DATA ORGANIZATION IN PARALLEL COMPUTERS

THE KLUWER INTERNATIONAL SERIES
IN ENGINEERING AND COMPUTER SCIENCE

PARALLEL PROCESSING AND
FIFTH GENERATION COMPUTING

Consulting Editor

Doug DeGroot

Other books in the series:

PARALLEL EXECUTION OF LOGIC PROGRAMS
John S. Conery ISBN 0-89838-194-0

PARALLEL COMPUTATION AND COMPUTERS FOR
ARTIFICIAL INTELLIGENCE
Janusz S. Kowalik ISBN 0-89838-227-0

MEMORY STORAGE PATTERNS IN PARALLEL PROCESSING
Mary E. Mace ISBN 0-89838-239-4

SUPERCOMPUTER ARCHITECTURE
Paul B. Schneck ISBN 0-89838-234-4

ASSIGNMENT PROBLEMS IN PARALLEL
AND DISTRIBUTED COMPUTING
Shahid H. Bokhari ISBN 0-89838-240-8

MEMORY PERFORMANCE OF PROLOG ARCHITECTURES
Evan Tick ISBN 0-89838-254-8

DATABASE MACHINES AND KNOWLEDGE BASE MACHINES
Masaru Kitsuregawa ISBN 0-89838-257-2

PARALLEL PROGRAMMING AND COMPILERS
Constantine D. Polychronopoulos ISBN 0-89838-288-2

DEPENDENCE ANALYSIS FOR SUPERCOMPUTING
Utpal Banerjee ISBN 0-89838-289-0

DATA ORGANIZATION IN PARALLEL COMPUTERS

by

Harry A.G. Wijshoff
University of Utrecht
and
Center for Supercomputing Research and Development
University of Illinois (Urbana-Champaign)

KLUWER ACADEMIC PUBLISHERS
Boston/Dordrecht/London

Distributors for North America:
Kluwer Academic Publishers
101 Philip Drive
Assinippi Park
Norwell, Massachusetts 02061 USA

Distributors for the UK and Ireland:
Kluwer Academic Publishers
Falcon House, Queen Square
Lancaster LA1 1RN, UNITED KINGDOM

Distributors for all other countries:
Kluwer Academic Publishers Group
Distribution Centre
Post Office Box 322
3300 AH Dordrecht, THE NETHERLANDS

Library of Congress Cataloging-in-Publication Data

Wijshoff, Harry A. G., 1960-
Data organization in parallel computers / by Harry A.G. Wijshoff.
p. cm. — (The Kluwer international series in engineering and computer science. Parallel processing and fifth generation computing)
Bibliography: p.
Includes index.
ISBN 0-89838-304-8
1. Data structures (Computer science) 2. Parallel processing (Electronic computers) I. Title. II. Series.
QA76.9.D35W53 1988
005.7'3—dc19 88-13881
CIP

Printed in the United States of America

Contents

Preface

The organization of data is clearly of great importance in the design of high performance algorithms and architectures. Although there are several landmark papers on this subject, no comprehensive treatment has appeared. This monograph is intended to fill that gap.

We introduce a model of computation for parallel computer architectures, by which we are able to express the intrinsic complexity of data organization for specific architectures. We apply this model of computation to several existing parallel computer architectures, e.g., the CDC 205 and CRAY vector-computers, and the MPP binary array processor.

The study of data organization in parallel computations was introduced as early as 1970. During the development of the ILLIAC IV system there was a need for a theory of possible data arrangements in interleaved memory systems. The resulting theory dealt primarily with storage schemes also called skewing schemes for 2-dimensional matrices, i.e., mappings from a 2-dimensional array to a number of memory banks. By means of the model of computation we are able to apply the theory of skewing schemes to various kinds of parallel computer architectures. This results in a number of consequences for both the design of parallel computer architectures and for applications of parallel processing.

In order to study thoroughly the theoretical and practical aspects of data organization this work combines results in several, seemingly disparate, areas of mathematics and computer science, e.g., abelian group theory, integral matrix theory, theory of codes, computer architectures and parallel algorithms. Care has been taken, however, to provide the necessary background in sufficient detail, so that the text is self-contained.

Acknowledgements

I could not have written this monograph without the help of many people. First of all I would like to thank Jan van Leeuwen for the stimulating discussions, his guidance and encouragement. The following persons I am grateful to: Henk Penning for his discussions about polyominoes during the very first beginning of my research in the area of data organization; my colleagues in the department of computer science at the University of Utrecht, Hans Bodlaender, Gerard Tel and Anneke Schoone, for their stimulating discussions, Pim Kars for carefully proofreading the manuscript; Ahmed Sameh and David Kuck for inviting me to CSRD; my colleagues at CSRD, in particular Kyle Gallivan, Stratis Gallopoulos, William Jalby, Constantine Polychronopoulos, Youcef Saad and Alex Veidenbaum, for the inspiring environment and for giving me a deeper appreciation for the practical implications of parallel processing; Els van der Pauw and my parents for their mental support.

Acknowledgments

DATA ORGANIZATION IN PARALLEL COMPUTERS

Chapter 1

Data Communication and Data Organization in Parallel Computations: Classification and Overview

1.1 Introduction

In the late nineteen sixties a number of computer architectures were introduced that deviate from the well-known von Neumann architecture and consist of several processors connected to memory through a number of data streams. Parallel computer architectures provide the capability of spreading a computation over a number of functional units (processors) which can perform sub-tasks of the computation in parallel. As long as the processors do not need to exchange information (data), they only have to be supplied with a suitable instruction stream and suitable data. More complications arise when, as happens in most cases, a computation asks for data exchanges between the processors, possibly via a shared memory module. Whenever a processor needs data from another processor, it has to suspend its own computation until the desired data have arrived. As waiting times slow down the computation, it is necessary to minimize the time of data transportation between the processors. For this reason a great variety of parallel computer architectures have been proposed and developed [HJ81,HS81]. Each architecture presents its own specific way of dealing with the problem of data routing. This state of affairs asks for some kind of classification scheme for parallel computer architectures. In the past two decades several attempts have been made to propose such a classification scheme [Fly72,Fen72,Han77,HJ81]. Whereas the existing classification schemes express the difference in computation power of parallel computer architectures quite well, they do not state anything about the communication abilities in these architectures. Nor can these classification schemes elucidate why certain application algorithms run faster or slower on different architectures, regardless the difference in computation power. Up to now the differences in performance due to the communication abilities of these architectures were explained by rather ad hoc methods . In this chapter we present a model of computation for parallel computer architectures and computations. By applying this model of computation to existing computer architectures we obtain a new classification scheme as well as a new computational viewpoint of parallel computations. In section 1.2 we briefly review the existing classification schemes for parallel computer architectures and we show their inadequacy for capturing the communication abilities of these architectures. In section 1.3 we introduce the model of computation for parallel computer architectures, by which we are able to express the intrinsic complexity of data routing for specific architectures. We apply this model of computation to several existing parallel computer architectures, e.g., the CDC 205 and CRAY 1 vector-computers, the ILLIAC IV and BSP array processors, the ICL DAP and MPP binary array processors. In section 1.4 we discuss the problem of data organization and data distribution in parallel computations. The study of data organization in parallel computations was introduced as early as 1970 [BK71]. During the development of the ILLIAC IV system [Bar68,KOMW67,Kuc68] there was a need for a theory of possible data arrangements in interleaved memory systems. The resulting theory dealt primarily with storage schemes also called skewing schemes for 2-dimensional matrices, i.e., mappings from a 2-dimensional array to a number of memory banks. By means of the model of computation introduced in section 1.3 we are able to apply the theory of skewing schemes to various kinds of parallel computer architectures. This results in a number of consequences for both the design of parallel computer architectures and for applications of parallel processing. Later chapters deal more exclusively with the theory of skewing schemes and related problems of data distribution.

1.2 Some Classification Schemes for Parallel Computer Architectures

In 1972 Flynn [Fly72] proposed a first classification scheme for parallel computer architectures. The classification scheme is based on the distinction between multiple instruction streams and one instruction stream, and between multiple data streams and one data stream. By this approach Flynn obtained four classes of computer architectures:

- Single Instruction stream-Single Data stream (SISD)
- Single Instruction stream-Multiple Data stream (SIMD)
- Multiple Instruction stream-Single Data stream (MISD)
- Multiple Instruction stream-Multiple Data stream (MIMD).

The four different kinds of architectures are illustrated in figure 1.1. Since the third class (MISD) is not incorporated in any existing parallel computer architecture, this leaves us with two essential classes of parallel computer architectures, viz. SIMD and MIMD. SIMD denotes any parallel computer architecture with only one instruction stream and synchronized processing elements. MIMD refers to any parallel computer architecture with multiple instruction streams and mostly asynchronous processing elements. Although the terms SIMD and MIMD are frequently used, they only give a vague distinction between the various kinds of parallel computer architectures.

The classification schemes introduced by Feng [Fen72], Händler [Han77] and Hockney and Jesshope [HJ81] provide a more detailed description of a parallel computer architecture. Whereas Feng's classification scheme only distinguishes the word length and the number of words that can be processed in one execution cycle, Händler's scheme is based on the hierarchical structure of parallel computer architectures. The latter classification scheme makes a distinction between three subsystem levels:

- Processor Control Unit (PCU) level,
- Arithmetic Logic Unit (ALU) level,
- Bit-Level Circuit (BLC) level.

Within each level the number of pipelined units and the segment length, i.e., the number of stages, of each unit is determined. This leads to a classification that expresses every (parallel) computer architecture by a triple: $< k \times k', d \times d', w \times w' >$, where

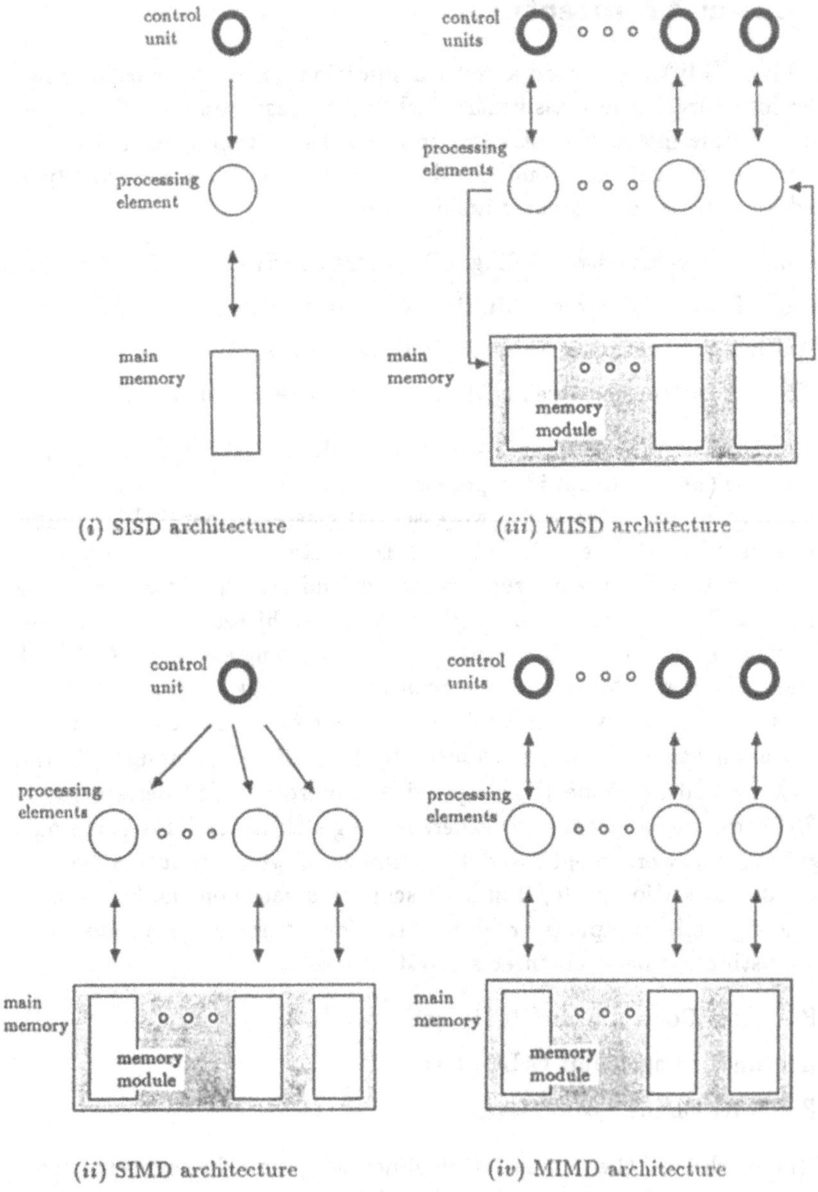

Figure 1.1: The classification scheme of Flynn.

$k =$ the number of processors (PCU's) within the architecture,
$k' =$ the number of PCU's that can be pipelined,
$d =$ the number of ALU's (or processing elements, PE's) under the control of one PCU,
$d' =$ the number of ALU's that can be pipelined,
$w =$ the word length of an ALU or of a PE,
$w' =$ the number of pipeline stages in all ALU's or in a PE.

Thus, e.g., the ILLIAC IV is represented by $< 1 \times 1, 64 \times 1, 64 \times 1 >$, the TI-ASC by $< 1 \times 1, 4 \times 1, 64 \times 8 >$, and the CRAY-1 by $< 1 \times 1, 12 \times 8, 64 \times (1 \sim 64) >$ (actually the pipeline degree of the ALU-level is variable with a maximal value equal to 8). Further, we can use the operators $\times$, $+$ and $\vee$ between triples, if a system consists of several distinct subsystems. For instance, the CDC 6600 is represented by $< 1 \times 1, 1 \times 10, 60 \times 1 >$ (the central processor) $\times < 10 \times 1, 1 \times 1, 12 \times 1 >$ (the I/O processors), and the C.mmp by $< 16 \times 1, 1 \times 1, 16 \times 1 > \vee < 1 \times 16, 1 \times 1, 16 \times 1 > \vee < 1 \times 1, 16 \times 1, 16 \times 1 >$, denoting the different operation modes in which the C.mmp can be used.

As can be noted, both Feng's and Händler's classification schemes express only the maximum computation power of a parallel computer architecture. The degradation of processing time due to communication costs cannot be explained by them. So, we need a more powerful tool for describing the data communication abilities of a parallel computer architecture. In our opinion this can only be achieved by focusing attention on the data management of a computer system, rather than on the functional units and processing elements. This is exactly where the classification schemes above fail; they give no information about the locations where the data is stored and about the interconnection structure of these locations.

1.3 Data Communication in Parallel Computer Architectures: a New Computational Viewpoint of Parallel Computations

Parallel computations in which the data exchanges between the processes have no regular structure do not allow for a clear determination of the exact communication costs. This is because the actual behavior, i.e., the patterns of data exchanges between the processes, of such a computation at run-time are unpredictable. Some examples of these computations are data-flow computations, object oriented computations, functional language based computations, and distributed computations. By means of statistical methods and simulation studies some estimates on the communication costs of these computation have been derived [MV84,Gen84,LMM85]. However, these estimates are obtained by taking the average communication costs of a number of possible computations, and this does not say anything about the performance during a particular computation. Because of this we restrict ourselves to computations which do have regularly structured data exchanges between the processes, i.e., computations in which the patterns of data exchanges between the processes are not totally depending on the progress of the computation. Most of the computations performed by vector and array processors, such as the ILLIAC IV, the BSP, the ICL DAP, the MPP, the CRAY 1/2, the CDC 205, and the FUJITSU VP-200, are regularly structured. Obviously these regularly structured computations are coupled with SIMD architectures; MIMD architectures are not necessarily inadequate to perform these regularly structured computations, though.

1.3.1 A Model of Computation for Regularly Structured Computations

In our opinion a regularly structured computation is nothing more than a number of data transfers between one-dimensional arrays of data. To be precise, our model of computation $\mathcal{COM}$ consists of a number of *levels* $1, 2, ..., r (r \geqslant 1)$ with each level i $(1 \leqslant i \leqslant r)$ consisting of a *one-dimensional array of data locations of unit size*

$$L_i = \{L_i(0), L_i(1), ..., L_i(n_i - 1)\},\ n_i \geqslant 1.$$

See figure 1.2. Let w be the size of the data locations, normally given in bits. Between every two consecutive levels i and $i-1 (2 \leqslant i \leqslant r)$ data transfers can be performed. Access patterns denote the locations of the data elements that can be transferred in parallel. Consequently data transfers are determined by the *sets of access patterns*

$$\mathcal{U}_i = \{U_1, U_2, ..., U_{p_i}\},\ \text{and}\ \mathcal{V}_i = \{V_1, V_2, ..., V_{q_i}\},$$

with for all j, $1 \leqslant j \leqslant p_i$, $\{L_i(x) | x \in U_j\} \subseteq L_i$, and for all j, $1 \leqslant j \leqslant q_i$, $\{L_{i-1}(y) | y \in V_j\} \subseteq L_{i-1}$. For each access pattern $U \in \mathcal{U}_i$ (or $V \in \mathcal{V}_i$) we can define an *instance*

$$a + U = \{a + x | x \in U\},$$

with $a \geqslant 0$ such that $a + U \subseteq \{0, 1, .., n_i - 1\}$. The data transfers between level i and level $i - 1$ are injective maps f from an instance $a + U$, $U \in \mathcal{U}_i$, to an instance $b + V$, $V \in \mathcal{V}_i$ (or vice versa). The impact of a data transfer f is such that the contents of the location $L_{i-1}(b + y)$ are replaced by the contents of the locations $L_i(f^{-1}(b+y))$, for $y \in V$. The contents of $L_i(a+x)$, $x \in U$, remain unchanged.

For i, $2 \leqslant i \leqslant r$, let $\mathcal{F}_{i,i-1}$ be the *set of all admissible data transfers*

$$f : a + U \rightarrow b + V,$$

with $U \in \mathcal{U}_i$ and $V \in \mathcal{V}_i$ and $\mathcal{F}_{i-1,i}$ be the set of all admissible data transfers from an instance $b + V$, $V \in \mathcal{V}_i$, to an instance $a + U$, $U \in \mathcal{U}_i$. For each i the data transfers f of $\mathcal{F}_{i,i-1}$ and of $\mathcal{F}_{i-1,i}$ take a unit amount of time t_i. Data transfers on different levels can be done independently and in parallel (when there occurs no conflict in the access patterns of two consecutive levels). On each level i the data transfers of $\mathcal{F}_{i,i-1}$ or $\mathcal{F}_{i-1,i}$ have to be done one after the other.

On the highest level 1 we have two different types of data transfers. The first type of data transfers is similar to the data transfers between two consecutive levels, except that it consists of data transfers that are injective maps from an instance $a + U_1$, $U_1 \in \mathcal{U}_1$, to an instance $b + U_2$, $U_2 \in \mathcal{U}_1$(!), where $\mathcal{U}_1$ is the set of access patterns on L_1. Let $\mathcal{F}_1$ be the set of all admissible data transfers from an instance $a + U_1$, $U_1 \in \mathcal{U}_1$, to an instance $b + U_2$, $U_2 \in \mathcal{U}_1$. We assume that all $f \in \mathcal{F}_1$ take a unit amount of time t_1 in order to be elaborated, and have to be elaborated one after the other.

The second type of data transfers on level 1 consists of transfers of data combined with an operation. Let

$$\{\vartheta_1, \vartheta_2, ..., \vartheta_n\}$$

be the *set of admissible operations*, for instance a ϑ_i can be a floating point addition of two vectors, a vector product of two vectors, and so on. Data transfers of this type, determined by the set $\mathcal{U}_0$ of access patterns on L_1, are mappings

$$f : \{\vartheta_i(x_1, x_2, ..., x_{s_1}, y_1, y_2, ..., y_{s_2})\} \rightarrow c + U_3,$$

with $\{x_1, x_2, ..., x_{s_1}\} = a + U_1$, and $\{y_1, y_2, ..., y_{s_2}\} = b + U_2$, for some a, b, c and $U_1 \in \mathcal{U}_0$, $U_2 \in \mathcal{U}_0$, and $U_3 \in \mathcal{U}_0$. The instances $a + U_1$ and $b + U_2$ have to be disjoint. The impact of a data transfer f of this type is that the contents of $L_1(c + z)$ is replaced by $f^{-1}(c + z)$, $z \in U_3$. Let $\mathcal{F}_0$ be the set of all

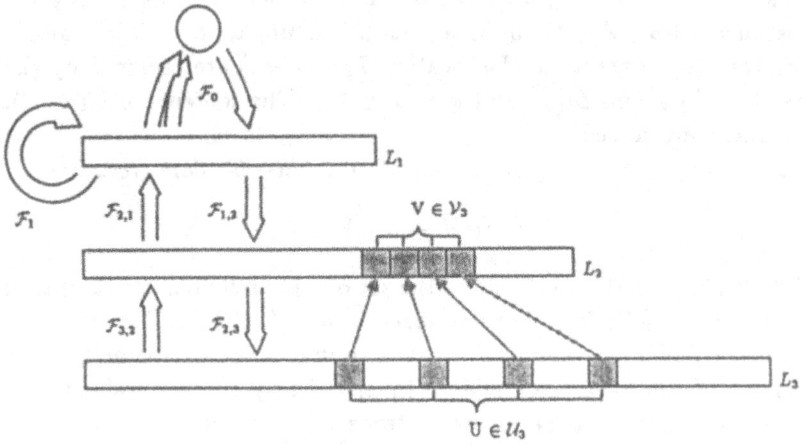

Figure 1.2: A three-level model of computation.

admissible data transfers of this type, and let for all $f \in \mathcal{F}_0$, t_0 be the unit amount of time to perform f, not including the time for the actual operation ϑ_i. Figure 1.2 shows a three-level model of computation.

Usually we represent a function $f \in \mathcal{F}_{i,i-1}(f \in \mathcal{F}_{i-1,i}, f \in \mathcal{F}_0$, or $f \in \mathcal{F}_1)$ by a mapping $f' : \{0, 1, ..., k-1\} \rightarrow \{0, 1, ..., l-1\}$, such that for every access pattern $U \in \mathcal{U}_i$ and $V \in \mathcal{V}_i$, the ith location of U is mapped to location $f'(i)$ of V under f.

Concluding, the model of computation $\mathcal{COM}$ is parameterized by the following entities:

- $\vartheta_1, \vartheta_2, ..., \vartheta_n$: the operations that can be performed
- r: the number of levels
- $n_1, n_2, ..., n_r$: the number of data locations in the levels $i\,(1 \leqslant i \leqslant r)$
- w: the size of the data locations
- $\mathcal{U}_0, \mathcal{U}_1, \mathcal{U}_2, \mathcal{V}_2, ..., \mathcal{U}_r, \mathcal{V}_r$: the sets of access patterns on the levels $i\,(1 \leqslant i \leqslant r)$
- $\mathcal{F}_0, \mathcal{F}_1, \mathcal{F}_{1,2}, \mathcal{F}_{2,1}, ..., \mathcal{F}_{r-1,r}, \mathcal{F}_{r,r-1}$: the sets of admissible data transfers on the levels $i\,(1 \leqslant i \leqslant r)$
- $t_0, t_1, ..., t_r$: the amount of time to perform the data transfers on the levels $i\,(1 \leqslant i \leqslant r)$

The model of computation can be more specified by allowing that the data transfers take place under the control of a MASK, which means that only a certain subset of the access pattern is actually transferred. Further, the data transfer functions could be pipelined. In that case the time required by such a data transfer is represented by two parameters T_i and t_i, where T_i denotes the pipeline delay and t_i is the time to perform one stage of the pipeline. A particular instance $\mathcal{COM}_{...}$ of the model of computation will be called a Parallel Processing Machine (PPM, for short). The sets of access patterns and data transfers are the main characteristics of a Parallel Processing Machine. They reflect the communication abilities of a parallel computer architecture. This will be worked out in the next sections.

1.3.2 Classification of Some Existing Parallel Computer Architectures

In this section we examine a number of representative vector and array processors and test our model of computation for these parallel computer architectures.

1.3.2.1 Vector/Pipeline Processors

Recently developed and commercially available vector/pipeline computers are, for instance, the CRAY 1, the CDC 205 and the FUJITSU VP-200 [HB85]. The CRAY 1 [Rus78] comprises a number of working registers, large instruction buffers and data buffers, and 12 functional pipeline units. The CPU contains a computation section, a memory section and an I/O section.

Figure 1.3 shows the overall system architecture. The main memory can hold up to 4 Mwords and is sixteen-way interleaved to provide the desired data transport to the functional units. The memory cycle time is 50 ns, and the transfer of data can be done in one, two or four words per clock period. Thus, the transfer of data may vary from a maximum of four 64-bit words per clock period (a databus bandwidth of 80 Mword/s) when the words are drawn from separate memory banks to a minimum of one word per four clock periods (20 Mwords/s) when the words are drawn from the same memory bank.

The actual parallel processing is being done through the 8 vector registers, each comprising 64 64-bit words, and the six functional pipes: floating-point addition, floating-point multiplication, reciprocal approximation, integer addition, shift, and logical. The vector units perform operations on operands from a pair of V-registers or from a V-register and an S-register (one of the 8 64-bit floating-point scalar registers). The result is returned to a V-register or the vector mask register.

The standard vector length is 64, vector lengths of greater than 64 are handled under program control by dividing the vectors into groups of 64 words plus a remainder. The vectors are fetched from memory by setting the base address register and a vector increment register. So, vectors can be accessed from an arbitrary starting point with a constant stride. Note that vectors with a stride equal to a multiple of 16 cause memory bank conflicts and reduce the memory bandwidth to 20 Mword/s. Vectors with a stride equal to a multiple of 8 reduce the memory bandwidth to 40 Mword/s. Thus, we come to the following two-level PPM $\mathcal{COM}_{CRAY1}$, which is parameterized as follows:

- the operations: Floating Point Addition, Floating Point Multiplication, Reciprocal Approximation, Integer Addition, Shift, Logical, or a combination of these operations (chaining)
- $r = 2$
- $u_1 = 512$,
  $u_2 = 4194304$
- $w = 64$ (bit)
- $\mathcal{U}_0 = \{\{0, 8, 16, ..., 504\}\}$,
  $\mathcal{U}_1 = \emptyset$,
  $\mathcal{V}_2 = \{\{0, 8, 16, ..., 504\}\}$,
  $\mathcal{U}_2 = \{\{0, k, 2k, ..., 63k\} | k \geqslant 1\}$

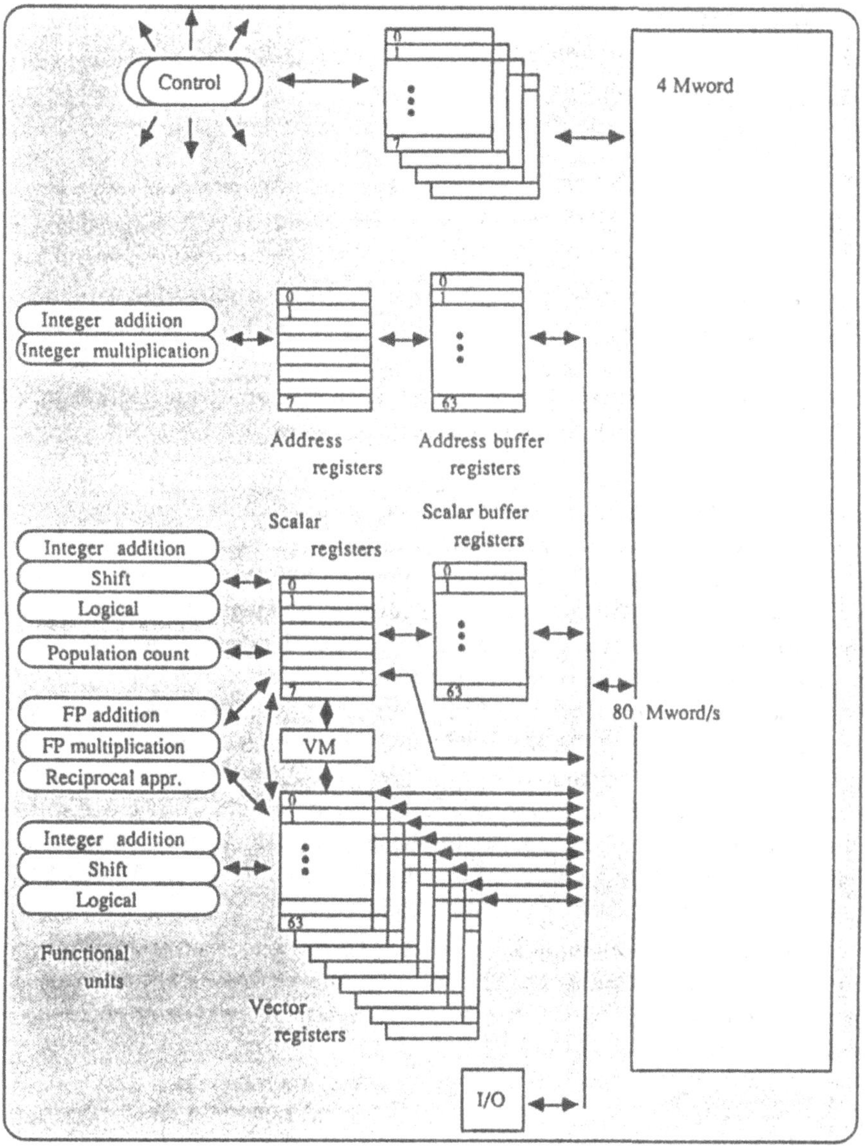

Figure 1.3: The overall system architecture of the CRAY 1.

- $\mathcal{F}_0, \mathcal{F}_{1,2}$ and $\mathcal{F}_{2,1}$ only consist of the identity,
  $\mathcal{F}_1 = \emptyset$

- t_0 is negligible,
  $t_2 = 800$ ns

Remarks

- the data locations of L_1 are related to the 8 vector registers in such a way that $L_1(i)$ represents word $\lfloor \frac{i}{8} \rfloor$ in vector register $i \bmod 8$
- the data locations of L_2 are in an obvious one to one relationship with the main memory
- t_2 actually varies from 800 ns to 3200 ns in case an access pattern from $\mathcal{U}_2$ is accessed, with k equal to a multiple of 16

The CDC 205 parallel computer architecture [Cor] differs from the CRAY 1 architecture in having a direct data path between main memory and the functional units. So, the CDC 205 has no vector registers. Further, a vector may contain up to 65635 consecutively addressed elements. If an access pattern does not consist of a sequence of consecutively stored elements, then this access pattern can be selected from a vector which includes this pattern. This is done by a control vector of bits. So, although an access pattern can be relatively small, a whole vector of 65635 elements has to be accessed to perform an operation on this access pattern. In addition, the selected access pattern from a vector can be stored into consecutive data locations in turn. These gather/scatter operations are implemented by microcode in hardware. The main memory is organized in 32 banks, each holding up to 131250 64-bit words. The memory bandwidth is 400 Mword/s.

To provide more communication abilities three particular instructions are implemented (in hardware): MASK, MERGE and COMPRESS. The MASK operation has two operands, vector A and vector B, which are combined under the control of a bit-vector Z to form a vector C, with $C_i = A_i$ if $Z_i = 1$ and $C_i = B_i$ if $Z_i = 0$. The MERGE operation is similar to the MASK operation, except that $C_i =$ the next element of A, if $Z_i = 1$, and $C_i =$ the next element of B, if $Z_i = 0$ ($C_1 = A_1$ if $Z_1 = 1$ and $C_1 = B_1$ if $Z_1 = 0$). The COMPRESS operation reduces a vector A to a vector C of smaller size under the control of a bit-vector Z.

This results in the following one-level PPM $\mathcal{COM}_{CDC205}$, which is parameterized as follows:

- the operations: Full Vector Addition, Full Vector Multiplication, Sparse Vector Addition, Sparse Vector Multiplication, Dot Product, Product of Elements, Max or Min of Elements, or combinations of two of these operations (short-stopping)
- $r = 1$
- $u_1 = 1048576(2^{20}) \sim 4194304(2^{22})$
- $w = 64$ (bit)
- $\mathcal{U}_0 = \{\{0, 1, 2, ..., k-1\} | k \leqslant 65635\}$,
  $\mathcal{U}_1 = U_1^1 \cup \bar{U}_1^1 \cup U_1^2 \cup \bar{U}_1^2$, with

  $U_1^1 = \{\{0, 1, 2, ..., k-1\} | k \leqslant 65635\}$,
  $\bar{U}_1^1 = \{A | \, A \subseteq \{0, 1, 2, ..., 65634\}\}$,
  $U_1^2 = \{\{0, 1, 2, ..., k-1, l, l+1, ..., 65634 - k + l\} | k < l\}$,
  $\bar{U}_1^2 = \{A \cup B | \; \exists k$ such that for
  $B' = \{x - k | x \in B\}$
  $A \cap B' = \emptyset$ and $A \cup B' = \{0, 1, 2, ..., 65634\}\}$

- $\mathcal{F}_0$ only consists of the identity ,
  $\mathcal{F}_1 = \mathcal{F}_1^1 \cup \mathcal{F}_1^2$, with
  for all $f \in \mathcal{F}_1^1 \; f : a + U \to b + V$, with $U \in \bar{U}_1^1, V \in U_1^1, |U| = |V|$,and $f(x) = x$, and with
  for all $f \in \mathcal{F}_1^2 \; f : a + U \to b + V$, with $U \in U_1^2$ or $U \in \bar{U}_1^2, V \in U_1^1$, and $f(x) = \pi(x)$
  such that there exists a k with
  for all $x \leqslant k - 1 : \pi(x) < \pi(x+1)$ and
  for all $x \geqslant k + 1 : \pi(x) < \pi(x+1)$
- $t_0 \approx 650\ \mu s$,
  $t_1 \approx 350\ \mu s$

Remarks

- the data locations of L_1 are in an obvious one to one relationship with the main memory
- actually $U_1^1 \subseteq \bar{U}_1^1$ and $U_1^2 \subseteq \bar{U}_1^2$, but for notational purposes we have distinguished these sets
- the functions of $\mathcal{F}_1^1$ represent the COMPRESS operation
- the functions of $\mathcal{F}_1^2$ represent the MERGE and MASK operations
- the gather and scatter operation have been included in the other operations

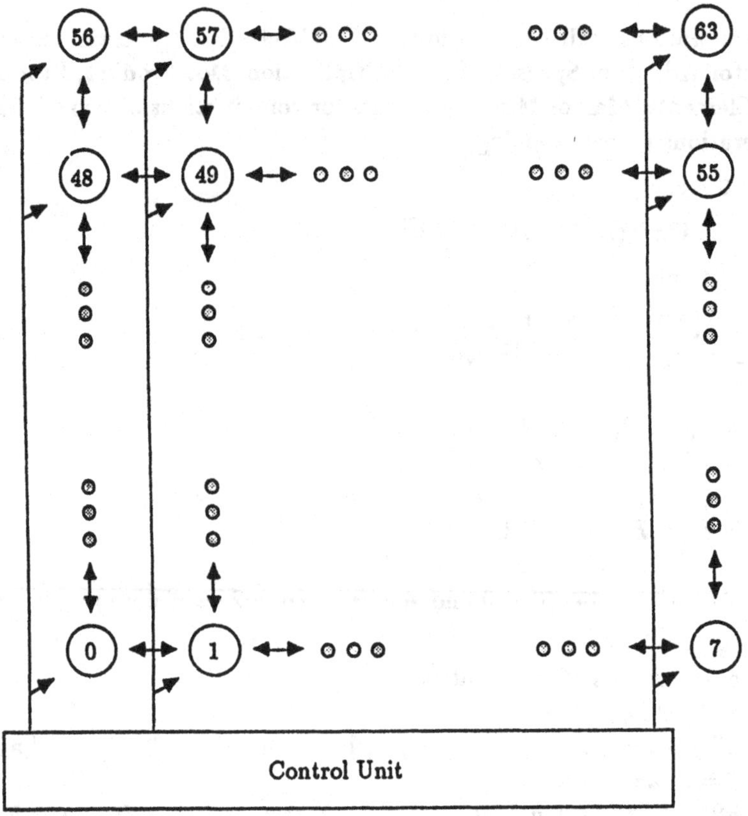

Figure 1.4: The grid connection of the ILLIAC IV.

The FUJITSU VP-200 [LMM85] has characteristics from both the CDC 205 and the CRAY 1. An instance of the computational model can be obtained for this pipelined computer, in a similar way.

1.3.2.2 Array Processors

The ILLIAC IV computer [Bar68] was one of the first parallel computer architectures consisting of a large number of individual processing elements. It comprises 64 (128, 256, 512) processing elements which are arranged in a grid (mesh), see figure 1.4.

So, processing element i is connected to the neighboring processing elements $i+1$, $i-1$, $i+8$, and $i-8$. The end connections are wrapped around, so that processing element 63 connects to 0, 62, 7, and 55.

Each processing element consists of a local memory and four 64-bit registers: operand registers A and B, shift register S, and a routing/result register R. Further a processing element provide a 240 ns ADD time and a 400 ns MULTIPLY time for 64-bit operands. All processing elements are controlled by one control unit and execute the same instruction stream. However, a processing element has the ability to ignore an instruction depending on an enable bit. Addresses used by the processing elements for local operands contain three components: a fixed address contained in the instruction, an index value added from the control unit accumulator, and a local index value added at the processing element prior to transmission to its own memory. The access time of the local memory is 120 ns.

So we arrive at the two-level PPM $\mathcal{COM}_{ILLIACIV}$, parameterized as follows:

- operations: Add, Multiply, Boolean, Shift, Division
- $r = 2$
- $u_1 = 256$,
  $u_2 = 131072$
- $w = 64$ (bit)
- $\mathcal{U}_0 = \{\{0, 4, 8, ..., 252\}\}$,
  $\mathcal{U}_1 = \mathcal{V}_2 = \{\{0, 4, 8, ..., 252\}\}$,
  $\mathcal{U}_2 = \{A| \; |A| = 64$ and all $x \in A$ are different mod 64 $\}$
- $\mathcal{F}_0$ only consists of the identity,
  $\mathcal{F}_1 = \{f_1, f_2, f_3, f_4\}$, with
  $f_1(x) = (x + 4) \bmod 64$,
  $f_2(x) = (x - 4) \bmod 64$,
  $f_3(x) = (x + 32) \bmod 64$,
  $f_4(x) = (x - 32) \bmod 64$,
  $\mathcal{F}_{1,2}$ and $\mathcal{F}_{2,1}$ only consist of the identity
- t_0 is negligible,
  $t_1 =$ "the time required to fetch a word from the R register of a neighboring processing element",
  $t_2 = 120$ ns

Remarks

- the data locations of L_1 are related to the registers in each processing element in such a way that $L_1(i)$ represents the following register :
  the A register, if $i \bmod 4 = 0$,

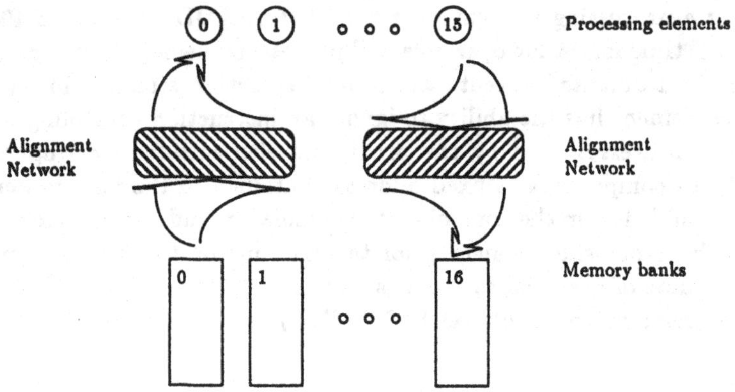

Figure 1.5: The functional structure of the BSP computer.

the B register, if $i \bmod 4 = 1$,
the C register, if $i \bmod 4 = 2$,
the D register, if $i \bmod 4 = 3$

- actually, the functions of $\mathcal{F}_0$ only act on $\{\vartheta(x_1, x_2, ..., x_{64}, y_1, ..., y_{64})\}$, with $\{x_1, x_2, ..., x_{64}\} = U$, and $\{y_1, y_2, ..., y_{64}\} = 1 + U$, for some $U \in \mathcal{U}_0$ and the functions of $\mathcal{F}_1$ only act on $3 + U$, for some $U \in \mathcal{U}_1$
- the access patterns of $\mathcal{U}_2$ are not as irregular as they appear to be; this is because the local addresses have to be computed by each processing element under the control of one control unit

The BSP computer [KS82,Sto77] is the successor of the ILLIAC IV computer. It consists of 16 processing elements and 17 memory banks. Unlike the ILLIAC IV in which the processing elements are connected by an interconnection network and each processing element has its own local memory, the BSP provides an input/output alignment network for routing the operands from the memory banks to the processing elements, and another alignment network for data transfers in the opposite direction. See figure 1.5. Both alignment networks contain full crossbar switches.

The processing elements address the memory banks via d-ordered vectors, i.e., sequences of memory addresses which are d apart from each other. The memory banks are organized in such a way that conflict-free access is guaranteed when d is not a multiple of 17. Each memory bank has a cycle time of 160 ns. This results in a memory bandwidth of 100 Mword/s.

So we obtain the following one-level PPM $\mathcal{COM}_{BSP}$, parameterized as follows:

- $r = 1$
- $u_1 = (17 \times 512 \times 1024 =)\ 8912896$
- $w = 64$ (bit)
- $$\begin{aligned}\mathcal{U}_0 = \mathcal{U}_1 = \{\{k,\ & ((k+d).524288 + \lfloor \tfrac{d}{17} \rfloor) \bmod 8912896, \\ & ((k+2d).524288 + \lfloor \tfrac{2d}{17} \rfloor) \bmod 8912896, \\ & \vdots \\ & ((k+15d).524288 + \lfloor \tfrac{15d}{17} \rfloor) \bmod 8912896\} \mid \\ & k \geqslant 0, d \geqslant 1 \text{ and } d \text{ is not a multiple of } 17\}\end{aligned}$$
- $\mathcal{F}_0 = \{f \mid f \text{ is an arbitrary permutation of } \{0, 1, ..., 15\}\}$,
  $\mathcal{F}_1 = \emptyset$
- $t_0 = 200$ ns

1.3.2.3 Bit-Slice Array Processors

Binary array processors are often used in image and signal processing environments, but they lend themselves also to other applications. In this section we shall study two representative binary array processors: the ICL DAP and the MPP which both consist of a number of 1-bit processing elements connected through a grid network.

The ICL DAP system [Fla82,HJ81] comprises 64×64 1-bit processing elements, which are arranged in a grid, which allows that the end connections are wrap-around. Each processing element is provided with an enable/disable control bit, a 1-bit full adder and a local memory of $4K \times 1$-bits. The access time of the local memory is 100 ns.

All the processing elements are controlled by the master control unit (MCU) which comprises 8 64-bit MCU registers and an instruction buffer. The instructions from the MCU are broadcast to all processing elements and give a 7-bit address, specifying the offset in local memory. Beside the data routing via the grid connections (each processing element is connected to its four neighbors), the ICL DAP has two "highways", i.e., two high-speed buses, with a bandwidth of 128106 bits/s. The column highway has one bit for each column of processing elements in the DAP array and the row highway has one bit for each row of processing elements in the DAP array. Both highways have access to the MCU registers. Further, the column highway provides the interface to the host computer and broadcasts the instructions from the instruction buffer to the processing elements.

So we get the 2-level PPM $\mathcal{COM}_{DAP}$, parameterized as follows:

- the operation: Full Add
- $r = 2$
- $u_1 = (64 \times 64 \times 4 \times 1024 =)\, 16777216$,
  $u_2 = (8 \times 64 =)\, 512$
- $w = 1$ (bit)
- $\mathcal{U}_0 = \mathcal{U}_1 = \{\{0, 4096, 8192, ..., 16773120\}\}$,
  $\mathcal{V}_2 = \mathcal{U}_1 \cup \{\{0, 4096, 8192, ..., 258048\}, \{0, 262145, 524288, ..., 1651507\}\}$,
  $\mathcal{U}_2 = \{\{0, 8, 16, ..., 504\}\}$
- $\mathcal{F}_0$ only consists of the identity,
  $\mathcal{F}_1 = \{f_1, f_2, f_3, f_4\}$, with

  $$f_1(x) = \begin{cases} x + 4096, \text{ if } x \neq 63k \text{ for some } k \geqslant 1, \\ x - 258048, \text{ otherwise} \end{cases}$$

  $$f_2(x) = \begin{cases} x - 4096, \text{ if } x \bmod 64 \neq 0, \\ x + 258048, \text{ otherwise} \end{cases}$$

  $$f_3(x) = \begin{cases} x + 262144 \text{ if } x < 16515072 \\ x - 16515072, \text{ otherwise} \end{cases}$$

  $$f_4(x) = \begin{cases} x - 262144, \text{ if } x \geqslant 262144 \\ x + 16515072, \text{ otherwise} \end{cases}$$

  $\mathcal{F}_{1,2} = \{I, f_1^{-1}, f_2^{-1}\}$, with f_1 and f_2 acting on $\mathcal{U}_1 \subseteq \mathcal{V}_1$ such that
  $f_1(x) = \lfloor \frac{x}{64} \rfloor$ and
  $f_2(x) = x \bmod 64$,
  $\mathcal{F}_{2,1}$ consists of the identity
- $t_0 = 100$ ns,
  $t_1 = 200$ ns,
  $t_2 = 500$ ns

Remarks

- the second level of data locations does not reflect the organization of main memory as in the previous models, but it provides additional data rearrangements for the first level
- of the access pattern $V_1 = \{0, 4096, 8192, ..., 258048\}$ of $\mathcal{V}_2$ only those instances $y_1 + V_1$ are taken with $y_1 \in \{0, 1, ..., 4095, 262144, 262145, ..., 266239, ..., 16515072, 16515073, ..., 16519167\}$
  and of the access pattern $V_2 = \{0, 262144, 524288, ..., 16515072\}$ only those instances $y_2 + V_2$ are taken with $y_2 \in \{0, 1, ..., 262143\}$
- the function f_1^{-1} and f_2^{-1} of $\mathcal{F}_{1,2}$ represent the columnwise and rowwise broadcasts that can be performed from a MCU register via the column highway to all processing elements
- the model $\mathcal{COM}_{DAP}$ reflects the normal bit-serial processing mode of the ICL DAP.

The MPP [Bat80,Pot85] comprises up to 128×128 (= 16384) 1-bit processing elements arranged in a grid. The grid connection allows three different types of wrap-around. Consequently the array of processing elements can have the topology of a cylinder, a torus, or a one-dimensional array (or a ring). See figure 1.6.

The processing elements are controlled by one control unit. Each processing element is provided with 6 1-bit registers, a shift register of variable size (2,6,10,14,18,22,26 or 30), a full adder and a local memory of 1024 bits. The 1-bit G register acts as a mask (disable/enable bit), the P register provides the communication with the four neighboring processing elements and the S register is used for feeding the processing elements with data from the main memory, also called the staging memory. See figure 1.7 for the functional structure of a processing element.

The staging memory contains up to 134 Mbits and it has a bandwidth of 1280 Mbit/s. The staging memory can be used as a data buffer and can also reformat the data. The data reformatting can be done because for any k, n and m all the data elements from the addresses: $k, k+n, k+2n, ..., k+127n, k+m, k+n+m, k+2n+m, ..., k+127n+m, ..., k+127m, k+n+127m, k+2n+127m, ..., k+127n+127m$, can be fetched and sent to the array of processing elements. The data transmission from the staging memory to the array of processing elements (and vice versa) proceeds by shifting the data via the S registers through the array, columnwise. The first column of processing elements receives the first 128 data elements and the last column sends out the last 128 data elements. One shifting step takes only one

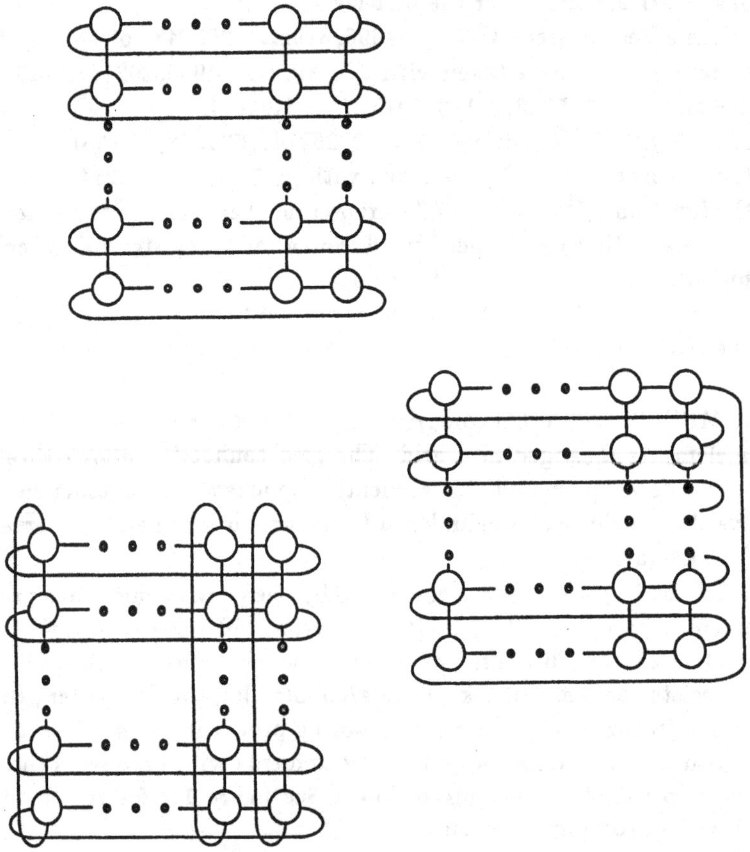

Figure 1.6: The possible grid connections of the MPP.

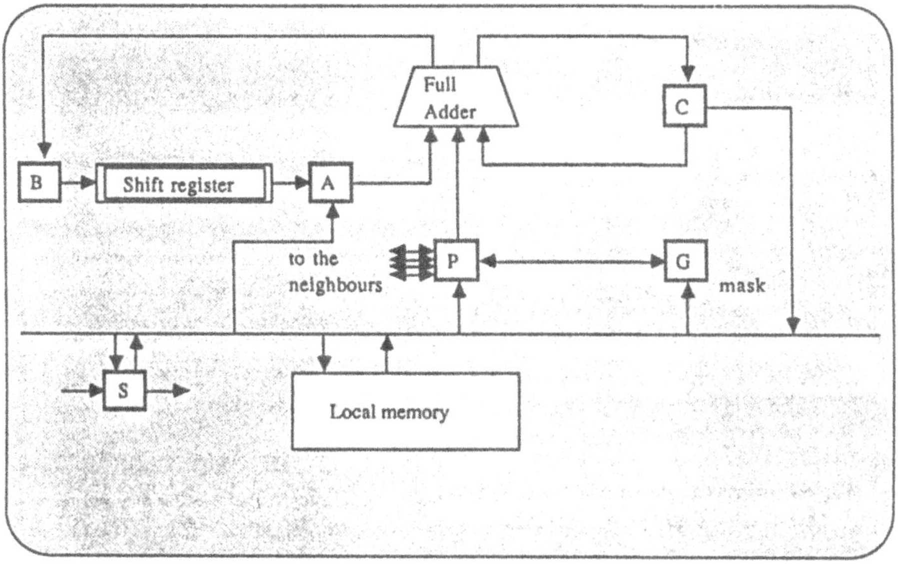

Figure 1.7: The functional structure of a processing element.

clockcycle (=100 ns). Further, the shift register provides a fast access time for the data elements. Each shift step takes only 1 clockcycle.

So we get the three-level PPM $\mathcal{COM}_{MPP}$ parameterized as follows:

- the operation: Full Add
- $r = 3$
- $u_1 = (34 \times 16384 =)\ 557056$,
  $u_2 = (1024 \times 16384 =)\ 16777216$,
  $u_3 = 134217728$
- $w = 1$ (bit)
- $\mathcal{U}_0 = \mathcal{U}_1 = \mathcal{V}_2 = \{\{0, 34, 68, ..., 557022\}\}$,
  $\mathcal{U}_2 = \mathcal{V}_3 = \{\{0, 1024, 2048, ..., 16777192\}\}$,
  $\mathcal{U}_3 = \{\{k, k+n, k+2n, ..., k+127n, k+m, k+n+m, k+2n+m, ..., k+127n+m, ..., k+127m, k+n+127m, k+2n+127m, ..., k+127n+127m\} | k \geqslant 0, n \geqslant 1 \text{ and } m \geqslant 1\}$,
- $\mathcal{F}_0$ only consists of the identity,
  $\mathcal{F}_1 = \{I, f, f_1, f_2, f_3, f_4\}$ with
  $f(x) = (x+1) \bmod 34$,
  and if the MPP has the topology of a cylinder or torus (like the ICL DAP):
  $$f_1(x) = \begin{cases} x + 34, \text{ if } x \neq 127k \text{ for some } k \geqslant 1 \\ x - 4318, \text{ otherwise} \end{cases}$$
  $$f_2(x) = \begin{cases} x - 34, \text{ if } x \bmod 127 \neq 0, \\ x + 4318, \text{ otherwise} \end{cases}$$
  $$f_3(x) = \begin{cases} x + 4352, \text{ if } x < 552704, \\ x - 552704, \text{ otherwise} \end{cases}$$
  $$f_4(x) = \begin{cases} x - 4352, \text{ if } x \geqslant 4352, \\ x + 552704, \text{ otherwise} \end{cases}$$
  and if the MPP has the topology of a one-dimension array (or ring) (like the ILLIAC IV):
  $f_1(x) = x + 34 \bmod 557056$,
  $f_2(x) = x - 34 \bmod 557056$,
  $f_3(x) = x + 4352 \bmod 557056$,
  $f_4(x) = x - 4352 \bmod 557056$
  $\mathcal{F}_{1,2}, \mathcal{F}_{2,1}, \mathcal{F}_{2,3}$ and $\mathcal{F}_{3,2}$ only consist of the identity

- t_0 is negligible,
  $t_1 = 100$ ns,
  $t_2 = 100$ ns,
  $t_3 = 12900$ ns $\approx 13\ \mu s$

Remarks

- the data locations of L_1 are related to the registers in each processing element in such a way that $L_1(i)$ represents the following register :
  the A register, if i mod 34 = 0,
  the C register, if i mod 34 = 1,
  the D register, if i mod 34 = 2,
  the B register, if i mod 34 = 3,
  and a location of the shift register, if i mod 34 $\geqslant$ 4
- the data locations of L_2 represent the local memories of each processing element
- the data locations of L_3 represent the staging memory
- actually, the functions of $\mathcal{F}_0$ only act on $\{V(x_1, ..., x_{16384}, y_1, ..., y_{16384})\}$ with $\{x_1, ..., x_{16384}\} = U$ and $\{y_1, ..., y_{16384}\} = 1+U$, for some $U \in \mathcal{U}_0$, the function I of $\mathcal{F}_1$ acts on the instances $a + U$, with $a \in \{0,1,2,3\}$ and $U \in \mathcal{U}_1$, the function f of $\mathcal{F}_1$ acts on the instances $a + U$, with $a \notin \{0,1,2\}$ and $U \in \mathcal{U}_1$, and the functions f_1, f_2, f_3 and f_4 of $\mathcal{F}_1$ act on $a + U$, with $a = 3$ and $U \in \mathcal{U}_1$
- the functions of $\mathcal{F}_{2,3}$ and $\mathcal{F}_{3,2}$ are routed via the S register, but for denotational reasons we have not included this fact into $\mathcal{COM}_{MPP}$
- we have assumed that the length of the shift register equals 30; the model can be easily adapted when the shift register has a length of less than 30.

1.3.2.4 Other Parallel Computer Architectures

A great variety of parallel computer architectures have been proposed and developed that do not rely on a grid network but on some other kind of interconnection structure for the processing elements. Common interconnection structures that can be distinguished are:

- n-dimensional grid networks
- tree networks
- pyramid networks

- ring networks
- one-dimensional arrays
- n-dimensional cube networks
- perfect shuffle networks

See figure 1.8. Some examples of parallel computer architectures that use these interconnection networks are: the EGPA (Erlangen General Purpose Array [HHS76]) and the HAP (Hierarchical Array Processor system [Shi86]) both using a pyramid network, the COSMIC CUBE [Pea77] based on the n-dimensional cube network, and the shuffle-exchange computer as studied by Stone [Sto71] and the FFT networks [Ber72] both using the perfect shuffle network.

All these interconnection networks have the following property: if the processing elements are controlled by one control unit, then there exists a mapping from the processing elements to the one-dimensional array such that all routing steps are represented by linear functions f, i.e., such that f or f^{-1} are of the form $(ax+b)$ mod N, for some a, b and N. For instance, we can number the nodes of the perfect shuffle network by 0,1,..., N-1 starting from the top to the bottom (see figure 1.8), so that the routing steps are represented by $f_1(x) = 2x \bmod N$, if the first edges of each node are taken, and $f_2(x) = (2x+1) \bmod N$, if the second edges are taken. Although the routing functions of e.g. the tree network, the perfect shuffle network and the n-dimensional cube network are of the form $(ax+b)$ mod N, with $a \geqslant 2$, they do not really offer new communication abilities over those which are presented in the previous sections. This is because these functions can be simulated by a number of functions $f : x \mapsto (x+b) \bmod N$ using a mask control, see also [TR86].

Recently, a tendency towards cluster organized parallel computer architectures can be observed. Cluster organized architectures consist of a number of processor clusters which are organized in a parallel computer architecture. Each cluster, in turn, is again a parallel computer architecture, possibly of a different kind as the architecture of the clusters. The CEDAR system [Sam86] and the SUPRENUM computer [Tro86] are examples of these architectures.

Even though cluster organized architectures may consist of different kinds of parallel computer architectures, they can also be incorporated into the model of computation of section 1.3.1. This is done by defining a Parallel Processing Machine B that reflects the parallel computer architecture of every clusters. On top of that, a Parallel Processing Machine A with increased

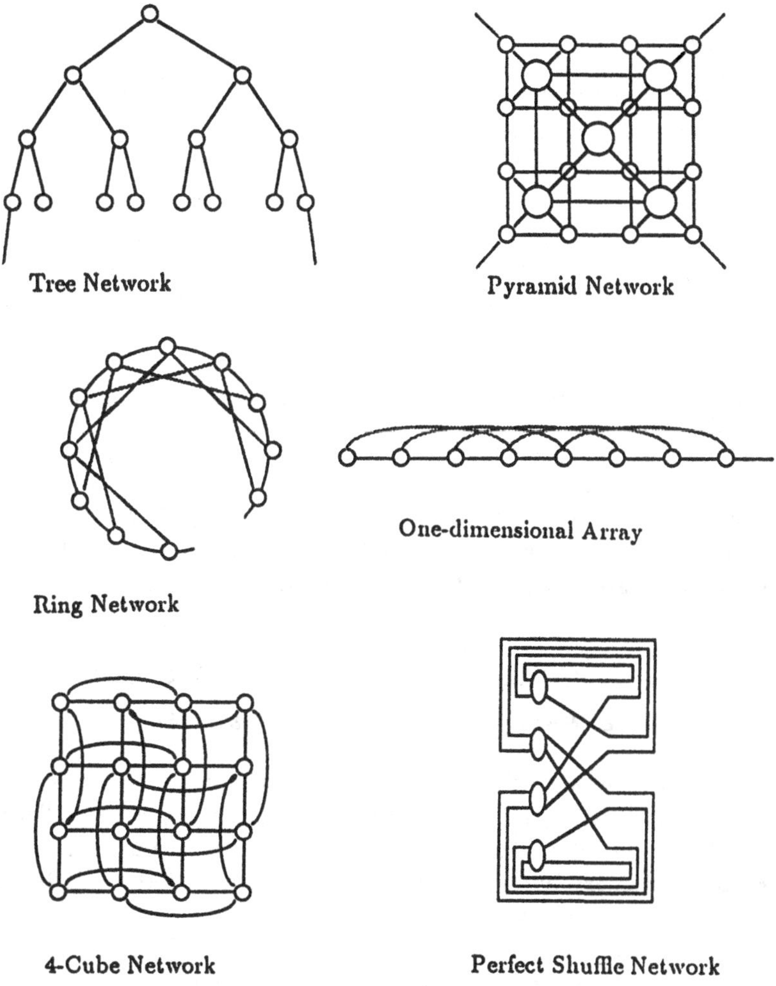

Figure 1.8: Some interconnection networks.

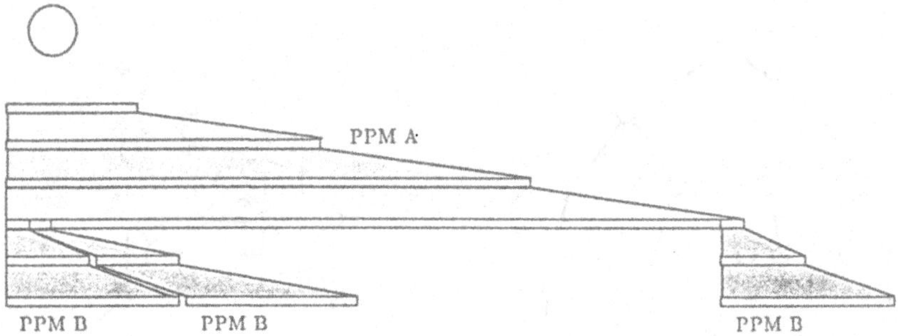

Figure 1.9: A cluster organized architecture incorporated into the model of computation.

word length is defined corresponding to the parallel computer architecture of the cluster in such a way that the data locations of the lowest level of A reflect the upperlevels of the PPMs B. See figure 1.9.

1.4 Data Organization in Parallel Computer Architectures: the Theory of Skewing Schemes

The issue of data organization in parallel computer architectures deals with the possible distributions of data over the data locations in a parallel computer architecture. The data locations can reside in main memory, data buffers, local memory within a processing element, and the registers provided in a processing element.

In terms of the model of computation from section 1.3, data organization concerns the possible mappings from some kind of data structure into the data locations of each level of the model. The theory which concerns the data organization in parallel computer architectures is also called the theory of skewing schemes.

1.4.1 Historical Notes

Skewing schemes were first presented by Budnik and Kuck [BK71] in the development of the ILLIAC IV system. The ILLIAC IV computer contains

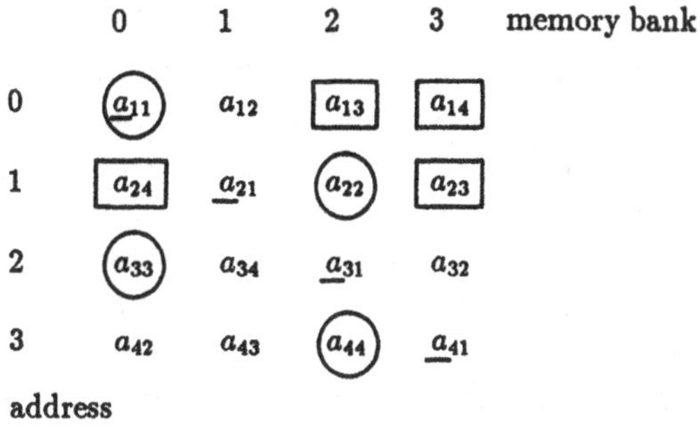

Figure 1.10: A storage scheme.

a number of memory banks which can be accessed in parallel, see also section 1.3.2.2. Within this context Budnik and Kuck (and others) have especially studied the problem of storing a 2-dimensional $N \times N$-matrix into a number (M) of memory banks numbered from 0 to $M-1$, such that certain vectors of interest, e.g., columns, rows, diagonals and blocks can be accessed conflict-free. Conflict-free access means that the elements of a vector are stored in different memory banks. Budnik and Kuck [BK71] defined storage schemes that map the elements of a row to successive memory banks modulo M in such a way that the elements of the first row start in memory bank 0, the elements of the second row start in memory bank S, for some $S \geqslant 0$, the elements of the third row start in memory bank $2S$, and so on. The case M=4, N=4 and S=1 is shown in figure 1.10. The elements of a 2×2 block are squared, the first column is underlined and the main diagonal is circled. Note that the main diagonal as well as the columns and rows can be accessed conflict-free, but the 2×2 block cannot be accessed conflict-free. S is called the skew of a storage scheme. The notion of skewing schemes originated from this early development.

Skewing schemes were further explored by Lawrie [Law75,LV82], who introduced the notion of linear skewing schemes. Linear skewing schemes are in fact a generalization of the storage schemes as defined by Budnik and Kuck. Lawrie defined the vectors of interest as d-ordered vectors and derived conditions for a linear skewing scheme to be conflict-free for a d-

ordered vector. In addition, he studied the alignment requirements for a BSP-like architecture, that are induced by a certain linear skewing scheme. The alignment requirements arise from the need to unscramble d-ordered vectors. For instance, the second row of the matrix in figure 1.10 is stored as: $a_{2,4}, a_{2,1}, a_{2,2}, a_{2,3}$. Whenever this row has to be processed adequately it should be presented to the processing elements as: $a_{2,1}, a_{2,2}, a_{2,3}, a_{2,4}$.

Shapiro [Sha75,Sha78b] has introduced skewing schemes which can be represented by a relatively small table of information, the so-called periodic skewing schemes. He also derived conditions for the existence of an arbitrary skewing scheme that is valid for a collection of vectors of interest (which he called templates). He showed that for certain classes of templates the existence of an arbitrary skewing scheme implies the existence of a linear (periodic) skewing scheme. Moreover, skewing schemes were studied in the context of image processing [CLR82,Sie81,vVM78].

1.4.2 Skewing Schemes

By means of the model of computation from section 1.3 we can apply the theory of skewing schemes to a broader range of applications.

Consider the PPM model $\mathcal{COM}$ of a certain parallel computer architecture. Define for each level i of $\mathcal{COM}$, k_i the maximum integer such that for all access patterns $U \in \mathcal{U}_i$ (and for all $U \in \mathcal{V}_{i+1}$) and for all $x \in U$ and $y \in U, x \neq y : x \text{ div } k_i \neq y \text{ div } k_i$. Then it appears that for existing parallel computer architectures $k_i | u_i$ for all i, where u_i is the number of data locations on level i, see section 1.3.2. Let the interleaving degree M_i of a level i be the number u_i/k_i. The number M_i is dictated by the specific architecture concerned. Thus, the number M_i can denote the number of memory banks (for instance, M_1 of $\mathcal{COM}_{BSP}$ equals 17) or the number of processing elements (for instance, M_1 of $\mathcal{COM}_{DAP}$ equals 4096) or the number of registers (for instance M_2 of $\mathcal{COM}_{DAP}$ equals 8).

Consider a (parallel) algorithm on some kind of data structure D, for instance, a d-dimensional matrix or a tree. Then the algorithm defines subsets of D which have to be processed in parallel. These subsets will be called templates. Because in most (parallel) algorithms these templates have a uniform "shape", we define with every template P the base-set $B_P \subseteq$ D of P, such that for all $a \in B_P$ $a \oplus P$ is a subset of D which has to be retrieved in parallel. $\oplus$ is an operation defined on the locations of D.

Definition 1.1
(i) *A template P on* D *is any (finite) subset of* D.

(ii) The base-set B_P of a template P is any subset of D.
(iii) An instance of P is a set $a \oplus P$, with $a \in B_P$.

One should not confuse the templates which are determined by the algorithm with the access patterns which are determined by the parallel computer architecture.

Let D be the data structure on which an algorithm is performed and let P be a template on D. Whenever two elements a and b of P are stored on level i of a PPM $\mathcal{COM}$ and the "distance" between a and b is less than M_i, then from the definition of M_i it follows that it is impossible to fetch a and b simultaneously. We define a skewing scheme s to be a mapping from the data structure D (or some subset of D) into the set $\{0, 1, ..., M_i - 1\}$ indicating which elements of D are stored in the first k_i data locations of L_i, which elements of D are stored in the second k_i data locations of L_i, and so on. Further, together with a skewing scheme s we define the address function η_s on D. The address function η_s is a mapping from D into the set $\{0, 1, ..., k_i - 1\}$ indicating the rank of an element of D in the set of k_i consecutive data locations in which the element is stored according to s. So, an element a of D is actually stored in the location $L_i(s(a).k_i + \eta_s(a))$. More precisely we have :

Definition 1.2
(i) A skewing scheme s for a data structure D *and level i of a* PPM *is a surjective map from* D *into* $\{0, 1, ..., M_i - 1\}$. *The address function η_s is a surjective map from* D *into* $\{0, 1, ..., k_i - 1\}$ *such that for all* $a, b \in$ D : *if* $s(a) = s(b)$ *then* $\eta_s(a) \neq \eta_s(b)$.
(ii) A skewing scheme s is valid for a collection of templates $C = \{P_1, P_2, ..., P_t\}$ *on* D *if* $\forall i, 1 \leqslant i \leqslant t, \forall a \in B_{P_i}, \forall m \in \{0, 1, ..., M_i - 1\} : |(a \oplus P_i) \cap s^{-1}(m)| \leqslant 1$.

1.4.3 The Interaction of Data Communication and Data Organization

Besides the fact that the model of computation puts the existing theory of skewing schemes into a broader range of application, it also allows a formalization of the interaction of data communication and data organization. In existing parallel computers these interactions were handled in a rather implementation oriented way.

From the previous sections can be concluded that the complexity of a parallel computation is mainly determined by the data rearrangements that occur. The data rearrangements abilities of a particular PPM $\mathcal{COM}$ are determined by the following entities:

- the complexity of the functions of $\mathcal{F}_i(= \mathcal{F}_{i-1,i} \cup \mathcal{F}_{i,i-1})$,
- the complexity of the access patterns on a level i,
- the time required by the functions of $\mathcal{F}_i$,
- the validity of a skewing scheme s,
- the complexity of a skewing scheme s,
- the complexity of the address function η_s belonging to s.

In this section we shall discuss the interrelation between these entities. First of all, the time required by the functions of $\mathcal{F}_i$ affects the computation speed negatively, whereas the use of a valid skewing scheme s on level i influences the computation speed positively. It is also clear that the complexity of the functions of $\mathcal{F}_i$ directly constrains the complexity of the skewing schemes to be implemented, which in turn constrains the validity of the skewing schemes to be implemented. In the same way we have that the complexity of the access patterns on level i is directly related to the complexity of the address function η_s.

Considering the various PPM's of existing parallel computer architectures we can distinguish between three types of data transfers and access patterns: constant data transfers (access patterns), functional data transfers (access patterns) and arbitrary data transfers (access patterns). Constant data transfers are characterized by the property that "consecutive" data locations are mapped to "consecutive" data locations (modulo k_i) and constant access patterns have the property that all pairs of consecutive elements are k apart for some constant k. Data transfers are functional if they can be described by a simple arithmetic function which can be computed in a relatively small number of operations. In a similar way a functional access pattern is defined.

Examples

1. All access patterns of $\mathcal{U}_0, \mathcal{U}_1, \mathcal{U}_2, \mathcal{V}_2$ and $\mathcal{V}_3$ of $\mathcal{COM}_{MPP}$ are constant access patterns.
2. All access patterns of $\mathcal{U}_3$ of $\mathcal{COM}_{MPP}$ are functional access patterns.
3. All the functions of $\mathcal{F}_0, \mathcal{F}_1, \mathcal{F}_2$, and $\mathcal{F}_3$ of $\mathcal{COM}_{MPP}$ are constant data transfers.
4. All access patterns of $\mathcal{U}_1$ of $\mathcal{COM}_{CDC205}$ are arbitrary .
5. All functions of $\mathcal{F}_0$ of $\mathcal{COM}_{BSP}$ are arbitrary.

Directly related to the constant and functional data transfers we can define compactly representable skewing schemes. Compactly representable skewing schemes also allow for a short representation and a fast computation. Further, a skewing scheme s and the corresponding address function η_s have to be evaluated at runtime. So, if for instance s is compactly representable and the evaluation of η_s takes considerably more time than the evaluation of s, then the speed-up gained by the computation of s is undone by the computation of η_s. Thus it is preferable to keep the complexity of a skewing scheme and the corresponding address function in balance (see, for instance, the BSP architecture [KS82]).

Concluding we can say that, because of the great enhancement of computation speed achieved by parallel computer architectures, the usual front-end processors are becoming more and more insufficient for supplying a parallel computer architecture with the desired data at acceptable transfer rates. Therefore, it is likely to assume that in the future parallel computers will be provided with still larger storage devices. This development demands a flexible and structured way of handling the large amounts of data. For instance, in the MPP the need for data rearrangements is resolved by allowing a great flexibility of the access patterns of $\mathcal{U}_3$; in the BSP this flexibility is achieved by the data transfers of $\mathcal{F}_0$. The model of computation as presented in this chapter provides a constructive way of dealing with the complexity of data rearrangements and the complexity of parallel computations.

Chapter 2

Arbitrary Skewing Schemes for d-Dimensional Arrays

This chapter (and also the remaining chapters) deals more exclusively with the data organization for parallel computer architectures. Within the context of the Parallel Processing Machine as introduced in chapter 1, this means that we study the validity and complexity of skewing schemes and the complexity of data transfer functions for each level of the PPM. In this chapter we consider arbitrary skewing schemes for d-dimensional arrays. Let D be a d-dimensional square array. D can effectively be viewed as the cartesian product Z_N^d, with $N \geqslant 0$ and $\mathsf{Z}_N = \{0, ..., N-1\}$. We also allow the case that $\mathrm{D} = \mathsf{Z}^d$. Application of definition 1.1 and 1.2, section 1.4.2, results in the following two definitions.

Definition 2.1
(i) A template P on D *is any finite subset* $\{a_1, a_2, ..., a_p\} \subseteq \mathrm{D}$, *with* $a_1 = (0, 0, ..., 0)$.
(ii) An instance $P(x)$, with $x \in \mathsf{Z}_N^d$, is the set $\{a_i \oplus_N x \mid a_i \in P\} \cap \mathrm{D}$. $\oplus_N$ *denotes the coordinate-wise addition modulo N.*

Note that the base set B_P, cf. definition 2.1(ii), equals Z_N^d for all templates P. For other choices of the base set B_P the reader is referred to section 3.3.

Definition 2.2
(i) A skewing scheme s for D *is a surjective mapping from* D *into the set* $\{0, 1, ..., M-1\}$, *for some integer* $M \geqslant 1$.
(ii) A skewing scheme s is valid for a collection of templates $C = \{P_1, P_2, ..., P_t\}$ *on* D *if* $\forall j, 1 \leqslant j \leqslant t\ \forall x \in \mathsf{Z}_N^d\ \forall m \in \{0, 1, ..., M-1\} : |P_j(x) \cap s^{-1}(m)| \leqslant 1$.

$$\begin{pmatrix}
11 & 6 & 0 & 2 & 3 & 10 & 9 & 8 & 1 & 4 & 7 & 5 \\
3 & 10 & 9 & 8 & 1 & 4 & 7 & 5 & 11 & 6 & 0 & 2 \\
1 & 4 & 7 & 5 & 11 & 6 & 0 & 2 & 3 & 10 & 9 & 8 \\
9 & 8 & 1 & 4 & 7 & 5 & 11 & 6 & 0 & 2 & 3 & 10 \\
7 & 5 & 11 & 6 & 0 & 2 & 3 & 10 & 9 & 8 & 1 & 4 \\
0 & 2 & 3 & 10 & 9 & 8 & 1 & 4 & 7 & 5 & 11 & 6 \\
11 & 6 & 0 & 2 & 3 & 10 & 9 & 8 & 1 & 4 & 7 & 5 \\
3 & 10 & 9 & 8 & 1 & 4 & 7 & 5 & 11 & 6 & 0 & 2 \\
1 & 4 & 7 & 5 & 11 & 6 & 0 & 2 & 3 & 10 & 9 & 8 \\
9 & 8 & 1 & 4 & 7 & 5 & 11 & 6 & 0 & 2 & 3 & 10 \\
7 & 5 & 11 & 6 & 0 & 2 & 3 & 10 & 9 & 8 & 1 & 4 \\
0 & 2 & 3 & 10 & 9 & 8 & 1 & 4 & 7 & 5 & 11 & 6
\end{pmatrix}$$

Figure 2.1: A skewing scheme for a 2-dimensional array.

(iii) $\mu(C)$ *is equal to the minimum number* M *for which there exists a skewing scheme* $s : \mathbb{Z}_N^d \rightarrow \{0, 1, ..., M-1\}$ *that is valid for* C.

Example

An example of a skewing scheme $s : \mathbb{Z}_{12} \times \mathbb{Z}_{12} \rightarrow \{0, 1, ..., 11\}$ is given in figure 2.1. The values in the matrix indicate the s-values of the corresponding elements of the matrix. Note that s is valid for rows, anti-diagonals, and 2×6-blocks, but that s is not valid for columns, diagonals and 6×2-blocks.

Skewing schemes for d-dimensional arrays were mainly studied in the context of image processing and numerical computations, see also section 1.4.1. Within this framework, M reflects the number of memory banks provided by a specific architecture, the s-values indicate the memory banks in which the data elements are stored, and the templates correspond to the typical operands of image processing and numerical computations: rows, columns, $p \times q$-blocks, diagonals, etc. So, as can be concluded from chapter 1, the concepts of skewing schemes and validity of skewing schemes are applicable to various architectures and applications. We will normally refer to the interleaving degree M as the number of memory banks, numbered from 0 to $M-1$. The values in the range of a skewing scheme will denote the memory banks in which the data elements are stored.

First we present some results concerning the validity of skewing schemes. In section 2.2, section 2.3 and section 2.4 we study skewing schemes that are valid for block templates, $[x_1, x_2, ..., x_d]$-lines, and polyominoes, respectively.

As tessellations of the d-dimensional space (viz. the 2-dimensional plane) by templates play an important role in this chapter, we first introduce some notions.

Definition 2.3
(i) A partial tessellation of $\mathbb{Z}^d$ by a template P is any collection of disjoint (non-overlapping) instances of the template P.
(ii) A partial tessellation of $\mathbb{Z}^d$ by a template P is said to be total if every point of $\mathbb{Z}^d$ is in exactly one instance of P in the collection.

If no adjective is added we assume a tessellation to be total. If there exists a total tessellation of $\mathbb{Z}^d$ using a template P then we say that P tessellates $\mathbb{Z}^d$. In figure 2.2 an example of a tessellation of the plane by the template $\{(0,0),(0,1),(0,2),(1,0),(2,0)\}$ is depicted. We can designate one fixed element of a template P, e.g., (0,0,...,0), as the "handle" of P. An instance of P is obtained by adding a fixed displacement to all locations of P. By this we can define a tessellation of the d-dimensional space by P by means of the set of points in which the handles of the instances of P are located.

Definition 2.4
(i) The defining set of a (partial) tessellation by a template P is the set consisting of all points $x \in \mathbb{Z}^d$, such that $P(x)$ is part of the tessellation.
(ii) A tessellation is periodic if its defining set is a d-dimensional lattice.

A d-dimensional lattice is the set of points obtained as the integer linear combinations $\lambda_1.\vec{x}_1 + \lambda_2.\vec{x}_2 + ... + \lambda_d.\vec{x}_d$ of d integral independent vectors $\vec{x}_1, \vec{x}_2, ..., \vec{x}_d$ (the basis of the lattice).

WARNING. When we speak of a tessellation of the d-dimensional space using a template of some sort we shall require throughout this text that the templates in a tessellation all have equal orientation, i.e., we do not consider rotations and reflections of the objects when discussing tessellations unless explicitly stated otherwise.

2.1 The General Case

It would be very useful if we could study skewing schemes without regard of the bounds of the particular array concerned. The following result, due

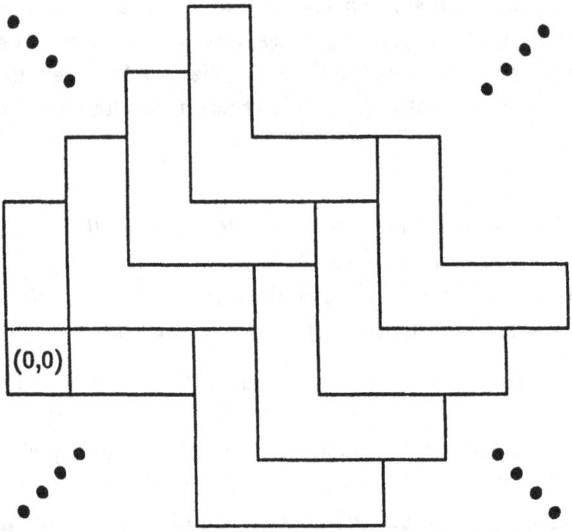

Figure 2.2: A tessellation of the plane.

to Shapiro [Sha75], proves that there exists a valid skewing scheme s for all d-dimensional arrays $\mathbf{Z}_N^d, N \geqslant 0$, if and only if there exists a valid skewing scheme s for the infinite d-dimensional array $\mathbf{Z}^d$.

Theorem 2.1 [Sha75] *Given a collection C of templates on a d-dimensional array and a number $M \geqslant 0$. Then there exists a skewing scheme $s : \mathbf{Z}_N^d \rightarrow \{0, 1, ..., M-1\}$ that is valid for C, for all $N \geqslant 0$, if and only if there exists a skewing scheme $s : \mathbf{Z}^d \rightarrow \{0, 1, ..., M-1\}$ that is valid for C.*

Actually Shapiro has proved this result only for 2-dimensional arrays, but his proof can be generalized to the d-dimensional case in an obvious way. So from now on, whenever we speak about skewing schemes for d-dimensional arrays, we mean skewing schemes from $\mathbf{Z}^d$ to $\{0, 1, ..., M-1\}$, unless stated otherwise.

A second result of Shapiro [Sha78b] determines the validity of skewing schemes for a collection of templates of equal size. Shapiro showed that there is a valid skewing scheme for a template P if and only if P tessellates the d-dimensional space. As the argument is important, we briefly digress and include our simplified proof of this fact (cf. theorem 2.2 below).

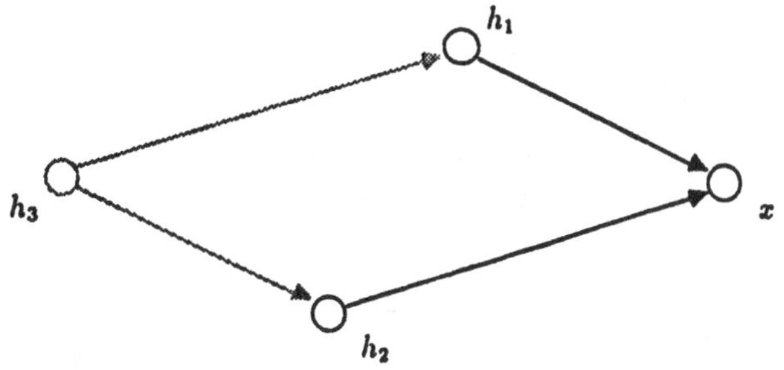

Figure 2.3: The parallelogram spanned by h_1, x and h_2.

Lemma 2.1 *Let P_1 and P_2 be instances of P with handles located in $h_1 \in \mathbb{Z}^d$ and $h_2 \in \mathbb{Z}^d$ respectively. P_1 and P_2 overlap if and only if h_1 and h_2 can be covered by a single instance of P.*

Proof Suppose P_1 and P_2 overlap in a point x. It means that $(x - h_1)$ and $(x - h_2)$ both lead into a point of the template when used as displacements from the handle.

Let h_3 be the "fourth" corner of the parallelogram spanned by h_1, x and h_2 (see figure 2.3) and imagine an instance P_3 of P located with its handle in h_3. It follows that both h_1 and h_2 must be covered by this instance P_3. The converse is established along similar lines. □

Lemma 2.2 *Let P_1 and P_2 be disjoint instances of P. If an instance P_3 overlaps P_1 and P_2 then the points it covers in P_1 are distinct from the points it covers in P_2 even when considered as elements of the same template.*

Proof Let the handles of P_1, P_2 and P_3 be located in h_1, h_2 and h_3 respectively. Suppose that P_3 covers a point x of P_1 and a point y of P_2 that are identically located with respect to h_1 and h_2 (respectively). It follows that, as displacements, $(x - h_1)$ and $(y - h_2)$ are identical. Let h_4 be the "fourth" corner of the parallelogram spanned by h_1, x and h_3 (see figure 2.4) and imagine an instance P_4 of P located with its handle in h_4. Observe that h_4, h_3, y and h_2 form a parallelogram as well and that as a result $(h_1 - h_4) = (x - h_3)$ and $(h_2 - h_4) = (y - h_3)$. As x and y are both covered by P_3, it follows that h_1 and h_2 are both be covered by P_4 and thus, using lemma 2.1 that P_1 and P_2 must overlap. This contradicts the disjointness of P_1 and P_2. □

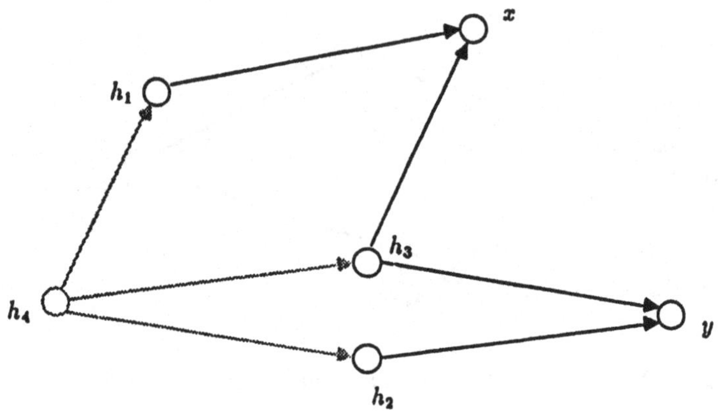

Figure 2.4: The displacements of h_1, h_2, h_3 and h_4.

Theorem 2.2 *There exists a valid skewing scheme s for* $\{P_1, P_2, ..., P_t\}$, $|P_i| = N$, *for all i, using N memory banks if and only if each* P_i *tessellates the d-dimensional space with the same defining set.*

Proof $\Rightarrow$ Let s be a valid skewing scheme for $\{P_1, P_2, ..., P_t\}$. Consider the arrangement A in which an instance of P_i is located at every point p with $s(p)$=0. (Note that every instance of P_i must have one point assigned to memory bank 0 and thus A is not empty.) Any two instances P_i^1 and P_i^2 in A must be disjoint. (If not, then lemma 2.1 would ensure the existence of an instance P_i^3 containing two points mapped to 0, contradicting the fact that s was valid.) To prove that A is a tessellation we need to show that every point q is covered. Consider the N possible instances P_i^j of P_i that cover q and let their handles be located in points p_j $(1 \leqslant j \leqslant N)$. The p_j must all be assigned to different memory banks (or else another contradiction could be derived with lemma 2.1) and thus there is exactly one p_k such that P_i^j covers q and $s(p_k)$=0. This P_i^j is indeed in A by definition. It is obvious that all tessellations so obtained have the same defining set.
$\Leftarrow$ Consider a tessellation by a template P_i. Number the points of P_i from 0 to $N-1$ and consider the skewing scheme s obtained by repeating this numbering throughout all instances in the tessellation and assigning to each point the value it got in the numbering. To prove that s is valid for P_i, consider an arbitrary instance P_i^1 of P_i. If P_i^1 coincides with an instance from the tessellation, then its points are trivially assigned to different memory

banks. Otherwise lemma 2.2 shows that P_i^1 takes disjoint bytes out of every instance of P_i in the tessellation that it intersects when viewed as parts of the original template. Thus all points in P_i^1 are assigned different numbers even now. □

Corollary 2.1 *Let P be a template on a d-dimensional array. Then there exists a skewing scheme $s : \mathbb{Z}^d \to \{0, 1, ..., M-1\}$ that is valid for P, where M is the size of a minimal template P' which contains P and which tessellates the d-dimensional space.*

It remains open whether the skewing scheme so obtained uses the minimum number of memory banks needed for skewing a template P. In this respect the following results can be helpful.

Theorem 2.3 *Let P be a template on a d-dimensional array. If there exists a skewing scheme $s : \mathbb{Z}^d \to \{0, 1, ..., M-1\}$ with $M \geqslant |P|$ that is valid for P, then there exists a partial tessellation of $\mathbb{Z}^d$ which covers a fraction of $\frac{|P|}{M}$ of the d-dimensional space.*

Proof The argument of the only if-part of the proof of theorem 2.2 can also be applied to this case and directly yields the desired result. □

The reverse implication of theorem 2.3 is not obviously fulfilled. However, if there exists a partial tessellation of $\mathbb{Z}^d$ by a template P that covers at least a fraction $\alpha\,(0 < \alpha \leqslant 1)$ of the d-dimensional space and which is periodic (cf. definition 2.4), then we can obtain a skewing scheme $s : \mathbb{Z}^d \to \{0, 1, ..., M-1\}$ that is valid for P and with $M = |P|/\alpha$. This is because in a periodic (partial) tessellation the "neighborhood" of each instance of P belonging to the tessellation is the same. Therefore we can extend P to a template P', with $|P'| = |P|/\alpha$ such that a tessellation is obtained by positioning the handles of the instances of P' in the points of the defining set of the periodic tessellation by P, cf. proposition 3.10. See figure 2.5 for an example. However, a partial tessellation of a template P that covers a maximal part of the d-dimensional space cannot always be obtained by a regular tessellation, see also section 2.4.5.

Another tool for determining the validity of a skewing scheme is provided by the conflict-region of a template P.

Definition 2.5 *Let P be a template on a d-dimensional array. The conflict-region C_P of P is the set $\bigcup_{-x \in P} P(x)$.*

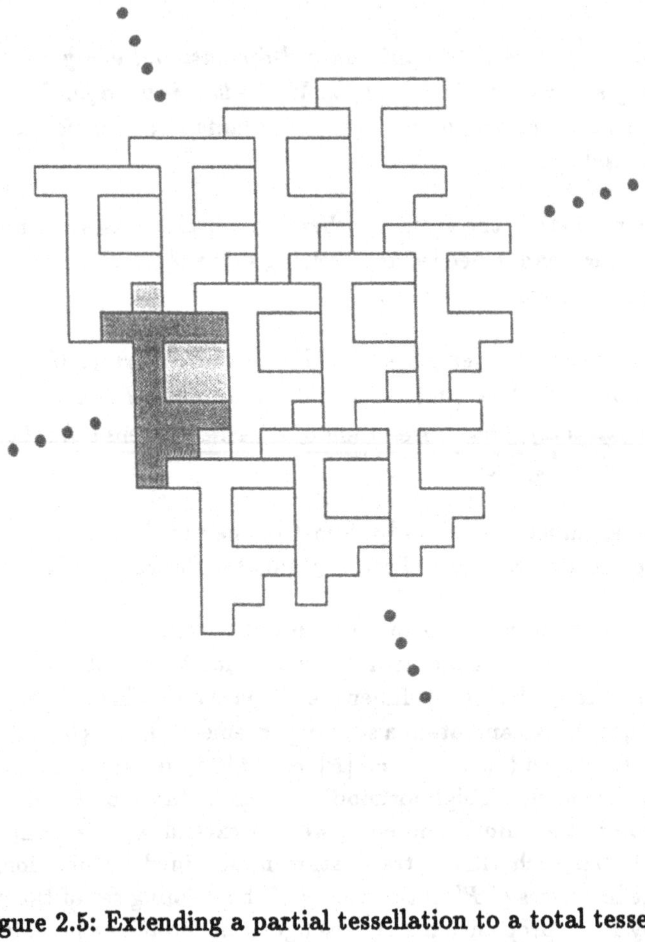

Figure 2.5: Extending a partial tessellation to a total tessellation.

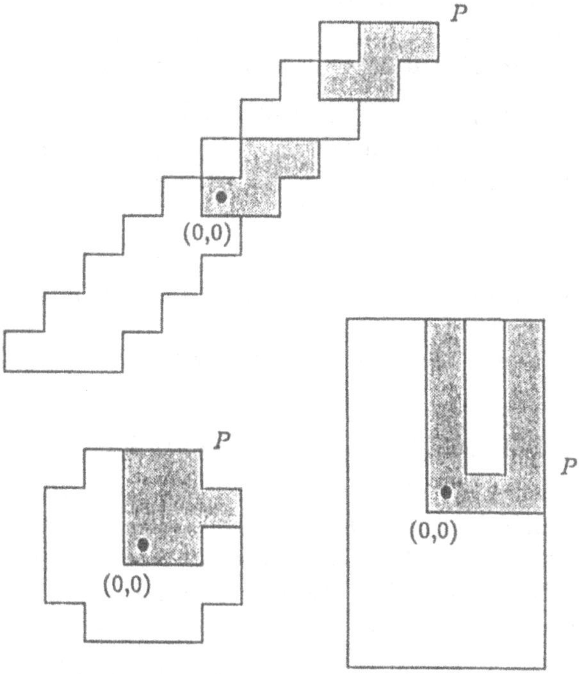

Figure 2.6: The conflict-regions of some templates.

The conflict-region of a template P is the set of points that are forced to be stored into a memory bank different from $(0,0,...,0) \in \mathbb{Z}^d$ in a valid skewing scheme for P. In figure 2.6 some examples of templates on the plane are depicted together with their conflict-region.

Lemma 2.3 *$x \in C_P$ iff $-x \in C_P$*

Proof Directly from definition 2.5. □

Theorem 2.4 *Let P be a template on a d-dimensional array. If there exists a set $\{P(x_1), P(x_2), ..., P(x_n)\}$ of instances of P such that*
(i) for all i, $1 \leqslant i \leqslant n$, $P(x_i) \subseteq C_P$ and $0 \notin P(x_i)$, and
(ii) for all $i, j, 1 \leqslant i, j \leqslant n$, $x_i - x_j \in C_P$,
then every skewing scheme s that is valid for P uses at least $|P| + n$ memory banks.

Proof If $P(x_i) \subseteq C_P$ and $0 \notin P(x_i)$, then from definition 2.5 and lemma 2.3 it follows that x_i has to be stored into a memory bank different from the elements of $P(0, 0, ..., 0)$. Further (ii) implies that all the x_i's in turn have to be stored into different memory banks also. □

Theorem 2.4 does not always yield the best possible bound on the minimum number of memory banks needed by a skewing scheme in order to be valid for a template P. This is illustrated by the following examples.

Examples

1. Consider the template P={(0,0),(1,0),(0,1),(1,1),(2,1),(0,2),(1,2)}. For this template P, theorem 2.4 yields the bound 7, whereas the minimum number of memory banks to skew P conflict-free equals 8.
2. An example of a template for which the bound of theorem 2.4 is optimal is provided by

$$P = \{(0,0),(1,0),(2,0),(0,1),(2,1),(0,2),(2,2),(0,3),(2,3),(0,4),(2,4)\}.$$

Consider the instances $P(-1,-1), P(-1,-2), P(-1,-3), P(-1,-4)$. Then these instances fulfill the constraints of theorem 2.4 (see figure 2.7) and we infer that at least $|P| + 4 = 15$ memory banks are needed for a valid skewing scheme for P. This is optimal in the sense that there does indeed exist a skewing scheme s valid for P that uses 15 memory banks.

The results so far give rather ad hoc methods for determining the minimum number of memory banks to obtain a skewing scheme that is valid for some kind of template. Define the following problem: given a collection of templates $\mathcal{C}$, determine the minimum number, $\mu(\mathcal{C})$, of memory banks for which there exists a skewing scheme that is valid for $\mathcal{C}$ (MINIMUM SKEWING). MINIMUM SKEWING is probably NP-complete, but we are not able to prove it. For the case that D is a k-ary tree, however, the problem is NP-complete, see chapter 4. In the remainder of this section we will mention some specific results for MINIMUM SKEWING for the one-dimensional case (cf. [TvLW86]).

For a given template $P = \{a_1, a_2, ..., a_p\}$, where $a_1 < a_2 < ... < a_p$, on a one-dimensional array, let $H(P)$ be the smallest integer $M \geqslant 1$ such that the numbers $a_1 \bmod M, a_2 \bmod M, ..., a_p \bmod M$ are all distinct. Let $L(P)$ be the chromatic number of the "template graph" corresponding to P defined as the graph of $2l$ points $(l = a_p - a_1 + 1) : 1, 2, ..., l, l+1, ..., 2l$ with an edge between x and y and only if there exists integers i and j such that $|x - y| = |a_i - a_j|$. The proofs of the following two theorems can be found in [TvLW86].

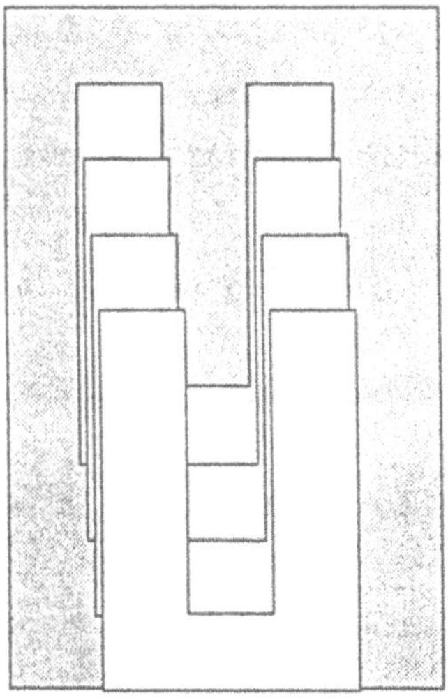

Figure 2.7: A template for which the bound of theorem 2.4 is optimal.

Theorem 2.5 *For every template $P = \{a_1, a_2, ..., a_p\}$ on a one-dimensional array:*

$$L(P) \leqslant \mu(P) \leqslant H(P) \leqslant a_p - a_1 + 1.$$

Theorem 2.6 *For every template $P = \{a_1, a_2, ..., a_p\}$ on a one-dimensional array:*

$$\mu(P) \leqslant d(P) + 1, \text{ with } d(P) = |\{|a_i - a_j| \mid i \neq j, a_i \in P \text{ and } a_j \in P\}|.$$

Examples

1. Let P be the set $\{0, 1, 2, 3, 4\}$, then the skewing scheme $s : \mathbb{Z} \to \{0, 1, 2, 3, 4\}$ defined by $s(x) = x \bmod 5$, is valid for P. See figure 2.8. Hence $|P| = 5$ and $\mu(P) = 5$. Furthermore $L(P) = 5$, $H(P) = 5$ and $d(P) = 4$.
2. Let P be the set $\{0, 1, 2, 5, 8\}$, then the skewing scheme $s : \mathbb{Z} \to \{0, 1, ..., 8\}$ defined by $s(x) = x \bmod 9$, is valid for P. See figure 2.9. Thus $|P| = 5$ and $\mu(P) = 9$. Furthermore $L(P) = 9$, $H(P) = 9$ and $d(P) = 8$.
3. Let P be the set $\{0, 3, 7, 12\}$, then the skewing scheme $s : \mathbb{Z} \to \{0, 1, 2, 3, 4\}$ defined by $s(x) = \lfloor \frac{x}{3} \rfloor \bmod 9$, is valid for P. See figure 2.10 . Thus $|P| = 4$ and $\mu(P) = 5$, but $L(P) = 5$, $H(P) = 8$ and $d(P) = 6$.

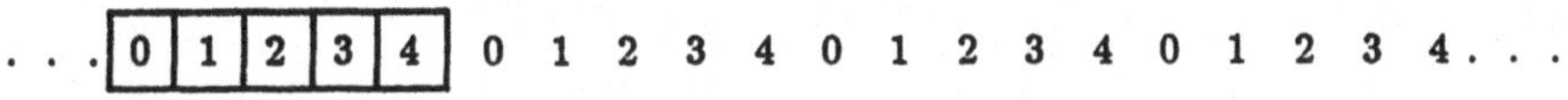

Figure 2.8: A one-dimensional skewing scheme valid for $\{0,1,2,3,4\}$.

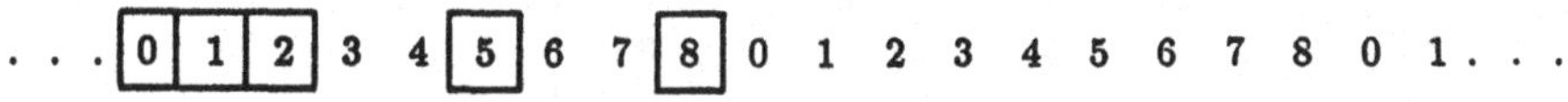

Figure 2.9: A one-dimensional skewing scheme valid for $\{0,1,2,5,8\}$.

Figure 2.10: A one-dimensional skewing scheme valid for $\{0,3,7,12\}$.

Define a (k,l,m)-template P as the set $\{0,1,...,k-1,k+l,k+l+1,...,k+l+m-1\}$.

Theorem 2.7 [TvLW86] *A (k,l,m)-template P tessellates the one-dimensional line iff $(k+m)|l$ or $k=m$ and $k|l$.*

Theorem 2.8 [TvLW86] *For every (k,l,m)-template P:*

$$\mu(P) \leqslant \begin{cases} \lceil (l \bmod k)/(l \operatorname{div} c) \rceil + c & \text{if } k=m \\ \lceil (l \bmod c)/(l \operatorname{div} c) \rceil + c & \text{otherwise,} \end{cases}$$

where $c=k+m$.

2.2 The Validity of Skewing Schemes for Block Templates

Image processing and pattern recognition require simultaneous access to templates that are "block shaped". See for instance the access patterns of the staging memory of the MPP design (section 1.3.2.2).

Definition 2.6 *A $(p_1,k_1)\times(p_2,k_2)\times ... \times(p_d,k_d)$-block template B on a d-dimensional array is the set $\{(i_1k_1,i_2k_2,...,i_dk_d)|\ 0\leqslant i_1<p_1, 0\leqslant i_2<p_2,...,0\leqslant i_d<p_d\}$.*

Call $(k_1, k_2, .., k_d)$ the stretch of a block template B. Several studies of parallel memory organizations suited for fast access to block templates can be found in e.g. [Pot85,vVM78]. However, most of the research done on this subject focuses on block templates on 2-dimensional arrays and presupposes that the stretch of the block templates equals (1,1). In this section we study the validity of skewing schemes for block templates with general stretch values.

The following result follows from theorem 2.2.

Lemma 2.4 *Let B be a $(p_1, 1) \times (p_2, 1)$-block template and let $s : \mathbb{Z}^2 \to \{0, 1, ..., N-1\}, N = p_1p_2$, be a skewing scheme valid for B. Then there exist integers $\alpha_j, j \in \mathbb{Z}, (\alpha_0 = 0)$ such that either*
(i) for all $m \in \{0, 1, ..., N-1\}$:

$$\{(x_1 - x_2, y_1 - y_2) |\, s(x_1, y_1) = s(x_2, y_2) = m\} = \{ip_1, \alpha_i + jp_2) |\, i, j \in \mathbb{Z}\}, \text{ or,}$$

(ii) for all $m \in \{0, 1, ..., N-1\}$:

$$\{(x_1 - x_2, y_1 - y_2) |\, s(x_1, y_1) = s(x_2, y_2) = m\} = \{\alpha_j + ip_1, jp_2) |\, i, j \in \mathbb{Z}\}.$$

Proof If there exists a skewing scheme $s : \mathbb{Z}^2 \to \{0, 1, ..., N-1\}$ that is valid for P, then by theorem 2.2 there exists a tessellation τ of the plane such that for all $m \in \{0, 1, ..., N-1\}$ the points $s^{-1}(m)$ correspond, possibly after a translation by a suitable vector $\vec{x} \in \mathbb{Z}^2$, to the defining set of the tessellation τ. Clearly we only need to distinguish between two different types of tessellations of the plane by B, see figure 2.11. If τ is of type 1 then (i) is fulfilled, and if τ is of type 2 then (ii) is fulfilled. □

Lemma 2.5 *Let B_1 be a $(p_1, 1) \times (p_2, 1)$-block template and B_2 a $(q_1, 1) \times (q_2, 1)$-block template, $p_1 < q_1$ and $p_1p_2 = q_1q_2 = N$. Then the existence of a skewing scheme $s : \mathbb{Z}^2 \to \{0, 1, ..., N-1\}$ that is valid for B_1 and B_2 implies that $p_1 | q_1$.*

Proof Let s be a skewing scheme that is valid for B_1 and B_2. Suppose $p_1 \nmid q_1$. Consider any slice of the plane of width q_1 and height N. Then there is a partition of this slice consisting of exactly q_2 blocks B_2 (see figure 2.12). Consequently there are exactly q_2 points within this slice with a s-value of m, for every $m \in \{0, 1, ..., N-1\}$. Let $m_0 \in \{0, 1, ..., N-1\}$ and let (a, b) be a point in this slice with b minimal and $s(a, b) = m_0$. The validity of s

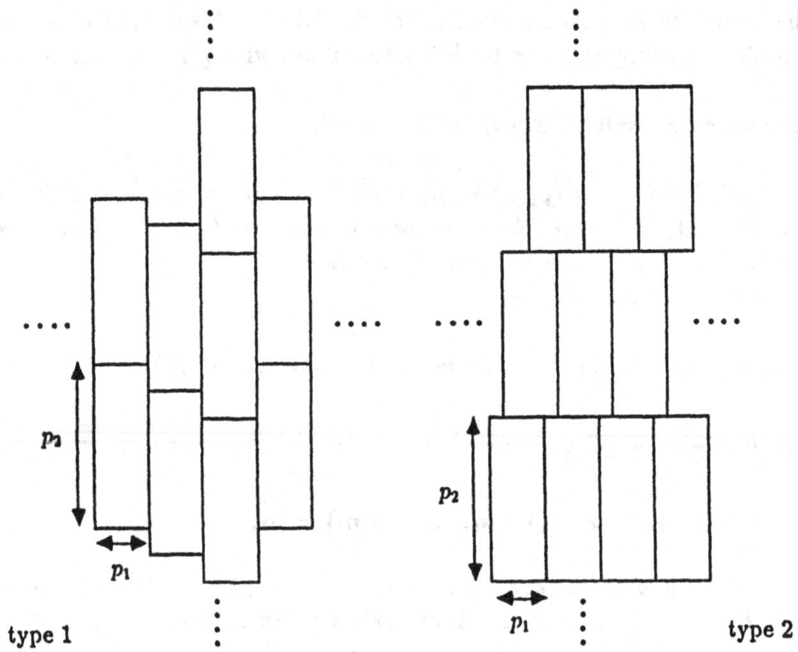

Figure 2.11: Two different types of tessellation of the plane.

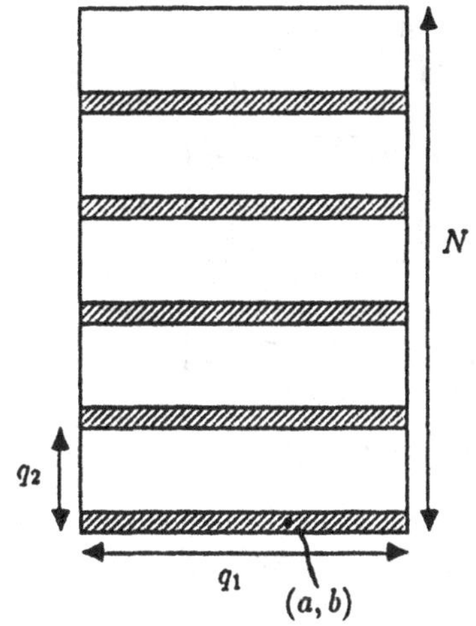

Figure 2.12: The points with s-value equal to m_0.

implies that the other $q_2 - 1$ points with s-value equal to m_0 are contained in the shaded strips of figure 2.12. In each strip there is exactly one such a point. From the assumption that $q_1 > p_1$ follows that there is a slice L' with width p_1 and height N, which also contains (a, b) and which in turn is contained in slice L. This slice L' can be partitioned into p_2 blocks B_1. By the same argument as above, in slice L' there are p_2 strips each containing exactly one point with s-value m_0. When we overlay these two slices L and L' (see figure 2.13) then from $q_2 \nmid p_2$ it follows that there is at least one shaded strip of L' that is not contained in a strip of L. This implies that there are more than q_2 points in slice L with s-value m_0. Contradiction. □

Consider the property P:

$$\begin{aligned}&\text{for all } (x, y) \in \mathbb{Z}^2 :\\ &\quad s(x, y) = s(x + k_1 a, y) \text{ iff } a = \lambda q_1 \text{ for some } \lambda \in \mathbb{Z}, \text{ and,}\\ &\quad s(x, y) = s(x, y + k_2 b) \text{ iff } b = \mu p_2 \text{ for some } \mu \in \mathbb{Z}.\end{aligned}$$

Theorem 2.9 *Let B_1 be a $(p_1, k_1)\times(p_2, k_2)$-block template and B_2 a $(q_1, k_1)\times(q_2, k_2)$-block template, $p_1 < q_1$ and $p_1 p_2 = q_1 q_2 = N$. Then there exists a skewing scheme $s : \mathbb{Z}^2 \to \{0, 1, ..., N-1\}$ that is valid for B_1 and B_2, which necessarily has property* P, *if and only if $p_1 | q_1$.*

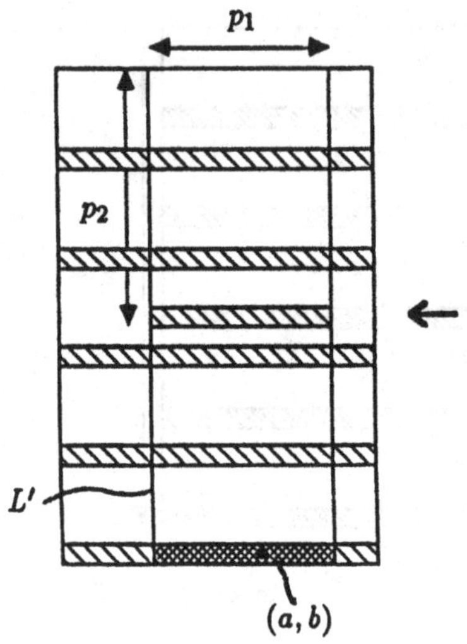

Figure 2.13: The other points with s-value equal to m_0.

Proof Note that the constraints induced by the validity of a skewing scheme s for B_1 and B_2 apply independently to each "coset" $\{(x+\lambda k_1, y+\mu k_2)|\lambda,\mu\in Z\}$. So, there exists a skewing scheme $s: Z^2 \to \{0,1,...,N-1\}$ that is valid for B_1 and B_2 if and only if there exist skewing schemes

$$s: \{(x+\lambda k_1, y+\mu k_2)|\lambda,\mu\in Z\} \to \{0,1,...,N-1\},$$

for each "coset" with $(x,y)\in Z^2$, that are valid for B_1 and B_2. Consider any "coset" $\{(x+\lambda k_1, y+\mu k_2)|\lambda,\mu\in Z\}, (x,y)\in Z^2$. Then this "coset" can be viewed as (is isomorphic to) Z^2 and the block templates B_1 and B_2 translate into the block templates $\bar{B}_1$ and $\bar{B}_2$, with dimensions $(p_1,1)\times(p_2,1)$ and $(q_1,1)\times(q_2,1)$. Thus the if-part follows directly from lemma 2.5. Assume that $p_1|q_1$. From lemma 2.4 it follows that if there exists a skewing scheme $\bar{s}: Z^2\to\{0,1,...,N-1\}$ that is valid for $\bar{B}_1$ and $\bar{B}_2$, then $\bar{s}$ has the property that there exist integers α_j $(j\in Z), \alpha_0=0$, and integers β_j $(j\in Z), \beta_0=0$, such that for all $m\in\{0,1,...,N-1\}$:

$$\begin{aligned}\{(x_1 - x_2, y_1 - y_2) | \, \bar{s}(x_1, y_1) = \bar{s}(x_2, y_2) = m\} \\ = \{(ip_1, \alpha_i + jp_2 | \, i, j \in \mathbb{Z}\} \\ = \{(\beta_j + iq_1, jq_2) | \, i, j \in \mathbb{Z}\}.\end{aligned}$$

Note that the other three possibilities lead to contradiction. Thus,

$$\begin{aligned}& s(x, y) = s(x + k_1 a, y), \text{ for some } (x, y) \in \mathbb{Z}^2 \\ & \quad \text{iff } \bar{s}(x, y) = s(x + a, y), \text{ for some } (x, y) \in \mathbb{Z}^2 \\ & \quad \text{iff } (a, 0) = (i_1 p_1, \alpha_{i_1} + j_1 p_2) = (\beta_{j_2} + i_2 q_1, j_2 q_2), \\ & \quad \text{for some } i_1, i_2, j_1, j_2 \in \mathbb{Z} \\ & \quad \text{iff } a = i_2 q_1, \text{ for some } i_2 \in \mathbb{Z} \ (\beta_0 = 0).\end{aligned}$$

In the same way we get that $s(x, y) = s(x, y + k_2 b)$ iff $b = j_1 p_2$ for some $j_1 \in \mathbb{Z}$.

Consider the tessellation τ of the plane by $\bar{B}_1$ and $\bar{B}_2$ which has as defining set $\{(\lambda p_1 + \mu q_1, \lambda q_2) | \lambda, \mu \in \mathbb{Z}\}$, see figure 2.14. By theorem 2.2 there exists a skewing scheme that is valid for $\bar{B}_1$ and $\bar{B}_2$. Let $\bar{s} : \mathbb{Z}^2 \rightarrow \{0, 1, ..., N-1\}$ be the skewing scheme that is implied by the tessellation τ. Define the skewing scheme $s : \mathbb{Z}^2 \rightarrow \{0, 1, ..., N-1\}$ by

$$s(x, y) = \bar{s}(\lfloor \frac{x}{k_1} \rfloor, \lfloor \frac{y}{k_2} \rfloor).$$

Then s is valid for B_1 and B_2 and s acts on each "coset" $\{(x + \lambda k_1, y + \mu k_2) | \lambda, \mu \in \mathbb{Z}\}$ as a periodic skewing scheme with defining set $\{(\lambda p_1 + \mu q_1, \lambda q_2) | \lambda, \mu \in \mathbb{Z}\}$. □

In fact s can be chosen to be a skewing scheme acting on each "coset"

$$\{(x + \lambda k_1, y + \mu k_2) | \, \lambda, \mu \in \mathbb{Z}\}$$

as a periodic skewing scheme with underlying lattice $\{(\lambda p_1 + \mu q_1, \lambda q_2) | \, \lambda, \mu \in \mathbb{Z}\}$ (see section 3.2). Thus, if there exists a skewing scheme valid for two block templates B_1 and B_2 of equal size then there exists a multi-periodic (in the sense of section 3.3) skewing scheme valid for B_1 and B_2.

Corollary 2.2 *There does not exist a skewing scheme $s : \mathbb{Z}^2 \rightarrow \{0, 1, ..., N-1\}$ that is valid for more than 2 different block templates, which have an equal stretch and size N.*

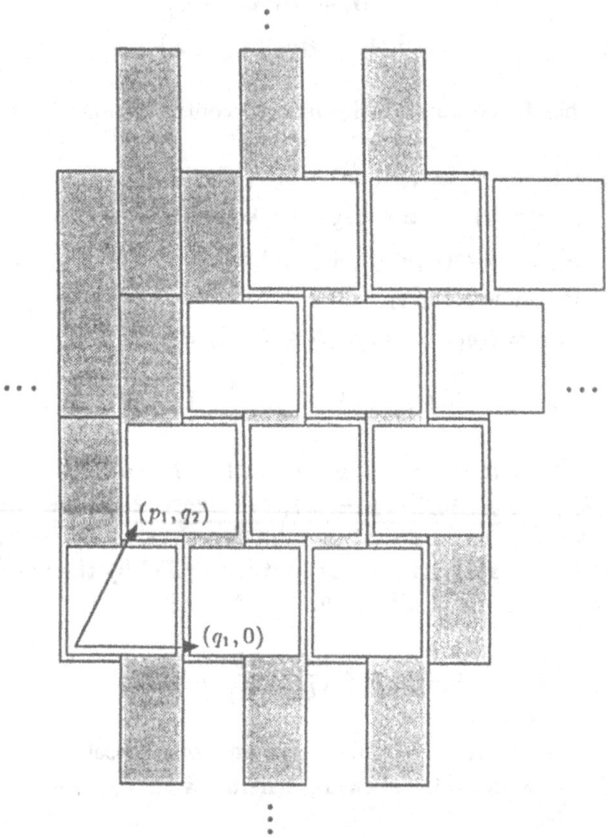

Figure 2.14: A tessellation of the plane by both $\bar{B}_1$ and $\bar{B}_2$.

Proof Let B_1 be a $(p_1, k_1) \times (p_2, k_2)$-block template, B_2 a $(q_1, k_1) \times (q_2, k_2)$-block template, and B_3 a $(r_1, k_1) \times (r_2, k_2)$-block template, and let $p_1 < q_1 < r_1$ and $p_1 p_2 = q_1 q_2 = r_1 r_2 = N$. Suppose $s : \mathbb{Z}^2 \rightarrow \{0, 1, ..., N-1\}$ is valid for B_1, B_2 and B_3. Then from theorem 2.9 follows that for all $(x, y) \in \mathbb{Z}^2$ $s(x, y) = s(x + k_1 a, y)$ iff $a = \lambda q_1$ for some $\lambda \in \mathbb{Z}$ iff $a = \lambda' r_1$ for some $\lambda' \in \mathbb{Z}$. Contradiction. □

Corollary 2.2 generalizes an observation by Voorhis and Morrin [vVM78], who proved it for the very restricted case that the block templates have dimensions $(1, 1) \times (pq, 1)$, $(p, 1) \times (q, 1)$ and $(pq, 1) \times (1, 1)$.

For the case that block templates have unequal stretches the following theorem is useful.

Theorem 2.10 *Let for i, $1 \leqslant i \leqslant t$, B_i be a $(p_1^i, k_1^i) \times (p_2^i, k_2^i) \times ... \times (p_d^i, k_d^i)$-block template on a d-dimensional array. Then there exists a (periodic) skewing scheme $s : \mathbb{Z}^d \rightarrow \{0, 1, ..., N-1\}$ that is valid for $\{B_1, B_2, ..., B_t\}$ and with $N = q_1 q_2 ... q_d$, where for all $j, 1 \leqslant j \leqslant d : q_j =$ "the smallest number q such that $q \geqslant p_j^i$ and $\gcd(q, k_j^i) = 1$ for all $i, 1 \leqslant i \leqslant t$".*

Proof Assign to each point x of the "block" $\{(x_1, x_2, ..., x_d) | 0 \leqslant x_i < q_i\}$ a different value $\eta(x) \in \{0, 1, ..., N-1\}$. Define the skewing scheme $s : \mathbb{Z}^d \rightarrow \{0, 1, ..., N-1\}$ by $s(x_1 x_2, ..., x_d) = \eta(x_1 \bmod q_1, x_2 \bmod q_2, ..., x_d \bmod q_d)$. We claim that s is valid for $\{B_1, B_2, ..., B_t\}$. Suppose that there exists a B_i and a point $x \in \mathbb{Z}^d$ such that there are two distinct points $(a_1, a_2, ..., a_d)$, $(b_1, b_2, ..., b_d) \in B_i(x)$ with $s(a_1, a_2, ..., a_d) = s(b_1, b_2, ..., b_d)$. Then there are $\lambda_1, \lambda_2, ..., \lambda_d$ such that

$$\begin{aligned} -p_1^i < \; & \lambda_1 < p_1^i, \\ -p_2^i < \; & \lambda_2 < p_2^i, \\ & \vdots \\ -p_d^i < \; & \lambda_d < p_d^i, \text{ and} \end{aligned}$$

$$(b_1, b_2, ..., b_d) = (a_1 + \lambda_1 k_1^i, a_2 + \lambda_2 k_2^i, ..., a_d + \lambda_d k_d^i).$$

Because $(a_1, a_2, ..., a_d) \neq (b_1, b_2, ..., b_d)$, there exists at least one λ_j with $\lambda_j \neq 0$. Because $q_j \geqslant p_j^i$ and $\gcd(k_j^i, q_j) = 1$ we have that $\lambda_j k_j^i = 0 \bmod q_j$. Thus $(a_1 \bmod q_1, a_2 \bmod q_2, ..., a_d \bmod q_d) \neq (b_1 \bmod q_1, b_2 \bmod q_2, ..., b_d \bmod q_d)$ and $s(a_1, a_2, ..., a_d) \neq s(b_1, b_2, ..., b_d)$. Contradiction. □

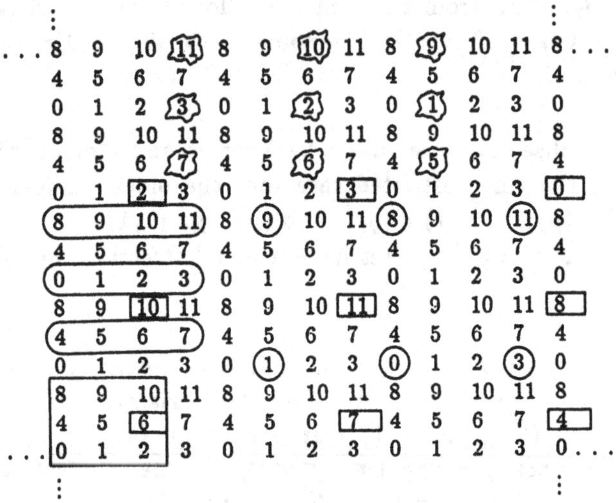

Figure 2.15: A skewing scheme that is valid for block templates with unequal stretches.

Example
In figure 2.15 a skewing scheme $s : Z^d \rightarrow \{0, 1, ..., 11\}$ is depicted that is valid for a $(3,1) \times (3,1)$-block template, a $(3,5) \times (3,4)$-block template, a $(3,3) \times (2,5)$-block template, a $(3,3) \times (3,2)$-block template and a $(4,1) \times (3,2)$-block template.

Corollary 2.3 *Let N be as in* theorem 2.10. *Then*

$$N \leqslant 2^d p_1 p_2 ... p_d$$

with $p_1 = \max_{1 \leqslant i \leqslant t} p_1^i, p_2 = \max_{1 \leqslant i \leqslant t} p_2^i, ..., p_d = \max_{1 \leqslant i \leqslant t} p_d^i$.

Proof By Bertrand's postulate [HW79] the smallest prime $\geqslant x$ is $\leqslant 2x$. So, we can choose for each q_j in theorem 2.10 a number $\leqslant 2.\max_{1 \leqslant i \leqslant t} p_j^i$. □

Corollary 2.4 *Let for each i, $1 \leqslant i \leqslant t$, B_i be a $(p_1, k_1^i) \times (p_2, k_2^i) \times ... \times (p_d, k_d^i)$-block template on a d-dimensional array. Further, let for each $i, 1 \leqslant i \leqslant t$, and $j, 1 \leqslant j \leqslant d$:*

$$k_j^i = 2^n \text{ for some } n \geqslant 0.$$

Then there exists a skewing scheme $s : \mathbb{Z}^d \to \{0, 1, ..., N-1\}$ that is valid for $\{B_1, B_2, ..., B_t\}$ with

$$N \leqslant (p_1 + 1)(p_2 + 1)...(p_d + 1)$$

Proof Either p_j or $p_j + 1$ is odd, and the result follows directly from theorem 2.10. □

2.3 The Validity of Skewing Schemes for $[x_1, x_2, ..., x_d]$-Lines

$[x_1, x_2, ..., x_d]$-lines can be seen as 1-dimensional subsets of $\mathbb{Z}^d$. Their importancy for numerical computations was already discerned by Budnik and Kuck [BK71], whose notion of d-ordered vectors, see also section 1.4.1, arose from the specific $[x_1, x_2, ..., x_d]$-lines: rows, columns and diagonals of a d-dimensional array.

Definition 2.7 *A $[x_1, x_2, ..., x_d]$-line P on a d-dimensional array $\mathbb{Z}_N^d$ is the set $\{(\lambda x_1 \bmod N, \lambda x_2 \bmod N, ..., \lambda x_d \bmod N) \mid 0 \leqslant \lambda \leqslant N-1\}$.*

Shapiro [Sha78a] proved that for $[x_1, x_2, ..., x_d]$-lines linear skewing schemes are as powerful as arbitrary skewing schemes. A skewing scheme $s : \mathbb{Z}^d \to \{0, 1, ..., M-1\}$ is linear if s can be represented by $s(x_1, x_2, ..., x_d) = (a_1 x_1 + a_2 x_2 + ... + a_d x_d) \bmod M$ for some integers $a_1, a_2, ..., a_d$, see also section 1.4.1 and section 3.1.

Theorem 2.11 [Sha78a] *Given a collection C of $[x_1, x_2, ..., x_d]$-lines of equal size N on a d-dimensional array. Then there exists a skewing scheme $s : \mathbb{Z}^d \to \{0, 1, ..., N-1\}$ that is valid for C if and only if there exists a linear skewing scheme $s : \mathbb{Z}^d \to \{0, 1, ..., N-1\}$ that is valid for C.*

For a study of the validity of linear skewing schemes for $[x_1, x_2, ..., x_d]$-lines see section 3.1.2. This section focuses on arbitrary but very special skewing schemes for 2-dimensional $n \times n$-arrays that are valid for both the [1,0]-line (rows), and the [0,1]-line (columns). These skewing schemes are well-known as *Latin squares*.

2.3.1 Latin Squares

A Latin square of order n is an $n \times n$-array $\mathbf{a}$ over the integers $1, ..., n$, such that each integer i $(1 \leqslant i \leqslant n)$ occurs exactly once in each row and exactly once in each column of $\mathbf{a}$. In this section we study a special type of Latin square that received attention in the early 70's (according to [Hil73] on a suggestion of J. Dénes). Its importance here derives from the fact that these squares represent (arbitrary) skewing schemes that are valid for rows, columns, and the two main diagonals.

A Latin square $\mathbf{a}$ is called double diagonal (dd, for short) if each integer i $(1 \leqslant i \leqslant n)$ also occurs exactly once on the main diagonal and exactly once on the off diagonal. The following result is due to Hilton [Hil73].

Theorem 2.12 *There exist double diagonal Latin squares for all orders n with $n \geqslant 1, n \neq 2, 3$.*

Hilton used sophisticated techniques to prove his results. In 1972 Gergely [Ger74] gave a much simpler proof of theorem 2.12 using the elegant method of "projecting transversals". His proof is easily seen to imply a linear time algorithm for constructing a double diagonal Latin square of given order. The major part of this section is devoted to a proof that a suitable direct ("Kronecker") product construction can be developed for double diagonal Latin squares.

Theorem 2.13 *Any double diagonal Latin square of order p $(p \geqslant 1)$ can be composed with a suitable diagonal Latin square of order q $(q = 1$ or $q \geqslant 4$ when $p = 1$, and $q \geqslant 1$ otherwise) to obtain a double diagonal Latin square of order pq.*

The algorithm of composition will be explained below. In theorem 2.13 the "suitable" Latin square can be any double diagonal Latin square when $q = 1$ or $q \geqslant 4$, because the class of double diagonal Latin squares is obviously closed under direct (Kronecker-) product and double diagonal Latin squares exist for every such order (cf. theorem 2.12).

Hilton ([Hil73], p.683) notes that for $n \equiv \pm 1 \pmod 6$ a double diagonal Latin square is obtained by taking $\mathbf{a}(i, j) \equiv j + 2i - 2 \pmod n$. By using theorem 2.13 one can construct double diagonal Latin squares for all remaining orders $n > 6$ from double diagonal squares of order $n \leqslant 6, n \neq 2, 3$ and thus obtain a simple alternative proof of theorem 2.12.

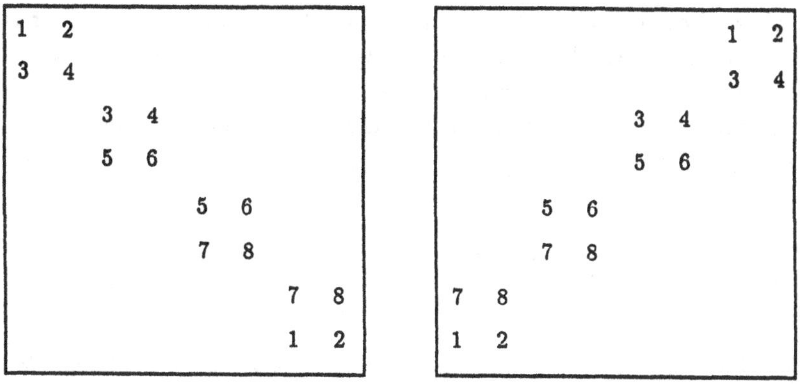

Figure 2.16: Diagonals in non-permuted order.

2.3.2 Composition of Double Diagonal (dd) Latin Squares

Let **a** be a dd-Latin square of order p over the (barred) symbol set $\bar{1}, ..., \bar{p}$ and let $q \geqslant 1$. Without loss of generality let $p \geqslant 4$ (cf. theorem 2.12). If $q \geqslant 4$ then theorem 2.12 implies that there exists a dd-Latin square **b** of order q over the symbol set $1, ..., q$. Replace every $\bar{i}$-cell of **a** $(1 \leqslant i \leqslant p)$ by the instance of **b** with $(i - 1)q$ added to each entry. The result is easily seen to be a dd-Latin square of order pq. (Note that this is essentially the observation in [Hil73, page 683].) Thus theorem 2.13 remains to be proven for $q = 2$ and $q = 3$. We will show that in both cases a suitable replacement of every $\bar{i}$-cell of **a** $(1 \leqslant i \leqslant p)$ can be deviced.

Theorem 2.14 *Given a double diagonal Latin square **a** of order p $(p \geqslant 4)$, it can be "composed" to a double diagonal Latin square of order $2p$.*

Proof Begin by replacing every $\bar{i}$-cell of **a** $(1 \leqslant i \leqslant p)$ as indicated by the following substitution.

$$1 \rightarrow \begin{array}{|c|c|} \hline 1 & 2 \\ \hline 3 & 4 \\ \hline \end{array} \qquad 2 \rightarrow \begin{array}{|c|c|} \hline 3 & 4 \\ \hline 5 & 6 \\ \hline \end{array} \qquad \cdots \qquad p \rightarrow \begin{array}{|c|c|} \hline 2p-1 & 2p \\ \hline 1 & 2 \\ \hline \end{array}$$

Note that this guarantees that every symbol from $1, ..., 2p$ occurs exactly once in every row, on the main diagonal and on the off diagonal (figure 2.16 shows example diagonals in non-permuted order).

However, the columns are not right. To correct this we shall make changes in the cells, while preserving the transversal property for all rows and for the main and off diagonals. The changes consist of "flipping" the upper two entries (the "upper track") and/or the lower two entries (the "lower track") in the appropriate cells. Call an unflipped pair of entries positive, a flipped pair negative. Being positive or negative implies a notion of "orientation" in the tracks of the cells:

1 2 (positive)	2 1 (negative)	1 2 (positive)	2 1 (negative)
3 4 (positive)	3 4 (positive)	4 3 (negative)	4 3 (negative)

Observation 2.1 *Flipping the entries in the upper track or in the lower track of a cell does not affect the "Latin square property" for the rows.*

An $\bar{r}$-cell and an $\bar{s}$-cell of a are said to be in column-conflict if the cells are in the same column and have symbols in a same position. There can only be two sorts of column-conflict for an $\bar{r}$-cell:
(i) its upper track is equal to and has the same orientation as the lower track of an $\bar{s}$-cell in the same column, and
(ii) its lower track is equal to and has the same orientation as the upper track of an $\bar{s}$-cell in the same column.

Observation 2.2 *The upper (lower) track of an $\bar{r}$-cell can create a column-conflict with exactly one lower (upper) track of a cell in the same column.*

(To be precise, the first type of column-conflict occurs with the $\bar{s}$-cell with $s = r - 1$ ($s = p$ if $r = 1$) and the second type occurs with the $\bar{s}$-cell with $s = r + 1$ ($s = 1$ if $r = p$).) A column-conflict can be resolved by flipping one of the tracks involved. Clearly one should not flip the track of the cell that lies on the main or off diagonal, if this happens to be the case, because it would destroy the transversal property on the diagonal without there being a reason for it. A problem arises if both cells involved in a column-conflict lie on a diagonal.

Flipping the upper (lower) track of a cell on a diagonal will give rise to a "diagonal-conflict" with the lower (upper) track of exactly one other cell on the same diagonal. (Compare this to observation 2.2 , but note that this time the conflicting tracks have opposite orientation).

Observation 2.3 *If an $\bar{r}$-cell and an $\bar{s}$-cell are in column-conflict and the $\bar{r}$-cell lies on a diagonal, then flipping the conflicting track in the $\bar{r}$-cell creates a diagonal-conflict precisely with the (unique) $\bar{s}$ cell on the same diagonal.*

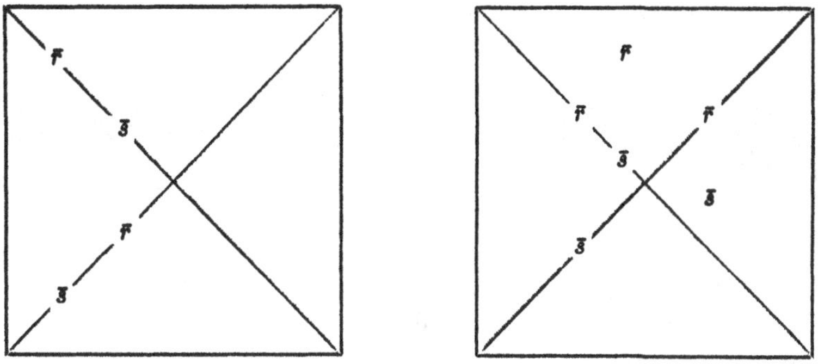

(*i*) (*ii*)

Figure 2.17: The possible cases of two cells which are both in column-conflict and lie on a diagonal.

Now consider the case that an $\bar{r}$-cell and an $\bar{s}$-cell are in column-conflict, and both lie on a diagonal (which means that we must flip in a diagonal cell which causes a diagonal-conflict). There are essentially two different cases to distinguish.

Case I. The $\bar{s}$-cell and $\bar{r}$-cell involved in the diagonal-conflicts according to observation 2.3 are in the same column (see figure 2.17(*i*)). The conflicts can all be resolved by flipping the appropriate track of both the $\bar{r}$-cell and the $\bar{s}$-cell on one of the diagonals. Note that the diagonal remains a transversal in doing so.

Case II. The $\bar{s}$-cell and $\bar{r}$-cell involved are not in the same column (see figure 2.17(*ii*)).

The column- and diagonal-conflicts can now be resolved by flipping the appropriate track of the $\bar{r}$-cell and the $\bar{s}$-cell on one of the diagonals (i.e., starting with the $\bar{r}$-cell that was in column-conflict), with the suitable flip in the off-diagonal $\bar{r}$-cell in the same column as the latter $\bar{s}$-cell. The resulting changes on the one diagonal leave it a correct transversal.

Thus we have shown that all column-conflicts can be resolved. The resulting Latin square is correct and dd, and of the desired order. □

Theorem 2.15 *Let* **a** *be a double diagonal Latin square of order* p $(p \geqslant 4)$, *then it can be "composed" to a double diagonal Latin square of order* $3p$.

Proof The argument is very similar to theorem 2.14. Begin by replacing every $\bar{\imath}$-cell of **a** $(1 \leqslant i \leqslant p)$ as follows.

$$
1 \rightarrow
\begin{array}{|c|c|c|}
\hline
1 & 2 & 3 \\
\hline
4 & 5 & 6 \\
\hline
7 & 8 & 9 \\
\hline
\end{array}
\qquad
2 \rightarrow
\begin{array}{|c|c|c|}
\hline
4 & 5 & 6 \\
\hline
7 & 8 & 0 \\
\hline
10 & 11 & 12 \\
\hline
\end{array}
\qquad \cdots \qquad
p \rightarrow
\begin{array}{|c|c|c|}
\hline
3p-2 & 3p-1 & 3p \\
\hline
1 & 2 & 3 \\
\hline
4 & 5 & 6 \\
\hline
\end{array}
$$

Note that this guarantees again that all rows are right, and it can easily be verified that the main and off diagonal are right as well. A problem arises because of column-conflicts.

Observe that a track of a cell can be in conflict with precisely two other tracks (of the same "contents", and in separate cells) in the same column. A column-conflict can be resolved by shifting one of the tracks over one position (cyclically) and a second over two. If one of the three tracks occurs in a cell on the diagonal, then this track should obviously be the one that remains unaffected (and thus leaves the diagonal a correct transversal).

If two of the three tracks involved in a column-conflict lie on a diagonal (clearly this is the worst case that can occur), then it cannot be avoided that a track of one cell on the diagonal is shifted and a diagonal-conflict is created. If the column-conflict was created by the upper/lower/middle track of an $\bar{r}$-cell, an $\bar{s}$-cell and a $\bar{t}$-cell with (say) the $\bar{r}$-cell on the main diagonal and the $\bar{t}$-cell on the off diagonal, then the diagonal-conflict involves again the $\bar{r}$-cell and the $\bar{s}$- and $\bar{t}$-cells on the particular diagonal. Considering the possible cases as in the proof of theorem 2.14 shows that the column-conflict and the subsequent diagonal-conflict can always be resolved by appropriate cyclic shifts of the tracks.

Removing all column-conflicts leads to a correct dd-Latin square of order $3p$. $\qquad\qquad\qquad\qquad\qquad\qquad\qquad\qquad\qquad\qquad\qquad\qquad\qquad\qquad\square$

The construction used in theorem 2.14 and theorem 2.15 clearly generalizes and gives a simple and uniform method of building a double diagonal Latin square of order pq from one of order p $(p \geqslant 4)$ for every integer $q \geqslant 1$. The construction requires only linear time in the size of the resulting square.

2.4 The Validity of Skewing Schemes for Polyominoes (Rookwise Connected Templates)

In this section we settle an important conjecture of Shapiro [Sha78b] and prove that for templates that have the shape of a polyomino there exists a valid skewing scheme s from Z^2 into $\{0, 1, ..., N-1\}$ if and only if there exists a valid *periodic* skewing scheme s from Z^2 into $\{0, 1, ..., N-1\}$. A skewing scheme $s : Z^2 \rightarrow \{0, 1, ..., N-1\}$ is periodic if there exists a 2-dimensional lattice $L = \{\lambda_1\vec{x}_1 + \lambda_2\vec{x}_2 | \lambda_1 \in Z, \lambda_2 \in Z\}$, such that for all $a \in L, b \in L$ and $x \in Z^2 : s(x + a) = s(x + b)$, cf. definition 2.4 (*ii*). For a more detailed definition of periodic skewing schemes see section 3.2. In order to exclude ambiguity we shall refer throughout this section to points $x \in Z^2$ as cells.

Definition 2.8 *A polyomino is a data template of which the cells form a rookwise connected set with no "holes" (when embedded in the plane).*

Rook-wise connectedness means that every two cells of the template can be connected by a chain of cells within the template, with every two consecutive cells of the chain sharing a full side. The proof of Shapiro's conjecture relies on theorem 2.2. We show that when a polyomino of size N tessellates the plane, then it tessellates the plane periodically, i.e., with its instances arranged according to a 2-dimensional lattice. As a corollary we show that the existence of a valid skewing scheme for a polyomino of size N can be decided in polynomial time.

2.4.1 Definitions and Preliminary Results

In this section we fix a polyomino P of size N and introduce some notions pertaining to its set of instances $P(x, y)$.

Definition 2.9 *The relative position π of cells (x_1, y_1) and (x_2, y_2) is the "bi-directional" vector $r = \pm(x_2 - x_1, y_2 - y_1)$ The relative position of $P(x_1, y_1)$ and $P(x_2, y_2)$ is the relative position of (x_1, y_1) and (x_2, y_2).*

It is best to think of r as a vector pointing "both ways". Intuitively it is the vector needed to go from one cell to the other. (Observe that the relative position of (x_1, y_1) and (x_2, y_2) is equal to the relative position of (x_2, y_2) and (x_1, y_1).) In polyominoes $P(x_1, y_1)$ and $P(x_2, y_2)$ all corresponding cells have the same relative position, namely the relative position of $P(x_1, y_1)$ and $P(x_2, y_2)$.

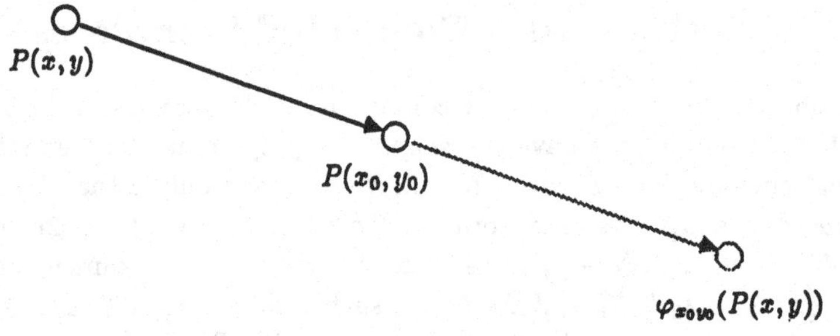

Figure 2.18: The buddy of a polyomino.

Definition 2.10 *$P(x_1,y_1)$ and $P(x_2,y_2)$ overlap if there exist elements (a_i,b_i) and (a_j,b_j) of P such that $(a_i+x_1,b_i+y_1)=(a_j+x_2,b_j+y_2)$.*

Lemma 2.6 *$P(x_1,y_1)$ and $P(x_2,y_2)$ overlap if and only if P contains two elements that are in the same relative position as $P(x_1,y_1)$ and $P(x_2,y_2)$.*

Proof Clearly $P(x_1,y_1)$ and $P(x_2,y_2)$ overlap if and only if for some i and j: $(a_i,b_i) = (a_j,b_j)+(x_2-x_1,y_2-y_1)$ or, equivalently, $(a_j,b_j) = (a_i,b_i)+(x_2-x_1,y_2-y_1)$. □

Let $P(x_0,y_0)$ be a fixed instance of P. With every polyomino $P(x,y)$ there is a second polyomino (its "buddy") that has the same relative position to $P(x_0,y_0)$.

Definition 2.11 *The buddy of $P(x,y)$ with respect to $P(x_0,y_0)$ is the instance $\varphi_{x_0y_0}(P(x,y)) = P(2x_0-x,2y_0-y)$.*

Observing that $(2x_0-x,2y_0-y)=(x_0,y_0)+(x_0-x,y_0-y)$ it should be clear (see figure 2.18) that the buddy of $P(x,y)$ is symmetrically located at the "opposite" side of the polyomino $P(x_0,y_0)$. It also follows that buddies are paired, i.e., if P_1 is the buddy of P_2 then P_2 is the buddy of P_1. The following properties of $\varphi_{x_0y_0}$ are worth noting.

Lemma 2.7 *$\varphi_{x_0y_0}$ preserves relative positions.*

Proof We have to establish that $\varphi_{x_0y_0}P(x_1,y_1)$ and $\varphi_{x_0y_0}P(x_2,y_2)$ have the same relative position as $P(x_1,y_1)$ and $P(x_2y_2)$. A simple calculation

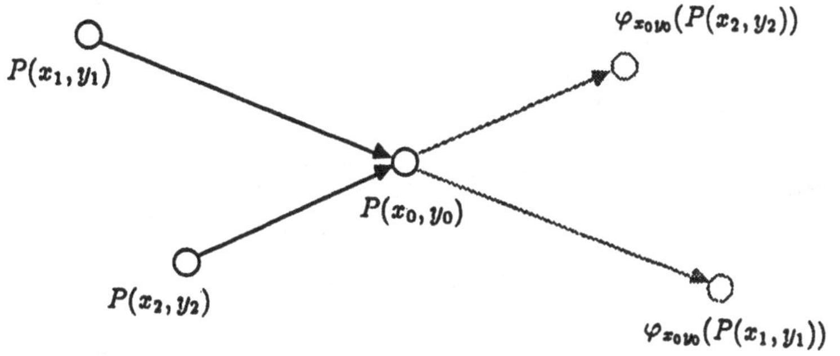

Figure 2.19: $\varphi_{x_0y_0}$ preserves relative positions.

would suffice, but the argument is best seen from a geometric interpretation (see figure 2.19). In fact it is useful to think of $\varphi_{x_0y_0}$ as a reflection of the designated cells around (x_0, y_0) that "carries" the polyomino along in an unreflected manner. This certainly preserves the relative position of corresponding cells throughout the mapping. □

Using lemma 2.6 it follows in particular that $\varphi_{x_0y_0}$ maps disjoint instances of P to disjoint images.

Lemma 2.8 *$\varphi_{x_0y_0}$ does not introduce overlap, i.e., if $P(x,y)$ and $P(x_0,y_0)$ are disjoint then $\varphi_{x_0y_0}(P(x,y))$ is disjoint from these instances as well.*

Proof Let $P(x,y)$ and $P(x_0,y_0)$ be disjoint. Using lemma 2.6 and lemma 2.7 we easily conclude that $\varphi_{x_0y_0}(P(x,y))$ must be disjoint from $P(x_0,y_0)$ as well. Suppose $\varphi_{x_0y_0}(P(x,y))$ is not disjoint from $P(x,y)$ and actually overlaps it in cell $\gamma = (u,v)$. The situation is shown in figure 2.20 where for simplicity we have set $P \equiv P(x,y), P_0 \equiv P(x_0,y_0)$ and $\varphi \equiv \varphi_{x_0y_0}(P(x,y))$.

By observing how γ is located with respect to the handles of $P(x,y)$ and $\varphi_{x_0y_0}(P(x,y))$ we can identify four more cells $(\alpha,\beta,\delta,\mu)$ that are of interest because of their similar location with respect to the handles of $P(x,y), P(x_0,y_0)$ or $\varphi_{x_0y_0}(P(x,y))$ Note that $\alpha,\beta,...$ are on a straight line, with a relative position equal to $\pm(x_0 - x, y_0 - y)$ between every consecutive two. Figure 2.20 shows to which polyomino each of the $\alpha,\beta,...$ must belong. As $\alpha \in P(x,y)$ and $\gamma \in P(x,y)$ and P is a polyomino, there must be a rookwise connected chain π of cells leading from α to γ that uses only cells within $P(x,y)$. As β and δ (both $\in P(x_0,y_0)$) are in the same relative

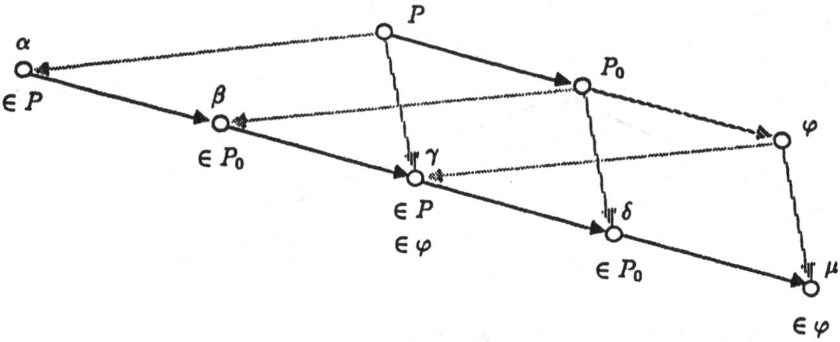

Figure 2.20: $\varphi_{x_0 y_0}$ does not introduce overlap.

position, the chain π' obtained by shifting π over the vector $(x_0 - x, y_0 - y)$ must connect them and run entirely within the polyomino $P(x_0, y_0)$. (This is because π really is a chain that is fixed for the template.) Because α, γ and β, δ are interlaced, π and π' necessarily intersect. Any cell where the chains intersect will belong to both $P(x, y)$ and $P(x_0, y_0)$. This contradicts the fact that they are disjoint. □

Lemma 2.8 is a special case of some results of Levi [Lev34]. Note that lemma 2.7 holds for templates in general, but that lemma 2.8 makes essential use of the fact that we deal with polyominoes. In later sections "buddying" will be important in analyzing disjoint placements of polyominoes around an instance $P(x_0, y_0)$.

2.4.2 Tessellations of the Plane by Polyominoes

Tessellations (or "tilings") are a familiar subject in mathematics. We require the objects in a tessellation to have an equal orientation. In the following we assume that polyominoes are sets of cells on the two-dimensional grid. (Recall that polyominoes have no holes.) We say that two polyominoes border each other if they have at least one gridpoint in common.

Definition 2.12 *The boundary B of the (embedded) polyomino P is the set of gridlines of unit length that bound the interior of P from the exterior. The size of B is denoted by $|B|$. The boundary $B(x, y)$ of $P(x, y)$ is B shifted by a vector (x, y).*

We number the gridlines in B going around clockwise as $r_0, r_1, \ldots$ starting from a fixed reference element $r_0 \in B$. Shifting over a vector (x, y) this numbering translates into a numbering $r_0(x, y), r_1(x, y), \ldots$ of $B(x, y)$. Note that numbers like $r_i(x, y)$ are merely names of gridlines with respect to some $P(x, y)$.

Notice that a partial tessellation may contain holes, e.g. cells which are not covered by any instance of this tessellation. The "boundary" of any such hole is formed by the parting and rejoining boundaries of the enclosing instances. The entire boundary will be called the *interior boundary* I of the instances with respect to the hole. Whenever a collection of instances forms no hole then the *exterior boundary* E of that collection is defined as the collection of gridlines belonging to exactly one instance. The length of I (or E, respectively) will be denoted as $|I|(|E|)$. In the remaining part of this section we shall prove that a hole formed by two or three instances of P cannot be covered by further instances of P.

Lemma 2.9 *Given three nonoverlapping instances* $P(x_0, y_0), P(x_1, y_1)$ *and* $P(x_2, y_2)$, *with* $P(x_i, y_i)$ *bordering* $P(x_{i\pm1 \bmod 3}, y_{i\pm1 \bmod 3})$ *for* $0 \leqslant i \leqslant 2$. *Let* $\vec{a} = (x_1 - x_0, y_1 - y_0)$, $\vec{b} = (x_2 - x_0, y_2 - y_0)$ *and* $\vec{c} = (x_2 - x_1, y_2 - y_1)$. *Then for all* (x, y) *the instances* $P(x, y)$, $P((x, y) \pm \vec{a})$, $P((x, y) \pm \vec{b})$ *and* $P((x, y) \pm \vec{c})$ *do not overlap each other* (*see* figure 2.21).

Proof Let $P(x, y) \equiv P_0, P((x, y) + \vec{a}) \equiv P_1, P((x, y) + \vec{b}) \equiv P_2$, $P((x, y) + \vec{c}) \equiv P_3, P((x, y) - \vec{a}) \equiv P_4, P((x, y) - \vec{b}) \equiv P_5$ and $P((x, y) - \vec{c}) \equiv P_6$.

Note that P_0 does not overlap with any P_i. For e.g. P_1 we can make the following observations:

1. P_1 and P_0 do not overlap ($P(x_1, y_1)$ and $P(x_0, y_0)$ do not overlap).
2. P_1 and P_2 do not overlap ($P(x_1, y_1)$ and $P(x_2, y_2)$ do not overlap).
3. P_1 and P_6 do not overlap ($P(x_2, y_2)$ and $P(x_0, y_0)$ do not overlap).
4. P_1 and P_4 do not overlap, because of 1 and lemma 2.8.

Because the polyominoes are (rookwise) connected and have the same form and orientation, we also observe:

5. P_1 and P_3 do not overlap, and
6. P_1 and P_5 do not overlap.

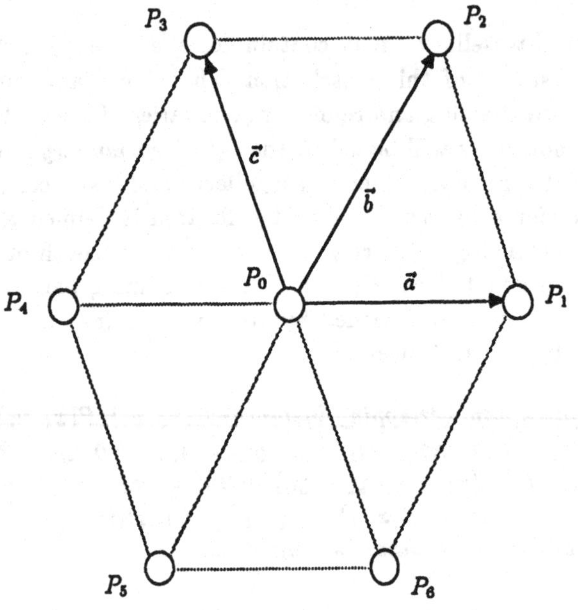

Figure 2.21: The disjointness of $P_0, P_1, P_2, P_3, P_4, P_5$ and P_6.

The reason for this is that P_1 cannot reach around P_2 and P_0 (or P_0 and P_6, respectively) to intersect P_3 or P_5. Note that P_2 and P_0 (and P_0 and P_6, respectively) border each other.

By symmetry, similar observations hold for $P_2, P_3, ..., P_6$. Hence P_0, P_1 through P_6 do not overlap each other. (Note that P_1 borders P_2 borders P_3 borders ... borders P_6 borders P_1. So P_0 is totally enclosed by $P_1 ... P_6$). □

The next two lemmas will put restrictions on the sizes of the interior and exterior boundary of a collection of instances of P.

Lemma 2.10 *Given a polyomino P, with boundary B.*
(i) Let two instances of P form a hole h and have a gridline in common. Then the size of the interior boundary I of these instances with respect to h is strictly less than $|B|$.
(ii)Let three instances of P form a hole h and at least two of them have a gridline in common. Then the size of the interior boundary of these instances with respect to h is strictly less than $|B|$.

Proof We shall first give a proof of the second part of the lemma, because it is the more difficult one.

(*ii*) Let $P(x_0, y_0) \equiv P_0, P(x_1, y_1) \equiv P_1$ and $P(x_2, y_2) \equiv P_2$ be three nonoverlapping instances, which form a hole h. Furthermore two of them have a gridline in common. Consider the set S of gridlines belonging to the interior boundary of $\{P_0, P_1, P_2\}$ with respect to hole h or to at least 2 instances (see figure 2.22). Clearly $|S| \geqslant |I| + 1$. We will prove that S consists of gridlines belonging to disjoint parts of the boundary B. By this we mean that if $r_k(x_i, y_i), r_l(x_j, y_j) \in S$ and $r_k(x_i, y_i) \neq r_l(x_j, y_j)$ then $k \neq l$.

Whenever $r_k(x_i, y_i), r_l(x_i, y_i) \in S$ and $r_k(x_i, y_i) \neq r_l(x_i, y_i)$ then it trivially follows that k cannot be equal to l. Suppose now $r_k(x_i, y_i), r_l(x_j, y_j) \in S, i \neq j, r_k(x_i, y_i) \neq r_l(x_j, y_j)$ and $k = l$. Let $i = 0$ and $j = l$. Because of symmetry the other cases can be handled analogously.

From lemma 2.9 follows that $P_0, P_1, P_2, P(x_0+x_2-x_1, y_0+y_2-y_1) \equiv P_3$, and $P(2x_0 - x_1, 2y_0 - y_1) \equiv P_4$ do not overlap each other. Note that the relative positions of P_2, P_0 and P_1 to each other are the same as those of P_3, P_4 and P_0 to each other. So we can extend both P_2 and P_3 to P_2' and P_3' in such a way that P_2' exactly covers P_2 and the hole h, and P_3' exactly covers P_3 and the corresponding hole (see figure 2.23). Furthermore P_0, P_1, P_2', P_3' and P_4 do not overlap each other. We assumed that $k = l$. Thus both P_2' and P_3' border P_0 along the same gridline $r_k(x_0, y_0)$ (if $r_k(x_1, y_1) \notin B(x_0, y_0)$) or both P_1 and P_4 border P_0 along a gridline $r_{k'}(x_0, y_0)$ with $r_{k'}(x_0, y_0) =$

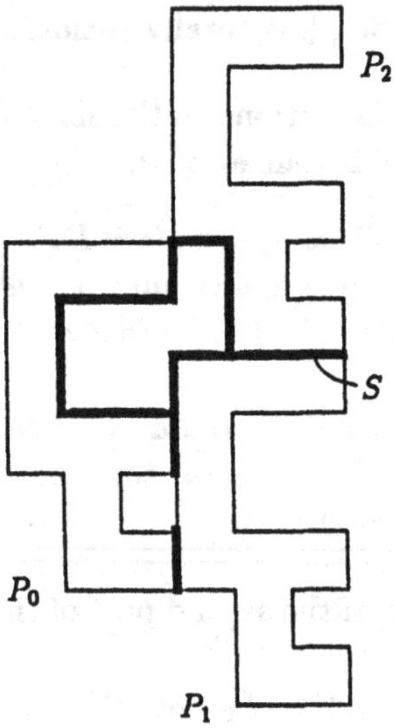

Figure 2.22: Three instances which form a hole such that at least two of them have a gridline in common.

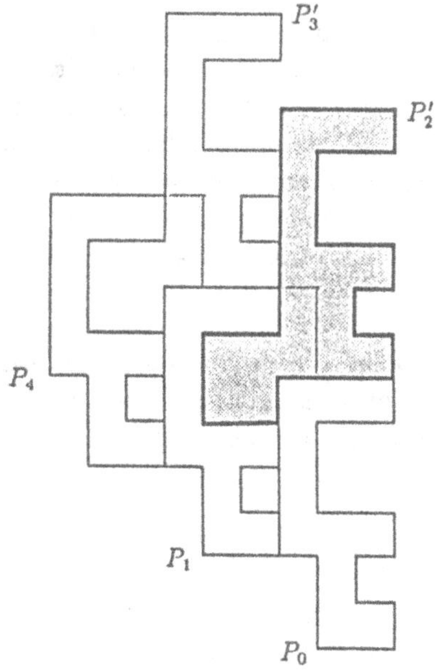

Figure 2.23: The extension of P_2 and P_3 to P_2' and P_3'.

$r_k(x_1, y_1)$ (if $r_k(x_1, y_1) \in B(x_0, y_0)$). This however contradicts the fact that P_0, P_1, P_2', P_3' and P_4 do not overlap each other.

It follows now that the set S consists of gridlines belonging to disjoint parts of the boundary B. So $|S| \leqslant |B|$. Together with $|S| \geqslant |I| + 1$ this gives $|I| < |B|$.

(*i*) Let $P(x_0, y_0) \equiv P_0$ and $P(x_1, y_1) \equiv P_1$ be two nonoverlapping instances which form a hole h and have a gridline in common. Consider again the set S of gridlines belonging to the interior boundary of P_0 and P_1 with respect to h or to both $B(x_0, y_0)$ and $B(x_1, y_1)$. Then because of lemma 2.8 P_0, P_1 and $P_2 \equiv \varphi_{x_1 y_1}(P(x_0, y_0))$ do not overlap each other.

Extend both P_0 and P_1 to P_0' and P_1' in the same way as in (*ii*). Then again P_0', P_1' and P_2 do not overlap each other. Similar to the proof of (*ii*) a contradiction occurs if we assume that two gridlines of S correspond to the same gridline of B. □

Lemma 2.11 *Given a polyomino P with boundary B. Let E be the exterior boundary of any nonempty finite collection of instances of P, which do not overlap each other and form no hole. Then $|E| \geqslant |B|$.*

Proof See [WvL84]. □

Theorem 2.16
(*i*) *If $P(x_1, y_1)$ and $P(x_2, y_2)$ form a hole and have a gridline in common, then there exists no total tessellation using P which contains both $P(x_1, y_1)$ and $P(x_2, y_2)$.*
(*ii*) *If $P(x_1, y_1)$, $P(x_2, y_2)$ and $P(x_3, y_3)$ form a hole and have a gridline in common, then there exists no total tessellation using P which contains both $P(x_1, y_1)$, $P(x_2, y_2)$ and $P(x_3, y_3)$.*

Proof (*i*) From lemma 2.10(*i*) and lemma 2.11.
(*ii*) From lemma 2.10(*ii*) and lemma 2.11. □

2.4.3 Conditions for Periodic Tessellations by Polyominoes

Recall the definition of the boundary $B(x, y)$ of an embedded polyomino $P(x, y)$ and its numbering. Now suppose that some partial or total tessellation τ is given. We say that $P(x_1, y_1), ..., P(x_k, y_k)$ *partially surround* the instance $P(x_0, y_0)$ if the polyominoes (including $P(x_0, y_0)$) are all disjoint, but for all $i > 0 : B(x_i, y_i) \cap B(x_0, y_0) \neq \emptyset$. We say that $P(x_1, y_1), ..., P(x_k, y_k)$ *completely surround* $P(x_0, y_0)$ if, in addition, each gridline of $B(x_0, y_0)$ is contained in some $B(x_i, y_i)$ $(i > 0)$. The size of a (partial or complete) surrounding will be the number (k) of distinct polyominoes in it. It is clear that the boundary of $B(x_0, y_0)$ splits up in a number of consecutive segments $[r_{i_0}(x_0, y_0), ..., r_{i_1}(x_0, y_0)], [r_{i_2}(x_0, y_0), ..., r_{i_3}(x_0, y_0)], ..., (r_0 \leqslant r_{i_0} \leqslant r_{i_1} < r_{i_2} \leqslant r_{i_3} < ...)$ that are the borderlines with instances $P(x_i, y_i)$. We will assume that each segment is maximal for the particular $P(x_i, y_i)$.

Lemma 2.12 *If τ is a total tessellation, then each $P(x, y)$ that surrounds $P((x_0, y_0) \in \tau$ generates exactly one, contiguous segment on the boundary.*

Proof Directly from theorem 2.16. □

Definition 2.13 *A partial segmentation of $B(x_0, y_0)$ is any set of (maximal and disjoint) indexed segments $I_0, I_1, ...$ along $B(x_0, y_0)$ that are the borderline with some $P(x, y) \in \tau$. A segmentation is called total if $\bigcup_i I_i = B(x_0, y_0)$.*

A segmentation of $B(x, y)$ will be denoted by $\text{Seg}(B(x, y))$. The number of segments in it will be denoted by $|\text{Seg}(B(x, y))|$. Its "length" is defined in an obvious manner. Clearly partial surroundings lead to partial segmentations and complete surroundings lead to complete segmentations of $B(x_0, y_0)$. Surroundings and the segmentations they induce are the key to a further understanding of periodic tessellations.

Definition 2.14 *A tessellation τ is regular if the same segmentation is induced in every $B(x, y)$ with $P(x, y) \in \tau$, i.e., $\text{Seg}(P(x_1, y_1)) = \text{Seg}(P(x_2, y_2))$ for every $P(x_1, y_1)$ and $P(x_2, y_2)$ in the tessellation.*

Lemma 2.13 *If a tessellation τ is periodic then τ is regular.*

Proof Follows from the observation that in a periodic tessellation the relative positions of the surrounding polyominoes must be the same for every $P(x, y) \in \tau$. □

The reverse, regularity implies periodicity, is valid too, and will be proved later in this section.

Lemma 2.14 *There exists a regular tessellation using P if and only if there exist an instance $P(x_0, y_0)$ and a complete surrounding $P(x_1, y_1), ..., P(x_k, y_k)$ of it such that $\text{Seg}(P(x_i, y_i)) \subseteq \text{Seg}(P(x_0, y_0))$ $(i > 0)$.*

Proof (Note that the segmentations of the $P(x_i, y_i)$ referred to in the second part of the lemma will be partial for $i > 0$.)
$\Rightarrow$ Let τ be regular. Consider any $P(x_0, y_0) \in \tau$ and the polyominoes (of τ) completely surrounding it. The desired property now follows immediately from definition 2.14.
$\Leftarrow$ Suppose there exists a complete surrounding $P(x_1, y_1), ..., P(x_k, y_k)$ of $P(x_0, y_0)$ such that $\text{Seg}(P(x_i, y_i)) \subseteq \text{Seg}(P(x_0, y_0))$ $(i > 0)$. Because we can shift the entire configuration anywhere, one can surround $P(x_0, y_0)$ wherever (x_0, y_0) is located. Observe that $|\text{Seg}(P(x_0, y_0))| = k$, by virtue of lemma 2.12. Consider any $P(x_i, y_i)$ $(1 \leqslant i \leqslant k)$ and surround it by polyominoes just like $P(x_0, y_0)$. Because of the assumed property of the original segmentations the new polyominoes "grip" with the existing ones without conflict. Repeating this, every polyomino can be surrounded and the tessellation that results must be regular. □

Given a (partial or total) tessellation τ, let G_τ be the graph of boundaries of the instances $P(x, y) \in \tau$. The nodes of G_τ will be the (grid)points where at least three boundaries meet. The length of an edge e will be the number of unit-length gridlines it is composed of, denoted as $|e|$. Clearly G_τ is a planar graph with nodes of degree 3 or 4.

Definition 2.15 *A three-node (four-node) is any gridpoint g where three (four) nonoverlapping instances of P meet. The branches of g are the three (four) edges that meet in g (taken in consecutive order).*

We normally refer to the three- and four-nodes of some G_τ with τ total but the definition applies to any local configuration of some $P(x_0, y_0)$ and a (partial or complete) surrounding. In the latter case we speak of three-nodes (four-nodes) admitted by P. An edge will simply extend to either a node or a gridpoint where two boundaries part.

Lemma 2.15 *Suppose P admits a three-node g with branches T_1, T_2 and T_3. Then there exists with every $P(x_0, y_0)$ a partial surrounding $P(x_1, y_1), ...,$ $P(x_6, y_6)$ such that $P(x_i, y_i) \cap P(x_{i+1}, y_{i+1}) \neq \emptyset$ for $1 \leqslant i \leqslant 6$ (and $x_7 \equiv x_1, y_7 \equiv y_1$). The length of the partial segmentation induced is $2.|T_1| + 2.|T_2| + 2.|T_3|$.*

Proof Suppose P admits a three-node g as described. It means that for any $P(x_0, y_0) \equiv P_0$ we can find two additional nonoverlapping instances $P(x_1, y_1) \equiv P_1$ and $P(x_2, y_2) \equiv P_2$ that surround it, with the three of them

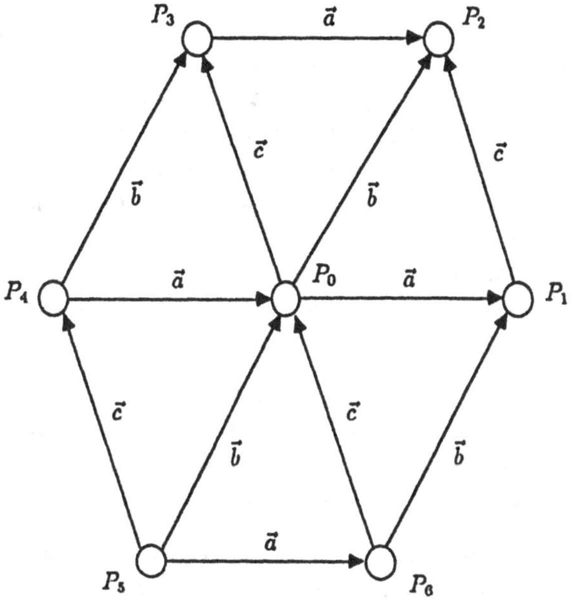

Figure 2.24: The construction of a surrounding of a polyomino.

meeting in g. Furthermore $B(x_0, y_0) \cap B(x_1, y_1) \neq \emptyset$, $B(x_1, y_1) \cap B(x_2, y_2) \neq \emptyset$, and $B(x_2, y_2) \cap B(x_0, y_0) \neq \emptyset$. We apply lemma 2.9 to P_0, P_1 and P_2 and obtain the situation as shown in figure 2.24. Observe that $P_0, P_1, ..., P_6$ do not overlap each other and that the relative position of P_0 and P_1 is the same as that of P_4 and P_0 and of P_3 and P_2 and of P_5 and P_6 and so on. So $P(x_i, y_i) \cap P(x_{i+1}, y_{i+1}) \neq \emptyset$ for $1 \leqslant i \leqslant 6$ (and $x_7 \equiv x_1, y_7 \equiv y_1$).

Finally consider the partial segmentation induced on the boundary of $P(x_0, y_0)$. From theorem 2.16 now follows that no other instances of P but P_1 through P_6 can border $P(x_0, y_0)$. Each $P_i (1 \leqslant i \leqslant 6)$ gives rise to exactly one segment along $B(x_0, y_0)$. This identifies the 6 segments along $B(x_0, y_0)$, with a total length equal to $|T_1|+|T_3|+|T_1|+|T_2|+|T_2|+|T_3| = 2.(|T_1|+|T_2|+|T_3|)$.

□

Lemma 2.16 *Suppose P admits a four-node g with branches T_1, T_2, T_3 and T_4. Then there exists with every $P(x_0, y_0)$ a partial surrounding $P(x_1, y_1), ...,$ $P(x_4, y_4)$ such that the length of the partial segmentation induced on $B(x_0, y_0)$ is equal to $2.|T_1| + 2.|T_4|$ (respectively $2.|T_4| + 2.|T_3|$, $2.|T_3| + 2.|T_2|$ and*

$2.|T_2| + 2.|T_1|)$.

Proof Suppose P admits a four-node g as described. So for every $P(x_0, y_0) \equiv P_0$ we can find three additional nonoverlapping instances $P(x_1, y_1) \equiv P_1$ and $P(x_2, y_2) \equiv P_2$ and $P(x_3, y_3) \equiv P_3$ that surround it, with the three of them meeting in g. Let P_0 border P_1 along T_1, P_1 border P_2 along T_2, P_2 border P_3 along T_3 and P_3 border P_0 along T_4. Consider P_3, P_0, P_1, then these three instances meet the conditions as stated in lemma 2.9. So we obtain again a situation as shown in figure 2.24. By means of the same arguments as in the previous proof this gives the desired result. Note that $B(x_1, y_1) \cap B(x_3, y_3) \neq \emptyset$. The other partial surroundings are obtained by considering P_2, P_3, P_0 (resp. P_1, P_2, P_3 and P_0, P_1, P_2). □

Lemma 2.17 *Let τ be a regular tessellation using P. Then either (a) every node of G_τ is a three-node and every $P(x, y) \in \tau$ is completely surrounded by 6 other instances of P, or (b) every node of G_τ is a four-node and every $P(x, y) \in \tau$ is completely surrounded by 4 other instances of P.*

Proof Let τ be a regular tessellation of the plane using P. Consider an arbitrary node g of G_τ. Clearly g is either a three-node or a four-node.

In case g is a three-node there are three instances P_0, P_1 and $P_2 \in \tau$ that meet at g as specified in the beginning of the proof of lemma 2.15. This identifies three relative positions (the "vectors" $\pm\vec{a}$, $\pm\vec{b}$ and $\pm\vec{c}$ in figure 2.24) which, because of the regularity of τ, must always lead from one instance of P in τ to another one that necessarily also belongs to τ. It is easily verified that for this reason each of the polyominoes P_3 to P_6 constructed in the proof of lemma 2.15 can be justified as a polyomino actually belonging to τ. As any hole between two consecutive P_i's $(i > 0)$ and the boundary of P_0 would be too small to fit in another instance of P (because of theorem 2.16) and yet τ is total, it follows that the polyominoes P_1 to P_6 must be a complete surrounding of P_0. Again arguing from the assumed regularity of τ, this means that every polyomino in τ is surrounded likewise in exactly the same manner. In particular, each node of G_τ necessarily appears as a three-node.

In case g is a four-node one can argue as before that the polyominoes $P(x_1, y_1)$, $P(x_2, y_2)$, $P(x_3, y_3)$ and $P(x_4, y_4)$ of lemma 2.16 must all belong to τ and form a complete surrounding of P_0. Since τ is regular, it follows that every polyomino in τ is surrounded in exactly the same manner and (hence) that every node of G_τ is a four-node. □

Lemma 2.18 *Let τ be a regular tessellation of the plane using P. Then the underlying set of points (x, y) such that $P(x, y) \in \tau$ forms a lattice.*

Proof Let τ be regular. By lemma 2.17 we know that τ must either consist of *(a)* polyominoes that are all surrounded in exactly the same manner by 6 other instances, or of *(b)* polyominoes that are all surrounded likewise by 4 other instances of P. The lattice we are after is generated by the vectors from which all relative positions within τ can be obtained by "iteration". It follows from the proof of lemma 2.15 (viz. figure 2.24) that two vectors will do in case *(a)*. (Note in figure 2.24 that e.g. $\vec{c}$ is integrally dependent on $\vec{a}$ and $\vec{b}$ and that $\vec{a}$ and $\vec{b}$ "generate" the entire tessellation.) By the same argument it follows from the proof of lemma 2.16 that two vectors suffice in case *(b)* as well. □

Theorem 2.17 *A (total) tessellation τ is periodic if and only if τ is regular.*

Proof Directly from lemma 2.13 and definition 2.4 together with lemma 2.18. □

Thus, "regularity" exactly characterizes periodic tessellations, and all results we obtained for regular tessellations are valid for periodic tessellations as well. With respect to this, see also section 3.2.

Corollary 2.5 *Let τ be an arbitrary (partial or total) tessellation of the plane using P. For all three-nodes of G_τ we have: $|T_1|+|T_2|+|T_3| \leqslant \frac{1}{2}|B|$ and for all four-nodes of G_τ we have: $|T_1|+|T_4| \leqslant \frac{1}{2}|B|$ (resp. $|T_4|+|T_3| \leqslant \frac{1}{2}|B|$, $|T_3|+|T_2| \leqslant \frac{1}{2}|B|$ and $|T_2|+|T_1| \leqslant \frac{1}{2}|B|$). Here T_1, T_2 and T_3 (and T_4) are the branches of the three-node (four-node) in question and B is the boundary of P.*

Proof Consider any three-node g of G_τ. By lemma 2.15 every $P(x_0, y_0)$ can be partially surrounded by a set of polyominoes (not necessarily from τ) that induce a partial segmentation of $B(x_0, y_0)$ of length $2.(|T_1|+|T_2|+|T_3|)$. Hence $|T_1|+|T_2|+|T_3| \leqslant \frac{1}{2}|B|$. Likewise it follows from lemma 2.16 that for every four-node g of G_τ : $|T_1|+|T_4| \leqslant \frac{1}{2}|B|$ respectively $|T_4|+|T_3| \leqslant \frac{1}{2}|B|$, $|T_3|+|T_2| \leqslant \frac{1}{2}|B|$ and $|T_2|+|T_1| \leqslant \frac{1}{2}|B|$. □

The final result of this section is important because it establishes a local condition that is necessary and sufficient for the existence of a periodic tessellation.

Theorem 2.18 *There exists a periodic tessellation of the plane using the polyomino P with boundary B if and only if*

(*) *P admits a three-node g with branches* T_1, T_2, T_3 *such that* $|T_1|+|T_2|+|T_3| = \frac{1}{2}|B|$, *or*

(**) *P admits a four-node g with branches* T_1, T_2, T_3 *and* T_4 *such that* $|T_1| + |T_2| + |T_3| + |T_4| = |B|$.

Proof $\Rightarrow$ Let τ be a periodic tessellation of the plane using P. By lemma 2.17 and theorem 2.17 we know that G_τ consists of either three-nodes or four-nodes. If G_τ consists of three-nodes (and, hence P admits a three-node) then the argument in lemma 2.17 shows that the surrounding of any $P(x_0, y_0)$ as constructed in proof of lemma 2.15 must be complete. It follows that $2.(\,|T_1| + |T_2| + |T_3|) = |B|$, or, $|T_1| + |T_2| + |T_3| = \frac{1}{2}|B|$, for any three-node in G_τ. If G_τ consists of four-nodes (and, hence, P admits a four-node) then the argument in lemma 2.17 shows likewise that the surroundings constructed in the proof of lemma 2.16 must be complete. Thus $|T_1|+|T_4| = \frac{1}{2}|B|$ and $|T_2| + |T_3| = \frac{1}{2}|B|$. It follows that $|T_1| + |T_2| + |T_3| + |T_4| = |B|$ in this case.

$\Leftarrow$ Suppose P satisfies (*). Observing the length of the induced segmentation, it follows that the surrounding of $P(x_0, y_0)$ constructed in the proof of lemma 2.16 necessarily is a complete surrounding. Observing the relative positions of $P(x_0, y_0)$ and its surrounding polyominoes, it follows that for each of the $P(x_i, y_i)$: $\text{Seg}(B(x_i, y_i)) \subseteq \text{Seg}(B(x_0, y_0))$. So the conditions of lemma 2.14 are satisfied and the surrounding can be extended to a regular (hence, periodic) tessellation of the entire plane.

If P satisfies (**) rather than (*), then from corollary 2.5 follows that $|T_1| + |T_4| = \frac{1}{2}|B|$ and a similar argument carries through, based on the construction of a surrounding in the proof of lemma 2.16 and shows with lemma 2.14 that again a periodic tessellation can be obtained using P. □

2.4.4 Obtaining Periodic Tessellations from Arbitrary Tessellations; a Proof of Shapiro's Conjecture

The detailed analyses of the preceding sections will now be used to settle Shapiro's conjecture and prove that whenever there is a tessellation of the plane using the polyomino P, there must exist a periodic tessellation using P. Let τ be an arbitrary tessellation of the plane using P. The key idea is a detailed analysis of the "grid"-graph G_τ. Imagine that each edge of G_τ is cut into two equal halves and that the length of each half is charged to the appropriate end-point.

Definition 2.16 *The support of a node $g \in G_\tau$, denoted by:* $\mathrm{Sup}_\tau(g)$ *or just by:* $\mathrm{Sup}(g)$*, is equal to the total charge thus accumulated at g, i.e.,* $\mathrm{Sup}_\tau(g) = \frac{1}{2}\Sigma|e|$*, with the summation extending over all (3 or 4) edges incident to g.*

(The reason for looking at the edge-lengths in G_τ should be clear, for the edges are the "branches" of the three-nodes and four-nodes in the graph. The halving is only introduced to simplify later accounting procedures and to avoid that entire edges are counted twice: once at every end-point.) The proof of Shapiro's conjecture heavily relies on the criteria for periodic tessellations in theorem 2.18 and uses the following surprising fact.

Lemma 2.19 *In every tessellation of the plane using P there exists a three-node as in (*) or a four-node as in (**).*

Proof Let N be sufficiently large and consider an arbitrary $N \times N$ window on G_τ. Let G'_τ be the (planar) graph of nodes and edges obtained by only considering the polyominoes of τ that are strictly located within the window. Clearly G'_τ is a connected and finite section of G_τ, with a contour C bounding the graph from its "exterior". Among the nodes along C there are likely to be many that are remnants of three-nodes or four-nodes that lost at least one branch (because it was sticking out of the window). Let K be the number of polyominoes of τ strictly contained in the window and (hence) spanning G'_τ. Define factors ε (depending on τ, K and N) such that

$\varepsilon_1.K$ = the number of three-nodes along C that have degree 2 in G'_τ,
$\varepsilon'_1.K$ = the number of three-nodes along C that (still) have degree 3 in G'_τ,
$\varepsilon_2.K$ = the number of four-nodes along C that have degree 2 in G'_τ,
$\varepsilon'_2.K$ = the number of four-nodes along C that have degree 3 in G'_τ,
$\varepsilon''_2.K$ = the number of four-nodes along C that (still) have degree 4 in G'_τ.

Claim 2.1 *For N sufficiently large each factor ε is less than $\frac{1}{2.|B|}$, where B is the size of the boundary of P.*

Proof Note that the size of the polyomino is fixed. Thus K increases quadratically in N for $N \to \infty$. On the other hand, it is easily seen that $|C|$ increases at most linearly in N. Thus the number of nodes along C can be made less than any factor times K, by choosing N sufficiently large. □

For a further analysis of G'_τ we define the following values. In each case an expression is obtained either by direct reasoning or by carefully accounting the "contributions" to three-nodes ($\frac{1}{3}$ from each incident polyomino), four-nodes ($\frac{1}{4}$ from each incident polyomino) and edges ($\frac{1}{2}$ from the "initial" node in the clockwise ordering of B):

$$\begin{aligned}
\alpha_{ij} &= \text{the number of polyominoes within the window (hence in } G'_\tau\text{)} \\
&\quad\ \text{that have } i \text{ three-nodes and } j \text{ four-nodes on their boundary,} \\
\alpha_{i*} &= \text{the number of polyominoes etc. that have } i \text{ three-nodes on their boundary} \\
&= \sum_j \alpha_{ij}, \\
\alpha_{*j} &= \text{the number of polyominoes etc. that have } j \text{ four-nodes on their boundary} \\
&= \sum_i \alpha_{ij}, \\
t &= \text{the number of three-nodes within the window (hence in } G'_\tau\text{)} \\
&= \sum_i \frac{i}{3}.\alpha_{i*} + \frac{2}{3}.\varepsilon_1 K + \frac{1}{3}.\varepsilon'_1 K, \\
f &= \text{the number of four-nodes within the window (hence in } G'_\tau\text{)} \\
&= \sum_j \frac{j}{4}.\alpha_{*j} + \frac{3}{4}.\varepsilon_2 K + \frac{2}{4}.\varepsilon'_2 K + \frac{1}{4}.\varepsilon''_2 K, \\
n &= \text{the total number of nodes within the window (hence in } G'_\tau\text{)} \\
&= t + f, \\
e &= \text{the total number of edges within the window (hence in } G'_\tau\text{)} \\
&= \sum_{i,j} \frac{i+j}{2}.\alpha_{ij} + \frac{1}{2}.\varepsilon_1 K + \frac{1}{2}.\varepsilon'_1 K + \frac{1}{2}.\varepsilon_2 K + \frac{1}{2}.\varepsilon'_2 K + \frac{1}{2}.\varepsilon''_2 K, \\
p &= \text{the total number of parts in which the plane is divided by } G'_\tau \\
&= K + 1.
\end{aligned}$$

Note that $\sum_i \alpha_{i*} = \sum_j \alpha_{*j} = K$.

Claim 2.2

$$f = -\frac{1}{2}t + \frac{1}{2}\varepsilon_1 K + \varepsilon_2 K + \frac{1}{2}\varepsilon'_2 K + K - 1.$$

Proof Since G'_τ is planar we can apply Euler's well-known formula: $n+p = e+2$. Substituting the expressions for n, p and e (etc.) we obtain

$$t + f + K + 1 = e + 2$$

$$\Rightarrow \sum_i \frac{i}{3}.\alpha_{i*} + \frac{2}{3}.\varepsilon_1 K + \frac{1}{3}.\varepsilon_1' K + \sum_j \frac{j}{4}.\alpha_{*j} + \frac{3}{4}.\varepsilon_2 K + \frac{2}{4}.\varepsilon_2' K + \frac{1}{4}.\varepsilon_2'' K +$$

$$K + 1 = \sum_{i,j} \frac{i+j}{2}.\alpha_{ij} + \frac{1}{2}.(\varepsilon_1 + \varepsilon_1' + \varepsilon_2 + \varepsilon_2' + \varepsilon_2'')K + 2$$

$$\Rightarrow \sum_i \frac{i}{6}.\alpha_{i*} + \sum_j \frac{j}{4}.\alpha_{*j} = \frac{1}{6}\varepsilon_1 K - \frac{1}{6}\varepsilon_1' K + \frac{1}{4}\varepsilon_2 K - \frac{1}{4}\varepsilon_2'' K + K - 1.$$

Multiplying the latter equation by 2, the left-hand side contains terms that remind of $t + 2f$. Straightforward manipulation shows:

$$\begin{aligned} t + 2f &= (\sum_i \frac{i}{3}.\alpha_{i*} + \sum_j \frac{j}{2}.\alpha_{*j}) + \frac{2}{3}\varepsilon_1 K + \frac{1}{3}\varepsilon_1' K + \frac{3}{2}\varepsilon_2 K + \varepsilon_2' K + \frac{1}{2}\varepsilon_2'' K \\ &= \varepsilon_1 K + 2\varepsilon_2 K + \varepsilon_2' K + 2K - 2, \end{aligned}$$

and the expression claimed for f easily follows. □

Suppose by way of contradiction that τ (hence G'_τ) does not contain any three-nodes satisfying (*) nor any four-nodes satisfying (**). By corollary 2.5 this means that for every three-node g : $|T_1|+|T_2|+|T_3| \leqslant \frac{1}{2}|B|-1$ (note that $|B|$ is always even) and for every four-node g : $|T_1|+|T_2|+|T_3|+|T_4| \leqslant |B|-1$, where, T_1, etc., are the branches of the node. It means that for every three-node g : $\text{Sup}(g) \leqslant \frac{1}{4}|B| - \frac{1}{2}$. Let L be the total edge length of G'_τ. Note that $L < \sum_{g \in G'_\tau} \text{Sup}(g)$. (The <-sign holds because there is at least one node along the contour of G'_τ that "lost" a branch which is still accounted for in its support.) Using the expression for f from claim 2.2 we can bound L as follows:

$$\begin{aligned} L &< \sum_{\substack{g \in G'_\tau \\ (g \text{ three-node})}} \text{Sup}(g) + \sum_{\substack{g \in G'_\tau \\ (g \text{ four-node})}} \text{Sup}(g) \\ &\leqslant t.(\frac{1}{4}|B| - \frac{1}{2}) + f.(\frac{1}{2}|B| - \frac{1}{2}) \\ &< t.(\frac{1}{4}|B| - \frac{1}{2}) + (-\frac{1}{2}t + \frac{1}{2}\varepsilon_1 K + \varepsilon_2 K + \frac{1}{2}\varepsilon_2' K + K)(\frac{1}{2}|B| - \frac{1}{2}) \\ &= -\frac{1}{4}t + (\frac{1}{4}\varepsilon_1 + \frac{1}{2}\varepsilon_2 + \frac{1}{4}\varepsilon_2')K.(|B| - 1) + \frac{1}{2}K.|B| - \frac{1}{2}K \\ &\leqslant \frac{1}{2}K.|B| + \{(\frac{1}{4}\varepsilon_1 + \frac{1}{2}\varepsilon_2 + \frac{1}{4}\varepsilon_2').|B| - \frac{1}{2}\}K. \end{aligned}$$

As N was chosen sufficiently large, it easily follows from claim 2.1 that $\frac{1}{4}\varepsilon_1 + \frac{1}{2}\varepsilon_2 + \frac{1}{4}\varepsilon_2' < \frac{1}{2.|B|}$. Thus our estimate on L reduces to

$$L < \frac{1}{2}K.|B|.$$

On the other hand, if we let each of the K polyominoes in G_τ' contribute one half of every bounding edge (which indeed properly divides the length of every edge over its two bordering polyominoes) then it easily follows that

$$L \geqslant K.\frac{1}{2}|B| = \frac{1}{2}K.|B|,$$

a contradiction. We conclude that G_τ' (hence τ) must contain a three-node satisfying (*) or a four-node satisfying (**). □

Corollary 2.6 *In every tessellation of the plane using P there exist infinitely many three-nodes as in (*) or infinitely many four-nodes as in (**).*

Proof The proof of lemma 2.19 shows that for N sufficiently large there is a three-node satisfying (*) or a four-node satisfying (**) in every $N \times N$ window on G_τ. The argument is easily completed from here. □

Theorem 2.19 *Let P be a polyomino. If it is possible at all to tessellate the plane using P, then there exists a periodic tessellation of the plane using P.*

Proof The result follows at once from lemma 2.19 and theorem 2.18. (Note the additional observations for periodic tessellations in section 2.4.3). □

2.4.5 Final Comments

It is important to note that the result of theorem 2.19 is entirely effective. First of all, whenever a tessellation using a polyomino P is given in some computable manner, then the proof of lemma 2.19 shows that one can compute (by inspecting any $N \times N$ window) a three-node satisfying (*) or a four-node satisfying (**). Secondly, the results underlying theorem 2.18 show that there is an effective way to determine the two generating vectors (i.e., the basis) of the lattice of points where the polyominoes P in a periodic tessellation must be placed. Clearly, given theorem 2.19 only the second observation is important, for one can always determine by trying whether P admits a three-node or a four-node with the desired property.

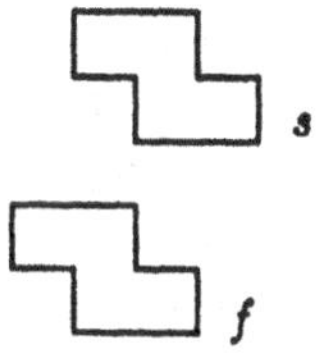

Figure 2.25: A template which is not rookwise connected.

Theorem 2.20 *Given a polyomino P, there exists an algorithm that is polynomial in the size of P to decide whether P can tessellate the plane or not.*

Proof By theorem 2.19 we only need to test the conditions for a periodic tessellation using P as expressed in theorem 2.18. Take an instance of P and test at every (grid)point along the boundary whether 3 or 4 instances can be fitted without overlap and satisfying the length condition for the branches at the node so created. There are only polynomially many cases to consider, and each test takes at most $O(|B|^2)$ (hence, polynomial) time. □

The study of plane tessellations (tilings, pavings) with regular objects has a long history in mathematics. It has repeatedly been the subject of M.Gardner's column in the Scientific American [Gar77]. A systematic study of tessellations with sets of polyominoes was made by Golomb [Gol66]. In the late sixties Golomb [Gol70] proved that the question whether an arbitrary finite set of polyominoes tiles the plane (rotational symmetries etc. allowed) is equivalent to Wang's domino problem ([Wan65]) and hence algorithmically undecidable. If the set contains only one polyomino, the decidability question is reportedly still open (Göbel [Gob79]). Thus the results we proved in this section, and theorem 2.20 in particular, may be viewed as a partial answer to this question for a restrictive class of tessellations (requiring polyominoes to have a fixed orientation).

Severe problems arise if we attempt to generalize theorem 2.19 and e.g. relax the condition that P is a polyomino. The template T shown in figure 2.25 provides an example that Shapiro's conjecture does not remain valid if we do so.

It is easily verified that T tessellates the plane. But the following argument shows that it cannot tessellate the plane periodically. Name the two components f ("first") and s ("second"). Whenever we try to place a second instance of T to fill the narrow gorge between f and s, we get either an f on an f or an s on an s, and it is easily seen that this cannot be repeated without conflict. Yet there may be a way to relax the condition of periodicity in such a manner that a suitable modification of Shapiro's conjecture remains valid.

Other problems arise if we no longer insist that tessellations have to be total. For instance, it is not true that the existence of a partial tessellation with a certain density using a polyomino P implies the existence of a periodic partial tessellation with the same density using P. To illustrate this see figure 2.26, in which a partial tessellation is shown, which covers $\frac{9}{11}$ of the plane. If we want to tessellate the plane in a periodic way with this polyomino then at most $\frac{8}{11}$ of the plane can be covered. (The example is due to H.L.Bodlaender.)

Even the generalization of theorem 2.19 to higher dimensions is not obviously fulfilled. Stein [Ste72] has shown that for the 5- and 10- dimensional space there exist templates which tessellate only nonperiodically. For the dimensions d, $d \geqslant 3$ and $d \neq 5, 10$ the question remains open.

The existence of periodic tessellations in general, using sets of objects and allowing symmetries, is a hard problem for which only a few results have been proved. It is known (see Gardner [Gar77]) that there exists a set of 2 polygons which tile the plane nonperiodically only.

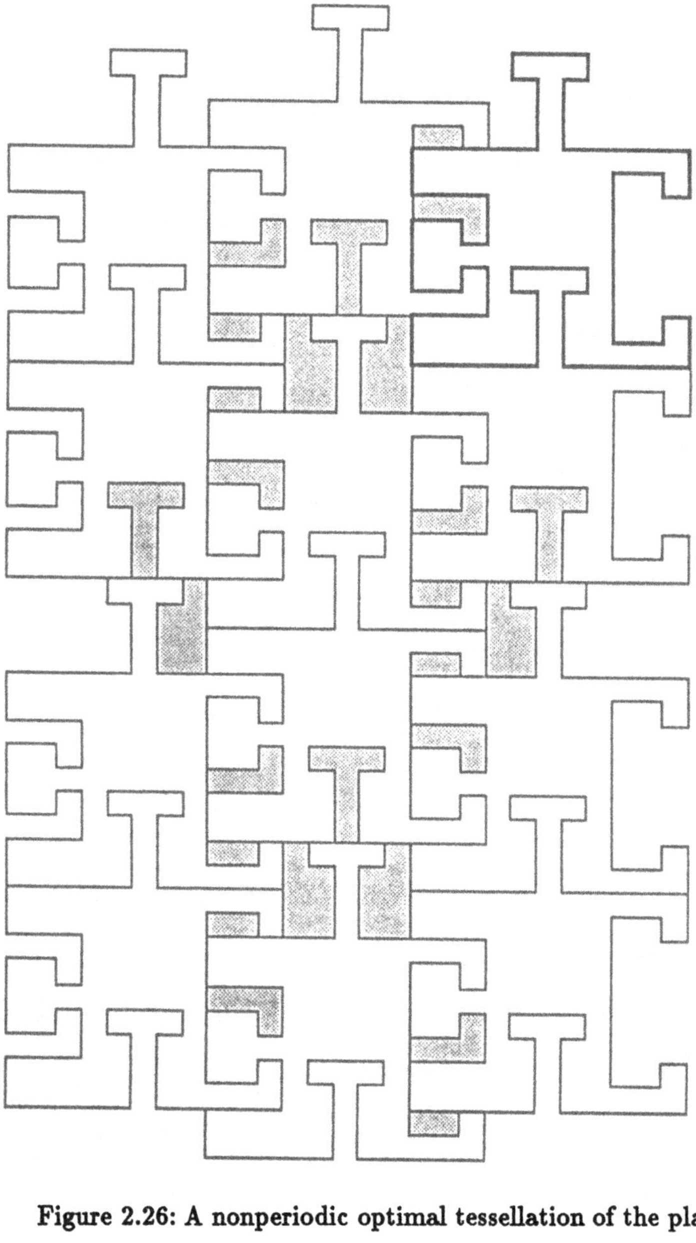

Figure 2.26: A nonperiodic optimal tessellation of the plane.

Chapter 3

Compactly Representable Skewing Schemes for *d*-Dimensional Arrays

In general, arbitrary skewing schemes are not of much practical interest. There are two reasons why arbitrary skewing schemes do not fit the purposes for which they are meant. First of all the system architecture determines the data transfer functions which, in turn, determine the skewing schemes that are possible, see section 1.4.3. Secondly, skewing schemes have to be evaluated at run-time in order to determine the locations of the data elements to be fetched. As this affects the overall performance of the system the use of arbitrary skewing schemes either implies a considerable degradation of the performance (especially when these schemes are used in the upper levels of the computation model) or requires the existence of large look-up tables in each processing element to compute the locations of the data elements. Both of these possibilities are mostly undesirable.

In practically all architectures of parallel computers skewing schemes were introduced which allow a compact representation and can be evaluated fast. Traditionally only "linear" skewing schemes are considered, defined by $s(i_1, i_2, ..., i_d) = \lambda_1.i_1 + \ldots + \lambda_d.i_d \bmod M$ for suitably chosen coefficients $\lambda_1, \lambda_2, ..., \lambda_d \in \mathbf{Z}$ [BK71,Law75]. More generally, Shapiro [Sha78b] defined a skewing scheme to be "periodic", and thus compactly represented, if the skewing scheme can be represented by a small-sized table to which all arguments can be reduced by the use of a proper modulus.

In this chapter we shall revise and extend the existing theory of compactly representable skewing schemes. Because 2-dimensional compactly representable skewing schemes for 2-dimensional arrays received considerable attention in the literature [vLW83], a substantial part of this chapter deals with 2-dimensional compactly representable skewing schemes. Although most of the results as obtained in this part directly follow from the results presented later on in this chapter, we have chosen for this approach because of its "historical" interest. In section 3.1 we reconcile the results obtained by Budnik, Kuck and Lawrie [BK71,Law75] for linear skewing schemes, and we derive bounds on the minimum number of memory banks (the interleaving degree) for linear skewing schemes to be valid for a collection of standard vectors from a matrix. In section 3.2 we first redefine the notion of 2-dimensional periodic skewing schemes as introduced by Shapiro and we show that periodic skewing schemes can be represented by a single arithmetic expression. Secondly we generalize the theory of 2-dimensional periodic skewing schemes to periodic skewing schemes for d-dimensional arrays and we show that periodic skewing schemes have an elegant foundation in both the mathematical theory of integral lattices and the theory of finite abelian groups. In section 3.3 we study compactly representable skewing schemes, viz. multi-periodic skewing schemes, that are specially suited for templates whose base-sets (cf. definition 1.1) are proper subsets of $\mathbf{Z}^d$, i.e. lattices $\subseteq \mathbf{Z}^d$.

3.1 Linear Skewing Schemes

The simplest and most commonly used skewing schemes are the "linear" skewing schemes for 2-dimensional arrays of Budnik and Kuck [BK71], defined by

$$s(i,j) = a.i + b.j \bmod M,$$

$0 \leqslant i, j \leqslant N-1$ (see also Lawrie [Law75]). In the literature several conditions on a, b and M have been formulated such that s is conflict-free on, e.g. rows, columns and several diagonals. Very often M is assumed to be a prime number, so $\mathbf{Z}_M$ is a cyclic group and various desirable properties of s are ensured almost regardless of the values of a and b chosen.

We shall analyze and extend the existing theory of 2-dimensional linear skewing schemes, most notably concerning the conditions that have been formulated for the conflict-free access of standard vectors from a matrix. In section 3.1.1 we discuss the equivalence of linear skewing schemes. In section 3.1.2 we review and slightly extend the known results for so-called d-

ordered vectors. In section 3.1.3 we formulate precise conditions for a linear skewing scheme to be conflict-free on rows, columns and (circulant) backward and forward diagonals. In section 3.1.4 we study the use of linear skewing schemes for retrieving sets of elements by multiple (conflict-free) fetches.

3.1.1 The Equivalency of Linear Skewing Schemes

In this section we will prove several facts allowing a full range of values for i and j, i.e., we consider the behavior of linear skewing schemes s with $s(i,j) = a.i + b.j \bmod M, 0 \leqslant i,j \leqslant M-1$. Frequently we will refer to s as an (a,b) scheme (cf. Lawrie [Law75]). We do so because in practice s is likely to be used for all $N \times N$ matrices with $N \leqslant M$. Note that s does not necessarily use all memory banks! From the elementary theory of linear congruences the following result is straightforward.

Proposition 3.1 *A linear skewing scheme* $s(i,j) = a.i + b.j \bmod M$ *uses all memory banks 0 to* $M-1$ *if and only if* $\gcd(a,b,M) = 1$.

Linear skewing schemes with $\gcd(a,b,M) = 1$ will be called *proper*, and will be the only ones we consider. (If a scheme is not proper, one can factor out $\gcd(a,b,M)$ and do the skewing in $M/\gcd(a,b,M)$ memory banks.) Further we assume that $a \not\equiv 0 \pmod M$ and $b \not\equiv 0 \pmod M$.

By varying the choice of a and b it seems that there can be up to $(M-1)^2 = O(M^2)$ different linear skewing schemes. Many do not differ in an essential manner.

Definition 3.1 *The (linear) skewing schemes s and s' are equivalent if there is a permutation Π on $0...M-1$ such that $s = \Pi \circ s'$.*

Thus, two skewing schemes are equivalent if they are identical after a suitable renaming of the memory banks. The equivalence-concept is geared to the linearity of the schemes we consider, as it ensures that bank 0 is always named the same. (Observe that necessarily $\Pi(0) = 0$ in the definition.)

Definition 3.2 *The null-set of a linear skewing scheme* $s(i,j) = a.i + b.j \bmod M$ *is the set* $L_s = \{(i,j) \mid a.i + b.j \equiv 0 \pmod M, 0 \leqslant i,j < M\}$.

Lemma 3.1 *Two linear skewing schemes s and s' are equivalent if and only if $L_s = L_{s'}$.*

Consider two proper linear skewing schemes $s(i,j) = a.i + b.j \bmod M$ and $s'(i,j) = a'.i + b'.j \bmod M$. Define the determinant $\Delta(s,s')$ by

$$\Delta(s,s') = \begin{vmatrix} a & b \\ a' & b' \end{vmatrix}.$$

Theorem 3.1 *Two proper linear skewing schemes s and s' are equivalent if and only if $\Delta(s,s') \equiv 0 \pmod{M}$.*

Proof By lemma 3.1 it is necessary and sufficient for s and s' to be equivalent that $a.i + b.j \equiv 0 \pmod{M} \Leftrightarrow a'.i + b'.j \equiv 0 \pmod{M}$, for all $0 \leqslant i,j < M$. Restricting to $j = 0$ ($i = 0$) first, we need that $a.i \equiv 0 \pmod{M} \Leftrightarrow a'.i \equiv 0 \pmod{M}$ and $b.j \equiv 0 \pmod{M} \Leftrightarrow b'.j \equiv 0 \pmod{M}$, and thus obtain that $\gcd(a,M) = \gcd(a',M)$ and $\gcd(b,M) = \gcd(b',M)$. Writing $u = \gcd(a,M)$ and $v = \gcd(b,M)$ it follows that $a = u.a_1, b = v.b_1, a' = u.a_2$ and $b' = v.b_2$ for suitable integers a_1, a_2, b_1 and b_2 that are relatively prime to M. Note that $\gcd(u,v) = 1$ (because s is proper and thus $\gcd(a,b,M) = 1$) and (hence) $u.v|M$. By $a_1^{-1}, \ldots$ we shall denote the inverses mod M of $a_1, \ldots$.

Now $u.a_1.i + v.b_1.j \equiv 0 \pmod{M} \Leftrightarrow v.j = -a_1.b_1^{-1}.u.i + \lambda.M$ for some integer λ, and we get valid solutions i,j whenever $v|a_1.b_1^{-1}.u.i$. But v has no common divisor $\neq 1$ with u nor with a_1 and b_1^{-1} (the latter because any common divisor is also a divisor of M and a_1 and b_1 are relatively prime to M) and thus we get valid solutions precisely when $v|i$, which means $i = \mu.v$ for $\mu = 0, 1, \ldots, M/v-1$. The corresponding j-values follow after substitution. For the equivalence of s and s' to hold this means that we must have

$$\begin{aligned} u.a_2.i + v.b_2.j &= u.a_2.i + b_2(-a_1.b_1^{-1}.u.i + \lambda M) \\ &\equiv -(u.a_1.b_2.b_1^{-1} - u.a_2)\, i \pmod{M} \\ &\equiv -(a.b_2 - a'.b_1)\, b_1^{-1}.\mu.v \pmod{M} \\ &\equiv -(a.b' - a'.b)\, b_1^{-1}.\mu \pmod{M} \\ &\equiv -\Delta(s,s').b_1^{-1}.\mu \pmod{M} \\ &\equiv 0 \pmod{M}, \end{aligned}$$

which is true if and only if $\Delta(s,s') \equiv 0 \pmod{M}$. By a completely analogous argument one shows that this condition is necessary and sufficient for $u.a_2.i + v.b_2.j \equiv 0 \pmod{M} \Rightarrow u.a_1.i + v.b_1.j \equiv 0 \pmod{M}$.

Conversely, let $\Delta(s,s') = a.b' - a'.b \equiv 0 \pmod{M}$. It follows that $\gcd(a,M)|a'.b$ and hence, by properness, that $\gcd(a,M)|a'$. In the same way

$\gcd(a', M)|a$, and we obtain that necessarily $\gcd(a, M) = \gcd(a', M)$. By the same token we get that $\gcd(b, M) = \gcd(b', M)$. It is easily seen that the preceding argument can now be reversed completely to show that indeed $a.i + b.j \equiv 0 \pmod M \Leftrightarrow a'.i + b'.j \equiv 0 \pmod M$, i.e., that s and s' are equivalent. □

Theorem 3.2 *Every proper* (a, b) *scheme is equivalent to a* $(\gcd(a, M), c)$ *scheme for some* c *depending on* a, b *and* M.

Proof Write $u = \gcd(a, M)$ and let $a = u.a_1 \bmod M$ for a suitable a_1 relatively prime to M. By theorem 3.1 it suffices to show that there is a solution x to the equation

$$\begin{vmatrix} a & b \\ u & x \end{vmatrix} = a.x - b.u \equiv 0 \pmod M.$$

Take $x = a_1^{-1}.b \bmod M$ and observe that

$$a.x - b.u = u.a_1.a_1^{-1}.b - b.u \equiv 0 \pmod M$$

as was to be shown. □

Lemma 3.2 *Every equivalence class of proper linear skewing schemes is uniquely represented by a* (d, c) *scheme with* $0 < d, c < M$, $(d, c) = 1$, $d|M$ *and fixed value of* $c \bmod (M/d)$.

Proof First we observe that no (proper) (d, c) scheme can be equivalent to a (proper) (e, f) scheme for $d|M$, $e|M$ and $d \neq e$. For otherwise by theorem 3.1

$$\begin{vmatrix} d & c \\ e & f \end{vmatrix} = d.f - e.c \equiv 0 \pmod M$$

and (as in the proof of theorem 3.1) it follows from the properness of the schemes that $\gcd(d, M) = \gcd(e, M)$, hence $d = e$, a contradiction.

Next we note that a proper (d, c) scheme and a proper (d, c') scheme are equivalent if and only if $c \equiv c' \pmod{M/d}$. For by theorem 3.1 the necessary and sufficient condition for equivalence is

$$\begin{vmatrix} d & c \\ d & c' \end{vmatrix} = d(c - c') \equiv 0 \pmod M$$

and hence that c and c' differ by a multiple of M/d. □

Let $\sigma(M)$ denote the sum of the positive divisors of M.

Theorem 3.3 *There are at most $\sigma(M) - 2$ essentially different (,i.e., non-equivalent) proper linear skewing schemes for a given number of memory banks M.*

Proof By lemma 3.2 there are at most M/d non-equivalent $(d, *)$ schemes for every d with $1 \leqslant d < M, d|M$. In fact, for $d = 1$ there are only $M - 1$ schemes. Thus the total number of non-equivalent proper schemes is bounded by

$$\sum_{\substack{d|M \\ d \neq M}} M/d - 1 = \sum_{d|M} M/d - 2 = \sum_{d|M} d - 2 = \sigma(M) - 2.$$

□

As $\sigma(M)$ =O(M loglog M), with an average of $O(M)$ ([HW79]), theorem 3.3 proves the earlier claim that the number of non-equivalent proper linear skewing schemes really is substantially less than M^2 for $M \to \infty$. A generalized version of this result for linear skewing schemes of the d-dimensional Z^d into Z_M is derived in section 3.2.2.2, where it is proven that for this case a bound of $O(M^{d-1} \log\log M)$ holds. Note that for M prime the number of non-equivalent proper linear skewing schemes is $\sigma(M) - 2 = M - 1$.

3.1.2 *d*-Ordered Vectors

The subject of d-ordered vectors naturally arises in relation to linear skewing schemes $s(i, j) = a.i + b.j \bmod M$. For if we consider a matrix row (i fixed), then we see that its elements are "ordered" into successive memory banks that are b apart mod M. Likewise, the elements of any matrix column (j fixed) appear "ordered" in banks that are a apart mod M.

Definition 3.3 *A d-ordered k-vector is a vector of k elements whose i^{th} logical element $(0 \leqslant i < k)$ is stored in memory bank $c + d.i \bmod M$, for some arbitrary constant c.*

d-Ordered vectors were first discussed in Budnik and Kuck [BK71] and in Lawrie [Law75]. In general one would like to have storage schemes such that all vectors of interest can be retrieved as d-ordered k-vectors without conflict, for some suitably chosen d and k. Essentially only the following result is known (Lawrie [Law75]).

Theorem 3.4 *A d-ordered k-vector can be accessed conflict-free if and only if* $M \geqslant k.\text{gcd}(d, M)$.

Theorem 3.4 provides a uniform bound of $M/\text{gcd}(d, M)$ on the maximum size of "conflict-free" d-ordered vectors. It is advantageous to have $\text{gcd}(d, M) = 1$, which is guaranteed e.g. when M is prime. Larger d-ordered vectors will have to be retrieved in r "fetches", for some $r > 1$. Note that we make no assumption about the way an ordered vector is actually split up for this. Theorem 3.4 can now be generalized in the following way.

Theorem 3.5 *A d-ordered k-vector can be accessed in r conflict-free fetch operations if and only if* $M \geqslant (\lfloor \frac{k-1}{r} \rfloor + 1)\text{gcd}(d, M)$.

Proof We may assume that $r > 1$. From theorem 3.4 it follows in particular that the largest set of elements from a d-ordered vector that can be accessed conflict-free has size $M/\text{gcd}(d, M)$ and that this amounts to taking exactly one datum from each memory bank holding elements from the d-ordered vector. (Thus every maximum set can in fact be retrieved as a d-ordered subvector!) This implies that we may assume without loss of generality that d-ordered k-vectors are retrieved in full batches of $M/\text{gcd}(d, M)$ elements and a "remainder".

Now assume that a d-ordered k-vector can be accessed in r conflict-free fetches. It follows that $k \leqslant r.M/\text{gcd}(d, M)$. Write $k = \alpha.r + \beta$ for $0 \leqslant \beta < r$ and distinguish two cases. If $r|k$ (hence $\beta = 0$) then $\alpha = k/r = \lfloor \frac{k-1}{r} \rfloor + 1$ and $M \geqslant \alpha.\text{gcd}(d, M)$. If $r \nmid k$ then we obtain $\alpha = \lfloor \frac{k-1}{r} \rfloor$ and

$$\begin{aligned} \alpha.r + \beta &\leqslant r.M/\text{gcd}(d, M) - 1 \\ \Rightarrow \alpha + \frac{\beta + 1}{r} &\leqslant M/\text{gcd}(d, M) \\ \Rightarrow \alpha + 1 &\leqslant M/\text{gcd}(d, M) \end{aligned}$$

whence $M \geqslant (\alpha + 1)\text{gcd}(d, M)$. This proves the bound on M for both cases.

To prove the converse, we rephrase the earlier interpretation of theorem 3.4 once again and observe that a d-ordered k-vector can be retrieved in r conflict-free accesses if and only if no memory bank holds more than r elements of the d-ordered vector. If $M \geqslant (\lfloor \frac{k-1}{r} \rfloor + 1).\text{gcd}(d, M)$ then this is exactly what happens because it forces a bound on k (basicly $k \geqslant r.M/\text{gcd}(d, M)$) so the elements of the vector that are stored in banks in the order

$$c \bmod M, c + d \bmod M, ..., c + (\frac{M}{gcd(d, M)} - 1)d \bmod M, c \bmod M, ...$$

are not "wrapped" over the same bank more than r times. □

Corollary 3.1 *A d-ordered k-vector can be accessed in* $\lfloor\frac{(k-1).\gcd(d,M)}{M}\rfloor+1$ *conflict-free fetch operations (where each fetch operation retrieves a d-ordered subvector), and this is best possible.*

Proof By the analysis in theorem 3.5 the (optimal) method for accessing a d-ordered k-vector is in full batches of $M/\gcd(d,M)$ elements and a "remainder". Writing $k = \alpha.M/\gcd(d,M) + \beta$ for $\alpha \geqslant 0$ and $0 \leqslant \beta < M/\gcd(d,M)$ it follows that α fetches are necessary and sufficient for $\beta = 0$ and $\alpha + 1$ fetches are necessary and sufficient for $\beta > 0$. One easily verifies that the precise formula for α and $\alpha + 1$, respectively, is as given above. □

Finally note that two d-ordered vectors are either stored in the same set of $M/\gcd(d,M)$ memory banks or in disjoint ones, depending on the value of c (the "offset") mod $\gcd(d,M)$. Thus up to $\gcd(d,M)$ different d-ordered vectors can be retrieved conflict-free in one cycle.

3.1.3 The Validity of Linear Skewing Schemes for Rows, Columns and (Anti-)Diagonals

We shall now consider storing an $N \times N$ matrix into M memory banks, for some M, such that a choice of "vectors of interest", viz. rows, columns and (anti-)diagonals, can be accessed conflict-free. Note that these templates are all $[x_1, x_2]$-lines in the sense of section 2.3. We shall make use of a suitable (proper) linear skewing scheme s with $s(i,j) = a.i + b.j \bmod M$, $0 \leqslant i,j < N$ where a and b (and M) are yet to be determined. The following observations are immediate (see Lawrie [Law75]):

each row is a b-ordered N-vector,
each column is an a-ordered N-vector,
the main diagonal is an $(a+b)$-ordered N-vector,
the main anti-diagonal is an $(a-b)$-ordered N-vector,

the latter provided that $a \neq b$. Note that all other diagonals and anti-diagonals are likewise "ordered" k-vectors for suitable $k < N$. We conclude the following.

Proposition 3.2 *A linear skewing scheme provides conflict-free access to all non-circulant (anti-)diagonals of a matrix if and only if it provides conflict-free access to the main (anti-)diagonal.*

Proof Directly from linearity, or from theorem 3.4. □

Applying theorem 3.4 we obtain simple conditions on a, b and M for conflict-free access to rows, columns and diagonals (cf. Lawrie [Law75]):

$$(*)\begin{cases} M \geqslant N.\gcd(b, M) & \text{for rows,} \\ M \geqslant N.\gcd(a, M) & \text{for columns,} \\ M \geqslant N.\gcd(a+b, M) & \text{for diagonals,} \\ M \geqslant N.\gcd(a-b, M) & \text{for anti-diagonals (provided } a \neq b\text{).} \end{cases}$$

Proposition 3.3 *In order to have conflict-free access to rows, columns, diagonals and anti-diagonals using a linear skewing scheme, it is sufficient to choose M as the smallest prime number $\geqslant \min(N, 5)$.*

Proof This is immediate from (*) taking e.g. $a = 1$ and $b = 2$. □

The choice of M implied by proposition 3.3 will normally not be the smallest possible. Discussions in e.g. Lawrie [Law75] show that there are "non-prime" cases where $M = N$. We show the following.

Theorem 3.6 *In order to have conflict-free access to rows, columns, diagonals and anti-diagonals using a linear skewing scheme, the smallest number of memory banks required is*

$$M = \begin{cases} N & \text{if } 2 \nmid N \text{ and } 3 \nmid N, \\ N+1 & \text{if } 2|N \text{ and } N \equiv 0, 1 \pmod 3, \\ N+2 & \text{if } 2 \nmid N \text{ and } 3|N, \\ N+3 & \text{if } 2|N \text{ and } N \equiv 2 \pmod 3. \end{cases}$$

Proof First let $2 \nmid N$. If also $3 \nmid N$ then take $a = 1$ and $b = 2$ and observe that all gcd's in (*) are 1 when $M = N$. Thus all inequalities are satisfied for this smallest choice of M. If $3|N$ then necessarily $N = 6v + 3$, for some v. Now note that M cannot be equal to N. For otherwise at least one of the gcd's in (*) would be $\geqslant 3$ because with any choice of a and b at least one of $a, b, a+b$ and $a-b$ will have a factor 3. The next best choice $M = N + 1$ (=even) will not do either because with any choice of a and b at least two of $a, b, a+b$ and $a-b$ will have a factor 3. Observe that $M = N + 2 (= 6v + 5)$ is neither even nor divisible by 3 and (thus) taking $a = 1$ and $b = 2$ satisfies (*) and makes $M = N + 2$ the smallest number of memory banks to use in this case.

Next let $2|N$. If $N \equiv 2 \pmod 3$ then necessarily $N = 6v + 2$, for some v. By the same argument as above we must choose M equal to the first number

$\geqslant N$ that is neither even nor divisible by 3 in order that valid a and b can be chosen, hence $M = N + 3 = 6v + 5$ and we can again take $a = 1$ and $b = 2$. If $N \equiv 0, 1 \pmod 3$ then N is of the form $6v$ or $6v + 4$, for some v. In both cases $M = N$ is not possible for satisfying (*) but $M = N + 1$ is, again with $a = 1$ and $b = 2$. □

Corollary 3.2 *If it is possible to have conflict-free access at all to rows, columns, diagonals and anti-diagonals using a linear skewing scheme, then it is possible to achieve this using the scheme* $i + 2.j \bmod M$.

Proof From the preceding analysis it follows that for the required conflict-free accesses M must necessarily be non-divisible by 2 or 3 (otherwise a contradiction occurs for any choice of a and b), or it is much larger that the minima given in theorem 3.6 (but then the smaller number we need is available too). From the proof we conclude that one can always use $i + 2.j \bmod M$ for a skewing scheme, with a suitable choice of M. □

Other bounds will result if the set of vectors of interest is changed. We shall study the case of conflict-free access to rows, columns and full circulant diagonals and anti-diagonals. Historically the case $M = N$ has received most attention, not just within the context of vector processing. In the statistical analysis of experiments any assignment of bank-numbers 1 to N to the cells of an $N \times N$ matrix such that (in our terminology) conflict-free access is provided to rows, columns and all circulant diagonals and anti-diagonals is called a Knut Vik design (after Vik [Vik24]). In 1973 Hedayat and Federer [HF75] showed that no Knut Vik designs exist for N even, and in 1977 Hedayat [Hed77] completed the analysis by relying on some observations of Euler [Eul82] and proved that Knut Vik designs of order N exist if and only if N is not divisible by 2 and 3. In terms of (general) skewing schemes the result was observed independently by Shapiro [Sha78b] (see also [Sha78a]), who noticed that the problem of providing conflict-free access to rows, columns and all circulant diagonals and anti-diagonals is very similar to the problem of positioning N non-attacking "superqueens" on an $N \times N$ chessboard. Superqueens were introduced as early as 1918 by Polya [Pol18], who was the first to derive the complete conditions for the problem to be solvable. Restated in our terminology, the result is as follows.

Theorem 3.7 *Let* $2 \nmid N$ *and* $3 \nmid N$. *Then there exists a (proper) linear skewing scheme using* $M = N$ *banks that provides conflict-free access to rows, columns and all circulant diagonals and anti-diagonals.*

For all other values of N we need a larger number of memory banks M to attain the same effect. Consider the following collection of conditions for a linear skewing scheme:

$$(**)\begin{cases} ax \not\equiv 0 & \text{for all } x \in \{1, ..., N-1\}, \\ bx \not\equiv 0 & \text{for all } x \in \{1, ..., N-1\}, \\ (b+a)x \not\equiv 0 & \text{for all } x \in \{1, ..., N-1\}, \\ (b-a)x \not\equiv 0 & \text{for all } x \in \{1, ..., N-1\}, \\ (b+a)x \not\equiv bN & \text{for all } x \in \{1, ..., N-1\}, \\ (b-a)x \not\equiv bN & \text{for all } x \in \{1, ..., N-1\}, \end{cases}$$

where equivalences $\equiv$ are taken modulo M.

Lemma 3.3 *Conditions (**) are necessary and sufficient for the existence of a linear skewing scheme using M banks that provides conflict-free access to rows, columns and all circulant diagonals and anti-diagonals.*

Proof We shall accumulate the necessary and sufficient conditions for each of the sets of vectors.

(i) *Rows.*

For the elements of the ith row to be stored in different banks it is required that $ai+bj_1 \not\equiv ai+bj_2 \pmod M$, i.e., that $b(j_1-j_2) \not\equiv 0$ for all $0 \leqslant j_1, j_2 < N$ with $j_1 \neq j_2$. This translates into the second condition of (**).

(ii) *Columns.*

By a completely analogous argument this leads to the first condition of (**).

(iii) *Circulant diagonals.*

The kth circulant diagonal ($0 \leqslant k < N$) consists of the "vector" of cells $(i, (i+k) \bmod N)$ for $0 \leqslant i < N$. The ith element is thus mapped to bank $(a+b)i+bk \bmod M$ if $0 \leqslant i < N-1-k$, and to bank $(a+b)i+bk-bN \bmod M$ if $N-k \leqslant i < N$. To require that different cells are mapped to different banks we must consider the (three) possible combinations of ranges for cell-indices i_1 and i_2:

$0 \leqslant i_1, i_2 \leqslant N-1-k$: this immediately leads to the requirement that $(a+b)x \not\equiv 0$ for all $x \in \{1, ..., N-1-k\}$.

$N-k \leqslant i_1, i_2 \leqslant N-1$: this likewise leads to the requirement that $(a+b)x \not\equiv 0$ for all $x \in \{1, ..., k-1\}$.

$0 \leqslant i_1 \leqslant N-1-k$ and $N-k \leqslant i_2 \leqslant N-1$ (or with i_1 and i_2 interchanged): the inequivalences $(a+b)i_1+bk \not\equiv (a+b)i_2+bk-bN \pmod M$ now translate to the requirement that $(a+b)x \not\equiv bN$ for $x \in \{1, ..., N-1\}$.

Combining the conditions for k from 0 to $N-1$ leads to the third and fifth condition of (**).

(iv) *Circulant anti-diagonals.*

The kth circulant anti-diagonal ($0 \leqslant k < N$) consists of the cells $(i, (N-1-i+k) \bmod N)$ for $0 \leqslant i < N$. The ith element is thus mapped to bank $(a-b)i + b(k-1) \bmod M$ if $0 \leqslant i \leqslant k-1$, and to bank $(a-b)i + b(k-1) + bN \bmod M$ if $k \leqslant i < N$. An analysis like in case (iii) leads to the fourth and sixth condition of (**) in order that different cells of any circulant anti-diagonal are mapped to distinct banks. □

It is useful to rephrase conditions (**) as an extension of the earlier set (*):

$$(**') \begin{cases} M \geqslant N.\gcd(a, M), & \\ M \geqslant N.\gcd(b, M), & \\ M \geqslant N.\gcd(b+a, M), & \\ M \geqslant N.\gcd(b-a, M), & \\ (b+a)x \not\equiv bN & \text{for all } x \in \{1, ..., N-1\} \\ (b-a)x \not\equiv bN & \text{for all } x \in \{1, ..., N-1\}. \end{cases}$$

Using lemma 3.3 one can prove several effective upperbounds on the required number of memory banks M for conflict-free linear skewing of the vectors we consider. We will treat the case in which only conflict-free access to rows, columns and circulant (forward) diagonals is desired separately. From the analysis above is easily derived that necessary and sufficient conditions for this case are:

$$(***) \begin{cases} ax \not\equiv 0 & \text{for all } x \in \{1, ..., N-1\} \\ bx \not\equiv 0 & \text{for all } x \in \{1, ..., N-1\} \\ (b+a)x \not\equiv 0 & \text{for all } x \in \{1, ..., N-1\} \\ (b+a)x \not\equiv bN & \text{for all } x \in \{1, ..., N-1\}. \end{cases}$$

Theorem 3.8 *Let M be the smallest prime number $\geqslant N$ with $M \neq N+1$. Then there exists a linear skewing scheme using M memory banks that provides conflict-free access to rows, columns and all circulant (forward) diagonals. ($N \neq 2$.)*

Proof If N is prime and > 2, then the conditions of (***) are easily seen to be satisfied with $M = N$ and $a = b = 1$. If N is not prime, then certainly $M > N+1$ and we can reason as follows. By theorem 3.2 we may assume without loss of generality that $a = 1$. Conditions (***) thus translate to the requirement that an integer b exists with $1 \leqslant b \leqslant N-2$ such that

$N^{-1}(1 + b^{-1})$ has no inverse (mod M) in the set $\{1, ..., N-1\}$. But if we let b range over all $M-2$ distinct values 1 to $M-2$, then we get exactly $M-2$ distinct values for the inverses of $N^{-1}(1+b^{-1})$. As $M > N+1$ (hence $M-2 > N-1$) it now follows by a simple application of the pigeonhole principle that at least one of these inverses must lie outside of the forbidden range $1, ..., N-1$, and the corresponding b will do for our purposes. (Observe that indeed no b can exist if $M = N+1, M$ prime.) □

Corollary 3.3 *Any linear skewing scheme that provides conflict-free access to rows, columns and all circulant (forward) diagonals using a minimum number of memory banks M is equivalent to a $(1, c)$ scheme, for some c with* $\gcd(c, M) = 1$. $(N \neq 2)$.

Proof By Bertrand's postulate (cf. [HW79]) the smallest prime greater than $x \geqslant 2$ is $\leqslant 2x - 1$. Thus it follows from theorem 3.8 that the smallest number of memory banks M needed for the desired type of linear skewing satisfies $M < 2N$, and from (***) we see that the choice of a is constrained by $\gcd(a, M) = 1$. By theorem 3.2 we conclude that any linear skewing scheme with this property is equivalent to a $(1, c)$ scheme. The condition on c follows again from (***). □

Theorem 3.9 *Let M be the smallest prime number $> 2N+1$. Then there exists a linear skewing scheme using M memory banks that provides conflict-free access to rows, columns and all circulant diagonals and anti-diagonals.*

Proof By theorem 3.2 we may assume without loss of generality that $a = 1$. Conditions (**′) now translate into the requirement that there exists an integer b with $2 \leqslant b \leqslant M-2$ such that both $N^{-1}(1+b^{-1})$ and $N^{-1}(1 - b^{-1})$ have inverses outside of the set $\{1, ..., N-1\}$ (mod M). Consider the collection of pairs

$$\{(N^{-1}(1+b^{-1}))^{-1}, (N^{-1}(1-b^{-1}))^{-1}\}$$

for b from 2 to $M-2$. This gives precisely $M-3$ distinct pairs, and the values that appear in the first (or second) coordinate as inverses are necessarily all distinct. Thus striking out all pairs that have a "forbidden" first or second coordinate eliminates at most $2(N-1)$ pairs and (hence) leaves at least $M - 3 - 2(N-1) = M - (2N+1) \geqslant 1$ pairs with both coordinates outside of the range $1, ..., N-1$. Choosing for b the integer corresponding to one of these pairs will do for our purposes. □

In case $3 \nmid N$ the bound on M given in theorem 3.9 can be improved to the smallest prime number $\geqslant 2N+1$ (but also recall theorem 3.7). To show this we only need to consider the situation that $2N+1$ is prime and hence $M = 2N+1$. Necessarily $N = 3v+2$, for some v. It can be verified that $2^{-1} \equiv N+1$, $N^{-1} \equiv 2N-1$ and $(2N)^{-1} \equiv 2N$. Consider the linear skewing scheme determined by $a = 1$ and $b = M-2 = 2N-1$. Clearly $b+a \not\equiv 0$ and $b-a \not\equiv 0$ (provided $N > 1$), and it follows that we only need to verify the last two conditions of (**).
(i) Suppose $2N.x \equiv (2N-1)N$. Then $x \equiv 2^{-1}.(2N-1) \equiv (N+1).(2n-1) \equiv 2N$, and thus $(b+a)x \equiv bN$ has no solution in the range $1, ..., N-1$.
(ii) Suppose $(2N-2)x \equiv (2N-1)N$, or $3x = 2N$. This means that we seek a solution $x \in \{1, ..., 2N\}$ to the equation $3x = 2N + \lambda(2N+1) = (2+2\lambda)3v + 4 + 5\lambda$. For $\lambda = 1$ we get as a (necessarily unique) solution $x = 4v+3 = \frac{4}{3}N+\frac{1}{3}$, which is outside the range $1...N-1$. Thus $(b-a)x \equiv bN$ has no solution in the latter range.

It follows that the conditions (**) are satisfied for this choice of a and b. The result is only of interest if a prime number of memory banks is provided, and certainly does not give the best possible bound. For if $3 \nmid N$ then it is easily seen that (**) can be satisfied with $a = 1$, $b = 2$ and $M = 2N$ (i.e., $2N$ memory banks are sufficient).

3.1.4 Conflict-Free Access through Multiple Fetches

In section 3.1.2 we anticipated that "vectors of interest" can be retrieved by performing (at most) r conflict-free fetches from the given set of M memory banks, for some $r \geqslant 1$. This certainly applies to the case of retrieving circulant diagonals (cf. section 3.1.3) which, after all, can be obtained by at most 2 conflict-free fetches using a skewing scheme that is valid for non-circulant (i.e., ordinary) diagonals. Using theorem 3.6 it follows that no more than $N+3$ memory banks are needed to skew an $N \times N$ matrix and have conflict-free access to rows, columns and all circulant diagonals, if only we allow up to 2 retrieval operations per "vector". (Compare this to theorem 3.8.) In this section we shall examine the effect of multiple fetches more closely.

We shall first consider the simple case of accessing rows, columns and (ordinary) diagonals of an $N \times N$ matrix using a linear skewing scheme and

r-fold fetching. Consider the following conditions.

$$(****)\begin{cases} M \geqslant (\lfloor \frac{N-1}{r} \rfloor + 1)\gcd(a, M), \\ M \geqslant (\lfloor \frac{N-1}{r} \rfloor + 1)\gcd(b, M), \\ M \geqslant (\lfloor \frac{N-1}{r} \rfloor + 1)\gcd(b + a, M), \\ M \geqslant (\lfloor \frac{N-1}{r} \rfloor + 1)\gcd(b - a, M), \\ (a < b). \end{cases}$$

Lemma 3.4 *Conditions (****) are necessary and sufficient for the existence of a linear skewing scheme using M banks that provides conflict-free access to rows, columns, diagonals and anti-diagonals in at most r fetches per vector.*

Proof The comments at the beginning of section 3.1.3 apply to characterize the "vectors of interest" as d-ordered vectors of size (at most) N, for the proper values of d. In theorem 3.5 was shown that such vectors can be retrieved in at most r conflict-free fetches if and only if one has $M \geqslant (\lfloor \frac{N-1}{r} \rfloor + 1)\gcd(d, M)$. Substituting the pertinent values of d here leads to the conditions (****) as claimed. □

Theorem 3.10 *In order that there exists a linear skewing scheme that provides conflict-free access to rows, columns, diagonals and anti-diagonals in at most r fetches per vector the number of memory banks M required need to be no larger than $\lfloor \frac{N-1}{r} \rfloor + 4$.*

Proof The analysis in theorem 3.6 (of the very similar conditions in (*)) shows that the smallest M needed to satisfy (****) need to be no larger than $(\lfloor \frac{N-1}{r} \rfloor + 1) + 3 = \lfloor \frac{N-1}{r} \rfloor + 4$. □

Actually the analysis of theorem 3.6 shows that the smallest value for M needed in theorem 3.10 is precisely equal to "the smallest number $\geqslant \lfloor \frac{N-1}{r} \rfloor +$ 1 that is not divisible by 2 and 3". This leads to an interesting observation about the trade-off between the number of memory banks M and r. (We simply take $r = 2$.)

Proposition 3.4 *Consider the existence of linear skewing schemes for conflict-free access to rows, columns, diagonals and anti-diagonals.*
(i) If $2|N$ but $3 \nmid N$ and $4 \nmid N$, then one can "skew" an $N \times N$ matrix in $N/2$ banks and retrieve rows, etc., in at most 2 fetches per vector, but it is impossible to skew it in N banks and retrieve rows, etc., in a single fetch.
(ii) If $2 \nmid N$ and $3 \nmid N$ and $N \not\equiv 1 \pmod{12}$, then one can skew an $N \times N$ matrix in N banks and retrieve rows, etc., in a single fetch but it is impossible to skew it in $\lfloor N/2 \rfloor$ banks and retrieve rows, etc., in 2 fetches per vector.

Proof (*i*) If $2|N$ but $3 \nmid N$ and $4 \nmid N$, then $\lfloor \frac{N-1}{2} \rfloor + 1 = N/2$ and $2 \nmid N/2$ and $3 \nmid N/2$. Hence $N/2$ memory banks suffice for retrieving rows, etc., in at most 2 fetches. On the other hand theorem 3.6 shows that at least $N+1$ banks are needed if we want to retrieve rows, etc., in a single fetch.
(*ii*) If $2 \nmid N$ and $3 \nmid N$ then N banks suffice for conflict-free access to rows, etc., in one fetch (theorem 3.6). If in addition $N \not\equiv 1 \pmod{12}$ and hence N is of the form $12v+5$, $12v+7$ or $12v+11$ then the smallest $M \geqslant \lfloor \frac{N-1}{2} \rfloor + 1$ not divisible by 2 and 3 is equal to $6v+5$, $6v+5$ and $6v+7$, respectively. Thus the smallest M required to be able to retrieve rows, etc., in 2 fetches is $> \lfloor N/2 \rfloor$ in each case. □

It is of some interest to consider the effect of multiple fetches if conflict-free access is required to more general templates in a matrix than only rows, columns and diagonals. We shall prove that there are linear schemes for skewing an $N \times N$ matrix in $N + O(1)$ memory banks such that every connected template of N cells can be retrieved conflict-free in $O(\sqrt{N})$ fetches. We shall first consider the case of rookwise connected templates, i.e., templates in which every two cells are connected by a path of consecutive cells such that any pair of consecutive cells share at least a full side.

Choose M as a perfect square, and consider the linear skewing scheme s defined by

$$s(i,j) = i - \sqrt{M}.j \bmod M$$

for $0 \leqslant i,j < N$. Observe that $s(i, j + \sqrt{M}) = s(i,j)$ and also that $s(i + \sqrt{M}, j+1) = s(i,j)$. Further it is clear that s maps the cells of any $\sqrt{M} \times \sqrt{M}$ sub-array (viewed as a template) to different banks, i.e., s is conflict-free on $\sqrt{M} \times \sqrt{M}$ blocks. It means that an $N \times N$ matrix is stored by splitting (covering) it into approximately N^2/M sub-arrays of size $\sqrt{M} \times \sqrt{M}$ that are each stored as a full-size vector in the M banks available, with small "cut off" effects along the boundary but an otherwise fully periodic pattern.

Lemma 3.5 *Let (i_1, j_1) and (i_2, j_2) be two different cells of the matrix. If $s(i_1, j_1) = s(i_2, j_2)$ then either the i-coordinates or the j-coordinates of the two cells differ by at least $\sqrt{M}$.*

Proof This is immediate from the "periodicity" of s, and also from the fact that no two cells that are mapped to the same bank can lie within one $\sqrt{M} \times \sqrt{M}$ block. □

Now consider an arbitrary, rookwise connected template T of t cells. If $t \leqslant \sqrt{M}$ then T necessarily fits in a $\sqrt{M} \times \sqrt{M}$ "box" and can obviously be accessed conflict-free with a single fetch.

Theorem 3.11 *Using s to store an $N \times N$ matrix into M memory banks, any rookwise connected template of t cells can be retrieved by means of (at most) $\lfloor (t-1)/\sqrt{M} \rfloor + 1$ conflict-free fetches of vectors from the M memory banks.*

Proof (The proof requires some familiarity with the Steiner tree problem in the plane, cf. Melzak [Mel61].) Consider the memory banks that receive elements under s from the given instance of T positioned in the domain of the matrix. Suppose bank α receives the largest number of elements from T, and let this largest number be l.

Claim 3.1 *The elements of the given instance of T can be retrieved by means of (exactly) l conflict-free fetches of vectors from the M memory banks.*

We shall proceed by estimating l. Consider the matrix as an $N \times N$ square of cells on the two-dimensional grid, and let the cells be labeled with the name of the memory bank they are mapped to under s. Let V be the collection of cells labeled α that are "covered" by the instance of T. Clearly $l = |V|$. Because T is rookwise connected, every two cells of V are connected by a "rectilinear" chain of cells that runs entirely within T. Consider some minimum collection of chains needed to connect all cells this way. It yields a tree-like substructure of T, with the property that "edges" (chains) may intersect or even partly overlap. Thus we have a tree on a super-set of V (the additional cells can appropriately be called Steiner cells, in analogy to the Steiner tree problem [Mel61]), with cells connected by "simple" rectilinear chains. We conclude that T must contain a "rectilinear Steiner tree" on V, and thus have at least as many cells as a Steiner minimal tree on V with rectilinear edges. Let the length of such a Steiner minimal tree be l_s. It follows that $t \geqslant l_s$.

Using lemma 3.5 it is fairly straightforward to find a lowerbound of about $(l-1)\sqrt{M}$ on the length $l_{\min}$ of a "classical" minimum spanning tree of V. This translates to a lowerbound for l_s by using a theorem of Hwang [Hwa76], who showed that $l_s \geqslant \frac{2}{3} l_{\min}$. (Note that l_s can be smaller than $l_{\min}$ because edges that partly coincide with other edges do not contribute the overlapped parts to the length twice.)

Claim 3.2 $l_s \geqslant (l-1)\sqrt{M}+1$.

Proof Hanan's theorem [Han66] asserts that there is a Steiner minimal tree with rectilinear distance that is contained in the (sub-)grid obtained by taking precisely the rows and columns of the cells in V. (Thus Steiner cells necessarily occur at grid-points only, and edges between Steiner cells and/or cells of V either are straight paths or paths with one "hook"). By the nature of s columns are at least a distance $\sqrt{M}$ apart, and thus horizontal line segments that connect cells of V must contain at least $\sqrt{M}-1$ cells (only counting the part between the two columns spanned). Also observe that within a column the occurring cells of V must lie a distance of at least $\sqrt{M}$ apart, and thus vertical line segments that connect cells of V must be at least $\sqrt{M}-1$ cells in length.

Now "charge" cells of the Steiner minimal tree to V in the following manner. Choose an arbitrary cell of V as the root of the tree, and orient all edges away from the root. (This implies a notion of "distance" from the root, measured by the number of points of V visited on a path.) Label every edge by "h" or "v", depending on whether it is a horizontal or a vertical connection. (Hooks are labeled by "h".) Note that h-edges account for at least $\sqrt{M}-1$ cells. Begin by charging 1 to the root, to account for the one cell it occupies. Suppose we have completed the charging to cells of V at distance i from the root. Consider any cell p of V at distance i from the root, and all cells q of V at distance $i+1$ reached from p. The cells are connected to p by a (sub-)tree of labeled edges and Steiner cells as "internal nodes". For every leaf q determine the lowest edge in the tree labeled h and mark it by q.

Case (a) There is no edge labeled h on the path from q to the root (p).

It means that all edges on this path are labeled v, and thus we have a straight vertical connection between two points of V in one column. Charge $\sqrt{M}-1$ (for the length of the vertical line segment) and 1 (for the cell q occupies), hence a total of $\sqrt{M}$ cells to q. (Note that Steiner points on this vertical line segment can only have outgoing h-edges beside the v-edges now accounted for, and no other leaf can be charged the same cells as q.)

Case (b) The h-edge marked by q has no other marks.

It means that this edge can be uniquely assigned to q and we can again charge $\sqrt{M}-1$ (for the horizontal line segment) and 1 (for the cell of q), hence a total of $\sqrt{M}$ cells to q.

Case (c) The h-edge marked by q has other marks as well.

Note that in this case the h-edge necessarily ends in a Steiner cell, with one outgoing v-edge continuing on to q over a path of further v-edges. Say (without loss of generality) that the path leads from the Steiner cell downwards. The only possibility for the h-edge to be marked by another leaf as well is that there is a cell of V, that necessarily lies in the same column as q and is vertically connected to it. Now charge the usual $\sqrt{M}$ cells to q (for the h-edge) and $\sqrt{M}$ cells to the other leaf for the vertical line segments.

It follows (by carrying out this procedure for cells of V at increasing distance from the root) that all $l-1$ cells of V beside the root can be charged a unique set of $\sqrt{M}$ cells. Hence we obtain $l_s \geqslant (l-1)\sqrt{M}+1$. □

We now complete the proof of theorem 3.11 as follows. By claim 3.1 we need l conflict-free fetches to retrieve T. By claim 3.2 we have $t \geqslant l_s \geqslant (l-1)\sqrt{M}+1$, hence $l \leqslant \lfloor (t-1)/\sqrt{M} \rfloor + 1$. Thus we can retrieve T by means of at most $\lfloor (t-1)/\sqrt{M} \rfloor + 1$ fetches. □

By choosing for M a square close to N, the following result is immediate. (Take, e.g., $M = \lfloor \sqrt{N} \rfloor^2$.)

Corollary 3.4 *There is a linear skewing scheme using no more than N memory banks, such that every rookwise connected template of N cells in an $N \times N$ matrix can be retrieved in at most $\sqrt{N}+2$ conflict-free fetches.*

For arbitrary, connected templates T (including ,e.g., diagonals) a precise analysis as in theorem 3.11 is hard, but the following somewhat weaker bound can be obtained.

Theorem 3.12 *Using s to store an $N \times N$ matrix into M memory banks, any connected template of t cells can be retrieved by means of at most $\lfloor 2t/\sqrt{M} \rfloor + 1$ conflict-free fetches.*

Proof Follow the same argument as in theorem 3.11 until after claim 3.1. To estimate l we now reason as follows. Enclose every cell of V by a "box " of cells that are at most $\lceil \frac{1}{2}\sqrt{M} \rceil$ away from it, measured in cells along a connected (but not necessarily rookwise connected) chain. Note that the boxes indeed are squares, and that the boxes thus surrounding the cells of V are all disjoint. Assuming $l > 1$, the connectedness of T requires that in every box so distinguished there is a chain of cells leading from the middle cell to the boundary. This accounts for at least $\lceil \frac{1}{2}\sqrt{M} \rceil$ cells of T per box, hence $t \geqslant l \lceil \frac{1}{2}\sqrt{M} \rceil$ and $l \leqslant \lfloor 2t/\sqrt{M} \rfloor$. The bound stated in the theorem is thus correct, including the case that t is small yet $l = 1$. □

Choosing again $M = \lfloor\sqrt{N}\rfloor^2 (\approx N)$ it follows that every connected template of N cells in an $N \times N$ matrix can be retrieved in at most $2\sqrt{N}+O(1)$ conflict-free fetches, using the linear skewing scheme s.

3.2 Periodic Skewing Schemes

Shapiro [Sha78b] defined a skewing scheme s for a 2-dimensional array to be periodic with period N if $s(i,j) = s(i \pm k_1.N, j \pm k_2.N)$ for any (i,j) and any (integer) k_1 and k_2. In the next section we redefine the notion of periodic skewing schemes for 2-dimensional arrays and derive results concerning the validity of these skewing schemes. In section 3.2.2 we consider the structure of periodic skewing schemes more generally. The theory of periodic skewing schemes is generalized to the d-dimensional case. It is shown that these periodic skewing schemes allow a compact representation and can be evaluated fast. Also the relationship between periodic skewing schemes and linear skewing schemes is explored. Further, in section 3.2.3 a detailed account is given of the connection between periodic skewing schemes and the theory of finite abelian groups. By this approach we are able to prove that the periodic skewing schemes can be completely classified into equivalence "types", and a normal form theorem is derived. Section 3.2.2 and section 3.2.3 are based on [WvL85] and [TvLW84], respectively. An important conclusion will be that the theory of skewing schemes, which originated from certain needs in engineering, can be reduced to well-known frameworks in mathematics. In view of the application of this theory, we will elaborate on the connections as concretely as possible.

3.2.1 Periodic Skewing Schemes for 2-Dimensional Arrays

Compactly representable skewing schemes for d-dimensional arrays received considerable attention in the literature, for the case $d = 2$. Therefore in this section we particularly deal with periodic skewing schemes for 2-dimensional arrays.

3.2.1.1 Periodic Skewing Schemes Redefined

Definition 3.4 *A skewing scheme $s : Z \to \{0, ..., M-1\}$ is called regular if and only if the following property is satisfied for all points p and q: if $s(p) = s(q)$ then any pair of points that are in the same relative position as p and q are mapped to equal banks.*

Note that a regular skewing scheme necessarily is periodic in the sense of Shapiro.

We first show that regular skewing schemes are closely connected to integral lattices as known in classical number theory (see Hardy and Wright [HW79]). A two-dimensional lattice L generated by integral vectors $\vec{x}$ and $\vec{y}$ (the basis of L) is the set of integer linear combinations $\lambda\vec{x} + \mu\vec{y}$. The set $\{\lambda\vec{x}+\mu\vec{y} \,|\, 0 \leqslant \lambda < 1, 0 \leqslant \mu < 1\}$ is the so-called fundamental parallelotope of L. The determinant of L is $\Delta(L) = |\det(\vec{x}\ \vec{y})|$. Points p and q are equivalent modulo L, notation $p \equiv_L q$, if $(p - q) \in L$.

Definition 3.5 *Let s be a regular skewing scheme. Any vector v that is the relative position* (cf. definition 2.9) *of two points p and q with $s(p) = s(q)$ is called a period of s.*

Proposition 3.5 *The periods of a regular skewing scheme form a discrete group in Z^2, and hence form a lattice.*

Let the lattice of periods of s be L. Let p be an arbitrary point and $s(p) = b$. Then all points of $p + L = p + \{\lambda\vec{x} + \mu\vec{y} \mid \lambda, \mu \in Z\}$ are mapped to bank b.

Proposition 3.6 *Let $s(p) = b$. Then $p + L$ is the collection of all points that are mapped to bank b, i.e., it characterizes the contents of this memory bank.*

Proof We only need to show that $q \in p + L$ when $s(q) = b$. Clearly $s(q) = s(p)$ implies that $(q-p) \in L$ (it is a period), and hence $q = p+(q-p) \in p + L$. □

Definition 3.6 *A skewing scheme $s : Z^2 \rightarrow \{1, ..., M\}$ is called periodic if there are M points $a_1, ..., a_M \in Z^2$ and a lattice L such that (i) the "cosets" $a_i + L$ are all disjoint but cover the entire Z^2 and (ii) s maps all points in $a_i + L$ to bank i ($1 \leqslant i \leqslant M$). (We will call s periodic "with lattice L", or that say L is the underlying lattice of s.)*

Proposition 3.7 *A skewing scheme s is periodic if and only if it is regular.*

Proof Let s be periodic with lattice L. If $s(p) = s(q)$, then p and q belong to the same $a_i + L$ and thus $(p - q) \in L$. It follows that all points that are in the same relative position as p and q belong the same $a_i + L$ and are thus mapped to equal banks. Hence s is regular. The converse easily follows from proposition 3.6. Let L be the lattice of periods, and choose for a_i any point that is mapped to bank i. □

Theorem 3.13 *Let s be a periodic skewing scheme using M memory banks, L the underlying lattice. Then $\Delta(L) = M$, i.e., the determinant of L is precisely equal to the number of memory banks used.*

Proof The result is well-known in the geometry of numbers (cf. Lekkerkerker [Lek69]) but we outline an intuitive argument.

Identify each cell with its "midpoint". Consider the template P_L of cells that have their midpoint inside the fundamental parallelotope of L. Now observe that (i) no two cells of P_L are equivalent modulo L (and thus the cells of P_L are all mapped to different banks) and (ii) every cell of the plane is equivalent to a cell of P_L modulo L (and thus every bank receives some cell of P_L). It follows that $|P_L| = M$.

On the other hand it can be seen that P_L covers exactly $\Delta(L)$ area. To this end, consider how P_L covers the fundamental parallelotope. Any cell of P_L fully contained in the parallelotope contributes a unit of 1 to $\Delta(L)$. Any cell p of P_L that has a part of area ϵ sticking out of the fundamental parallelotope (into one, two or three neighboring parallelotopes) only covers an area of $1 - \epsilon$ of it, but this is compensated for by the cells not belonging to the instance of P_L that are situated like p in a neighboring parallelotope and that have a part sticking out into the fundamental parallelotope. Hence the cells of P_L account for precisely $\Delta(L)$ total area, and $\Delta(L) = M$. □

Corollary 3.5 *Every periodic skewing scheme is valid for some template.*

Proof The instances of P_L are disjoint but cover the complete plane. By Shapiro's theorem ([Sha78b], see section 2.1) it follows that s is a valid skewing scheme for P_L. □

(Given that P_L tessellates the plane and has its instances arranged at every lattice point in the same manner, the conclusion of theorem 3.13 also follows from Hardy and Wright [HW79, thm. 41].)

In practice the domain of a (periodic) skewing scheme s will be an $N \times N$ matrix, for some $N > 0$. If s is valid for a template P, then it is valid for the matrix as long as we consider instances of P that are located entirely within the domain of the matrix. In some applications one also considers instances of P that lie in part across the border and uses the "wrap-around" convention for the points that stick out, i.e., their coordinates are reduced modulo N.

Theorem 3.14 *Let s be a periodic skewing scheme using M memory banks, and assume that s is valid for a template P. Then s is valid for P on any $N \times N$ matrix with $M|N$, allowing "wrap-around" of the instances of P.*

Proof Consider any point p of P that is involved in a "wrap-around", $p \in a_i + L$ (thus p is mapped to bank i) and $p = (a_{i_1} + \lambda x_1 + \mu y_1, a_{i_2} + \lambda x_2 + \mu y_2)$ for some integers λ and μ. Clearly point p is wrapped around to the cell p' with

$$p' = ((a_{i_1} + \lambda x_1 + \mu y_1) \bmod N, (a_{i_2} + \lambda x_2 + \mu y_2) \bmod N)$$

We shall prove that $p' \in a_i + L$, and thus p' is mapped to the same bank as p and no conflict is introduced because of the wrap-around. Let $N = \gamma M$ for some integer $\gamma > 0$. Clearly there exist integers α and β such that the following equalities hold for the coordinates of p':

$$(a_{i_1} + \lambda x_1 + \mu y_1) \bmod N = a_{i_1} + \lambda x_1 + \mu y_1 + \alpha N \qquad (3.1)$$
$$(a_{i_1} + \lambda x_2 + \mu y_2) \bmod N = a_{i_2} + \lambda x_2 + \mu y_2 + \beta N \qquad (3.2)$$

By theorem 3.13 $M = \Delta(L) = |\det\binom{x_1\ y_1}{x_2\ y_2}| = |x_1 y_2 - x_2 y_1|$ and hence $N = \gamma.|x_1 y_2 - x_2 y_1|$. By omitting the sign restriction on γ we can simply write $N = \gamma.(x_1 y_2 - x_2 y_1)$. Substituting this into the right-hand sides of equations 3.1 and 3.2 we obtain after some rearrangements:

$$(a_{i_1} + \lambda x_1 + \mu y_1) \bmod N = a_{i_1} + \lambda' x_1 + \mu' y_1$$
$$(a_{i_1} + \lambda x_2 + \mu y_2) \bmod N = a_{i_2} + \lambda' x_2 + \mu' y_2$$

with $\lambda' = \lambda + \alpha\gamma x_2 - \beta\gamma y_1$ and $\mu' = \mu - \alpha\gamma x_2 + \beta\gamma x_1$ (thus $\lambda', \mu' \in \mathbb{Z}$). Thus $p' = a_i + \lambda'\vec{x} + \mu'\vec{y} \in a_i + L$, as was to be shown. □

Crucial for the use of a periodic skewing scheme s is the question whether s-values can be efficiently computed. To compute $s(p)$ for a point $p = (i, j)$ one needs to determine the (unique) k such that $p \in a_k + L$ $(1 \leqslant k \leqslant M)$, where L is the lattice of s.

Proposition 3.8 *Every periodic skewing scheme s using M memory banks can be completely described by an $M \times M$ table* **a** *and a look-up procedure that is as simple as $s(i, j) = \mathbf{a}[i \bmod M, j \bmod M]$.*

Proof In the proof of theorem 3.14 it was shown that the value of $s(p)$ does not change if we reduce the coordinates of p modulo M (take $N = M$ in the argument). It means that all values of s are suitably summarized in a table that lists the s-value for all points (i, j) with $0 \leqslant i, j < M$. □

Proposition 3.8 reconciles our definition of periodic skewing schemes with the one proposed by Shapiro. From a practical point of view proposition 3.8 is not very useful, because the table is very large while only M essentially different values need to be recorded. A minimum table is obtained if we list the M different s-values of the points of the template P_L defined in the proof of theorem 3.13, and reduce points modulo L to a point of P_L. Because P_L is not a very regular template the look-up procedure is not elementary. We shall see in section 3.2.1.2 that P_L can be replaced by an equivalent template of a much more regular shape, and give a proof of the following result.

Theorem 3.15 *Every periodic skewing scheme s using M memory banks can be completely described by a table* $\mathbf{a}$ *of size M and a look-up procedure that is as simple as* $s(i,j) = \mathbf{a}[f(i,j)]$, *where $f(i,j)$ is a simple expression.*

Theorem 3.15 substantiates the claim that periodic skewing schemes are "finitely represented" and easy to compute.

3.2.1.2 Fundamental Templates and Their Use

We shall now delve deeper into the structure of periodic skewing schemes. We use L to denote a lattice, s its corresponding periodic skewing scheme.

Definition 3.7 *A fundamental domain of a lattice L is any domain $F \subseteq \mathbb{Z}^2$ such that*
(i) no two distinct points of F are equivalent modulo L and
(ii) every point of the plane is equivalent to a point of F modulo L.

We shall demonstrate that every lattice L has a fundamental template that is a rectangle[1]. We need the following observations. If we draw a horizontal line through any lattice point, then other lattice points on this line appear at regular distances called the "horizontal yardstick" of L. If we draw the horizontal lines through all lattice points (identifying lines that coincide), then the horizontal lines appear at regular distances called the "vertical yardstick" of L.

Lemma 3.6 *Let L be generated by integral vectors $\vec{x} = (x_1, x_2)$ and $\vec{y} = (y_1, y_2)$. Then the horizontal yardstick of L has size* $\Delta(L)/\gcd(x_2, y_2)$ *and the vertical yardstick of L has size* $\gcd(x_2, y_2)$.

[1] Whereas the underlying lattice theory is elementary, we have not found this observation in references like [Cox61] and [HC64].

Proof Lattice points have coordinates $(\lambda x_1+\mu y_1, \lambda x_2+\mu y_2)$ with $\lambda, \mu \in \mathbf{Z}$. The y-coordinates $\lambda x_2 + \mu y_2$ precisely range over all multiples of the gcd of x_2 and y_2, as is well known. Thus the vertical yardstick is as stated. To determine the horizontal yardstick, assume without loss of generality that $y_2 \neq 0$ and consider two lattice points $(\lambda_1 x_1 + \mu_1 y_1, \lambda_1 x_2 + \mu_1 y_2)$ and $(\lambda_2 x_1 + \mu_2 y_1, \lambda_2 x_2 + \mu_2 y_2)$ on the same horizontal line. Comparing y-coordinates we have

$$\begin{aligned} \lambda_1 x_2 + \mu_1 y_2 &= \lambda_2 x_2 + \mu_2 y_2 \\ \Rightarrow (\lambda_1 - \lambda_2) x_2 &= -(\mu_1 - \mu_2) y_2 \end{aligned}$$

and thus either (i) there is an integer α such that $\lambda_1 - \lambda_2 = \alpha.y_2/\text{gcd}(x_2, y_2)$ and $\mu_1 - \mu_2 = -\alpha.x_2/\text{gcd}(x_2, y_2)$, or (ii) $\mu_1 = \mu_2$ and $x_2 = 0$ (which implies that $\Delta(L) = |x_1 y_2|$ and $\Delta(L)/\text{gcd}(x_2, y_2) = |x_1|$). Now consider the difference in x-coordinate

$$(\lambda_1 - \lambda_2) x_1 + (\mu_1 - \mu_2) y_1$$

In case (i) this evaluates to $\alpha.(x_1 y_2 - x_2 y_1)/\text{gcd}(x_2, y_2)$ and thus gives exactly all multiples of $\Delta(L)/\text{gcd}(x_2, y_2)$ by varying α. In case (ii) we get $(\lambda_1 - \lambda_2) x_1$ and this also gives all multiples of $|x_1| = \Delta(L)/\text{gcd}(x_2, y_2)$, by varying λ_1 and λ_2. Thus the horizontal yardstick is as stated in the lemma. □

Theorem 3.16 *Let L be generated by integral vectors $\vec{x} = (x_1, x_2)$ and $\vec{y} = (y_1, y_2)$. Then the rectangle of size* $\text{gcd}(x_2, y_2)$ *(vertical) by* $\Delta(L)/\text{gcd}(x_2, y_2)$ *(horizontal) is a fundamental template of L.*

Proof Let the rectangle be R. Note that R has area equal to $\Delta(L)$, and thus consists of exactly $\Delta(L)$ points. We claim that R contains no two points p and q ($p \neq q$) that are equivalent modulo L. For suppose there were. Then (by shifting p and q) there would be two lattice points whose y-coordinates differ by less than the vertical yardstick (which means they must lie on the same horizontal line) and whose x-coordinates differ by less than the horizontal yardstick (which is impossible if they lie on the same horizontal line), a contradiction. Because there are no more than $M = \Delta(L)$ distinct memory banks, this implies that R must be a fundamental domain of L. (The same conclusion can be drawn from Hardy and Wright [HW79, thm. 42].) □

Corollary 3.6 *All fundamental templates of a 2-dimensional lattice are equivalent to a rectangle (modulo the lattice).*

Corollary 3.7 *Every periodic skewing scheme is valid for a rectangle.*

Theorem 3.16 is also of interest in conjunction with theorem 2.19, section 2.4.4 that asserts that every skewing scheme valid for a polyomino can be transformed into a periodic scheme. We conclude that whenever a polyomino tessellates the plane, then it can tessellate the plane periodically and is equivalent to a rectangle modulo the underlying lattice. A fundamental rectangle R naturally has the form of a table that we can use to obtain another "sample" periodic skewing scheme s_L with underlying lattice L. Let L be generated by integral vectors $\vec{x} = (x_1, x_2)$ and $\vec{y} = (y_1, y_2)$ and take R as in theorem 3.16. Write M for $\Delta(L)$ to denote the number of memory banks in use.

Theorem 3.17 *The mapping s defined by*

$$s(i,j) = (i - c_L.f(j)) \bmod M/\gcd(x_2,y_2) + (j \bmod \gcd(x_2,y_2)).M/\gcd(x_2,y_2)$$

(where f is a simple function specified below) is a periodic skewing scheme corresponding to L.

Proof Think of the lattice as being divided into horizontal strips of width $\gcd(x_2, y_2)$ and copies of R at every lattice point. (Thus each horizontal strip is a layer of R-"bricks".) All we need to do is locate a point (i, j) in the proper brick and assign it to the memory bank of the corresponding point. Clearly (i, j) is in the strip whose "bottom line" has y-coordinate fixed at $j - (j \bmod \gcd(x_2, y_2)) = f'(x_2, y_2, j)$, a multiple of $\gcd(x_2, y_2)$. To find the lattice points $(\lambda x_1 + \mu y_1, \lambda x_2 + \mu y_2)$ on this line, note that the equation $\lambda x_2 + \mu y_2 = f'(x_2, y_2, j)$ fixes (λ, μ) to a collection $(f'', f''') + \alpha.(y_2/\gcd(x_2, y_2), -x_2/\gcd(x_2, y_2))$, where f'' and f''' are a standard solution. (We assume that $y_2 \neq 0$ and omit the special case that $x_2 = 0$, compare the proof of lemma 3.6.) Then the x-coordinates of lattice points on the line are obtained by applying horizontal yardsticks beginning at $f(L, j) = f''.x_1 + f'''.y_1$. Thus (i, j) lies at position $((i - f(L, j)) \bmod M/\gcd(x_2, y_2), j \bmod \gcd(x_2, y_2))$ in its brick and its assignment to a memory bank easily follows. To complete the argument we show the existence of $f(L, j)$ factors. Let $a = x_2/\gcd(x_2, y_2)$, $b = y_2/\gcd(x_2, y_2)$ and $f(j) = (j - j \bmod \gcd(x_2, y_2))/\gcd(x_2, y_2)$, then a and b are relatively prime, $c = b^{-1} \bmod a$ exists, f'' and f''' can be chosen as $f''' = c.f(j)$ and $f'' = (1 - bc)/a.f(j)$ and $f(L, j) = (\frac{1-bc}{a}.x_1 + c.y_1).f(j) = c_L.f(j)$. (Note that $c_L = x_1/a + (acy_1 - bcx_1)/a = x_1/a - \Delta(L).c/x_2$.) A very similar argument holds in case $x_2 = 0$. □

By theorem 3.13 all other periodic skewing schemes induced by L can be obtained by a simple permutation of the memory bank numbers. In [WvL83b] another representation for periodic skewing schemes can be found.

3.2.1.3 The Validity of Periodic Skewing Schemes

We shall now deal with the problem of determining a periodic skewing scheme that is valid for a set of templates P_1 to P_t and uses a smallest number of memory banks M. First consider the case of a single template. We shall make use of Shapiro's theorem [Sha78b] (see also section 2.1) that relates (periodic) skewing schemes to (periodic) plane tessellations if the number of memory banks is to be $M = |P|$. In general (viz. if P does not tessellate the plane) the minimum number of memory banks required will be larger.

Proposition 3.9 *Let s be a periodic skewing scheme, P an arbitrary template. Then s is valid for P if and only if s is conflict-free on a single (arbitrary) instance of P.*

Proof We only need to show the if-part. Let s be conflict-free on an instance P' of P (located anywhere). Consider any other instance P'' of P and suppose there were two points $p, q \in P''$ with $s(p) = s(q)$. Then the two corresponding points of P' must be mapped to equal banks too, by the regularity of s (cf. proposition 3.7). Hence s would not be conflict-free on P', a contradiction. □

To obtain a periodic skewing scheme s valid for P one could enclose P by an $N \times N$ rectangle (N sufficiently large) and use a valid periodic scheme for the rectangle. Most likely this will not give a smallest number of memory banks.

Proposition 3.10 *Let s be a periodic skewing scheme using M memory banks that is valid for P. Then there is a template S of size M that encloses P such that s is valid for S (or equivalently, S tessellates the plane according to the underlying lattice).*

Proof Define s in the following manner. Consider an arbitrary instance of P laid down in the plane (and skewed conflict-free by assumption) and extend it to an instance of S by "appending" $M - |P|$ points to it, one point corresponding to every memory bank that did not receive an element from the instance of P. By construction this instance of S is skewed conflict-free and (hence) s is valid for S by proposition 3.9. The skewing scheme is valid because $M = |S|$, and by Shapiro's theorem this is equivalent to asserting that S tessellates the plane according to the same underlying lattice. □

Definition 3.8 *A minimal hull of a template P is a template S of smallest possible size that encloses P and periodically tessellates the plane.*

Clearly, the minimum number of memory banks required for a periodic skewing scheme valid for a template P is equal to the size of any minimal hull of P.

Theorem 3.18 *Every polyomino has a minimal hull that is again a polyomino.*

Proof Let P be a polyomino, and consider a periodic skewing scheme s that is valid for P and uses the smallest possible number of banks M. The underlying lattice L can be divided into horizontal layers of bricks as in theorem 3.16, each brick being a copy of the fundamental rectangle R and located at a lattice point. (Thus reductions modulo L can be computed as reductions "modulo R".) Lay down an instance of P and observe the finitely many parts $P^{(1)}$ to $P^{(l)}$,for some l, as they appear in different bricks. Each part is a polyomino within its brick, and when reduced modulo L to a single copy of R the parts appear as disjoint "islands" within R. (Disjointness follows because s was conflict-free on P.) Now extend the islands by adding bordering points such that they remain polyominoes but cover the entire R. Unfolding this and extending the polyominal parts $P^{(i)}$ likewise within the bricks where they are located effectively extends P to a larger polyomino of size M that must be a minimal hull by the same argument as in proposition 3.10. □

Now consider the problem of effectively computing the smallest number of memory banks required for a periodic skewing scheme to be valid for a set of templates P_1 to P_t. Suppose all templates can be fitted in an $N \times N$ rectangle. The rectangle is merely used to delimit the size of the templates. Clearly N^2 is an upperbound on the number of memory banks minimally required. The number of periodic skewing schemes to test that use N^2 memory banks or less is unfeasibly large, but fortunately many are equivalent, i.e., use the same underlying lattice.

Theorem 3.19 *The minimum number of memory banks required for a periodic skewing scheme that is valid for P_1 to P_t can be computed in time polynomial in N and t.*

Proof By theorem 3.13 we must test all lattices L that have $\triangle(L) \leqslant N^2$. For a given value k of the determinant there are at most $O(k^2)$ possible choices of a single base vector, hence $O(k^4)$ different lattices at all. Thus the number of lattices to inspect is polynomially bounded in N, and the lattice bases can be enumerated within this bound. With every lattice L a simple mapping s_L is associated that can act as a representative of all periodic skewing schemes that correspond to L. By proposition 3.9 the validity of s_L for each of the templates P_1 to P_t can be tested in linear time per template. The smallest value of $\triangle(L)$ that leads to a successful scheme is the minimum number of memory banks we were after. The method requires only polynomial time in N and t. □

Corollary 3.8 *For every set of templates P_1 to P_t that fit in an $N \times N$ box one can determine a valid periodic skewing scheme that uses the smallest possible number of memory banks in time polynomial in N and t.*

For $t = 1$ the method of theorem 3.19 is easily extended to an effective algorithm to compute a minimal hull of P. We only formulate this for the interesting case of a polyomino, cf. theorem 2.20.

Theorem 3.20 *For every polyomino P one can determine a smallest enclosing polyomino that periodically tessellates the plane in time polynomial in the size of P.*

Proof Theorem 3.18 implies that any smallest polyomino that encloses P and tessellates the plane must be a minimal hull. Thus apply the method of theorem 3.19 to find a lattice of minimum determinant that is valid for skewing P, and carry out the construction of an enclosing polyomino as in the proof of theorem 3.18. Since any polyomino P obviously fits in a $|P| \times |P|$ box (thus $N = |P|$ in theorem 3.19), the complete algorithm is easily seen to be polynomially bounded in $|P|$. □

3.2.2 Towards the Structure of Periodic Skewing Schemes

With the help of the theory of integral matrices we are able to generalize periodic skewing schemes to the d-dimensional case.

A d-dimensional lattice L^d generated by integral vectors $\vec{x}_1, ..., \vec{x}_d$ (the basis of the lattice) is the set of integral linear combinations $\lambda_1.\vec{x}_1 + ... + \lambda_d.\vec{x}_d$. The set

$$\{v_1.\vec{x}_1 + ... + v_d.\vec{x}_d \mid v_i \in \mathrm{R} \text{ and } 0 \leqslant v_i < 1\}$$

is called the fundamental parallelotope of L^d. Its volume is denoted as $\Delta(L^d)$, and is also called the determinant of L^d. Clearly one has $\Delta(L^d) = |\det(\vec{x}_1 ... \vec{x}_d)|$, and it can be shown that $\Delta(L^d)$ is independent of the particular basis chosen for L^d. Points $p = (p_1, ..., p_d)$ and $q = (q_1, ..., q_d)$ are said to be equivalent modulo L^d, notation: $p \equiv_{L^d} q$, if $(p - q) \in L^d$.

Fact 3.1 ([Lek69, page 23]) *The number of equivalence classes mod L^d is equal to $\Delta(L^d)$.*

Definition 3.9 *Let G be a finite set (e.g. a finite $\mathbb{Z}$-module) with $|G| = M$. A table t (for G) is any bijective map from G into $\{0, ..., M-1\}$.*

Definition 3.10 *Let $s : \mathbb{Z}^d \to \{0, ..., M-1\}$ be a skewing scheme using M memory banks. The scheme s is called periodic if and only if there exists a d-dimensional lattice L^d, a (surjective) homomorphism $\alpha : \mathbb{Z}^d \to \mathbb{Z}^d/_{L^d}$ with Ker $(\alpha) = L^d$, and a table for $\mathbb{Z}^d/_{L^d}$ such that $s = t \circ \alpha$.*

Compare this definition with definition 3.6. L^d is called the underlying lattice of s, and necessarily $\Delta(L^d) = M$. Thus t has exactly M entries. (Note that L^d is uniquely determined by s.) Figure 3.1 gives an example of a periodic skewing scheme restricted to $\mathbb{Z}_{12} \times \mathbb{Z}_{12}$, where L^d is a two-dimensional lattice with basis $\vec{x}_1 = (2, 2), \vec{x}_2 = (6, 2)$. Note that this skewing scheme is valid for every 2×6- and 6×2-block. The next proposition shows that in the definition of periodicity only the existence of a homomorphism of the desired kind is essential.

Proposition 3.11 *Let s be a periodic skewing scheme, $s = t \circ \alpha$. For every (surjective) homomorphism $\alpha' : \mathbb{Z}^d \to \mathbb{Z}^d/_{L^d}$ with* Ker$(\alpha') = L^d$ *there exists table t' such that $s = t' \circ \alpha'$.*

Proof Define a mapping $\psi : \mathbb{Z}^d/_{L^d} \to \mathbb{Z}^d/_{L^d}$ as follows. For every $y \in \mathbb{Z}^d/_{L^d}$ and x such that $\alpha'(x) = y$ let $\psi(y) = \alpha(x)$. Because Ker (α') = Ker (α) the value of $\psi(y)$ is well-defined and independent of the particular x with $\alpha'(x) = y$. It is easily verified that ψ is an automorphism of $\mathbb{Z}^d/_{L^d}$ and that $\psi \circ \alpha' = \alpha$. Hence $s = t \circ \alpha = t' \circ \alpha'$ with $t' = t \circ \psi$. □

It follows that in definition 3.10 we may always assume α to be the natural homomorphism from $\mathbb{Z}^d$ into $\mathbb{Z}^d/_{L^d}$.

Proposition 3.12 *A skewing scheme s is periodic if and only if there exist a lattice L^d and $a_0, ..., a_{M-1} \in \mathbb{Z}^d$ (where $M = \Delta(L^d)$) such that for all $0 \leqslant i \leqslant M-1$: $s^{-1}(i) = a_i + L^d$ and L^d is the underlying lattice of s.*

$$\begin{pmatrix}
8 & 9 & 10 & 11 & 6 & 7 & 8 & 9 & 10 & 11 & 6 & 7 \\
2 & 3 & 4 & 5 & 0 & 1 & 2 & 3 & 4 & 5 & 0 & 1 \\
10 & 11 & 6 & 7 & 8 & 9 & 10 & 11 & 6 & 7 & 8 & 9 \\
4 & 5 & 0 & 1 & 2 & 3 & 4 & 5 & 0 & 1 & 2 & 3 \\
6 & 7 & 8 & 9 & 10 & 11 & 6 & 7 & 8 & 9 & 10 & 11 \\
0 & 1 & 2 & 3 & 4 & 5 & 0 & 1 & 2 & 3 & 4 & 5 \\
8 & 9 & 10 & 11 & 6 & 7 & 8 & 9 & 10 & 11 & 6 & 7 \\
2 & 3 & 4 & 5 & 0 & 1 & 2 & 3 & 4 & 5 & 0 & 1 \\
10 & 11 & 6 & 7 & 8 & 9 & 10 & 11 & 6 & 7 & 8 & 9 \\
4 & 5 & 0 & 1 & 2 & 3 & 4 & 5 & 0 & 1 & 2 & 3 \\
6 & 7 & 8 & 9 & 10 & 11 & 6 & 7 & 8 & 9 & 10 & 11 \\
0 & 1 & 2 & 3 & 4 & 5 & 0 & 1 & 2 & 3 & 4 & 5
\end{pmatrix}$$

Figure 3.1: A periodic skewing scheme.

The following notion has proved useful in the theory (see e.g. section 3.1) and provides yet another characterization of periodicity.

Definition 3.11 *A skewing scheme s is called regular if and only if the following property is satisfied for all $p, q, \in \mathbb{Z}^d$: if $s(p) = s(q)$ then every pair of points $\in \mathbb{Z}^d$ that are in the same relative position as p and q is (also) mapped to equal memory banks.*

Lemma 3.7 *A skewing scheme s is periodic if and only if it is regular.*

Proof $\Rightarrow$ By proposition 3.12.
$\Leftarrow$ (Compare proposition 3.5.) Let any vector that is the relative position of two points p and q with $s(p) = s(q)$ be called a period of s. The crucial fact to observe is that the periods of s form a discrete group in $\mathbb{Z}^d$, and hence form a lattice L^d (see e.g. Weyl [Wey40, page 142]). This lattice is the underlying lattice for s. □

See also definition 3.4 and proposition 3.7.

3.2.2.1 A Representation of Periodic Skewing Schemes

We will argue that for every periodic skewing scheme $s : \mathbb{Z}^d \to \{0, ..., M-1\}$ there are a homomorphism α and a table t such that $s = t \circ \alpha$ and α can be expressed as a direct product of linear forms.

Definition 3.12 (cf. definition 3.7) *Given a d-dimensional lattice L^d. A fundamental domain F of L^d is any domain $\subseteq \mathbb{Z}^d$ such that (i) no two point of F are equivalent mod L^d, and (ii) every point $p \in \mathbb{Z}^d$ is equivalent mod L^d to a point of F. (Thus F has exactly one point for every equivalence class mod L^d and $|F| = \Delta(L^d)$.)*

Given a fundamental domain $F \subseteq \mathbb{Z}^d$, let $\delta_F : \mathbb{Z}^d \to F$ be defined such that for all $p \in \mathbb{Z}^d$ $\delta_F(p)$ is the unique $q \in F$ with $p \equiv_{L^d} q$. Any fundamental domain F can be regarded as an embedding of $\mathbb{Z}^d/_{L^d}$ into $\mathbb{Z}^d$ and thus inherits the structure of a finite $\mathbb{Z}$-module, with $\oplus$ and $\odot$ defined by $p \oplus q = \delta_F(p+q)$ and $\lambda \odot p = \delta_F(\lambda p)$. With this structure δ_F is a homomorphism, with Ker $(\delta_F) = L^d$.

Proposition 3.13 *Every fundamental domain F of L^d is (module-) isomorphic to $\mathbb{Z}^d/_{L^d}$.*

Proposition 3.14 *Let s be a periodic skewing scheme with underlying lattice L^d, and let F be a fundamental domain of L^d. There is a table t for F such that $s = t \circ \delta_F$.*

Proof By proposition 3.13 there is an isomorphism $\varphi : F \to \mathbb{Z}^d/_{L^d}$, hence $\varphi \circ \delta_F$ is a (surjective) homomorphism: $\mathbb{Z}^d \to \mathbb{Z}^d/_{L^d}$ with Ker $(\varphi \circ \delta_F) = L^d$. By proposition 3.11 there exists a table t' such that $s = t' \circ (\varphi \circ \delta_F)$. Take $t = t' \circ \varphi$. □

Next we show that for a suitable basis L^d has a fundamental domain that is "box-like", i.e., a polytope spanned by vectors along the coordinate axes. (See section 3.2.1.2 for the more special situation in the 2-dimensional case.) Let A be a $d \times d$ matrix with integer coefficients. For $1 \leqslant k \leqslant d$ define the kth determinantal divisor d_k of A by

$$d_k = \begin{cases} 0, & \text{if all } k \times k \text{ determinantal minors of } A \text{ are } 0 \\ \text{the gcd of all } k \times k \text{ determinantal minors of } A, & \text{otherwise} \end{cases}$$

and let

$$s_k = \frac{d_k}{d_{k-1}}$$

(where for consistency we define $d_0 \equiv 1$ and $\frac{0}{0} \equiv 0$). The coefficients s_k are known as the invariant factors of A.

Fact 3.2 ([New72], p.28) *The coefficients s_k $(1 \leqslant k \leqslant d)$ are integers and $s_1 | s_2 | \ldots | s_d$.*

Theorem 3.21 ([New72], p.36) *Let L^d be a d-dimensional lattice in $\mathbb{Z}^d$ with basis $\{\vec{x}_1, ..., \vec{x}_d\}$ (with respect to the standard basis of unit vectors in $\mathbb{Z}^d$). There exists a basis $U = \{\vec{u}_1, ..., \vec{u}_d\}$ of $\mathbb{Z}^d$ such that $s_1.\vec{u}_1, ..., s_d.\vec{u}_d$ is a basis of L^d, where s_1 through s_d are invariant factors of the matrix $A = (\vec{x}_1...\vec{x}_d)$.*

Note that $|\det(\vec{u}_1...\vec{u}_d)| = 1$ and that all s_k are non-zero (in the case of the theorem). Use the notation $(.., ..., ..)_U$ to denote a vector with respect to U.

Lemma 3.8 *The domain $F^* = \{(\lambda_1, ..., \lambda_d)_U | \ \lambda_k \in \mathbb{Z}_{s_k} \text{ for } 1 \leqslant k \leqslant d\}$ is a fundamental domain of L^d, where U and s_1 through s_d are as in the preceding theorem. Furthermore, the homomorphism $\delta_{F^*} : \mathbb{Z}^d \to F^*$ is given by $\delta_{F^*}((i_1, ..., i_d)_U) = (i_1 \bmod s_1, ..., i_d \bmod s_d)_U$.*

Proof Clearly F^* contains no two distinct point that differ by an integer linear combination of the base-vectors $s_1.\vec{u}_1, ..., s_d.\vec{u}_d$ of L^d. Thus $p \not\equiv_{L^d} q$ for any distinct $p, q \in F^*$. Let $\delta : \mathbb{Z}^d \to F^*$ be the homomorphism defined in the lemma. For every $(i_1, ..., i_d)_U \in \mathbb{Z}^d$ there are integers l_1 through l_d such that $(i_1, ..., i_d)_U - (i_1 \bmod s_1, ..., i_d \bmod s_d)_U = (l_1 s_1, ..., l_d s_d)_U)$ and hence for every $p \in \mathbb{Z}^d$: $p - \delta(p) \in L^d$, or: $p \equiv_{L^d} \delta(p)$. It follows that all equivalence classes mod L^d are uniquely represented in F^* (hence F^* is a fundamental domain) and $\delta = \delta_{F^*}$. □

Use $\sigma(x)$ to denote the order of any element x of a (finite) $\mathbb{Z}$-module. The following fact is well-known in the theory of finitely generated modules over a principal ideal domain.

Corollary 3.9 *Let L^d be a d-dimensional lattice in $\mathbb{Z}^d$. $\mathbb{Z}^d/_{L^d}$, or any fundamental domain of L^d, is (module-) isomorphic to a direct sum of d finite cyclic $\mathbb{Z}$-modules $< z_1 > \oplus ... \oplus < z_d >$ where $\sigma(z_k) = s_k$ for $1 \leqslant k \leqslant d$, and s_1 through s_d are as in the preceding theorem.*

Proof Immediate from proposition 3.13 and lemma 3.8. □

Another way of phrasing corollary 3.9 is to say that $\mathbb{Z}^d/_{L^d}$, or any fundamental domain of L^d, is (module-) isomorphic to the block B_{L^d} defined as

$$B_{L^d} = \{0, ..., s_1 - 1\} \oplus \{0, ..., s_2 - 1\} \oplus ... \oplus \{0, ..., s_d - 1\}.$$

Using this we can finally derive the main result concerning the representation of periodic skewing schemes.

Theorem 3.22 *Let s be a periodic skewing scheme and L^d its underlying lattice. There exists a (surjective) homomophism $\alpha : \mathbf{Z}^d \rightarrow B_{L^d}$ and a table t of B_{L^d} such that $s = t \circ \alpha$ and α is given by an expression of the type $a((i_1, ..., i_d)) = (L_1(i) \text{ mod } s_1, ..., L_d(i) \text{ mod } s_d)$, where $L_k(i) \equiv \lambda_{k,1}.i_1 + ... + \lambda_{k,d}.i_d$ is an integer linear form for $1 \leqslant k \leqslant d$ and B_{L^d} and s_1 through s_d are defined as before.*

Proof Let $U = \{\vec{u}_1, ..., \vec{u}_d\}$ be a basis for $\mathbf{Z}^d$ as implied by theorem 3.21. The matrix $(\vec{u}_1...\vec{u}_d)$ is unimodular, hence the mapping $\beta \equiv (\vec{u}_1...\vec{u}_d)^{-1}$ representing the linear transformation from standard coordinates to U-coordinates in $\mathbf{Z}^d$ is again described by an integral matrix. Because $\mathbf{Z}^d/_{L^d}, F^*$ and B_{L^d} are all fundamental domains of L^d (cf. lemma 3.8 and corollary 3.9) there are isomorphisms φ, ψ (cf. proposition 3.13) with $\varphi : F^* \rightarrow \mathbf{Z}^d/_{L^d}$ and $\phi : F^* \rightarrow B_{L^d}$ (where ψ is the natural isomorphism). Defining $\alpha' = \varphi \circ \delta_{F^*} \circ \beta$ we observe that $\alpha' : \mathbf{Z}^d \rightarrow \mathbf{Z}^d/_{L^d}$ is a homomorphism with Ker $(\alpha') = L^d$, and hence by proposition 3.11 there exists a table t' for $\mathbf{Z}^d/_{L^d}$ such that $s = t' \circ \alpha'$. Now let $\alpha = \varphi \circ \delta_{F^*} \circ \beta$ and $t = t' \circ \varphi \circ \psi^{-1}$. Then $\alpha : \mathbf{Z}^d \rightarrow B_{L^d}$ is again a homomorphism, t is a table for B_{L^d}, and $t \circ \alpha = t' \circ \varphi \circ \psi^{-1} \circ \psi \circ \delta_{F^*} \circ \beta = t' \circ \alpha' = s$. Furthermore α can be expressed as stated. (The kth coordinate expression of $\beta(i)$ provides the $L_k(i)$, and $\psi \circ \delta_{F^*}$ provides the reduction mod s_k.) □

3.2.2.2 Applications to the Theory of (Periodic) Skewing Schemes

We now show that various properties of periodic skewing schemes, often stated only for the 2-dimensional case, hold and have elegant proofs for all dimensions.

The particular "naming" (numbering) of the memory banks is of no importance for the property of conflict-free access to vectors. The following definition and results make this precise.

Definition 3.13 *Let s and r be d-dimensional (periodic) skewing schemes using an equal number of memory banks M. We say that s and r are equivalent, notation: $s \equiv r$, if and only if there exists a bijective map φ from $\{0, ..., M-1\}$ into $\{0, ..., M-1\}$ such that $s = \varphi \circ r$.*

The definition expresses that two skewing schemes are equivalent if and only if they are "equal" except for a change of table.

Proposition 3.15 *Let s and r be d-dimensional periodic skewing schemes using an equal number of memory banks M and underlying lattices L^d_s and L^d_r, respectively. Then $s \equiv r$ if and only if $L^d_s = L^d_r$.*

Proof $\Rightarrow$ Immediately from the characterization given in proposition 3.12. $\Leftarrow$ Let $s = t_s \circ \alpha_s$ and $r = t_r \circ \alpha_r$, as suggested by theorem 3.22. If $L_s^d = L_r^d$ (which determine the α's) then $\alpha_s = \alpha_r$. Consequently s and r are equivalent, using $\varphi = t_s \circ t_r^{-1}$. □

Theorem 3.23 *Let s be a periodic skewing scheme and L^d its underlying lattice. Then s is equivalent to a periodic skewing scheme s' defined by an expression of the type $s'(i) = \sum_1^d d_{k-1}.\ (L_k(i) \bmod s_k)$ for $i \in \mathbb{Z}^d$, where L_1 through L_d are integer linear forms and d_1 through d_d are integer factors determined by L^d as defined in* section 3.2.2.1.

Proof By theorem 3.22 we know that $s = t \circ \alpha$, for a (surjective) homomorphism $\alpha : \mathbb{Z}^d \to B_{L^d}$ as expressed in the theorem and a table t of B_{L^d}. Define a table t' of B_{L^d} by $t'(b_1, ..., b_d) = \sum_1^d s_1...s_{k-1}.b_k$. It follows that s must be equivalent to $s' = t' \circ \alpha$, and s' is expressed as in the theorem. Note that $s_1...s_{k-1} = d_{k-1}$. □

The theorem shows that every periodic skewing scheme is equivalent to a scheme that is described by a simple arithmetic expression. Explicit formulae for general 2-dimensional periodic skewing schemes can be found in [WvL83b], see also section 3.2.1.2.

Proposition 3.16 *Every linear skewing scheme is periodic.*

Proof Let s be defined by $s(i) = \lambda_1.i_1 + ... + \lambda_d.i_d \bmod M$. We show that s is regular, hence periodic by lemma 2.2. Assume that $s(p) = s(q)$ for two points $p = (p_1, ..., p_d)$ and $q = (q_1, ..., q_d)$, and let $v = (q - p)$ be the "relative position" of p and q. By substituting in the expression for s it follows that $\lambda_1.v_1 + ... + \lambda_d.v_d \equiv 0 \pmod{M}$. But this is precisely the condition for all pairs of points in relative position v to be mapped to equal banks, i.e., to have the same s-value. Thus s is regular. □

Whereas linear skewing schemes have the advantage of being very easy to evaluate, it can be argued that periodic skewing schemes in general give a greater flexibility for achieving some type of conflict-free access. Nevertheless we show that for M prime (more generally: M square-free) the full power of periodic skewing schemes can be obtained using the linear skewing schemes.

Theorem 3.24 *Let s be a periodic skewing scheme and L^d its underlying lattice with basis $\{\vec{x}_1, ..., \vec{x}_d\}$. Then s is equivalent to a linear skewing scheme if and only if $d_k = 1$ for $1 \leqslant k \leqslant d-1$ (equivalently: $s_k = 1$ for $1 \leqslant k \leqslant d-1$), where d_k (resp. s_k) is the kth determinantal divisor (resp. invariant factor) of the matrix $A = (\vec{x}_1 ... \vec{x}_d)$.*

Proof $\Rightarrow$ Let s be equivalent to a linear skewing scheme, thus $s = \varphi \circ s'$ for a bijective map $\varphi : \{0, ..., M-1\} \to \{0, ..., M-1\}$ and $s'(i) = \lambda_1.i_1 + ... + \lambda_d.i_d \bmod M$ for some integers $\lambda_1, ..., \lambda_d$ with $\gcd(\lambda_1, ..., \lambda_d, M) = 1$. From elementary number theory follows that there exists an $i^* \in \mathbb{Z}^d$ with $s'(i^*) = 1$. Thus $\{s'(\mu.i^*) \mid 0 \leqslant \mu < M\} = \{0, ..., M-1\}$ and (hence) $\{s(\mu.i^*) \mid 0 \leqslant \mu < M\} = \{0, ..., M-1\}$. It follows that $F = \{\mu.i^* | 0 \leqslant \mu < M\}$ is a fundamental domain of L^d. By corollary 3.9 F is isomorphic to a direct sum of cyclic modules $< z_1 > \oplus ... \oplus < z_d >$ with $\sigma(z_k) = s_k$ for $1 \leqslant k \leqslant d$. Because F is generated by one vector all but one of the modules must be trivial. Because $s_1 | s_2 | ... | s_d$ (fact 3.2) it follows that necessarily $s_1 = ... = s_{d-1} = 1$, or equivalently, $d_1 = ... = d_{d-1} = 1$.
$\Leftarrow$ Let $d_k = 1$ for $1 \leqslant k \leqslant d-1$, or equivalently, $s_k = 1$ for $1 \leqslant k \leqslant d-1$. It follows in particular that $d_d = s_d = \Delta(L^d) = M$. From theorem 3.23 it follows immediately that s is equivalent to a skewing scheme s' of the type $s'(i) = L_d(i) \bmod M$, by substitution. Clearly s' is linear. □

Corollary 3.10 *Let s be a periodic skewing scheme and L^d its underlying lattice. Then s is equivalent to a linear skewing scheme if and only if $\mathbb{Z}^d/_{L^d}$, or any fundamental domain of L^d, is cyclic.*

The condition in theorem 3.24 takes a particularly simple form for $d = 2$, as shown initially in [WvL83a] by a direct number-theoretic argument.

Corollary 3.11 *Let s be a 2-dimensional skewing scheme, and L^2 its underlying lattice with base-vectors $\vec{x} = (x_1, x_2)$ and $\vec{y} = (y_1, y_2)$. Then s is equivalent to a linear scheme if and only if* $\gcd(x_1, x_2, y_1, y_2) = 1$.

Corollary 3.12 *Let M be square-free (i.e., not divisible by the square of a prime). Then every periodic skewing scheme $s : \mathbb{Z}^d \to \{0, ..., M-1\}$ (using M banks) is equivalent to a linear scheme.*

Proof Let M be square-free, and suppose there was a periodic skewing scheme that was not equivalent to a linear scheme. By theorem 3.24 there must be a k with $1 \leqslant k \leqslant d-1$ such that $s_k > 1$. Let p be a prime factor of s_k. By fact 3.2 it follows that $p | s_d$, and (hence) $p^2 | \; s_1 ... s_d = \Delta(L^d) = M$. Contradiction. □

We note that the requirement that M is square-free in corollary 3.12 cannot be weakened. Let e.g. $M = 12$. The (partial) skewing scheme in figure 3.1 is periodic but not linear. One can even show that there does not exist any linear skewing scheme $s : \mathbb{Z}_{12} \times \mathbb{Z}_{12} \to \mathbb{Z}_{12}$, such that s is valid for every 2×6- and 6×2-block (possibly with "wrap-around").

3.2.3 The Finite Abelian Group Approach

In the group-theoretic setting a periodic skewing scheme (definition 3.10) is an epimorphism $s : \mathbb{Z}^d \to A$ with $\mathrm{Ker}(s) = L^d$, which implies that A is isomorphic to $\mathbb{Z}^d/_{L^d}$, a finite abelian group (cf. [Tap]). In this section we further extend the theory of periodic skewing schemes, by exploiting the close connections to the classical theory of finite abelian groups.
The mathematical background for this section is available from standard texts on algebra (e.g. Goldhaber & Ehrlich [GE70]) or group theory (viz. Kurosh [Kur56]). Throughout this section we use the following notations:

A	a finite abelian group of M elements,
$\mathrm{Aut}(A)$	the group of automorphisms of A,
$\oplus$	the direct sum (of abelian groups),
$\otimes$	the direct product (of automorphism groups),
$\twoheadrightarrow$	a surjection (e.g. an epimorphism).

3.2.3.1 Skewing Schemes and Conflict-Free Access

A general d-dimensional skewing scheme is defined to be any surjective mapping $s : \mathbb{Z}^d \twoheadrightarrow A$, where A is a finite set of M elements. The elements of A denote the M parallel memories that are available for storing data. Let "$\sim$" denote the equivalence relation on $\mathbb{Z}^d$ defined such that for all $p, q \in \mathbb{Z}^d : p \sim q$ iff $s(p) = s(q)$. Since A is finite, the equivalence $\sim$ is necessarily of finite index. Let $\mathbb{Z}^d/_\sim$ denote the set of equivalence classes of $\sim$ and $v : \mathbb{Z}^d \twoheadrightarrow \mathbb{Z}^d/_\sim$ the natural projection. It follows that there must exist a bijection ψ such that the following diagram commutes:

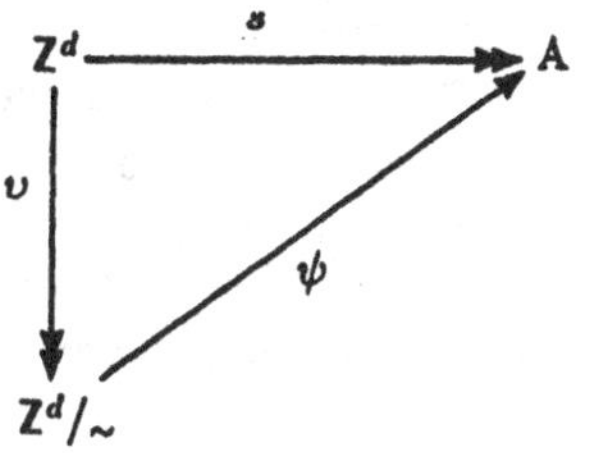

The following definition formalizes the notion of periodicity, definition 3.6 and definition 3.10.

Definition 3.14 *A skewing scheme $s : \mathbb{Z}^d \twoheadrightarrow A$ is called periodic if and only if $\sim$ is a congruence relation with respect to the free abelian group structure of $\mathbb{Z}^d$.*

If s is periodic, then $A \cong \mathbb{Z}^d/_\sim$ and (hence) A is identified with a finite abelian factor group of $\mathbb{Z}^d$ with (necessarily) d generators. Conversely every epimorphism $s : \mathbb{Z}^d \twoheadrightarrow A$ with A a finite abelian group is seen to be a periodic skewing scheme.

Skewing schemes are usually called equivalent (cf. definition 3.13) if they differ merely by the naming of the memory banks. More precisely, $s_1 : \mathbb{Z}^d \twoheadrightarrow A_1$ and $s_2 : \mathbb{Z}^d \twoheadrightarrow A_2$ are equivalent if and only if there is a bijection $\varphi : A_1 \rightarrow A_2$ such that $\varphi \circ s_1 = s_2$.

Proposition 3.17 *Let $s_1 : \mathbb{Z}^d \twoheadrightarrow A_1$ and $s_2 : \mathbb{Z}^d \twoheadrightarrow A_2$ be periodic skewing schemes, where A_1 and A_2 are finite abelian groups, and let $\varphi : A_1 \rightarrow A_2$ be a bijection such that $\varphi \circ s_1 = s_2$. Then φ is an isomorphism of abelian groups.*

The observation in proposition 3.17 leads to the following "program" for classifying the periodic skewing schemes $s : \mathbb{Z}^d \twoheadrightarrow A$, with A a finite abelian group. First let A run through the isomorphism types of all finite abelian groups with d generators. Next, for each such A consider the action of the automorphism group Aut(A) on the set of all epimorphisms (read: periodic skewing schemes) $s : \mathbb{Z}^d \twoheadrightarrow A$ defined by $\alpha(s) = \alpha \circ s$, for $\alpha \in$Aut(A). The orbits of this action precisely correspond to the equivalence classes of periodic skewing schemes.

Proposition 3.18 *A periodic skewing scheme $s : \mathbb{Z}^d \twoheadrightarrow A$ is linear if and only if A is a cyclic finite abelian group.*

Skewing schemes are designed such that desired collections ("vectors") of at most M elements each can be retrieved conflict-free from the parallel memories. In several studies of conflict-free access it has been suggested to choose M prime (see [Law75,LV82,WvL87]). This choice severely limits the type of skewing scheme that one can use, in view of the following fact.

Proposition 3.19 (cf. corollary 3.12) *If M is square-free (e.g. a prime), then every periodic skewing scheme using M memory banks is necessarily linear.*

Proof Every finite abelian group of square-free order is necessarily cyclic. Now apply proposition 3.18. □

A further observation is of interest. The rows, columns, and diagonals of a $N \times ... \times N$ (d-fold) matrix are easily parameterized into the form $p + \lambda q$

for fixed $p, q \in \mathbb{Z}^d$ and $\lambda \in \{0, ..., N-1\}$, and a periodic skewing scheme $s : \mathbb{Z}^d \twoheadrightarrow A$ will map the elements to banks $s(p) + \lambda s(q)$ (where the latter "+" denotes addition in A). This led Lawrie [Law75], see also section 3.1.2, to the paradigm of an "ordered" vector, which now takes the following form.

Definition 3.15 (cf. definition 3.3) *Let A be a finite abelian group. A γ-ordered k-vector ($\gamma \in A$, $k \geqslant 1$) is any vector of k elements whose i^{th} logical element is mapped under a periodic skewing scheme to bank $\delta + i\gamma$, for a suitable $\delta \in A$ and $0 \leqslant i < k$.*

Thus rows, columns, and diagonals are all γ-ordered k-vectors for suitable γ and k, when a periodic skewing scheme is used. Lawrie's main observation was that a γ-ordered k-vector with $\gamma \in \mathbb{Z}_M$ can be accessed conflict-free if and only if $M \geqslant k.\gcd(\gamma, M)$ (see [Law75,WvL87], section 3.1.2). The result is easily understood in the present framework. Let $\text{ord}(\gamma)$ denote the order of γ in A, an abelian group of M elements.

Proposition 3.20 *A γ-ordered k-vector ($\gamma \in A, k \geqslant 1$) can be accessed conflict-free if and only if $\text{ord}(\gamma) \geqslant k$.*

Proof Conflict-freeness means that $\delta + i\gamma \neq \delta + j\gamma$ for $i \neq j, 0 \leqslant i, j \leqslant k$. This is equivalent to the condition that $i\gamma \neq 0$ for $i = 1, ..., k-1$ and hence to $\text{ord}(\gamma) \geqslant k$. □

Note that when A is cyclic, the order of an element γg ($\gamma \in \mathbb{Z}, g$ a generator of A) is simply $M/\gcd(\gamma, M)$ and Lawrie's result follows. The following observation leads perhaps to the most compelling reason for the restriction to linear skewing schemes in practice.

Theorem 3.25 *Let s be a periodic skewing scheme using M memory banks, and suppose s yields conflict-free access to some γ-ordered k-vector for $k > M/2$. Then s is linear.*

Proof By proposition 3.20 we have $\text{ord}(\gamma) > M/2$ and, because $\text{ord}(\gamma) | M$ by elementary group theory, it follows that $\text{ord}(\gamma) = M$. Thus γ is a generator of A, and A is cyclic. The result now follows from proposition 3.18.

□

We conclude that if we want a periodic skewing scheme to be conflict-free on even a single row (or column or diagonal) of a $M \times ... \times M$ matrix, then the skewing scheme is necessarily linear. See section 3.1 for a further analysis of this case.

3.2.3.2 The Classification of Periodic Skewing Schemes

In order to work out the program for classifying the periodic skewing schemes as suggested in section 3.2.3.1 we have to delve deeply into the structure of finite abelian groups. First we review the (known) facts concerning the isomorphism types of finite abelian groups, which will enable us to derive the connection between periodic skewing schemes and d-tuples of linear forms rather directly (cf. section 3.2.2.2). Next we derive a characterization of Aut(A). The results will be used in section 3.2.3.3 to prove a normal form theorem for periodic skewing schemes, thus completing the classification effort.

Let A be an arbitrary finite abelian group of M elements, and let $M = p_1^{e_1} \dots p_r^{e_r}$ (the factorization of M into distinct primes). A has a unique decomposition as a direct sum $A = A_1 \oplus \dots \oplus A_r$, where the A_i are abelian p-groups of coprime order. (In fact, for $1 \leqslant i \leqslant r$, A_i is the Sylow subgroup of order $p_i^{e_i}$). For $1 \leqslant i \leqslant r$, let $\pi_i : A \twoheadrightarrow A_i$ be the implied projection morphism. For a periodic skewing scheme (or: epimorphism) $s : \mathbf{Z}^d \twoheadrightarrow A$, let $s_i = \pi_i \circ s$.

Proposition 3.21 *The mapping $s \mapsto (s_1, \dots, s_r)$ is a bijection between the set of all periodic schemes $s : \mathbf{Z}^d \twoheadrightarrow A$ and the set of all r-tuples $(t_1, \dots, t_r)$ of periodic skewing schemes $t_i : \mathbf{Z}^d \twoheadrightarrow A_i$ $(1 \leqslant i \leqslant r)$.*

We also note that Aut(A) =Aut(A_1) $\otimes \dots \otimes$Aut(A_r) and that, consequently, two periodic skewing schemes s and s' are conjugate under Aut(A) if and only if the corresponding s_i and s_i' are conjugate under Aut(A_i) for $1 \leqslant i \leqslant r$. This shows that the classification of periodic skewing schemes $s : \mathbf{Z}^d \twoheadrightarrow A$ reduces to the case where A can be assumed to be a finite abelian p-group.

To complete the description we note that a finite abelian p-group can be uniquely decomposed as the direct sum of cyclic p-groups. Hence $A_i \cong \mathbf{Z}_{p_i^{e_{i1}}} \oplus \dots \oplus \mathbf{Z}_{p_i^{e_{id}}}$ for suitable $e_{i1} \geqslant \dots \geqslant e_{id} \geqslant 0$ with $e_{i1} + \dots + e_{id} = e_i$ and $1 \leqslant i \leqslant r$, and assuming that A is a d-generator group. (The $p_i^{e_{i1}}, \dots, p_i^{e_{id}}$ are know as the invariant factors of the abelian p-group.) For $1 \leqslant i \leqslant d$, let $f_j = p_1^{e_{1j}} \dots p_r^{e_{rj}}$ denote the "invariant factors" of A. Observe that $f_{j+1} | f_j$ for $1 \leqslant j < d$ and by the Chinese Remainder Theorem one also has $\mathbf{Z}_{f_j} \cong \mathbf{Z}_{p_1^{e_{1j}}} \oplus \dots \oplus \mathbf{Z}_{p_r^{e_{rj}}}$. It follows that $A \cong \mathbf{Z}_{f_1} \oplus \dots \oplus \mathbf{Z}_{f_d}$, a direct sum of cyclic groups.

Theorem 3.26 (cf. theorem 3.23) *Every periodic skewing scheme $s : \mathbf{Z}^d \twoheadrightarrow A$ can be uniquely represented by a d-tuple $(L_1 \bmod f_1, \dots, L_d \bmod f_d)$, where L_1 through L_d are integer linear forms and f_1 through f_d are the invariant factors of A.*

Proof s uniquely corresponds to the d-tuple $(\bar{s}_1, ..., \bar{s}_d)$, where $\bar{s}_j = \pi_j \circ s$ and $\pi_j : A \twoheadrightarrow \mathbf{Z}_{f_j}$ are the projections corresponding to the composition above $(1 \leqslant j \leqslant d)$. By proposition 3.18 every $\bar{s}_j$ is a linear skewing scheme. □

Note that the component expressions for s are built up, using the Chinese Remainder Theorem, from the (linear) expressions corresponding to the projected skewing schemes: $\mathbf{Z}^d \twoheadrightarrow \mathbf{Z}_{p_k^{e_{kj}}}$ $(1 \leqslant k \leqslant r, 1 \leqslant j \leqslant d)$, which are all linear skewing schemes by proposition 3.18.

Restricting to the case of finite abelian p-groups A, assume that $A \cong \mathbf{Z}_{p^{e_1}} \oplus ... \oplus \mathbf{Z}_{p^{e_m}}$ for suitable $e_1 \geqslant ... \geqslant e_m > 0$ and $m \leqslant d$. For classifying the periodic skewing schemes in A's isomorphism type, we need a precise understanding of the action of Aut(A). Write the elements α of A as vectors $\alpha = (\alpha_1, ..., \alpha_m)^T$, where α_i is the residue of α in $\mathbf{Z}_{p^{e_i}}$ $(1 \leqslant i \leqslant m)$. A general result due to Shoda [Sho28, Satz 1] is the following.

Theorem 3.27 *The automorphisms of A can be represented by $m \times m$ matrices $\chi = (x_{ij})$ with columns that are generators of A and $p^{e_i - e_j} | x_{ij}$ for $i \leqslant j$.*

The action of χ on A and the composition of two automorphisms are derived from the usual matrix-vector and matrix-matrix product. A matrix χ represents a proper automorphism of A if and only if det $\chi \not\equiv 0 \pmod p$.

Theorem 3.28 *Let $A \cong \mathbf{Z}_{p^{e_1}} \oplus ... \oplus \mathbf{Z}_{p^{e_m}}$ be a finite abelian p-group, with $e_1 \geqslant ... \geqslant e_m > 0$. Aut$(A)$ is generated by all automorphisms ("matrices") χ having one of the following forms:*

(a) *χ interchanges the ith and j^{th} component of elements, for fixed i and j with $e_i = e_j$.*

(b) *χ multiplies a single (fixed) component of elements by a (fixed) integer $\not\equiv 0 \pmod p$.*

(c) *χ adds an integer multiple of the jth component to the ith component of elements, using a (fixed) integer multiplier divisible by $\lceil p^{e_i - e_j} \rceil$.*

Proof One easily verifies that the mappings χ of the form (a), (b) and (c) are automorphisms of A. Consider any automorphism of A and view it, using theorem 3.27, as a matrix $\chi = (x_{ij})$ with $p^{e_i - e_j} | x_{ij}$ for $i \leqslant j$ and det $\chi \not\equiv 0 \pmod p$. By repeated premultiplication with matrices of type (a), (b) and (c) one can transform χ into the identity matrix, by following a suitable version of the Gauss-Jordan algorithm. Thus the automorphisms of type (a), (b) and (c) generate Aut(A). □

3.2.3.3 A Normal Form for (General) Periodic Skewing Schemes

Let $s : \mathbb{Z}^d \twoheadrightarrow A$ be any d-dimensional periodic skewing scheme. By proposition 3.21 we may assume that A is a finite abelian p-group, and (hence) $A \cong \mathbb{Z}_{p^{e_1}} \oplus ... \oplus \mathbb{Z}_{p^{e_m}}$ for suitable $e_1 \geqslant ... \geqslant e_m > 0$ and $m \leqslant d$. As $\mathbb{Z}^d$ is a free abelian group (of rank d), the homomorphisms from $\mathbb{Z}^d$ to A uniquely correspond to the $m \times d$ matrices $T = (t_{ij})$ with $t_{ij} \in \mathbb{Z}_{p^{e_i}}$ whose columns can be regarded as the elements of A that are the images of the standard basis of $\mathbb{Z}^d$. A matrix T of this form represents a periodic skewing scheme (an epimorphism) if and only if the columns of T generate A. To obtain a classification of the periodic skewing schemes $s : \mathbb{Z}^d \twoheadrightarrow A$, we must classify the matrices T modulo the action of the automorphisms of A as described in theorem 3.27. The normal forms will be suitable representatives from the resulting equivalence classes.

For the analysis we have to delve into the subgroup structure of the component p-groups $\mathbb{Z}_{p^e}$ of A. A cyclic p-group $\mathbb{Z}_{p^e}$ has precisely $e+1$ subgroups, which are all cyclic p-groups and form a "tower" (or: a composition series). In fact, they are precisely the subgroups $p^k.\mathbb{Z}_{p^e}$ (generated by p^k) for $k = 0, 1, ..., e$. For $i \leqslant j$, let C_{ij} be a fixed system of coset representations of $p^{e_i - e_j}.\mathbb{Z}_{p^{e_i}}$ in $\mathbb{Z}_{p^{e_i}}$ and let $\tilde{C}_{ij}$ be a fixed system of coset representatives of $p^{e_i - e_j}.\mathbb{Z}_{p^{e_i}}$ in $p.\mathbb{Z}_{p^{e_i}}$. One may take $C_{ij} = \{0, 1, 2, ..., p^{e_i - e_j} - 1\}$ and, provided $e_i > e_j$, $\tilde{C}_{ij} = \{0, p, 2p, ... p^{e_i - e_j} - p\}$. If $e_i = e_j$ we let $\tilde{C}_{ij} = \{0\}$. Hence $|C_{ij}| = p^{e_i - e_j}$ and $|\tilde{C}_{ij}| = \lceil p^{e_i - e_j - 1} \rceil$.

Let $s : \mathbb{Z}^d \twoheadrightarrow A$ be a periodic skewing scheme, and T the matrix representing s. Denote the jth column of T by T_j $(1 \leqslant j \leqslant d)$.

Definition 3.16 *s is said to have normal form if the following properties hold:*

(i) there are columns indices $j_1, ..., j_m$ (written such that $j_k < j_l$ whenever $e_k = e_l$ and $k < l$) such that $T_{j_k} = (x_1, ..., x_{k-1}, 1, 0, ..., 0)^T$, with $x_i \in C_{ik}$ if $j_i < j_k$ and $x_i \in \tilde{C}_{ik}$ if $j_i > j_k$ for $1 \leqslant i < k$.

(ii) for every column index $j \notin \{j_1, ..., j_m\}$ and corresponding column $T_j = (x_1, ..., x_m)^T$ one has $x_i \in \mathbb{Z}_{p^{e_i}}$ if $j_i < j$ and $x_i \in p.\mathbb{Z}_{p^{e_i}}$ if $j_i > j$, for $1 \leqslant i \leqslant m$.

In the definition the columns $j_1, ..., j_m$ are called the basis columns of s (or: of T), and the remaining columns are called the non-basis columns of s. For every k $(1 \leqslant k \leqslant m)$ the index j_k refers to the left-most column of T having a generator of $\mathbb{Z}_{p^{e_k}}$ in its kth component. (Hence, trivially, the basis columns of T generate A.)

Theorem 3.29 *(Normal Form Theorem)*

(i) Every periodic skewing scheme $s : \mathbb{Z}^d \twoheadrightarrow A$ is equivalent to a periodic skewing scheme that has normal form.

(ii) Different periodic skewing schemes in normal form are not equivalent.

Proof (By proposition 3.17 two periodic skewing schemes $s_{1,2} : \mathbb{Z}^d \twoheadrightarrow A$ are equivalent if and only if s_1 and s_2 are conjugate under the action of Aut(A).)

(*i*) Let $s : \mathbb{Z}^d \twoheadrightarrow A$ be an arbitrary periodic skewing scheme, and T the $m \times d$ matrix representing s. We show that s can be transformed to normal form by a step-wise procedure, using the action of suitably chosen automorphisms of type (a), (b) and (c) (cf. theorem 3.28).

As the columns of T generate A, there must be a column of maximal order in A. Choose j_1 to be the index of the leftmost column of this kind, necessarily containing a generator of $\mathbb{Z}_{p^{e_1}}$ among its components. Use operations of type (a) and (b) to obtain an entry 1 in the first position of the column, and use operations of type (c) to make the lower entries vanish. Proceeding inductively, assume that we have obtained columns $j_1, ..., j_k$ as required in the normal form. Let $k < m$. Because the columns of T generate A and observing the structure of the columns $j_1, ..., j_k$, there must be a leftmost column j_{k+1} in T which has an entry in one of the components $k+1, k+2, ...$ which generates $\mathbb{Z}_{p^{e_{k+1}}}$. Use operations of type (a), (b) and (c) as before to obtain an entry 1 in position $k+1$ of the column and zeroes below it. (Note that these operations do not affect the structure of the columns $j_1, ..., j_k$ because they are zero in all positions $\geqslant k+1$.) As for the upper entries of column j_{k+1}, we observe the following. Let x_i be the entry in position i, for some $i < k+1$. Suppose that $x_i \notin p.\mathbb{Z}_{p^{e_i}}$, i.e., x_i is a generator of $\mathbb{Z}_{p^{e_i}}$, but $j_i > j_{k+1}$. This contradicts the choice of j_i. Hence we can use operations of type (c) in order to change the upper entries into coset representatives of the desired characteristic. (Note that again the structure of the columns $j_1, ..., j_k$ is not affected by these operations.) By continuing this process T is transformed to normal form.

(*ii*) Let $s, s' : \mathbb{Z}^d \twoheadrightarrow A$ be different periodic skewing schemes and T, T' the corresponding matrices, and suppose that both s and s' have normal form. We show that s and s' cannot be conjugate under the action of Aut(A).

Let $j_1, ..., j_m$ and $j'_1, ..., j'_m$ be the indexes of the basis columns of T and T', respectively. Suppose that the two sequences are not equal, i.e., let $j_1 = j'_1, ..., j_{i-1} = j'_{i-1}$ but $j_i \neq j'_i$ for some $1 \leqslant i \leqslant m$. Without loss of generality, let $j_i < j'_i$. By the structure of the basis columns it follows that $T_{j_1}, ..., T_{j_i}$ generate a subgroup of A whose order is greater than the order of the subgroup generated by $T'_{j_1}, ..., T'_{j_i}$. In this case T and T' cannot be conjugate under Aut(A). Suppose next that the two index sequences are equal, i.e., $j_i = j'_i$ for every $1 \leqslant i \leqslant m$. We show that any automorphism χ $\in$Aut(A) that maps the basis $T_{j_1}, ..., T_{j_m}$ (of A) onto the basis $T'_{j_1}, ..., T'_{j_m}$ (of A) must be the identity. Clearly T_{j_1} and $T'_{j_1} = \chi(T_{j_1})$ coincide, as both are equal to the first unit vector. Proceeding inductively, assume that T_{j_i} and $T'_{j_i} = \chi(T_{j_i})$ coincide for $i = 1, ..., k$. Let $k < m$. By order considerations we have $T'_{j_{k+1}} = \chi(T_{j_{k+1}})$. Because of the structure of the basis columns, there exist integer coefficients x_i $(1 \leqslant i \leqslant k)$ such that $T_{j_{k+1}} = u_{k+1} + \sum_1^k x_i.T_{j_i}$ (where u_{k+1} is the $(k+1)^{st}$ unit vector). It follows that $\chi(T_{j_{k+1}}) = \chi(u_{k+1}) + \sum_1^k x_i.\chi(T_{j_i}) = \chi(u_{k+1}) + \sum_1^k x_i.T_{j_i}$ and (hence) $T'_{j_{k+1}} - T_{j_{k+1}} = \chi(u_{k+1}) - u_{k+1}$. By theorem 3.27 (applied to χ) we conclude that the coset representatives in the upper diagonal positions of $T'_{j_{k+1}}$ and $T_{j_{k+1}}$ necessarily coincide. Thus $T_{j_{k+1}}$ and $T'_{j_{k+1}} = \chi(T_{j_{k+1}})$ coincide as complete vectors. By induction we conclude that χ must be the identity. This contradicts that s and s' are different. □

We conclude from theorem 3.29 that every periodic skewing scheme can be transformed to a unique (equivalent) normal form.

The existence of unique normal forms is useful for counting the number of "essentially different", i.e., non-equivalent, periodic skewing schemes. As an example, we count the number of non-equivalent periodic skewing schemes $s : \mathbb{Z}^d \twoheadrightarrow A$ where the underlying p-group A has the form $A \cong \mathbb{Z}_{p^e} \oplus ... \oplus \mathbb{Z}_{p^e}$ (m summands). One verifies that the normal forms are $m \times d$ matrices of the following form:

$$\begin{pmatrix}
y & .. & y & 1 & x & .. & x & 0 & x & .. & x & 0 & x & \cdots & \cdots & x & 0 & x & .. & x \\
y & .. & y & 0 & y & .. & y & 1 & x & .. & x & 0 & x & \cdots & \cdots & x & 0 & x & .. & x \\
\vdots & & \vdots & \vdots & y & .. & y & 0 & y & .. & y & 1 & x & \cdots & & \vdots & \vdots & \vdots & & \vdots \\
 & & & & \vdots & & \vdots & \vdots & y & .. & y & 0 & y & \cdots & & & & & & \\
 & & & & & & & & \vdots & & \vdots & \vdots & \vdots & & & & & & & \\
 & & & & & & & & & & & & & & & \vdots & \vdots & \vdots & & \vdots \\
\vdots & & \vdots & \vdots & \vdots & & \vdots & \vdots & \vdots & & \vdots & \vdots & \vdots & & \cdots & x & 0 & x & .. & x \\
y & .. & y & 0 & y & .. & y & 0 & y & .. & y & 0 & y & \cdots & \cdots & y & 1 & x & .. & x
\end{pmatrix}$$

where the basis columns (unit vectors in this case) occur in m selected positions $j_1, ..., j_m$ and the x's and y's denote arbitrary elements of $\mathbb{Z}_{p^e}$ and $p.\mathbb{Z}_{p^e}$, respectively. Every matrix (in normal form) represents a unique equivalence class of periodic skewing schemes, and conversely. The number of different normal forms is seen to be

$$\sum_{j_0<j_1<\ldots<j_m<j_{m+1}} \prod_{i=0}^{m} p^{(j_{i+1}-j_i-1)(i.e+(m-i)(e-1))}$$

where $j_0 = 0$ and $j_{m+1} = d+1$ are fixed and the summation ranges over all choices of $j_1, \ldots, j_m$. Further manipulations shows this number to be equal to

$$p^{(d-m)(m-1)(e+1)+\frac{1}{2}m(m-1)+d} \cdot \sum_{0<j_1<\ldots<j_m<d+1} \frac{1}{p^{j_1+\ldots+j_m}}.$$

3.2.3.4 The Number of Non-Equivalent Linear Skewing Schemes

In section 3.1.1 it is shown that the number of non-equivalent linear skewing schemes in the usual 2-dimensional case is surprisingly small and bounded by $O(M \text{ loglog } M)$, where M is the number of memory banks being used. In this section we apply our results on normal forms to obtain a precise expression for the number of non-equivalent linear skewing schemes in the general case and a feasible procedure for enumerating these schemes.

In section 3.2.3.1 we defined a linear skewing scheme to be any epimorphism $s : \mathbf{Z}^d \twoheadrightarrow \mathbf{Z}_M$. Let $M = p_1^{e_1} \ldots p_r^{e_r}$ (the factorization of M into distinct primes). By the Chinese Remainder Theorem $\mathbf{Z}_M$ can be decomposed as a direct sum $\mathbf{Z}_M = \mathbf{Z}_{p_1^{e_1}} \oplus \ldots \oplus \mathbf{Z}_{p_r^{e_r}}$. Every (projected) linear skewing scheme $s_i = \pi_i \circ s : \mathbf{Z}^d \twoheadrightarrow \mathbf{Z}_{p_i^{e_i}}$ can be described by a $1 \times d$ matrix T_i whose (single) row contains at least one component that is a generator of $\mathbf{Z}_{p_i^{e_i}}$. Observe that the results of section 3.2.3.3 apply (use $m = 1$, a direct approach is given in [Tap]). It follows that the non-equivalent s_i's can be enumerated by simply enumerating the normal forms, which are described as the $1 \times d$ matrices of the type $(y_1, \ldots, y_{j-1}, 1, x_{j+1}, \ldots, x_d)$ with $1 \leqslant j \leqslant d$, $x_k \in \mathbf{Z}_{p_i^{e_i}}$ $(j+1 \leqslant k \leqslant d)$, and $y_k \in p_i.\mathbf{Z}_{p_i^{e_i}}$ $(1 \leqslant k \leqslant j-1)$. According to proposition 3.21 and the arguments in section 3.2.3.2, the combinations of normal forms for the s_i $(1 \leqslant i \leqslant r)$ precisely characterize the equivalence classes of linear skewing schemes s. The enumeration of the non-equivalent linear skewing schemes now follows by a trivial algorithm.

Theorem 3.30 *The number of non-equivalent linear skewing schemes* $s : \mathbf{Z}^d \twoheadrightarrow \mathbf{Z}_M$ *is bounded by*

$$M^{d-1} \cdot \prod_{i=1}^{r} \frac{p_i}{p_i - 1}.$$

Proof There are precisely $\sum_{j=1}^{d} p_i^{(d-1)e_i-j+1} = (p_i^{e_i})^{d-1} \sum_{j=1}^{d} \frac{1}{p_i^{j-1}} = (p_i^{e_i})^{d-1} \cdot \frac{1-1/p_i^d}{1-1/p_i}$ different normal forms for every s_i $(1 \leqslant i \leqslant r)$. The number of non-equivalent linear skewing schemes is thus given by

$$\prod_{i=1}^{r} (p_i^{e_i})^{d-1} \cdot \frac{1-1/p_i^d}{1-1/p_i} = M^{d-1} \cdot \prod_{i=1}^{r} \frac{1-1/p_i^d}{1-1/p_i} < M^{d-1} \cdot \prod_{i=1}^{r} \frac{p_i}{p_i-1}.$$

□

Corollary 3.13 *The number of non-equivalent linear skewing schemes $s : Z^d \twoheadrightarrow Z_M$ is bounded by $O(M^{d-1} \log\log M)$.*

Proof Let $q_1, \ldots, q_r$ be the first r primes. From number theory it is known that there are constants c_1 and c_2 such that $\prod_1^r \frac{q_i}{q_i-1} \leqslant c_1 . \log q_r$ and $q_r \leqslant c_2 . r . \log r$. It follows that

$$\prod_1^r \frac{p_i}{p_i-1} \leqslant \prod_1^r \frac{q_i}{q_i-1} = O(\log r).$$

Clearly $r \leqslant \log M$, and the result follows by applying theorem 3.30. □

3.3 Multi-Periodic Skewing Schemes

In a hierarchically structured model of computation, see section 1.3, it is obvious that one should not consider all the instances of a certain template P, but only those which do not overlap too much. For, whenever a particular instance of P has been processed, it is likely that this instance is still kept in the data-buffers of the uppermost level. If the next instance of P which has to be processed overlaps the previous instance, then only the non-overlapped part of it needs to be fetched from the lower levels.

For this purpose, we shall consider only those instances $P(x)$ of P, with $x \in L$ and L a lattice $\subseteq Z^d$.

Definition 3.17 *Let L be a lattice $\subseteq Z^d$. A skewing scheme s is L-valid for P iff $\forall x \in L : s \restriction P(x)$ is an injection.*

Actually L is the base-set B_P of P, see definition 1.1. It appears that for commonly used templates P there always exists a lattice $L \subseteq Z^d$, such that

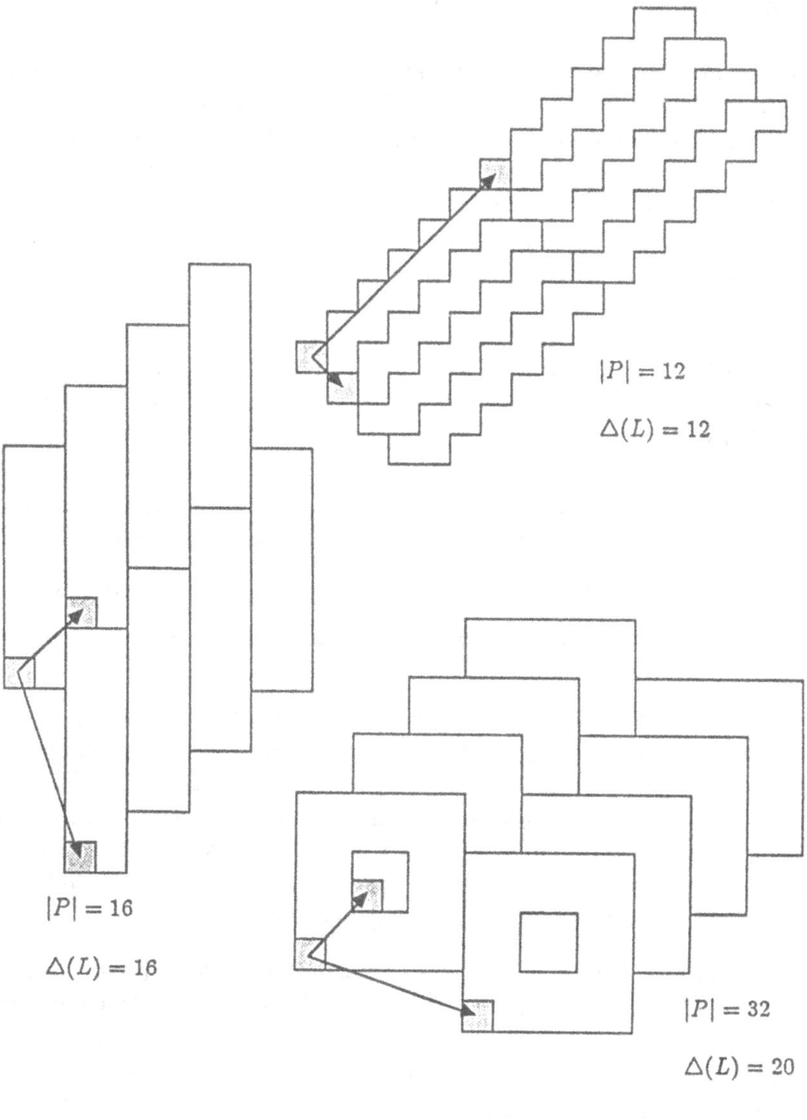

Figure 3.2: Some templates with corresponding lattices.

(i) $\Delta(L) = \Omega(|P|)$, and
(ii) for all $y \in Z^d$ there exists a $x \in L$ such that $y \in P(x)$.
See figure 3.2 for some examples (d=2).

In section 3.3.1 we show that periodic skewing schemes are too strong for just obtaining L-validity. Therefore we introduce a weaker and more general version of these schemes: the multi-periodic skewing schemes. It turns out that the multi-periodic skewing schemes also are an extension of the diamond schemes of Jalby et al. [JFJ84], and thus appear to be a suitable unified class of schemes for a great variety of purposes. We show in section 3.3.2 that multi-periodic schemes are quite suitable for skewing a collection of templates, such that they are L-valid for this collection of templates. In section 3.3.3 we show that multi-periodic skewing schemes can be compactly represented, like ordinary periodic schemes. Other studies which address this issue can be found in [JFJ84,FJL85]. All results presented in this section are from [TW85].

3.3.1 Multi-Periodic Skewing Schemes and Their Relationship with Other Compact Skewing Schemes

The following proposition is a direct generalization of proposition 3.9.

Proposition 3.22 *Given a periodic skewing scheme s, a template P and a lattice $L \subseteq Z^d$. Then s is L-valid for P iff s is valid for P.*

From proposition 3.22 follows that, while the property of L-validity is weaker than unrestricted validity, the two notions are equivalent for periodic skewing schemes. To take full advantage of the weaker requirement of L-validity we need a class of skewing schemes, which are as attractive as the periodic skewing schemes, but which are not as strictly tied to the lattice structure. The skewing schemes which fit these conditions are the multi-periodic skewing schemes, introduced in the following definitions.

Definition 3.18 *Let $L \subseteq Z^d$ be a lattice, with basis $\{\vec{x}_1, \vec{x}_2, ..., \vec{x}_d\}$. For every $a \in Z^d$ let $a + L = \{a + x | \ x \in L\} \cong Z^d$. Let η^a_L be the isomorphism: $\eta^a_L : a + L \rightarrow Z^d$, with $\eta^a_L(a + i_1.\vec{x}_1 + i_2.\vec{x}_2 + ... + i_d.\vec{x}_d) = (i_1, i_2, ..., i_d)$. The a-reduced skewing scheme s^a_L of a skewing scheme $s : Z^d \rightarrow \{0, 1, ..., M-1\}$ is defined by s^a_L: $Z^d \rightarrow A$, $A \subseteq \{0, 1, ..., M-1\}$, and $s^a_L(y) = s((\eta^a_L)^{-1}(y))$.*

Definition 3.19 *A skewing scheme $s : Z^d \rightarrow \{0, 1, ..., M-1\}$ is called multi-periodic if there exists a lattice $L \subseteq Z^d$ such that for all $a \in Z^d$: s^a_L is periodic. (L is called the underlying lattice of s.)*

Note that the periodic skewing schemes are multi-periodic.

Proposition 3.23 *Given a skewing scheme $s : \mathbb{Z}^d \to \{0, 1, ..., M-1\}$. If s is periodic, then s is multi-periodic.*

Proof Take $L = \mathbb{Z}^d$. □

We show that the multi-periodic skewing schemes are an extension of the diamond schemes as well. Diamond schemes were introduced by Jalby et al.[JFJ84]. We give the definition in our lattice-framework. Let S_M be the symmetric group, i.e., the group of permutations on M elements.

Definition 3.20 *A skewing scheme $s : \mathbb{Z}^d \to \{0, 1, ..., M-1\}$ is called a diamond scheme iff there exists a lattice $L \subseteq \mathbb{Z}^d$ with basis $\{\vec{x}_1, \vec{x}_2, ..., \vec{x}_d\}$, and d commuting permutations $\lambda_1, \lambda_2, ..., \lambda_d \in S_M$ such that for all $x \in \mathbb{Z}^d$ and for all $1 \leqslant i \leqslant d : s(x + \vec{x}_i) = \lambda_i(s(x))$. (L is called the underlying lattice of s.)*

Jalby et al.[JFJ84] actually defined the diamond schemes only for the case that the underlying lattice L is defined by an orthogonal basis. In order to prove that the multi-periodic schemes are an extension of the diamond schemes, we need the following characterization of periodic schemes.

Lemma 3.9 *Let $s : \mathbb{Z}^d \to \{0, 1, ..., M-1\}$ be a skewing scheme using M memory banks. Then s is periodic iff $\forall x \in \mathbb{Z}^d \ \exists \sigma_x \in S_M \ \forall y \in \mathbb{Z}^d : s(y + x) = \sigma_x(s(y))$.*

Proof The proof makes use of the following fact.

Fact 3.3 [lemma 3.7] *A skewing scheme s is periodic iff for all $x, y \in \mathbb{Z}^d$: if $s(x) = s(y)$, then for all x', y', with $x' - y' = x - y : s(x') = s(y')$.*

$\Rightarrow$ Let s be a periodic skewing scheme, and $x \in \mathbb{Z}^d$. Define σ_x as follows: if $s(y) = p, y \in \mathbb{Z}^d$, then $\sigma_x(p) = s(x + y)$. This definition is sound because, if $s(y) = p$ and $s(z) = p$ for $y \neq z$ then from fact 3.3 follows that $s(x + y) = s(x + z)$. It is obvious that σ_x fits the conditions.
$\Leftarrow$ Let y, z, y', z' be such that $s(y) = s(z)$ and $y' - z' = y - z$. Define $x = y' - y \ (= z' - z)$. Then $s(y') = \sigma_x(s(y))$ and $s(z') = \sigma_x(s(z))$. Hence $s(y') = s(z')$. From fact 3.3 it follows that s is periodic. □

Let Ran(s_L^q) denote the set $\{s_L^q(x) \mid x \in \mathbb{Z}^d\}$.

Theorem 3.31 *Let s be a skewing scheme defined on $\mathbb{Z}^d$. s is a diamond scheme with underlying lattice L iff*
(i) s is a multi-periodic skewing scheme with underlying lattice L, and
(ii) for all $a, b \in \mathbb{Z}^d$, with $a \not\equiv_L b$ is valid that Ran(s_L^a)$\cap$ Ran(s_L^b) $= \emptyset$ *, or, there exists a $y \in \mathbb{Z}^d$ such that for all $x \in \mathbb{Z}^d : s_L^b(x) = s_L^a(x+y)$.*

Proof $\Rightarrow$ Let $s : \mathbb{Z}^d \to \{0, 1, ..., M-1\}$ be a diamond scheme. Then there exist a d-dimensional lattice $L \subseteq \mathbb{Z}^d$ with basis $\{\vec{x}_1, \vec{x}_2, ..., \vec{x}_d\}$ and d commuting permutations $\lambda_1, \lambda_2, ..., \lambda_d \in S_M$, such that $\forall x \in \mathbb{Z}^d \, \forall 1 \leqslant i \leqslant d :$ $s(x + \vec{x}_i) = \lambda_i(s(x))$.

Consider an arbitrary $a \in \mathbb{Z}^d$. Then s_L^a: $\mathbb{Z}^d \to A_a$, $A_a \subseteq \{0, 1, ..., M-1\}$, and $s_L^a(x + \vec{e}_i) = \lambda_i(s_L^a(x))$, with $\{\vec{e}_1, \vec{e}_2, ..., \vec{e}_d\}$ the orthonormal basis of $\mathbb{Z}^d$. So given $y \in \mathbb{Z}^d$, y arbitrary, we can define $\sigma_y = \lambda_1^{y_1}\lambda_2^{y_2}....\lambda_d^{y_d}$, such that for all $x \in \mathbb{Z}^d : s_L^a(x+y) = \sigma_y(s_L^a(x))$. From lemma 3.9 it follows that s_L^a is a periodic skewing scheme. Consider Ran(s_L^a) and Ran(s_L^b), for $a, b \in \mathbb{Z}^d$. Then

$$\begin{aligned} \text{Ran}(s_L^a) &= \{\lambda_1^{i_1}\lambda_2^{i_2}...\lambda_d^{i_d}s(a) | \, i_1, i_2, ..., i_d \in \mathbb{Z}\} \text{ and} \\ \text{Ran}(s_L^b) &= \{\lambda_1^{i_1}\lambda_2^{i_2}...\lambda_d^{i_d}s(b) | \, i_1, i_2, ..., i_d \in \mathbb{Z}\}. \end{aligned}$$

Suppose Ran(s_L^a)$\cap$ Ran(s_L^b) $\neq \emptyset$. Then $s(b) \in$ Ran(s_L^a) and Ran(s_L^a) $=$ Ran(s_L^b). So there exist $i_1^*, i_2^*, ..., i_d^*$ such that $s(b) = \lambda_1^{i_1^*}.\lambda_2^{i_2^*}.....\lambda_d^{i_d^*}s(a)$. Take $y = (i_1^*, i_2^*, ..., i_d^*) \in \mathbb{Z}^d$. Then for all $x \in \mathbb{Z}^d$, $x = (x_1, x_2, ..., x_d)$:

$$\begin{aligned} s_L^b(x) = (s_L^b)(x_1, x_2, ..., x_d) &= s((\eta_L^b)^{-1}(x_1, x_2, ..., x_d)) \\ &= s(b + x_1\vec{x}_1 + x_2\vec{x}_2 + ... + x_d\vec{x}_d) \\ &= \lambda_1^{x_1}\lambda_2^{x_2}...\lambda_d^{x_d}s(b) \\ &= \lambda_1^{x_1+i_1^*}\lambda_2^{x_2+i_2^*}...\lambda_d^{x_d+i_d^*}s(a) \\ &= s(a + (x_1 + i_1^*)\vec{x}_1 + (x_2 + i_2^*)\vec{x}_2 + ... \\ &\quad +(x_d + i_d^*)\vec{x}_d) \\ &= s((\eta_L^a)^{-1}(x_1 + i_1^*, x_2 + i_2^*, ..., x_d + i_d^*)) \\ &= s_L^a(x+y) \end{aligned}$$

$\Leftarrow$ Let $s : \mathbb{Z}^d \to \{0, 1, ..., M-1\}$ be a multi-periodic skewing scheme, which satisfies the constraints of the theorem. Consider $a \in \{0, 1, ..., M-1\}$. From the periodicity of each s_L^a and from the constraints it follows that for all $x, y \in s^{-1}(a)$ and $z \in L : s(x+z) = s(y+z)$. Define $\lambda_1, \lambda_2, ..., \lambda_d \in S_M$ by $\lambda_i(a) = s(x + \vec{x}_i)$, for some $x \in s^{-1}(a)$. The soundness of this definition follows from the previous statement. And furthermore it is obvious that for all $x \in \mathbb{Z}^d, 1 \leqslant i \leqslant d : s(x + \vec{x}_i) = \lambda_i(s(x))$. □

Actually the set of permutations $\{\lambda_1^{i_1}\lambda_2^{i_2}...\lambda_d^{i_d} | \, i_1, i_2, ..., i_d \in \mathbb{Z}\}$ is a subgroup of S_M. And, hence, $\mathrm{Ran}(s_L^c) = \{\lambda_1^{i_1}\lambda_2^{i_2}...\lambda_d^{i_d}s(c) | \, i_1, i_2, ..., i_d \in \mathbb{Z}\}$ forms an orbit of the set $\{0, 1, ..., M-1\}$, for arbitrary $c \in \mathbb{Z}^d$. From elementary group theory it is known that the set of orbits form a partition of the set $\{0, 1, ..., M-1\}$.

Corollary 3.14 *If s is a periodic skewing scheme, then s is a diamond scheme.*

Proof From proposition 3.23 it follows that s is multi-periodic and s obviously satisfies the conditions of theorem 3.31. □

In the remainder of this section we shall examine the definition of the multi-periodic skewing schemes more thoroughly. We could for instance, extend these skewing schemes as well, by requiring that the s_L^a's are not strictly periodic, but multi-periodic themselves. Call these schemes multi-multi-periodic.

Definition 3.21 *A skewing scheme $s : \mathbb{Z}^d \to \{0, 1, ..., M-1\}$ is called multi-multi-periodic if there exists a lattice $L \subseteq \mathbb{Z}^d$ (the underlying lattice of s) such that for all $a \in \mathbb{Z}^d$: s_L^a is periodic, or, for all $a \in \mathbb{Z}^d$: s_L^a is multi-multi-periodic and all the s_L^a's have the same underlying lattice.*

Although it is not immediately obvious, we do not achieve anything with this extension. Every multi-multi-periodic scheme is just multi-periodic.

Lemma 3.10 *Let $s : \mathbb{Z}^d \to \{0, 1, ..., M-1\}$ be a skewing scheme. Then s is multi-multi-periodic iff s is multi-periodic.*

Proof Let $s : \mathbb{Z}^d \to \{0, 1, ..., M-1\}$ be multi-multi-periodic (write ${}^0s$ for s). Then $\exists t \geqslant 0$, such that for arbitrary $a \in \mathbb{Z}^d$: ${}^0s, {}^0s_L^a$ (write ${}^1s$), ${}^1s_L^a$ (write ${}^2s$), ..., ${}^ts_L^a$ (write ${}^{t+1}s$) are multi-multi-periodic but not periodic, and ${}^{t+1}s_L^a$ is periodic. Let $L_0, L_1, ..., L_t$ be lattices $\subseteq \mathbb{Z}^d$ such that L_i is the underlying lattice of ${}^is$, and let for each i : $\{\vec{x}_1^{(i)}, \vec{x}_2^{(i)}, ..., \vec{x}_d^{(i)}\}$ be a basis of L_i. Define the $d \times d$ matrices $A_0, A_1, ..., A_t$ by

$$A_0 = (\vec{x}_1 \, \vec{x}_2 \, ... \, \vec{x}_d)$$

and for all $1 \leqslant i \leqslant t$:

$$A_i = (A_{i-1}(\vec{x}_1^{(i)}) \; A_{i-1}(\vec{x}_2^{(i)}) \; ... \; A_{i-1}(\vec{x}_d^{(i)}))$$

Define the lattice L, with basis $\{\vec{x}_1, \vec{x}_2, ..., \vec{x}_d\}$, by $\vec{x}_j = A_t(\vec{x}_j^{(t)})$, then from definition 3.21 follows that for all $a \in \mathbb{Z}^d$: s_L^a is periodic, which ends the proof. □

Lemma 3.10 will be of use in the next section, where we shall study the L-validity of multi-periodic skewing schemes.

3.3.2 The L-Validity of Multi-Periodic Skewing Schemes

In this section we show that the multi-periodic skewing schemes lend themselves quite well for the L-valid skewing of one ore more templates P. We first need some notions.

Definition 3.22 *Given a collection of templates $C = \{P_1, P_2, ..., P_t\}$ and a lattice $L \subseteq \mathbb{Z}^d$. Define*
(i) $\mu_L(C)$ (respectively $\mu_L^p(C)$, $\mu_L^{mp}(C)$) as the minimum number M, such that there exists an arbitrary (resp. periodic, multi-periodic) skewing scheme $s : \mathbb{Z}^d \rightarrow \{0, 1, ..., M-1\}$ which is L-valid for each $P_i \in C$,
(ii) $\lambda_L^{mp}(C)$ as the minimum number δ, such that there exists a multi-periodic skewing scheme $s : \mathbb{Z}^d \rightarrow \{0, 1, ..., \mu_L^{mp}(C)\}$, that is L-valid for C and has an underlying lattice L' with $\Delta(L') = \delta$.

Note that for a periodic skewing scheme $s : \mathbb{Z}^d \rightarrow \{0, 1, ..., M-1\}$ the determinant of the underlying lattice L is equal to M.

The reason why we are interested in the number $\lambda_L^{mp}(C)$ is that this number is a measure for the representation-costs, as we shall see in section 3.3.3. An important means for determining the number $\mu_{\mathbb{Z}^d}^p(C)$ is the fundamental domain of a lattice.

Fact 3.4 *Given a template P and a periodic skewing scheme s with underlying lattice L. Let F be a fundamental domain of L. Then s is valid for P iff for every $x \in F$ there exists at most one $y \in P$ such that $x \equiv_L y$.*

Fact 3.5 *$\mu_{\mathbb{Z}^d}^p(C)$, C arbitrary, can be computed in time polynomial in N and t, with $N = \max\{|x|, x \in P_i \in C\}$.*

Fact 3.4 follows directly from the definition of the fundamental domain (definition 3.12). Fact 3.5 is an obvious generalization of theorem 3.19.

First we show that the multi-periodic skewing schemes are stronger than the periodic schemes in the sense that one may be able to skew collections of templates in fewer memory banks with the former.

Lemma 3.11 *For all $d > 0$ there exists a collection $\mathcal{C}$ of templates such that*

$$\mu^{p}_{\mathbb{Z}^d}(\mathcal{C}) > \mu^{mp}_{\mathbb{Z}^d}(\mathcal{C}).$$

Proof Let $\mathcal{C}$ consist of one template P, defined by $P = \{(0,0,...,0), (2,0,...,0)\}$. Then $\mu^{p}_{\mathbb{Z}^d}(\mathcal{C}) = 3$ and $\mu^{mp}_{\mathbb{Z}^d}(\mathcal{C}) = 2$. □

For the one-dimensional case this lemma can even be strengthened.

Theorem 3.32 *Given $\mathcal{C} = \{P_1, P_2, ..., P_t\}$, with all $P_i \subseteq \mathbb{Z}$. Then $\mu^{mp}_{\mathbb{Z}}(\mathcal{C}) = \mu_{\mathbb{Z}}(\mathcal{C})$.*

Proof Let $s : \mathbb{Z} \to \{0, 1, ..., \mu_{\mathbb{Z}}(\mathcal{C}) - 1\}$ be an arbitrary skewing scheme valid for $\mathcal{C}$, and let $a = \max_{k,l \in T_i} |k - l|$. Consider the a-tuples $t_0, t_1, t_2, ...$ with $t_i = (s(i), s(i+1), ..., s(i+a-1))$. By the pigeonhole principle there must exist p and q such that $t_p = t_q$. Define the skewing scheme $s' : \mathbb{Z} \to \{0, 1, ..., \mu_{\mathbb{Z}}(\mathcal{C}) - 1\}$ by $s'(i) = s(p + i \bmod (q-p))$. Then s' is valid for $\mathcal{C}$ also. Furthermore s' is multi-periodic with an underlying lattice defined by the basis $\{(q-p)\}$. □

So for the one-dimensional case the minimum number of memory banks $\mu_{\mathbb{Z}}(\mathcal{C})$ may be achieved by a multi-periodic skewing scheme, although the determinant of the underlying lattice of s is exponential in $\mu_{\mathbb{Z}}(\mathcal{C})$. The question whether this holds for higher dimensions also, seems to be more complicated and is left open. The following theorem gives a bound on the number of memory banks needed for L-validly skewing a collection of templates.

Theorem 3.33 *Given a collection of templates $\mathcal{C} = \{P_1, ..., P_t\}$, $P_i \subseteq \mathbb{Z}^d (1 \leqslant i \leqslant t)$, a d-dimensional lattice $L \subseteq \mathbb{Z}^d$ and a partition $\mathcal{B} = \{B_1, B_2, ..., B_r\}$ of a fundamental domain of L. Let $B_k = \{a^k_1, a^k_2, ... a^k_{r_k}\}$ for all $1 \leqslant k \leqslant r$. Then there exists a multi-periodic skewing scheme s, with underlying lattice L, such that s is L-valid for $\mathcal{C}$ and s uses M^* memory banks. Where*

$$M^* = \sum_{1 \leqslant k \leqslant r} \min_{x_1, x_2, ..., x_{|B_k|} \in \mathbb{Z}^d} \mu^{p}_{\mathbb{Z}^d}(\{\bigcup_i (P_1^{a^k_i} + x_i), \bigcup_i (P_2^{a^k_i} + x_i), ..., \bigcup_i (P_t^{a^k_i} + x_i)\}),$$

with $P_i^a = \eta^a_L(P_i \cap (a + L))$.

Proof Write C_k for $\mu^{p}_{\mathbb{Z}^d}(\{\bigcup_i (P_1^{a^k_i} + x_i), \bigcup_i (P_2^{a^k_i} + x_i), ..., \bigcup_i (P_t^{a^k_i} + x_i)\})$. Let for each B_k, $1 \leqslant k \leqslant r$: $x_1, x_2, ..., x_{|B_k|} \in \mathbb{Z}^d$ be arbitrary and $s_k : \mathbb{Z}^d \to \{0, 1, ..., M_k - 1\}$ be a periodic skewing scheme which is valid for C_k.

Construct the skewing scheme $s : \mathbb{Z}^d \rightarrow \{0, 1, ..., \sum_j M_j - 1\}$, by defining for each k, $1 \leqslant k \leqslant r : s\restriction\{a + L|a \in B_k\}$ by

$$s(y) = s(a_i^k + x) = s_k(\eta_L^{a_i^k}(y) - x_i) + \sum_{1 \leqslant j < k} M_j.$$

Then for each $k, l\ (k \neq l) : \{a + L|\ a \in B_k\} \cap \{a + L|\ a \in B_l\} = \emptyset$ and $\mathrm{Ran}(s\restriction\{a + L|a \in B_k\}) \cap \mathrm{Ran}(s\restriction\{a + L|a \in B_l\}) = \emptyset$. Thus s is defined sound and between the sets $\{a+L|a \in B_k\}$ and $\{a+L|a \in B_l\}$ "no conflicts" can occur. This means that there is no instance $P_j(x)$ of some template T_j such that $\exists p \in \{a + L|a \in B_k\}, q \in \{a + L|a \in B_l\}$ with $p, q \in T_j(x)$ and $s(p) = s(q)$. That "no conflicts" can occur on each set $\{a + L|a \in B_k\}$ itself, follows from the fact that s_k is valid for C_k. □

Theorem 3.34 *The number M^* can be computed in time polynomial in b, N and t, with $N = \max_{P_i \in C} |P_i|$, $b = \max_k \binom{N^2}{|B_k|} \cdot |B_k|!$*

Proof From fact 3.4 follows, that we do not have to consider for each B_k all possible choices of the points $x_1, x_2, ..., x_{|B_k|}$, but only those which belong to a fundamental domain of the underlying lattice of the periodic skewing scheme s_k concerned. Together with fact 3.5 this gives the desired result. □

Thus when we take a partition $\mathcal{B} = \{B_1, B_2, ..., B_r\}$ such that for all $1 \leqslant i \leqslant r : |B_i| \leqslant c$, for some constant c, then the number M^* can be computed in time polynomial in N and t. Because of the premisses, as stated in the introduction of 3.3, we may assume that for each template P_i and $a \in F$, F a fundamental domain of L, $|P_i \cap (a + L)|$ is small. With respect to this the following theorem and corollary are interesting.

Theorem 3.35 *Given a template $P \subseteq \mathbb{Z}^d$ and a lattice $L \subseteq \mathbb{Z}^d$, with basis $\{\vec{x}_1, \vec{x}_2, ..., \vec{x}_d\}$ and a fundamental domain F. If for all $a \in F$ there exists $b \in \mathbb{Z}^d$ such that $P \cap (a+L) \subseteq \{b, b \pm \vec{x}_1, b \pm \vec{x}_2, ..., b \pm \vec{x}_d\}$, but $P \cap (a+L) \neq \{b + \vec{x}_i, b - \vec{x}_i|\ i \in I_a\}$ for some $I_a \subseteq \{1, 2, ..., d\}$, then there exists a multi-periodic skewing scheme s with underlying lattice L, such that s is L-valid for P and s uses $|P|$ memory banks.*

Proof Let P satisfy the condition. Without loss of generality we assume that for all $1 \leqslant i \leqslant d : b + \vec{x}_i \in P \cap (a + L)$ or $b - \vec{x}_i \in P \cap (a + L)$. Then we have that for $a \in F$, a arbitrary,

$$\eta_L^a(P \cap (a + L)) \subseteq$$
$$\{(c_1, c_2, ..., c_d), (c_1 \pm 1, c_2, ..., c_d), (c_1, c_2 \pm 1, ..., c_d), ..., (c_1, c_2, ..., c_d \pm 1)\},$$

for some $(c_1, c_2, ..., c_d) \in \mathbb{Z}^d$, and

$$|\eta_L^a(P \cap (a+L))| \leqslant \begin{cases} 2d+1 \text{ if } (c_1, c_2, ..., c_d) \in \eta_L^a(P \cap (a+L)) \\ 2d-1 \text{ if } (c_1, c_2, ..., c_d) \notin \eta_L^a(P \cap (a+L)). \end{cases}$$

From fact 3.4 and theorem 3.33 follows that we only need to prove that for an arbitrary template P' , with $P' \subseteq \{(0,...,0), (\pm 1, 0, ..., 0), (0, \pm 1, 0, ..., 0), ..., (0, ..., 0, \pm 1)\} (= X^d)$,

$$|P'| \leqslant \begin{cases} 2d+1 \text{ if } (0,...,0) \in P' \\ 2d-1 \text{ if } (0,...,0) \notin P', \end{cases}$$

and with P' d-dimensional, which means that for all $1 \leqslant i \leqslant d$:

$$(\underbrace{0,...,0}_{i-1}, 1, \underbrace{0,...,0}_{d-i}) \in P' \text{ or } (\underbrace{0,...,0}_{i-1}, -1, \underbrace{0,...,0}_{d-i}) \in P'$$

there exists a periodic skewing scheme $s' : \mathbb{Z}^d \to \{0, 1, ..., |P'| - 1\}$, which is valid for P' . We shall prove a slightly stronger version of this statement.

Claim 3.3 *For all $P' \subseteq X^d$, P' d-dimensional, is valid that*
if $(0,...,0) \in P'$ *and* $|P'| = 2d+1$ *or if* $(0,...,0) \notin P'$ *and* $|P'| = 2d-1$
then *for all $s, t \in \mathbb{Z}$ there exist points $x_1, ..., x_t, y_1, ..., y_t, z_1, ..., z_s \in \mathbb{Z}^d$, such that for all $1 \leqslant j \leqslant t$: $\exists q_j \in \mathbb{Z}^d$ with $x_j - q_j = q_j - y_j$ and there exists a periodic skewing scheme $s : \mathbb{Z}^d \to \{0, 1, ..., |P'| + 2t + s - 1\}$ which is valid for $P' \cup \{x_i\}_{1 \leqslant i \leqslant t} \cup \{y_i\}_{1 \leqslant i \leqslant t} \cup \{z_i\}_{1 \leqslant i \leqslant s}$,*
else *for all $s \in \mathbb{Z}$ there exist points $z_1, z_2, ..., z_s \in \mathbb{Z}^d$, such that there exists a periodic skewing scheme $s : \mathbb{Z}^d \to \{0, 1, ..., |P'| + s - 1\}$ which is valid for $P' \cup \{z_i\}_{1 \leqslant i \leqslant s}$.*

Proof The proof is done by induction. For d=1 the templates to consider are:

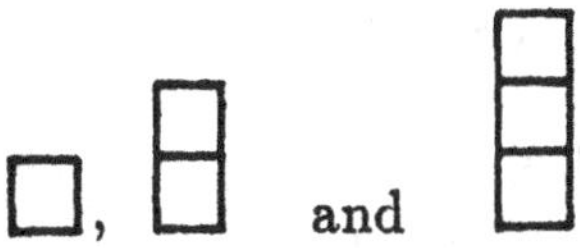

It can be verified that these templates meet the conditions. Let for $d = k$ the claim be valid and let $P' \subseteq X^{k+1}$, P' $(k+1)$-dimensional. Then we have two cases.

Case 1 $(0,...,0) \in P'$ and $|P'| = 2(k+1)+1$ or
$(0,...,0) \notin P'$ and $|P'| = 2(k+1)-1$.
Case 2 $(0,...,0) \in P'$ and $|P'| \leqslant 2(k+1)$ or
$(0,...,0) \notin P'$ and $|P'| \leqslant 2(k+1)-2$.

Consider **case 1**. Let $s, t \in \mathbb{Z}$ be arbitrary. If $(0,...,0) \in P'$ and $|P'| = 2(k+1)+1$, then there exists a j, $1 \leqslant j \leqslant k+1$, such that $|\{(\underbrace{0,...,0}_{i-1}, x, \underbrace{0,...,0}_{k-i+1}) | x \in \mathbb{Z}\} \cap P'| = 3$. Thus there exists a $P \subseteq X^k$, P k-dimensional, $(0,...,0) \in P$, and $|P| = 2k+1$, such that

$$\begin{aligned} P' &= \{(p_1, p_2, ..., p_{i-1}, 0, p_{i+1}, ..., p_{k+1}) |\ (p_1, p_2, ..., p_{i-1}, p_{i+1}, ..., p_{k+1}) \in P\} \\ &\quad \cup \{(\underbrace{0,...,0}_{i}, 1, \underbrace{0,...,0}_{k-i+1}), (\underbrace{0,...,0}_{i}, -1, \underbrace{0,...,0}_{k-i+1})\}. \end{aligned}$$

Then from the induction hypothesis follows that there exist points $x_1, ..., x_{t+1}$, $y_1, ..., y_{t+1}$, $z_1, ..., z_s \in \mathbb{Z}^d$, such that for all $1 \leqslant j \leqslant t+1$ there exists a q_j with $x_j - q_j = q_j - y_j$ (**) and such that there exists a periodic skewing scheme $s : \mathbb{Z}^d \to \{0, 1, ..., |P| + 2(t+1) + s - 1\}$ which is valid for $P \cup \{x_i\}_{1 \leqslant i \leqslant t+1}$ $\cup \{y_i\}_{1 \leqslant i \leqslant t+1}$ $\cup \{z_i\}_{1 \leqslant i \leqslant s}$ (*). Consider now

$$\begin{aligned} P' = \{&(p_1, p_2, ..., p_{i-1}, 0, p_{i+1}, ..., p_{k+1}) | \\ &(p_1, p_2, ..., p_{i-1}, p_{i+1}, ..., p_{k+1}) \in P - \{x_{t+1}, y_{t+1}\}\}. \end{aligned}$$

An analogous argument as in the proof of theorem 3.33 together with (*) provides the existence of a multi-periodic skewing scheme $s : \mathbb{Z}^{k+1} \to \{0, 1, ..., |P'| + 2t + s - 1\}$ which is valid for P'. With the use of (**) it turns out that s is periodic as well. The case that (0,...,0)$\in P'$ and $|P'| = 2(k+1)-1$ can be handled analogously.

Consider **case 2**. Let $s \in \mathbb{Z}$ be arbitrary. If (0,...,0)$\in P'$ and $|P'| \leqslant 2(k+1)$, then there exists a $1 \leqslant i \leqslant k+1$ such that $|\{(\underbrace{0,...,0}_{i-1}, x, \underbrace{0,...,0}_{k-i+1}) | x \in \mathbb{Z}\} \cap P'| = 2$. Thus there exists a $P \subseteq X^k$, P k-dimensional, such that

$$\begin{aligned} P' &= \{(p_1, p_2, ..., p_{i-1}, 0, p_{i+1}, ..., p_{k+1}) |\ (p_1, ..., p_{i-1}, p_{i+1}, ..., p_{k+1}) \in P\} \cup \\ &\quad \{(\underbrace{0,...,0}_{i-1}, 1, \underbrace{0,...,0}_{k-i+1})\} \text{ (or } \{(\underbrace{0,...,0}_{i-1}, -1, \underbrace{0,...,0}_{k-i+1})\}). \end{aligned}$$

Now a similar argument as in the above can be used to show the existence of points $z_1, ..., z_s \in \mathbb{Z}_d$ and a periodic skewing scheme $s : \mathbb{Z}^d \to \{0, 1, ..., |P'| +$

$s-1\}$ which is valid for $P' \cup \{z_i\}_{1 \leqslant i \leqslant s}$. The case that $(0,...,0) \notin P'$ and $|P'| \leqslant 2(k+1)-2$ can be handled analogously.

□

As a direct consequence we have:

Corollary 3.15 *Given a template $P \subseteq Z^d$ and a lattice $L \subseteq Z^d$, with basis $\{\vec{x}_1, \vec{x}_2, ..., \vec{x}_d\}$ and fundamental domain F. Suppose for all $a \in F$ there exists $b \in Z^d$, such that $P \cap (a+L) \subseteq \{b, b \pm \vec{x}_1, b \pm \vec{x}_2, ..., b \pm \vec{x}_d\}$. If there exist points $a_1, a_2, ..., a_s \in F$ such that for all $i, 1 \leqslant i \leqslant s : P \cap (a_i + L) = \{b + \vec{x}_i, b - \vec{x}_i | i \in I_{a_i}\}$, for some $I_{a_i} \subseteq \{1, 2, ..., d\}$, and if there exist integers $i_1, i_2, ..., i_t \in \{1, 2, ..., d\}$ such that for all $i, 1 \leqslant i \leqslant s$, there exists a i_j with $i_j \in I_{a_i}$, then there exists a multi-periodic skewing scheme $s : Z^d \to \{0, 1, ..., |P|-1\}$, which is L-valid for P and has an underlying lattice L' with basis*

$$\{\vec{x}_1, ..., \vec{x}_{i_1-1}, 2\vec{x}_{i_1}, \vec{x}_{i_1+1}, ..., \vec{x}_{i_2-1}, 2\vec{x}_{i_2}, \vec{x}_{i_2+1}, ..., \vec{x}_{i_t-1}, 2\vec{x}_{i_t}, \vec{x}_{i_t+1}, ..., \vec{x}_d\}.$$

Jalby et. al. [JFJ84] have given a weaker and slightly different version of theorem 3.35 and corollary 3.15. They have proven that for templates $P \subseteq Z^2$, with the property that for all $a \in F$ there exists a $b \in Z^2$, such that $P \cap (a+L) \subseteq \{b, b+\vec{x}_1, b+\vec{x}_2, b+\vec{x}_1+\vec{x}_2\}$, there exists a diamond scheme which uses $|P|$ memory banks.

Theorem 3.33 does not always yield a multi-periodic skewing scheme which uses the minimum number of memory banks, $\mu_L(C)$, as is shown in the next lemma.

Lemma 3.12 *There exists a collection of templates C, and a lattice L, such that $M^* > \mu_L(C)$.*

Proof Take the collection C, consisting of only one template

$$P = \{(0,0), (1,0), (3,0), (5,0), (0,1), (6,1)\} \subseteq Z^2$$

and let L be the lattice with basis $\{(1,0), (0,2)\}$. Then $M^* = 8$ as can be verified, while μ_L(C)=6 (see figure 3.3). □

```
...0 1 2 3 4 5 0 1 2 3 4 5 0 1 2 3 4 5 0 1 2 3 4 5...
...2 3 4 5 0 1 4 5 0 1 2 3 2 3 4 5 0 1 4 5 0 1 2 3...
   0 1 2 3 4 5 0 1 2 3 4 5 0 1 2 3 4 5 0 1 2 3 4 5
   2 3 4 5 0 1 4 5 0 1 2 3 2 3 4 5 0 1 4 5 0 1 2 3
   0 1 2 3 4 5 0 1 2 3 4 5 0 1 2 3 4 5 0 1 2 3 4 5
   2 3 4 5 0 1 4 5 0 1 2 3 2 3 4 5 0 1 4 5 0 1 2 3
   0 1 2 3 4 5 0 1 2 3 4 5 0 1 2 3 4 5 0 1 2 3 4 5
...2 3 4 5 0 1 4 5 0 1 2 3 2 3 4 5 0 1 4 5 0 1 2 3...
...0 1 2 3 4 5 0 1 2 3 4 5 0 1 2 3 4 5 0 1 2 3 4 5...
```

Figure 3.3: A skewing scheme that is valid for C.

Note that the multi-periodic skewing schemes as constructed in theorem 3.33 and theorem 3.35 are all diamond schemes by theorem 3.31. This is not a coincidence, because this subset of the multi-periodic skewing schemes has more structure than the general multi-periodic schemes, and for this reason the diamond schemes can be handled more easily in these cases. However, in general the diamond schemes are not as strong as the multi-periodic skewing schemes, as shown by the following lemma.

Lemma 3.13 *There exists a collection of templates C and a lattice L such that: if s is a diamond scheme that is L-valid for C and uses $\mu_L^{mp}(C)$ memory banks, then the determinant of the underlying lattice of $s \geqslant 2.\lambda_L^{mp}(C)$.*

Proof Take the same C as in lemma 3.12. Then the skewing scheme as denoted in figure 3.3 is a multi-periodic skewing scheme, which uses 6 memory banks and has an underlying lattice with basis $\{(3,0),(0,2)\}$. The best possible diamond scheme which uses 6 memory banks has an underlying lattice with basis $\{(1,0),(0,12)\}$. □

3.3.3 A Representation of Multi-Periodic Skewing Schemes

Recall section 3.2.2.1. Consider an arbitrary multi-periodic skewing scheme s, and let L be its underlying lattice. Because for each $a_U \in F^* : s_L^{a_U}$ is periodic, there exists a map α^{a_U} and t^{a_U} such that $t^{a_U} \circ \alpha^{a_U} = s_L^{a_U}$. Then from theorem 3.23 the following result follows.

Theorem 3.36 *Let s be a multi-periodic skewing scheme and L be its underlying lattice. Let $U = \{\vec{u}_1, \vec{u}_2, ..., \vec{u}_d\}$ and $s_1, s_2, ..., s_d$ be as in* lemma 3.23. *Then for all $x \in Z^d$*

$$s(x) = t^{(i_1 \bmod s_1, ..., i_d \bmod s_d)U} \circ s^{(i_1 \bmod s_1, ..., i_d \bmod s_d)U}(i_1 \text{over } s_1, ... i_d \text{over } s_d),$$

with $(i_1, i_2, ..., i_d) = (\vec{u}_1\vec{u}_2...\vec{u}_d)^{-1}(x)$.

Proof Immediate. □

Concluding we can say that a multi-periodic skewing scheme $s : Z^d \to \{0, 1, ..., M-1\}$, with underlying lattice L can be represented in the amount of space of approximately $|F^*|.(d^2+M) = \triangle(L).(d^2+M)$ memory locations.

Chapter 4

Arbitrary Skewing Schemes for Trees

Skewing schemes for d-dimensional arrays as studied in chapter 2 and chapter 3 received considerable attention in the literature. The reason is that d-dimensional arrays are at the basis of many scientific computations. However, for non-numerical computation trees are fundamental and nothing seems to be known about the possibilities of "skewing" such data structures. In this chapter and chapter 5 we want to initiate a study of skewing schemes for trees.

In order to define skewing schemes for trees we first have to consider how to represent trees. We assume that trees are infinite, complete, and k-ary, and that they have a fixed orientation (i.e., the trees are "rooted" by a node α_0). So when we mention trees throughout this chapter we mean trees T_k (T, for short), for any (fixed) value of $k \geqslant 2$, which have these restrictions. Note that an arbitrary finite k-ary tree can be seen as embedded in a tree T_k. In the following definition we give a way of labeling (numbering) the nodes (elements) of a tree. Let T_k be a tree with root α_0. Let the edges emanating from a node of T_k to its sons be labeled $e_1, ..., e_k$ from left to right. $\{e_1, e_2, ..., e_k\}^*$ denotes the set of all words over the alphabet $\{e_1, e_2, ..., e_k\}$.

Definition 4.1 *The mapping* lab : $T_k \rightarrow \{e_1, e_2, ..., e_k\}^*$ *is defined as*
(*i*) $\text{lab}(\alpha_0) = \varepsilon$,
(*ii*) *for all* $\alpha \neq \alpha_0$, $\text{lab}(\alpha) = \lambda_1\lambda_2...\lambda_n$, *with for all* i, $1 \leqslant i \leqslant n : \lambda_i \in \{e_1, e_2, ..., e_k\}$ *and* $\lambda_1\lambda_2...\lambda_n$ *is the sequence of labels on the unique path from* α_0 *to* α.

We usually identify a node α with the sequence $\text{lab}(\alpha)$, which uniquely defines it. In particular T_k can be identified with the (infinite) set $\{e_1, e_2, ..., e_k\}^*$. This representation of trees can also be found in the theory of codes [BP85], where a tree corresponds to the literal representation over a set of words of some alphabet A. In chapter 5 this connection will be explored further. Let $|\alpha|$ denote the length of (the word) α and let $\prec$ denote the ordering on a tree T_k defined by $\alpha \prec \beta$ iff $|\alpha| < |\beta|$, or $|\alpha| = |\beta|$ and α is less than or equal to than β in lexicographic order. For any α and β, $\alpha\beta$ $(\alpha.\beta)$ denotes the concatenation of (the words) α and β.

For each $\alpha \in T$ define Prefix(α) $= \{\beta | \exists\gamma : \beta\gamma = \alpha\}$ and Suffix(α) $= \{\gamma | \exists\beta : \beta\gamma = \alpha\}$.

Definition 4.2
(i) A template P on a tree T is any finite set of nodes $\{\alpha_1, \alpha_2, ..., \alpha_N\} \subseteq T$.
(ii) An instance $P(\gamma)$ *(or:* γP*),* $\gamma \in T$*, of a template P is the set* $\{\gamma\alpha_1, \gamma\alpha_2, ..., \gamma\alpha_N\}$.

Definition 4.3
(i) A skewing scheme for a tree T is a mapping $s : T \to \{0, 1, ..., M-1\}$.
(ii) A skewing scheme s is valid for a collection of templates $C = \{P_1, P_2, ..., P_t\}$ *if* $\forall 1 \leqslant i \leqslant t\, \forall\gamma \in T\, \forall j \in \{0, 1, ..., M-1\} : |P_i(\gamma) \cap s^{-1}(j)| \leqslant 1$.
(iii) $\mu_T(\{P_1, P_2, ..., P_t\})$ *is equal to the minimum number M such that there exists a skewing scheme* $s : T \to \{0, 1, ..., M-1\}$ *which is valid for* $\{P_1, P_2, ..., P_t\}$.

Note that there always exists a finite number M such that there exists a skewing scheme $s : T \to \{0, 1, ..., M-1\}$ which is valid for $\{P_1, P_2, ..., P_t\}$.

Example
Figure 4.1 shows (part of) the binary tree T_2, a template with some instances, and a skewing scheme that is valid for this template.

In this chapter we will study the underlying structure of the conditions forced by the validity of a skewing scheme on a tree T and give estimates on the number $\mu_T(C)$ for various collections C of templates. However, the general problem TREE SKEWING given by:

> Instance: A finite k-ary tree T of depth i, a collection C of templates on T,
> a positive integer $M \leqslant |\bigcup_{P \in C} P|$
> Question: Is $\mu_T(C) \leqslant M$

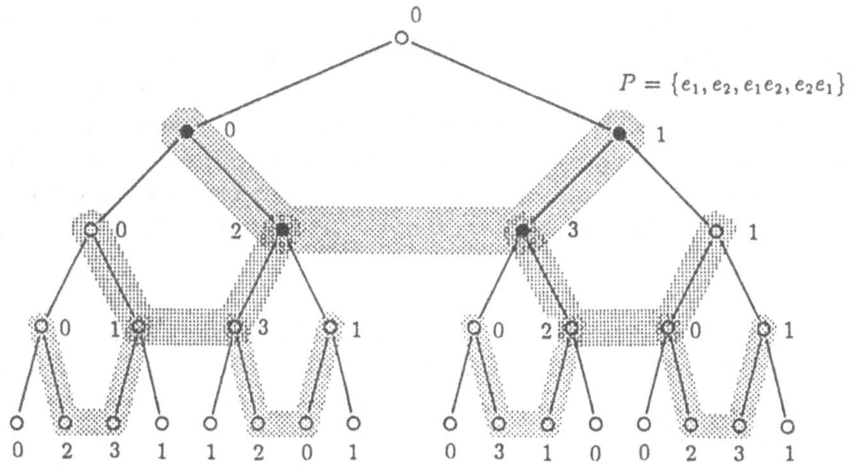

Figure 4.1: A skewing scheme for a tree T which is valid for a template P.

is NP-complete. Only those instances of a template of C are involved which fit the tree T. For the notion of NP-completeness, see [GJ78].

Theorem 4.1 TREE SKEWING *is* NP-*complete.*

Proof Because T is finite, any skewing scheme for T which uses M numbers can be represented in the size of T. Further the validity of a skewing scheme can be verified in time polynomial in the size of T, the number of templates in C and the maximal size of a template of C. So the problem TREE SKEWING is in NP. The NP-completeness of the problem TREE SKEWING will be proven by a transformation from the problem GRAPH K-COLORABILITY, which was proven to be NP-complete by Karp [Kar72]. The problem GRAPH K-COLORABILITY is given by:

> Instance: Graph $G = (V, E)$, positive integer $K \leqslant |V|$.
> Question: Is G K-colorable, i.e., does there exist a function $f : V \rightarrow \{1, 2, ..., K\}$ such that $f(u) \neq f(v)$ whenever $\{u, v\} \in E$.

Let $G = (V, E)$ and $K \leqslant |V|$ be an instance of GRAPH K-COLORABILITY. Let T be a k-ary tree of depth i and let $i \geqslant 0$ be the smallest integer such that $k^i \geqslant |V|$. The map $\eta : V \twoheadrightarrow \{\alpha | \alpha \in T \text{ and } |\alpha| = i\}$ is an arbitrary embedding of V into the nodes on the ith level of T. Define the collection C of templates on the tree T by $C = \{\{\alpha, \beta\} |$ there exists an edge $\{u, v\} \in E$ with $\alpha = \eta(u)$ and $\beta = \eta(v)\}$. Then $\mu_T(C) \leqslant K$ implies that there exists a function $f : V \rightarrow \{1, 2, ..., K\}$ such that $f(u) \neq f(v)$ whenever $\{u, v\} \in E$. And if G is K-colorable then the skewing scheme for T obtained by assigning to each node $\alpha = \eta(u)$, for some $u \in V$, the value $f(u) - 1$ and to the remaining nodes of T an arbitrary value $\in \{0, 1, ..., K - 1\}$ is valid for C. Thus $\mu_T(C) \leqslant K$. Further it is clear that the transformation is polynomial.

□

From the proof of theorem 4.1 we can conclude that even if we restrict the problem TREE SKEWING to collections C with for all $P \in C : |P| \leqslant 2$, the problem TREE SKEWING remains NP-complete. Even if we would restrict the problem TREE SKEWING to collections of templates C such that for a given polynomial computable and polynomial bounded injection $\varphi : \mathbb{Z}^+ \rightarrow \mathbb{Z}^+$, with $\varphi(x) \leqslant x$, and for all x and $P \in C : \max_{\alpha \in P} |\alpha| \leqslant \varphi(i)$, with i the depth of T, then again, by the same transformation as in the proof of theorem 4.1, TREE SKEWING is NP-complete. We only have to choose for the depth of T: $\varphi^{-1}(i)$ with i the smallest integer such that $k^i \geqslant |V|$.

In spite of this fact, in this chapter we are able to derive close to optimal bounds on the number $\mu_T(C)$. As a main result we will show that the existence of skewing schemes for trees is strongly related to the existence of skewing schemes for strips, where strips are bundles of one-dimensional arrays. The strips, in turn, are related again to d-dimensional arrays. This enables us to derive several bounds on the number $\mu_T(C)$.

This chapter is organized as follows. In section 4.1 we introduce some preliminary notions and results concerning skewing schemes for trees. Further, we give some rather ad hoc estimates on the number of memory banks needed in certain applications. In section 4.2 we introduce the notions of a strip and skewing schemes for strips. We will show that the existence of skewing schemes for strips is related to the existence of skewing schemes for d-dimensional arrays. In section 4.3 we give an exact characterization of the number $\mu_T(C)$ by reducing the problem of finding skewing schemes for trees to the problem of finding skewing schemes for strips. This characterization will be refined and simplified in section 4.4. In section 4.5 we show that the rather tedious characterization from the previous sections has some very nice consequences. Moreover we define classes of applications, for which the implied bounds on the number of memory banks needed are optimal. In section 4.6 we focus on the case that C contains only one template.

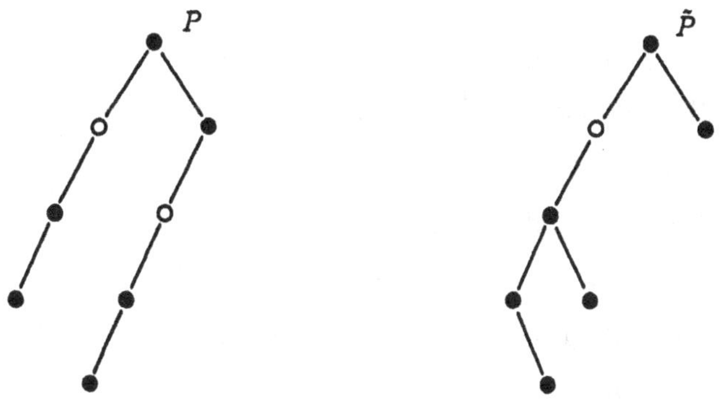

Figure 4.2: A template P for which $\mu_T(\{P\}) \neq \mu_T(\{\tilde{P}\})$.

4.1 The Validity of Skewing Schemes for Trees

In this section we present some preliminary notions and results concerning the validity of skewing schemes for trees. First we need the notion of a reversed template.

Definition 4.4 *Let the mapping* $tr : T \rightarrow T$ *be defined by* $tr(\lambda_1\lambda_2...\lambda_n) = \lambda_n\lambda_{n-1}...\lambda_1$. *Then*
(i) $\tilde{\alpha} = tr(\alpha)$ *is called the reversed node of* α
(ii) $\tilde{P} = \{tr(\alpha)|\alpha \in P\}$ *is the reversed template of* P.

Lemma 4.1 *In general it is not true that* $\mu_T(\{P\}) = M$ *iff* $\mu_T(\{\tilde{P}\}) = M$.

Proof Consider a binary tree T_2. Take $P = \{\varepsilon, e_1e_1, e_1e_1e_1, e_2, e_2e_1e_1, e_2e_1e_1e_1\}$. Then $\tilde{P} = \{\varepsilon, e_1e_1, e_1e_1e_1, e_2, e_1e_1e_2, e_1e_1e_1e_2\}$ (see figure 4.2). Then $\mu_T(\{P\}) = 6$ and $\mu_T(\{\tilde{P}\}) = 8$. □

With the aid of $\tilde{P}$ we can define the conflict-region $C_P(\alpha)$ of a node α and the conflict-number $c_P(\alpha)$ which denotes the number of different ways in which the template P can cover the node α. Let P be a template.

Definition 4.5
(i) The conflict-region $C_P(\alpha)$ *of a node* α *with respect to* P *is defined as*

$$C_P(\alpha) = \{\beta |\ \beta \in P \text{ and } \tilde{\beta} \text{ lies on the path from } \tilde{\alpha} \text{ to the root } \alpha_0\}.$$

(ii) The conflict-number $c_P(\alpha)$ of a node α with respect to P is defined as $c_P(\alpha) = |C_P(\alpha)|$.

The following two lemmas immediately follow from the definition.

Lemma 4.2 *For any template P and node $\alpha \in T$:*

$$c_P(\alpha) \leqslant |\{k| \, \exists \beta \in P \text{ with } |\beta| = k\}| \leqslant |P|.$$

Lemma 4.3 *For any template P and node $\alpha \in T$:*

$$\alpha \in P(\gamma) \text{ iff } \exists \beta \in C_P(\alpha) : \alpha = \gamma\beta.$$

The following theorem gives a rather crude estimate for $\mu_T(\{P\})$.

Theorem 4.2 *For any template P,*

$$\begin{aligned} |P| \leqslant \mu_T(\{P\}) &\leqslant \max_{\alpha\in T} \sum_{\beta\in C_P(\alpha)} |\{\gamma| \, \gamma \in P \text{ and } \gamma \prec \beta(\gamma \neq \beta)\}| + 1 \\ &\leqslant C(|P| - \frac{1}{2}C - \frac{1}{2}) + 1 \\ &\leqslant \frac{1}{2}|P|^2 - \frac{1}{2}|P| + 1 \end{aligned}$$

where $C = \max_{\alpha\in T} c_P(\alpha)$.

Proof Trivially $|P| \leqslant \mu_T(\{P\})$. The inequality $\mu_T(\{P\}) \leqslant M = \max_{\alpha\in T} \sum_{\beta\in C_P(\alpha)} |\{\gamma| \, \gamma \in P \text{ and } \gamma \prec \beta(\gamma \neq \beta)\}| + 1$ holds, because we can inductively construct a skewing scheme s that is valid for P and uses at most M memory banks. Let $T = \{\alpha_0, \alpha_1, \alpha_2, ...\}$ with for all $i \geqslant 0 : \alpha_i \prec \alpha_{i+1}$. Assign an arbitrary value $\in \{0, 1, ..., M-1\}$ to the root α_0 of T, and assign to each node α_i the smallest possible integer $\geqslant 0$ that does not conflict with the values at the previously assigned nodes $\alpha_0, \alpha_1, \alpha_2, ..., \alpha_{i-1}$, i.e., there exists no $\gamma \in T$ such that (1) $\alpha_i \in P(\gamma)$, and (2) there exists a $j \leqslant i-1$ such that $\alpha_j \in P(\gamma)$ and $s(\alpha_i) = s(\alpha_j)$. The skewing schemes s obtained in this fashion uses at most M memory banks, because by lemma 4.3

$$\begin{aligned} &|\{\alpha_j| \, \alpha_j \prec \alpha_i(\alpha_j \neq \alpha_i), \text{ and } \exists \gamma \in T : \alpha_i \in P(\gamma) \text{ and } \alpha_j \in P(\gamma)\}| \\ &\quad = |\{\alpha_j| \, \alpha_j \prec \alpha_i(\alpha_j \neq \alpha_i), \text{ and } \exists \delta \in T \, \exists \beta \in C_P(\alpha_i) : \\ &\qquad \alpha_i = \delta\beta \text{ and } \alpha_j \in P(\delta)\}| \\ &\quad = |\{\gamma| \, \exists \beta \in C_P(\alpha_i) : \alpha_i = \delta\beta, \gamma \prec \beta(\gamma \neq \beta) \text{ and } \gamma \in P\}| \\ &\quad = |\{\gamma| \, \exists \beta \in C_P(\alpha_i) : \gamma \prec \beta(\gamma \neq \beta), \text{ and } \gamma \in P\}| \\ &\quad \leqslant \sum_{\beta\in C_P(\alpha_i)} |\{\gamma| \, \gamma \prec \beta(\gamma \neq \beta) \text{ and } \gamma \in P\}| \\ &\quad \leqslant M - 1. \end{aligned}$$

The third inequality follows from the fact that for all $\alpha : \sum_{\beta \in C_P(\alpha)} |\{\gamma | \gamma \in P \text{ and } \gamma \prec \beta (\gamma \neq \beta)\}| \leqslant |P| - 1 + |P| - 2 + ... + |P| - C = C(|P| - \frac{1}{2}C - \frac{1}{2})$.

From $C \leqslant |P|$ immediately follows that $C(|P| - \frac{1}{2}C - \frac{1}{2}) \leqslant \frac{1}{2}|P|^2 - \frac{1}{2}|P|$.

□

A precise characterization of $\mu_T(\{P\})$ can be found in section 4.3. We continue this section with some applications of theorem 4.2.

Examples

In all examples we take $k = 2$, i.e., T is a binary tree.

1. Let P be the template $\{e_1e_1e_1, e_2, e_2e_1, e_2e_1e_1\}$. Then $\tilde{P}$ is the template $\{e_1e_1e_1, e_2, e_1e_2, e_1e_1e_2\}$, and for all α is valid that $c_P(\alpha) = 1$. Thus by theorem 4.2 follows that $4 = |P| \leqslant \mu_T(\{P\}) \leqslant |P| - \frac{1}{2} - \frac{1}{2} + 1 = 4$. P and $\tilde{P}$ are depicted in figure 4.3(i).

2. Let P be the template $\{\varepsilon, e_1, e_2e_1, e_2e_2e_1, e_1e_2e_2e_1, e_2e_1e_2e_2e_1, e_1e_2e_1e_2e_2e_1, e_1e_1e_2e_1e_2e_2e_1\}$. Then $\tilde{P}$ is the template $\{\varepsilon, e_1, e_1e_2, e_1e_2e_2, e_1e_2e_2e_1, e_1e_2e_2e_1e_2, e_1e_2e_2e_1e_2e_1, e_1e_2e_2e_1e_2e_1e_1\}$. Thus $\max_{\alpha \in T} c_P(\alpha) = 8$, and $\max_{\alpha \in T} c_{\tilde{P}}(\alpha) = 3$. See figure 4.3($ii$). Then the estimates for $\mu_T(\{P\})$ and $\mu_T(\{\tilde{P}\})$ given by theorem 4.2 become :

$8 = |P| \leqslant \mu_T(\{P\}) \leqslant 8.(8 - 4 - \frac{1}{2}) + 1 = 29$, and

$8 = |\tilde{P}| \leqslant \mu_T(\{\tilde{P}\}) \leqslant 3.(8 - 1\frac{1}{2} - \frac{1}{2}) + 1 = 19.$

On the other hand $\mu_T(\{P\}) = 8$ and $\mu_T(\{\tilde{P}\}) = 8$. Consider the skewing scheme $s : T \to \{0, 1, ..., 7\}$ defined by $s(\alpha) = |\alpha| \bmod 8$. Then s is valid for P and $\tilde{P}$.

3. For $d \geqslant 0$ consider the template $P_d = \{\alpha | \, |\alpha| \leqslant d\}$. P_d is the subtree of depth d. Then $P_d = \tilde{P}_d$, and from theorem 4.2 follows that $2^{d+1} - 1 = |P_d| \leqslant \mu_T(\{P_d\}) \leqslant (d+1)(2^{d+1} - 1 + \frac{1}{2}d - \frac{1}{2}) + 1 = O(|P_d|.\log|P_d|)$.

For some templates we can do better than suggested in the previous examples.

Definition 4.6 *A template P is called connected iff for all $\alpha \in P$ and for all β on the path from α to the root α_0 : $\beta \in P$.*

Theorem 4.3 *Let P be a template, with $\tilde{P}$ connected. Then $\mu_T(\{P\}) = |P|$.*

Proof Let $T = \{\alpha_0, \alpha_1, \alpha_2, ...\}$, with $\alpha_0 \prec \alpha_1 \prec \alpha_2 \prec ...$. Assign $|P|$ distinct numbers to the nodes of $P(\alpha_0)$, and for each $i \geqslant 1$ assign integers $\in \{0, 1, ..., |P| - 1\}$ to the nodes of $P(\alpha_i)$ in such a way that for all $\alpha \in P(\alpha_i)$

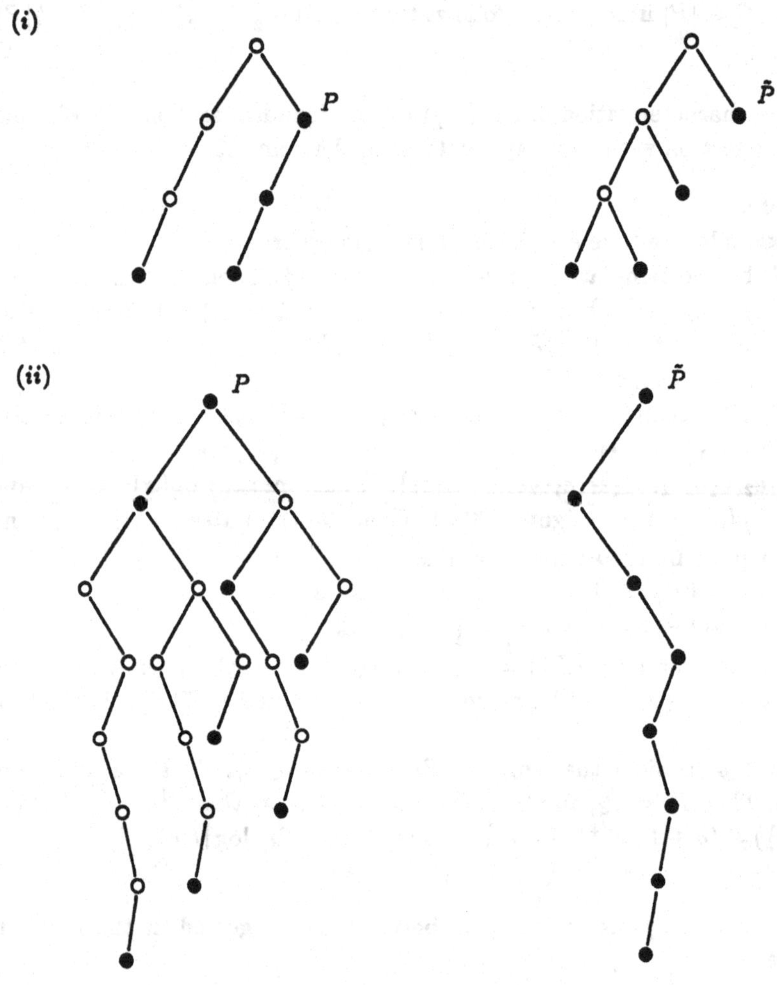

Figure 4.3: Some applications of theorem 4.2.

and $\beta \in P(\alpha_i) : s(\alpha) \neq s(\beta)$. That this can be done follows from the fact that for all α_i, α_j, with $\alpha_i \prec \alpha_j : P(\alpha_i) \cap P(\alpha_j) \subseteq P(\alpha_{j'})$, with $\alpha_{j'}$ determined by $\alpha_{j'} \prec \alpha_j$ and $|\alpha_{j'}|$ is maximal. □

With respect to theorem 4.3 the following two facts are quite surprising.

Proposition 4.1 *The implication: "if P is connected, then $\mu_T(\{P\}) = |P|$" is not true.*

Proof Take $k = 2$, i.e., T is a binary tree. Let P be the template $\{\varepsilon, e_1, e_1e_1, e_1e_1e_1, e_1e_1e_1e_2, e_1e_1e_2, e_2\}$. Then $|P| = 7$, but $\mu_T(\{P\}) = 8$. □

Proposition 4.2 *There exists a collection C of templates P with $\tilde{P}$ connected, such that $\mu_T(C) > \max_{P\in C}|P|$.*

Proof Take $k = 2$ and $C = \{P_1, P_2\}$ with $P_1 = \{\varepsilon, e_1, e_2\}$ and $P_2 = \{\varepsilon, e_1e_2, e_2\}$. Then both $\tilde{P}_1$ and $\tilde{P}_2$ are connected. But $\mu_T(C) = 4 > 3 = \max_{P\in C}|P|$. □

We can use theorem 4.3 for obtaining another estimate on $\mu_T(\{P\})$.

Theorem 4.4 *For any template P,*

$$\begin{aligned}\mu_T(\{P\}) &\leqslant \min\{|P'| \mid \tilde{P} \subseteq P' \text{ and } P' \text{ is connected}\} \\ &\leqslant \sum_{\alpha\in P} |\alpha|.\end{aligned}$$

Proof Directly from theorem 4.3. □

In some cases the estimate of theorem 4.2 yields better results than theorem 4.4. For instance, let P be the template $\{\alpha \mid |\alpha| = d\}$ (T is a binary tree). Then $C(|P| - \frac{1}{2}C - \frac{1}{2}) + 1 = |P| = 2^d$ (use that $C = 1$). And theorem 4.4 yields $\mu_T(\{P\}) \leqslant 2^{d+1} - 1$. But, e.g., in example 2, p. 149, theorem 4.4 yields $\mu_T(\{P\}) \leqslant 8$, which is optimal.

4.2 Skewing Schemes for Strips

In this section we introduce strips, skewing schemes for strips, and the notion of validity for these skewing schemes. The reason for introducing these auxiliary concepts is that they enable us to give an exact characterization of skewing schemes for trees in section 4.3. Moreover strips are closely related to d-dimensional arrays, for which there already exists a comprehensive theory on skewing schemes, see also chapter 2 and 3. Recall the results obtained for skewing schemes for 1-dimensional arrays, cf. section 2.1 and [TvLW86].

A strip is nothing but a bundle of 1-dimensional arrays, and a strip template is nothing but a bundle of 1-dimensional templates. Let $\mathbb{Z}^+ = \{x \mid x \in \mathbb{Z} \text{ and } x \geqslant 0\}$.

Definition 4.7
(i) A strip S is a copy of the set $\mathbb{Z} \times \mathbb{Z}^+$.
(ii) A strip template ST on a strip S is any finite set of elements:
$\{(a_1^0, 0), (a_2^0, 0), ..., (a_{N_0}^0, 0), (a_1^1, 1), (a_2^1, 1), ..., (a_{N_1}^1, 1), ..., (a_1^t, t), (a_2^t, t), ..., (a_{N_t}^t, t)\} \subseteq S$, *such that* $t \geqslant 0$, *for all* $0 \leqslant j \leqslant t : 0 \leqslant a_1^j < a_2^j < ... < a_{N_j}^j$, *and there exists a* $j, 0 \leqslant j \leqslant t$ *such that* $a_1^j = 0$.
(iii) An instance $ST(x)$, $x \in \mathbb{Z}$, of a strip template ST is the set $\{(a + x, b) \mid (a, b) \in ST\}$.

Beside these strip templates which can be shifted in a "horizontal" direction, we also define templates on a strip, which can be shifted in a "vertical" direction.

Definition 4.8
(i) A transversal template TT on a strip S is any finite subset $\{c_1, c_2, ..., c_N\}$ of $\mathbb{Z}$.
(ii) The projections of a transversal template TT are the sets

$$\pi_0(TT) = \{b_1^0, b_2^0, ...\},$$
$$\pi_1(TT) = \{b_1^1, b_2^1, ...\},$$
$$\vdots$$
$$\pi_t(TT) = \{b_1^t, b_2^t, ...\},$$

such that for all $0 \leqslant j \leqslant t : 0 \leqslant b_1^j < b_2^j < ...$, *for all* $0 \leqslant i \leqslant t$, $0 \leqslant j \leqslant t$, $i \neq j : \pi_i(TT) \cap \pi_j(TT) \neq \emptyset$, *and such that for each* $c_i \in TT$ *there exists a* m_i *and* j_i *such that* $c_i = b_{j_i}^{m_i} \in \pi_{m_i}(TT)$.
(iii) An instance $TT(x, y), x \in \mathbb{Z}$ *and* $y \geqslant 0$, *is the set* $\{(x, b_{j_1+y}^{m_1}), (x, b_{j_2+y}^{m_2}), ..., (x, b_{j_N+y}^{m_N})\}$, *with* m_i *and* j_i *as determined in (ii).*

The sets $\pi_0(TT), \pi_1(TT), ..., \pi_t(TT)$ can be seen as a strip S' embedded in one "column" of the strip S, and the transversal template TT can be seen as a strip template on the strip S'. This is illustrated in figure 4.4.

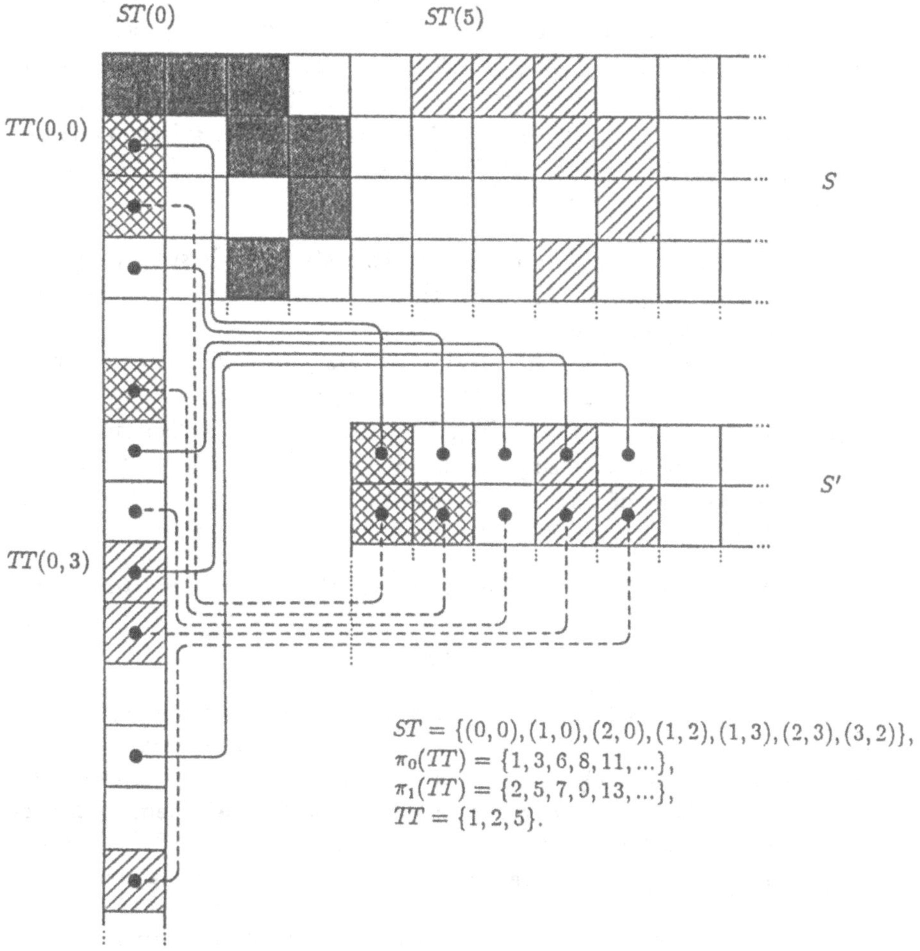

Figure 4.4: The transversal templates seen as embedded strip templates.

Definition 4.9
(i) A skewing scheme for a strip S is a mapping $s : S \to \{0, 1, ..., M-1\}$.
(ii) A skewing scheme s is valid for a collection of strip and transversal templates $\{ST_1, ST_2, ..., ST_n, TT_1, TT_2, ..., TT_m\}$, m and n both finite, if $\forall 1 \leqslant i \leqslant n \, \forall x \in \mathbf{Z} \, \forall j \in \{0, 1, ..., M-1\} : |ST_i(x) \cap s^{-1}(j)| \leqslant 1$, and if $\forall 1 \leqslant i \leqslant m \, \forall x \in \mathbf{Z} \, \forall y \geqslant 0 \, \forall j \in \{0, 1, ..., M-1\} : |TT_i(x, y) \cap s^{-1}(j)| \leqslant 1$.
(iii) $\mu_S(\{ST_1, ST_2, ..., ST_n, TT_1, TT_2, ..., TT_m\})$ is equal to the minimum numer M such that there exists a skewing scheme $s : S \to \{0, 1, ..., M-1\}$ which is valid for that collection of templates.

The collection C of templates on a strip consists of both strip templates and transversal templates. Although this is mathematical imprecise , for denotational purposes we define C in this way.

Define for each $c \in \mathbf{Z}$ the cut strip $S^c = \{x | x \geqslant c\} \times \mathbf{Z}^+$. Then again we can define a strip template ST on S^c, a transversal template TT, a skewing scheme $s : S^c \to \{0, 1, ..., M-1\}$ and $\mu_{S^c}(C)$ with C a collection of strip templates and transversal templates on S^c, in a similar way as for a strip S. As a consequence of a result obtained by Shapiro[Sha78b], we have the following lemma.

Lemma 4.4 *For every $c \in \mathbf{Z}$, and C a collection of strip and transversal templates,*

$$\mu_S(C) = \mu_{S^c}(C).$$

Proof $\mu_S(C) \geqslant \mu_{S^c}(C)$ trivially. Let s^c be a skewing scheme for S^c valid for C, which uses $\mu_{S^c}(C) = M$ memory banks. Let $d \, (\in \mathbf{Z})$ be arbitrary, then $s^d : S^d \to \{0, 1, ..., M-1\}$ defined by $s^d(x, y) = s^c(x + c - d, y)$ is valid for C too. So we have that for every $d \in \mathbf{Z}$ there exists a skewing scheme s^d for the strip S^d, which is valid for C and uses only M memory banks. The remainder of the proof can be given analogously to the proof of [Sha78b, appendix]. □

Let C be a collection $\{P_1, P_2, ..., P_t\}$ of templates, i.e., finite subsets of $\mathbf{Z}^d$, on a d-dimensional array $\mathbf{Z}^d$, cf. definition 4.1. Let $\mu_{\mathbf{Z}^d}(C)$ denote the minimum number M such that there exists a skewing scheme $s : \mathbf{Z}^d \to \{0, 1, ..., M-1\}$ which is valid for C.

Theorem 4.5 *Let $d \geqslant 2$, $\mathbf{Z}^d$ a d-dimensional array, and C_1 a set of templates on $\mathbf{Z}^d$. Then there exists a (necessarily) infinite set C_2 of transversal templates on a strip S, such that*

$$\mu_{\mathbf{Z}^d}(C_1) = \mu_S(C_2).$$

Proof Because $\mathbb{Z}^d$ is countable, there exists a bijection η from $\mathbb{Z}^d$ to $\mathbb{Z}^+$. Define a set C_2 of transversal templates on a strip S by

$$C_2 = \{TT \mid \text{there exist } x \in \mathbb{Z}^d, P \in C_1, \text{ and } 1 \leqslant i \leqslant d \text{ such that } TT = \eta(P(x)), \pi_0(TT) = X_0^i, \pi_1(TT) = X_1^i, ..., \pi_t(TT) = X_{t_i}^i, \text{ with } \{X_0^i, X_1^i, ..., X_{t_i}^i\} = \{\{(a_1, a_2, ..., a_{i-1}, y, a_{i+1}, a_{i+2}, ..., a_d) | y \in \mathbb{Z}\} | (a_1, a_2, ..., a_d) \in P(x)\}.$$

Note that except for the trivial case that for all $P \in C_1 : |P| \leqslant 1$, C_2 is infinite. It can be verified that C_2 "satisfies" the theorem. □

Thus, we have shown that the problem of finding skewing schemes for d-dimensional arrays can be reduced to the problem of finding skewing schemes for strip data-structures. In section 4.4 it will be shown that finding skewing schemes for tree data-structures also reduces to finding suitable skewing schemes for strips. We conclude this section by stating two conjectures, which we are unable to prove.

Conjecture 4.1 *Let $C = \{ST_1, ..., ST_n, TT_1, ..., TT_m\}$, be a finite collection of strip and transversal templates on a cut strip S^0. Let $l = \max_{(a,b) \in ST_i} a$, and let $s : \{0, 1, ..., 2l-1\} \times \mathbb{Z}^+ \to \{0, 1, ..., M-1\}$ be an "incomplete" skewing scheme on S^0 which is valid for C, $M \leqslant \mu_S(C)$. Then there exists a skewing scheme $s' : S^0 \to \{0, 1, ..., M'-1\}$, such that $s' \upharpoonright \{0, 1, ..., l-1\} \times \mathbb{Z}^+ = s \upharpoonright \{0, 1, ..., l-1\} \times \mathbb{Z}^+$, $M \leqslant M' \leqslant \mu_S(C)$, and s' is valid for C.*

Conjecture 4.2 *Let C and l be as in the previous conjecture. Then for every "incomplete" skewing scheme $s : \{0, 1, ..., 2l-1\} \times \mathbb{Z}^+ \to \{0, 1, ..., M-1\}$ valid for C, holds $M \geqslant \mu_S(C)$.*

4.3 An Exact Characterization of the Number $\mu_T(\{P_1, P_2, ..., P_t\})$

To capture the underlying structure of the conditions that are forced by the validity of a skewing scheme for a collection of templates on a tree T, we define certain subsets of the tree T, called lines (or: bundles of lines). These bundles of lines allow a direct translation to a strip S, on which a collection ST of strip templates and a collection TT of transversal templates can be defined which correspond to the collection of templates on T. Theorem 4.6 shows that $\mu_T(\{P_1 P_2, ... P_t\})$ is equal to the minimum number of memory banks needed by a skewing scheme on a strip S to be valid for ST and TT.

Definition 4.10 *Let T be a (k-ary) tree. A line ${}_{\alpha}l_{\beta}^{\lambda}$ (l, for short) is the set*

$$\{\alpha\beta, \alpha\lambda\beta, \alpha\lambda^2\beta, ...\} \subseteq T, \text{ with}$$

(i) $\lambda \in T$, $\lambda \neq \varepsilon$ such that there exists no $\bar{\lambda} \in T, s > 1$ with $\lambda = \bar{\lambda}^s$,
(ii) $\alpha \in T$, such that $\lambda \notin$ Suffix(α) and
(iii) $\beta \in T$, such that Prefix(β) $\cap$ Prefix(λ) $= \{\varepsilon\}$.
λ, α, and β are called the period, head, *and* tail *of the line l, respectively.*

The conditions on λ, α, and β imply that a line is uniquely represented. Furthermore a line is fully determined by any two distinct nodes ϱ and σ which are elements of l.

Lemma 4.5 *Let $\varrho = \varrho_1\varrho_2...\varrho_n$ and $\sigma = \sigma_1\sigma_2...\sigma_m$ be elements of T. Then there exists a line l with $\varrho \in l$ and $\sigma \in l$ iff there exist i, j ($i < j$) such that $\varrho_1...\varrho_i = \sigma_1...\sigma_i$ and $\varrho_{i+1}...\varrho_n = \sigma_j...\sigma_m$ or such that $\sigma_1....\sigma_i = \varrho_1...\varrho_i$ and $\sigma_{i+1}...\sigma_m = \varrho_j...\varrho_n$.*

Proof Directly from definition 4.10. □

Definition 4.11
(i) A line ${}_{\alpha}l_{\beta}^{\lambda}$ is called primary iff $\alpha \in$ Suffix(λ).
(ii) Two primary lines ${}_{\alpha}l_{\beta}^{\lambda}$ and ${}_{\varrho}l_{\sigma}^{\mu}$ are called related iff $\beta = \sigma$ and $\lambda = \mu$.
(iii) Two primary lines ${}_{\alpha}l_{\beta}^{\lambda}$ and ${}_{\varrho}l_{\sigma}^{\mu}$ with $\lambda = \lambda_1...\lambda_n, \alpha = \alpha_1...\alpha_m$ and $\varrho = \varrho_1...\varrho_l$, are called associated iff there exist i ($1 \leqslant i \leqslant n$), and j ($1 \leqslant j \leqslant$ min(m, l)) such that $\lambda_{i+1}...\lambda_n\lambda_1...\lambda_i = \mu$, and $\alpha_1...\alpha_j = \varrho$ or $\varrho_1...\varrho_j = \alpha$.

Note that the relationships "related" and "associated" are equivalences.

Example
In figure 4.5 an example of a binary tree is shown, together with some lines. The (primary) lines l, l_1 and l_2 (of figure 4.5) are related to each other, the (primary) lines l, m, and m_2 are associated.

Definition 4.12 *Let l be an arbitrary line, $l = {}_{\alpha}l_{\beta}^{\lambda}$. The corresponding primary line* prim(l) *is the line ${}_{\alpha'}l_{\beta}^{\lambda}$, with $\alpha' \in$ Suffix(α) $\cap$ Suffix(λ), $\alpha' \neq \alpha$ and $|\alpha'|$ is maximal. The* base *of the line l is the node $\gamma \in T$ such that $\{\gamma\varrho | \varrho \in$ prim(l)$\} = l$.*

For each line there is exactly one corresponding primary line. As we bundled a set of 1-dimensional arrays to get a strip, we now bundle a set of lines on a tree T, which are primary and associated to each other, to get a bundle on T.

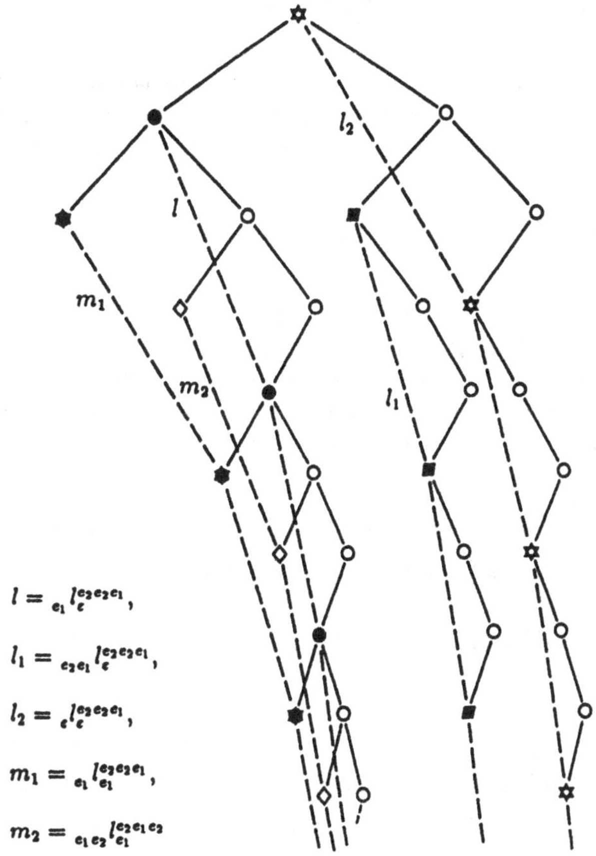

Figure 4.5: Lines on a tree T.

Definition 4.13 *Let l be a primary line, and $C = \{P_1, P_2, ..., P_t\}$ a collection of templates on a tree T.*
(i) The bundle $B_l^{(0)}$ of the line l is defined by

$$B_l^{(0)} = \{\gamma| \text{ there exists a primary line } m, \text{ which is associated with } l, \text{ such that } \gamma \in m, \text{ and there exists a primary line } m' \text{ which is related to } m, \text{ such that } |m' \cap P_k| \geqslant 1 \text{ for some } P_k \in C\}.$$

(ii) The collection $TL_l^{(1)}$ of lines is defined by

$$TL_l^{(1)} = \{m| \text{ there exist primary lines } m_1 \text{ and } m_2, \text{ associated with } l, \text{ such that } m_1 \neq m_2,\ m_1 \subseteq B_l^{(0)},\ m_2 \subseteq B_l^{(0)}, \text{head}(m_1)\text{tail}(m_1) \in m, \text{ and } \text{head}(m_2)\text{tail}(m_2) \in m, \text{ and there exists a primary line } m' \text{ which is related to } \text{prim}(m), \text{ such that } |m' \cap P_k| \geqslant 1, \text{ for some } P_k \in C\}.$$

Furthermore $\widetilde{TL}_l^{(1)}$ is a maximal subset of $TL_l^{(1)}$ such that for all $m_1 \in \widetilde{TL}_l^{(1)}$, $m_2 \in \widetilde{TL}_l^{(1)}$, and $m_1 \neq m_2$, m_1 is not associated with m_2.

(iii) The bundle $B_l^{(1)}$ of the line l is defined by

$$B_l^{(1)} = B_l^{(0)} \cup \{\gamma| \text{ there exists a primary line } m \text{ which is associated with } l, \text{ such that } \gamma \in m, \text{ and there exists a line } m' \in \widetilde{TL}_l^{(1)}, \text{ such that there exists a primary line } {}_\alpha l_\beta^\lambda \subseteq B^{(0)}_{\text{prim}(m')} \text{ with } m \cap {}_{\gamma\alpha} l_\beta^\lambda \neq \emptyset \text{ and } \gamma = \text{base}(m')\}.$$

(iv) For $i \geqslant 2$:

$TL_l^{(i)}$ is defined similar to $TL_l^{(1)}$ except that $B_l^{(0)}$ has to be replaced by $B_l^{(i-1)}$, $\widetilde{TL}^{(i)}$ is a maximal subset of $TL_l^{(i)}$ which contains no elements which are associated to each other, and
$B_l^{(i)}$ is defined similar to $B_l^{(1)}$ except that $B_l^{(0)}$ has to be replaced by $B_l^{(i-1)}$ and $\widetilde{TL}_l^{(1)}$ by $\widetilde{TL}_l^{(i)}$.

(v) *The collection of transversal lines TL_l of l is defined by*

$TL_l = \{m|$ *there exists a* $i \geqslant 1$ *such that* $m \in \widetilde{TL}_l^{(i)}\}$.

(vi) *The bundle $B_l^{\mathcal{C}}$ of l with respect to l is defined by*

$B_l^{\mathcal{C}} = \{\alpha|$ *there exists a* $i \geqslant 0$ *such that* $\alpha \in B_l^{(i)}\}$.

An instance $B_l^{\mathcal{C}}(\gamma)$ of the bundle $B_l^{\mathcal{C}}$ is defined by $\alpha \in B_l^{\mathcal{C}}$ iff $\gamma\alpha \in B_l^{\mathcal{C}}(\gamma)$.

Because of the complexity of definition 4.13 some examples of bundles $B_l^{\mathcal{C}}$ are listed below.

Examples

In all examples T is a binary tree, whose edges are labeled by e_1 and e_2.
1. Let P be the template $\{e_2e_1, e_2e_1e_2\}$, and let l be the line ${}_{\varepsilon}l^{e_1}_{\varepsilon}$. Then for all lines m associated with l: period(m) $= e_1$. So all lines m', which are related to a line m which is associated with l, have period e_1. Thus $B_l^{(0)} = {}_{\varepsilon}l^{e_1}_{e_2e_1} \cup {}_{\varepsilon}l^{e_1}_{e_2e_1e_2}$. Because only the lines $m_1 = {}_{\varepsilon}l^{e_1}_{e_2e_1}$ and $m_2 = {}_{\varepsilon}l^{e_1}_{e_2e_1e_2}$ have the property that they are primary, $m_1 \neq m_2$, $|\text{tail}(m_1)| \leqslant |\text{tail}(m_2)|$, and $m_1 \subseteq B_l^{(0)}$ and $m_2 \subseteq B_l^{(0)}$ we have that for all lines $m \in TL_l^{(1)}$ both $e_2e_1e_2$ and $e_1^ke_2e_1$, for some $k \geqslant 0$, are element of m. Applying lemma 4.5 yields that $TL_l^{(1)} = \emptyset$. Hence $B_l^{\mathcal{C}} = {}_{\varepsilon}l^{e_1}_{e_2e_1} \cup {}_{\varepsilon}l^{e_1}_{e_2e_1e_2}$, with $\mathcal{C} = \{P\}$. See also figure 4.6(i).
2. Let $\mathcal{C} = \{P\}$, with $P = \{\varepsilon, e_1, e_2, e_1, e_2e_2e_1\}$, and $l = {}_{\varepsilon}l^{e_1}_{\varepsilon}$. Then, similar to example 1, we get $B_l^{(0)} = {}_{\varepsilon}l^{e_1}_{\varepsilon} \cup {}_{\varepsilon}l^{e_1}_{e_2e_1} \cup {}_{\varepsilon}l^{e_1}_{e_2e_2e_1}$, and $TL_l^{(1)} = \{{}_{\varepsilon}l^{e_2}_{e_1}, {}_{\varepsilon}l^{e_2e_1}_{\varepsilon}, {}_{\varepsilon}l^{e_2e_2e_1}_{\varepsilon}\}(= \widetilde{TL}_l^{(1)})$. From this set $\widetilde{TL}_l^{(1)}$ we can construct $B_l^{(1)}$, and $TL_l^{(2)}$, and so on. Note that there are already an infinite number of distinct lines m, associated with l, with $m \subseteq B_l^{(1)}$. The sets $B_l^{(0)}$ and $\widetilde{TL}_l^{(1)}$ are shown in figure 4.6(ii).

Regarding definition 4.13 we can make two observations.

Lemma 4.6 *Let l be an arbitrary primary line. Then*

$$|\{m|m \subseteq B_l^{(0)}\}| \leqslant |\text{period}(l)|. \sum_{P \in \mathcal{C}} |P|.$$

Furthermore $|\{m|m \subseteq B_l^{(1)}$, m associated with $l\}|$ is infinite except for the case that $B_l^{(0)} = B_l^{(1)} = ... = B_l^{\mathcal{C}}$.

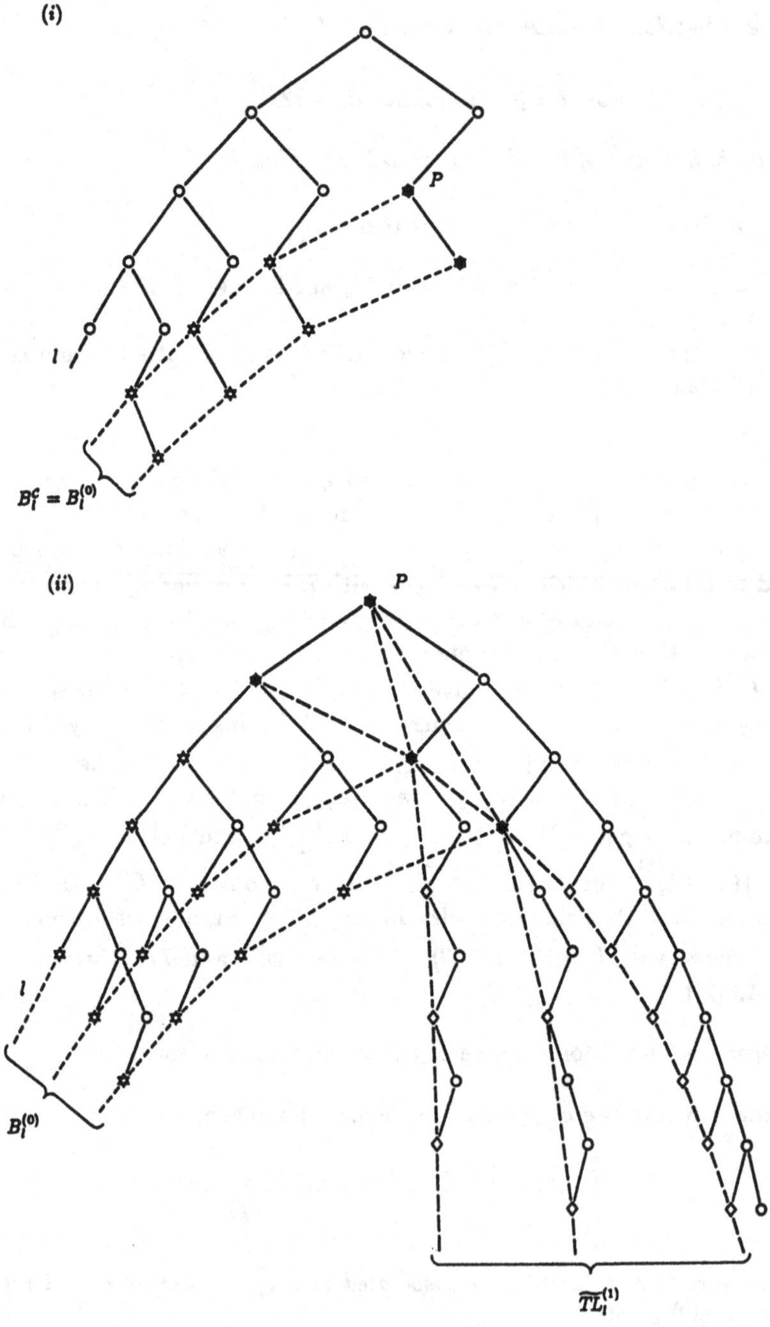

Figure 4.6: Some illustrations of the definition of the bundle B_l^c.

Proof From the definition of $B_l^{(0)}$ directly follows that

$$B_l^{(0)} = \bigcup_{\substack{m \\ \text{related to } l}} \bigcup_{\substack{m', \\ \text{associated with } m \\ \text{and } m' \cap P_k \neq \emptyset \\ \text{for some } P_k \in C}} \{\gamma \mid \text{there exists a primary line } m'' \text{ associated with } l \text{ and related to } m' \text{ such that } \gamma \in m''\}.$$

Together with the fact that $|\{m| m \text{ related to } l\}| \leqslant |\text{period}(l)|$, this gives the desired estimate on $|\{m| m \subseteq B_l^{(0)}\}|$.
That $|\{m| m \subseteq B_l^{(1)}, m \text{ associated with } l\}|$ is infinite except for the case that $B_l^{(0)} = B_l^C$, follows from the fact that $|\{m| m \subseteq B_l^{(1)}, m \text{ associated with } l\}|$ is infinite iff $TL^{(1)} \neq \emptyset$. □

Lemma 4.7 *Let l be an arbitrary primary line and let $i \geqslant 1$. Then*

$$B_l^{(i)} = B_l^{(i-1)} \cup \{(\text{period}(l))^s.\text{base}(m).\varrho | s \geqslant 0, m \in \widetilde{TL}_l^{(i)}, \textit{ and } \varrho \in B^{(0)}_{\text{prim}(m)}\}.$$

Proof Directly from definition 4.13. □

In order to get a unique representation of the bundle B_l^C, we need some kind of ordering on B_l^C.

Definition 4.14 *The standard decomposition $\mathcal{D}_{B_l^C}$ of a bundle B_l^C is the set $\{l_0, l_1, l_2, ...\}$, with $B_l^C = \bigcup_{i \geqslant 0} l_i$, for all i, j $(i \neq j)$: $l_i \neq l_j$, for all i, j $(i < j)$: $\text{tail}(l_i) \prec \text{tail}(l_j)$, and for all i : l_i is associated with l.*

Lemma 4.8 *Let l and m be two primary lines, with l related to m, and $\mathcal{D}_{B_l^C} = \{l_0, l_1, l_2, ...\}$. Then for all $i \geqslant 0$: $\text{tail}(l_i) = \text{tail}(m_i)$ and l_i is related to m_i.*

Proof Directly from the definitions. □

In the following we shall identify a bundle B_l^C with a cut strip S^0, and the instances $P(\gamma)$ of a template on a tree T, which have a non-empty intersection with B_l^C, with instances of strip and transversal templates on S^0.

Definition 4.15 *Let B_l^C be given, and let $\mathcal{D}_{B_l^C} = \{l_0, l_1, l_2, ...\}$. The corresponding cut strip $S^0_{B_l^C}$ is the set $\mathbf{Z}^+ \times \mathbf{Z}^+$, and the bijective map $\eta_{B_l^C}$: $B_l^C \to S^0_{B_l^C}$ is defined by $\eta_{B_l^C}(\gamma) = (t, r)$, with $r \in \mathbf{Z}^+$ and $t \in \mathbf{Z}^+$ such that $\gamma \in l_r = {}_\alpha l_\beta^\lambda \in D_{B_l^C}$ and $\gamma = \alpha\lambda^t\beta$.*

Definition 4.16 *Let l be a primary line, and $C = \{P_1, P_2, ..., P_t\}$ a collection of templates. The collection ST_l of strip templates on the strip $S^0_{B^c_l}$ is defined by*

$$ST_l = \{\eta_{B^c_m}(P_i) |\ P_i \in C \text{ and } m \text{ a primary line related to } l\}.$$

Note lemma 4.8 with respect to this definition 4.16. The strip templates of ST_l only act on $\eta_{B^c_l}(B^{(0)}_l)$.

Definition 4.17 *Let l be a primary line, and let $C = \{P_1, P_2, ..., P_t\}$ be a collection of templates.*
(i) Let for each $m' \subseteq TL_l$: $\{\{\text{base}(m').\varrho | \varrho \in m''\} | m'' \subseteq B^{(0)}_{\text{prim}(m')}\} = \{m_1, m_2, ..., m_k\}$, and let for each m with $\text{prim}(m)$ related to $\text{prim}(m')$ and $\text{base}(m) = \text{base}(m') = \gamma : \text{head}(\text{prim}(m)) = \alpha$ and $\text{head}(\text{prim}(m')) = \alpha'$. Then define for each $j, 1 \leqslant j \leqslant t$, the transversal template $TT_{m,j}$ on the strip $S^0_{B^c_l}$ by

$$TT_{m,j} = \bigcup_{1 \leqslant i \leqslant k} \eta_1(m_i \cap \{\gamma\alpha_1\varrho |\ \varrho \in P_j\}),$$

and for each i, $1 \leqslant i \leqslant k$, $\pi_i(TT_{m,j}) = \eta_1(m_i \cap B^c_l)$, with $\eta_1(\alpha) = j$ iff $\eta_{B^c_l}(\alpha) = (i,j)$, with $\alpha_1 \in T$ such that $\alpha' = \alpha_1\alpha$, if $|\alpha| < |\alpha'|$, and $\text{period}(m).\alpha' = \alpha_1\alpha$, otherwise.
(ii) The collection TT_l of transversal templates on the strip $S^0_{B^c_l}$ is defined by

$$TT_l = \{TT_{m,j} |\ 1 \leqslant j \leqslant t, \text{ and there exists a line } m' \in TL_l \text{ with } \text{prim}(m') \text{ related to } \text{prim}(m), \text{ and } \text{base}(m') = \text{base}(m)\}.$$

In figure 4.7 the connection between templates on a tree T and strip and transversal templates on a strip $S^0_{B^c_l}$ is illustrated. Recall within this context also figure 4.4.

We are ready now to state our main result.

Theorem 4.6 *Let T be a k-ary tree, and $C = \{P_1, P_2, ..., P_t\}$ a collection of templates on T. Then*

$$\mu_T(C) = \mu_{S^0_{B^c_l}}(ST_l \cup TT_l),$$

with $l = {}_e l^\lambda_e$, λ arbitrary.

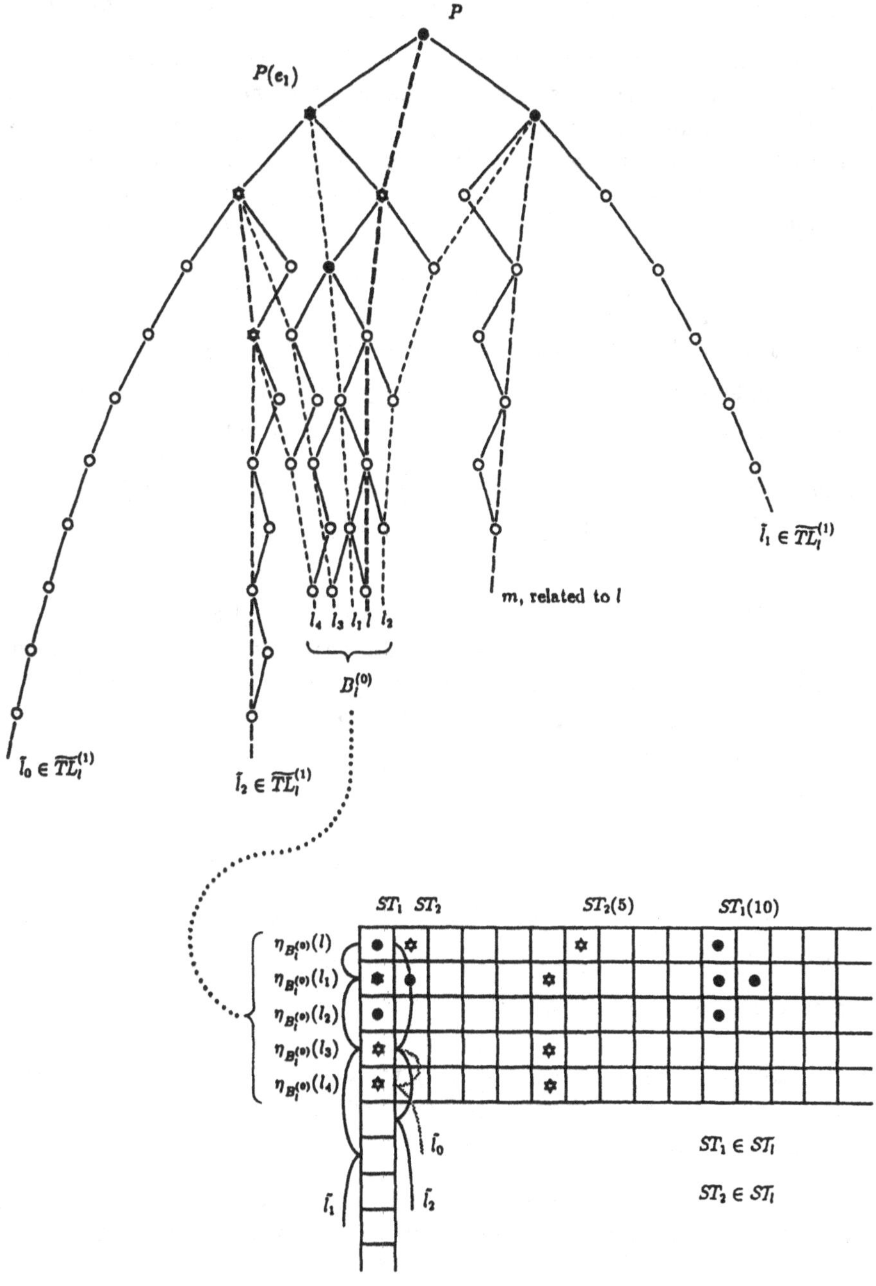

Figure 4.7: The relationship between templates on a tree T and strip and transversal templates on the strip $S^0_{B_l^c}$.

Proof For the sake of simplicity, let M denote the number $\mu_{S^0_{B_l^C}}(ST_l \cup TT_l)$. The proof proceeds by showing the existence of a skewing scheme $s : T \to \{0, 1, ..., M-1\}$, which is valid for C. This is all we need to prove because from the definitions it is clear that $\mu_T(C) \geqslant M$. The skewing scheme s is constructed by successively assigning values $\in \{0, 1, ..., M-1\}$ to nodes $\in T$, proceeding from level i to level $i+1$ and from the nth node in each level to the $(n+1)^{th}$ node. In each node γ the following two algorithms are performed.

Step I. Consider $B_l^C(\gamma)$. For this instance of the bundle B_l^C the collection $\Gamma = \{\alpha |\ \gamma\alpha \in B_l^C$ and $\gamma\alpha$ is already assigned by $s\}$ induces a "incomplete" skewing scheme s'_γ on $S^0_{B_l^C}$, defined by $\forall \alpha \in \Gamma : s'_\gamma(\eta_{B_l^C}(\alpha)) = s(\gamma\alpha)$. Extend this incomplete skewing scheme s'_γ to a complete skewing scheme s_γ on $S^0_{B_l^C}$, which is valid for the collection $ST_l \cup TT_l$ and uses only $\mu_{S^0_{B_l^C}}(ST_l \cup TT_l)$ numbers. Assign to all nodes $\gamma\alpha \in B_l^C(\gamma)$ the number $s_\gamma(\eta_{B_l^C}(\alpha))$.
Step II. If γ is not assigned to yet, then assign to γ an arbitrary number $\in \{0, 1, ..., M-1\}$.

First we shall prove that the construction actually can be done. Suppose we have arrived at a node γ, γ arbitrary. Then the next claim shows that for every pair of nodes ϱ and σ, $\varrho \in B_l^C(\gamma)$ and $\sigma \in B_l^C(\gamma)$, is valid that if there exists a node γ' and a template $P \in C$, with $\varrho \in P(\gamma')$ and $\sigma \in P(\gamma')$, then both ϱ and σ are assigned, or both ϱ and σ are not assigned yet. This means that the skewing scheme $s_\gamma : S^0_{B_l^C} \to \{0, 1, ..., M-1\}$, defined by

$$s_\gamma(i,j) = \begin{cases} s'_\gamma(i,j), \text{ if } (i,j) = \eta_{B_l^C}(\alpha) \text{ for some } \alpha \in \Gamma \\ s''(i,j), \text{ otherwise} \end{cases}$$

with $s'' : S^0_{B_l^C} \to \{0, 1, ..., M-1\}$ an arbitrary skewing scheme which is valid for $ST_l \cup TT_l$, is valid for $ST_l \cup TT_l$.

In the following we shall write $\gamma' \leqslant \gamma$ whenever γ' lies on the path from γ to the root α_0. Furthermore, each time when we write a node $\lambda \in T$ as $\lambda = \lambda_1 ... \lambda_n$, we tacitly assume that for all i, $1 \leqslant i \leqslant n$, $\lambda_i \in \{e_1, e_2, ..., e_k\}$.

Claim 4.1 *Let $P \in C$, and let ϱ, σ and γ be nodes $\in T$ such that $\varrho \in P(\gamma)$ and $\sigma \in P(\gamma)$. Then there does not exist nodes γ_1 and γ_2, with $\gamma_1 \lneqq \gamma_2 \leqslant \gamma$, $\varrho \in B_l^C(\gamma_1)$, $\sigma \in B_l^C(\gamma_2)$ and for all $\gamma' \lneqq \gamma_1$, $\gamma'' \lneqq \gamma_2 : \varrho \notin B_l^C(\gamma')$ and $\sigma \notin B_l^C(\gamma'')$.*

Proof Suppose there do exist nodes γ_1 and γ_2, with $\gamma_1 \lneq \gamma_2 \leqslant \gamma$, $\varrho \in B_l^C(\gamma_1)$, $\sigma \in B_l^C(\gamma_2)$ and for all $\gamma' \lneq \gamma_1, \gamma'' \lneq \gamma_2 : \varrho \notin B_l^C(\gamma')$ and $\sigma \notin B_l^C(\gamma'')$. $\varrho \in B_l^C(\gamma_1)$, thus $\varrho \in \{\gamma_1\alpha | \alpha \in {}_{\lambda_1...\lambda_k}l_\beta^{\lambda_{k+1}...\lambda_n\lambda_1...\lambda_k}(= m_1)\}$, with $\lambda_1...\lambda_n = \lambda$ ($l = {}_el_e^\lambda$), and $1 \leqslant k \leqslant n$. Let $\beta = \beta_1...\beta_p$. Then we can distinguish three cases.

Case 1 $\gamma = \gamma_1\lambda_1...\lambda_k(\lambda_{k+1}...\lambda_n\lambda_1...\lambda_k)^t\beta_1...\beta_i$, $t \geqslant 0$ and $i \leqslant p$.
Case 2 $\gamma = \gamma_1\lambda_1...\lambda_k(\lambda_{k+1}...\lambda_n\lambda_1...\lambda_k)^t\lambda_{k+1}...\lambda_i$, $t \geqslant 0$ and $i > k$, or
$\gamma = \gamma_1\lambda_1...\lambda_k(\lambda_{k+1}...\lambda_n\lambda_1...\lambda_k)^t\lambda_{k+1}...\lambda_n\lambda_1...\lambda_i$, $t \geqslant 0$ and $i < k$.
Case 3 $\gamma = \gamma_1\lambda_1...\lambda_i$, $i < k$.

Consider **case 1.**
Let $\varrho^{(1)}$ be the node with $\gamma\varrho^{(1)} = \varrho$. Then $\varrho^{(1)} \in P$ and $\varrho^{(1)} = \beta_{i+1}...\beta_p$. Consider the line $m_2 = {}_{\lambda_1...\lambda_j}l_{\beta_{i+j+1}...\beta_p}^{\lambda_{j+1}...\lambda_n\lambda_1...\lambda_j}$, with $\lambda_1...\lambda_j\beta_{i+j+1}...\beta_p = \beta_{i+1}...\beta_p$ and j maximal. Because m_2 is associated with l, and $\varrho^{(1)} = \beta_{i+1}...\beta_p \in m_2 \cap P$, it follows that $m_2 \subseteq B_l^{(0)}$.

Let μ be such that $|\mu|$ is minimal and there exists a $q \geqslant 1$ with $\mu^q = \lambda_1...\lambda_k\beta_1...\beta_i$. Let l_1 be the primary line ${}_el^\mu_{\beta_{i+1}...\beta_p}$. (In case that $\beta_{i+1} = \lambda_1$, take for l_1 the primary line associated with ${}_el_e^\mu$ such that $\beta_{i+1}...\beta_p \in l_1$. Further, this case can be handled analogously.) For this line l_1 both

$$\text{head}(m_1)\text{tail}(m_1) = \lambda_1...\lambda_k\beta_1...\beta_p = \mu^q\beta_{i+1}...\beta_p \in l_1 \text{ , and}$$
$$\text{head}(m_2)\text{tail}(m_2) = \lambda_1...\lambda_j\beta_{i+j+1}...\beta_p = \beta_{i+1}...\beta_p \in l_1.$$

Furthermore $\beta_{i+1}...\beta_p = \varrho^{(1)} \in P$. Thus, $l_1 \in TL_l^{(i)}$, for some $i \geqslant 1$. Applying lemma 4.7 gives $B_{l_1}^{(0)}(\lambda^v) \subseteq B_l^C$, for all $v \geqslant 0$. Consider σ, and let $\sigma^{(1)}$ be such that $\gamma\sigma^{(1)} = \sigma$. Then $\sigma^{(1)} \in P$. We can distinguish two cases.

Case 1.1 $\sigma^{(1)} = \mu^{q_1}\beta_{i+1}...\beta_{j_1}\sigma^{(2)}$, $q_1 \geqslant 0$ and j_1 with $p \geqslant j_1 > i$.
Case 1.2 $\sigma^{(1)} = \mu^{q_1}\mu_1...\mu_{j_1}\sigma^{(2)}$, $q_1 \geqslant 0$, $j_1 \leqslant n_1$, and $\mu_1...\mu_{n_1} = \mu$.

Consider **case 1.1.**
Let l_2 be the line ${}_el^\mu_{\beta_{i+1}...\beta_{j_1}\sigma^{(2)}}$. Then l_2 is primary, $\sigma^{(1)} \in l_2$, and l_2 is associated with l_1. Thus, $l_2 \subseteq B_{l_1}^{(0)}$. Hence,

$$\begin{aligned}
\sigma = \gamma\sigma^{(1)} &= \gamma_1\lambda_1...\lambda_k(\lambda_{k+1}...\lambda_n\lambda_1...\lambda_k)^t\beta_1...\beta_i\mu^{q_1}\beta_{i+1}...\beta_{j_1}\sigma^{(2)} \\
&= \gamma_1(\lambda_1...\lambda_n)^t\lambda_1...\lambda_k\beta_1...\beta_i\mu^{q_1}\beta_{i+1}...\beta_{j_1}\sigma^{(2)} \\
&= \gamma_1\lambda^t\mu^{q+q_1}\beta_{i+1}...\beta_{j_1}\sigma^{(2)} \\
&\in B_l^{(0)}(\gamma_1\lambda^t) \subseteq B_l^C(\gamma_1).
\end{aligned}$$

Contradiction. Figure 4.8 gives an illustration of case 1.1. The lines l, l_1, l_2, m_1 and m_2 are drawn starting from γ_1.

Case 1.2 can be handled analogously.

Consider **case 2**.
Then $\gamma = \gamma_1\lambda_1...\lambda_k(\lambda_{k+1}...\lambda_n\lambda_1...\lambda_k)^t\lambda_{k+1}...\lambda_i$ for some $t \geqslant 0$ and $i > k$. The case that $\gamma = \gamma_1\lambda_1...\lambda_k(\lambda_{k+1}...\lambda_n\lambda_1...\lambda_k)^t\lambda_{k+1}...\lambda_n\lambda_1...\lambda_i$ for some $t \geqslant 0$ and $i < k$ can be handled analogously. Let $\sigma^{(1)}$ be such that $\gamma\sigma^{(1)} = \sigma$. Then $\sigma^{(1)} \in P$. Furthermore let

$$\sigma^{(1)} = (\lambda_{i+1}...\lambda_n\lambda_1...\lambda_i)^v\lambda_{i+1}...\lambda_j\sigma^{(2)}, v \geqslant 0, j \geqslant i,$$

and $|\sigma^{(2)}|$ minimal. The case that $\sigma^{(1)} = (\lambda_{i+1}...\lambda_n\lambda_1...\lambda_i)^v\lambda_{i+1}...\lambda_n\lambda_1...\lambda_j$, $v \geqslant 0$, and $j < i$ can be handled analogously.

Consider the line $m = {}_{\lambda_1...\lambda_j}l_{\sigma^{(2)}}^{\lambda_{j+1}...\lambda_n\lambda_1...\lambda_j}$. Then m is primary and associated with l. Furthermore $\sigma^{(1)} = (\lambda_{i+1}...\lambda_n\lambda_1...\lambda_i)^v\lambda_{i+1}...\lambda_j\sigma^{(2)} \in {}_{\lambda_{i+1}...\lambda_j}l_{\sigma^{(2)}}^{\lambda_{j+1}...\lambda_n\lambda_1...\lambda_j}$, which is related to l'. Hence $l' \subseteq B_l^{(0)}$. Moreover we have

$$\begin{aligned}\sigma &= \gamma_1\lambda_1...\lambda_k(\lambda_{k+1}...\lambda_n\lambda_1...\lambda_k)^t\lambda_{k+1}...\lambda_i(\lambda_{i+1}...\lambda_n\lambda_1...\lambda_i)^v\lambda_{i+1}...\lambda_j\sigma^{(2)}\\ &= \gamma_1\lambda_1...\lambda_j(\lambda_{j+1}...\lambda_n\lambda_1...\lambda_j)^{t+v}\sigma^{(2)}\\ &\in \{\gamma_1\alpha \mid \alpha \in l'\} \subseteq B_l^{(0)}(\gamma_1) \subseteq B_l^{\mathcal{C}}(\gamma_1).\end{aligned}$$

Contradiction.

Case 3 can be handled analogously to case 2.

□

It remains to be proven that the skewing scheme s so obtained is valid for $\mathcal{C}$.

Claim 4.2 *For all $P \in \mathcal{C}$ and for all instances $P(\gamma)$ of P we have that for all $\varrho \in P(\gamma)$ and $\sigma \in P(\gamma), \sigma \neq \varrho : s(\sigma) \neq s(\varrho)$.*

Proof Because of claim 4.1 we only have to consider the case that both $\varrho \in B_l^{\mathcal{C}}(\gamma_1)$ and $\sigma \in B_l^{\mathcal{C}}(\gamma_1)$, for some $\gamma_1 \leqslant \gamma$, and both ϱ and σ are assigned by $B_l^{\mathcal{C}}(\gamma_1)$. $\varrho \in B_l^{\mathcal{C}}(\gamma_1)$ and $\sigma \in B_l^{\mathcal{C}}(\gamma_1)$, thus

$$\varrho \in \{\gamma_1\alpha \mid \alpha \in {}_{\lambda_1...\lambda_k}l_{\beta^{(1)}}^{\lambda_{k+1}...\lambda_n\lambda_1...\lambda_k}\}, \text{ and}$$

$$\sigma \in \{\gamma_1\alpha \mid \alpha \in {}_{\lambda_1...\lambda_k}l_{\beta^{(2)}}^{\lambda_{k+1}...\lambda_n\lambda_1...\lambda_k}\},$$

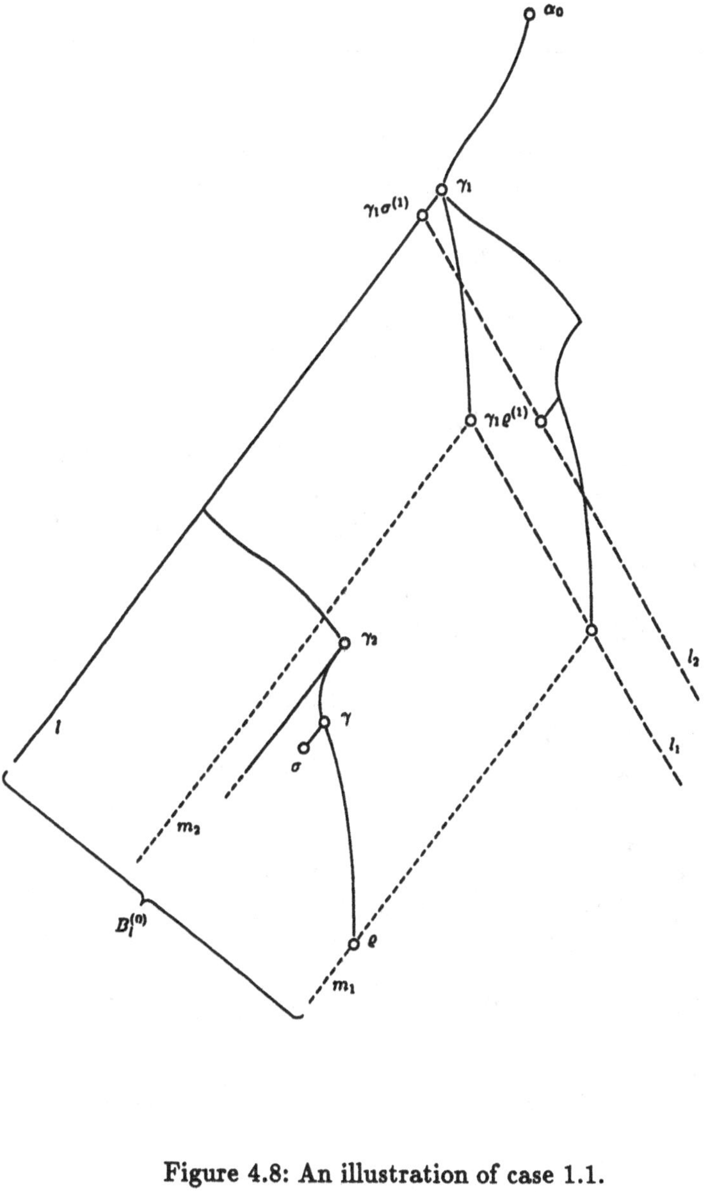

Figure 4.8: An illustration of case 1.1.

with $\lambda_1...\lambda_n = \lambda$ ($l = {}_e l_e^\lambda$), $1 \leqslant k \leqslant n$, and $1 \leqslant h \leqslant n$. So there exists $s \geqslant 0$ and $t \geqslant 0$ such that

$$\varrho = \gamma_1\lambda_1...\lambda_k(\lambda_{k+1}...\lambda_n\lambda_1...\lambda_k)^s\beta^{(1)}, \text{ and}$$
$$\sigma = \gamma_1\lambda_1...\lambda_h(\lambda_{h+1}...\lambda_n\lambda_1...\lambda_h)^t\beta^{(2)}.$$

Let $\varrho^{(1)}$ and $\sigma^{(1)}$ be such that $\gamma\varrho^{(1)} = \varrho$ and $\gamma\sigma^{(1)} = \sigma$. Then $\varrho^{(1)} \in P$ and $\sigma^{(1)} \in P$, and

$$\gamma^{(1)}\varrho^{(1)} = \lambda_1...\lambda_k(\lambda_{k+1}...\lambda_n\lambda_1...\lambda_k)^s\beta^{(1)}, \text{ and}$$
$$\gamma^{(1)}\sigma^{(1)} = \lambda_1...\lambda_h(\lambda_{h+1}...\lambda_n\lambda_1...\lambda_h)^t\beta^{(2)}, \text{ with } \gamma_1\gamma^{(1)} = \gamma.$$

We can now distinguish 9 cases.

Case 1 $\varrho^{(1)} = \lambda_j...\lambda_n(\lambda_1...\lambda_n)^{s'}\lambda_1...\lambda_k\beta^{(1)}$, and
$\sigma^{(1)} = \lambda_j...\lambda_n(\lambda_1...\lambda_n)^{t'}\lambda_1...\lambda_h\beta^{(2)}$, j, $1 \leqslant j \leqslant n$, $0 \leqslant s' \leqslant s$, and $0 \leqslant t' \leqslant t$.

Case 2 $\varrho^{(1)} = \lambda_j...\lambda_n(\lambda_1...\lambda_n)^{s'}\lambda_1...\lambda_k\beta^{(1)}$, and
$\sigma^{(1)} = \lambda_j...\lambda_h\beta^{(2)}$, j, $1 \leqslant j \leqslant n$, and $0 \leqslant s' \leqslant s$.

Case 3 $\varrho^{(1)} = \lambda_j...\lambda_k\beta^{(1)}$, and
$\sigma^{(1)} = \lambda_j...\lambda_n(\lambda_1...\lambda_n)^{t'}\lambda_1...\lambda_h\beta^{(2)}$, j, $1 \leqslant j \leqslant n$, and $0 \leqslant t' \leqslant t$.

Case 4 $\varrho^{(1)} = \lambda_j...\lambda_k\beta^{(1)}$, and
$\sigma^{(1)} = \lambda_j...\lambda_h\beta^{(2)}$, j, $1 \leqslant j \leqslant n$.

Case 5 $\varrho^{(1)} = \lambda_j...\lambda_n(\lambda_1...\lambda_n)^{s'}\lambda_1...\lambda_k\beta^{(2)}$, and
$\gamma^{(2)}\sigma^{(1)} = \lambda_1...\lambda_h\beta^{(2)}$, j, $1 \leqslant j \leqslant n$, $0 \leqslant s' \leqslant s$, and $\gamma^{(2)} \gneqq \lambda_1...\lambda_h$.

Case 6 $\gamma^{(2)}\varrho^{(1)} = \lambda_1...\lambda_k\beta^{(1)}$, and
$\sigma^{(1)} = \lambda_j...\lambda_n(\lambda_1...\lambda_n)^{t'}\lambda_1...\lambda_h\beta^{(2)}$, j, $1 \leqslant j \leqslant n$, $0 \leqslant t' \leqslant t$, and $\gamma^{(2)} \gneqq \lambda_1...\lambda_k$.

Case 7 $\varrho^{(1)} = \lambda_j...\lambda_k\beta^{(1)}$, and
$\gamma^{(2)}\sigma^{(1)} = \lambda_1...\lambda_h\beta^{(2)}$, j, $1 \leqslant j \leqslant n$, and $\gamma^{(2)} \gneqq \lambda_1...\lambda_h$.

Case 8 $\gamma^{(2)}\varrho^{(1)} = \lambda_1...\lambda_k\beta^{(1)}$, and
$\sigma^{(1)} = \lambda_j...\lambda_h\beta^{(2)}$, j, $1 \leqslant j \leqslant n$, and $\gamma^{(2)} \gneqq \lambda_1...\lambda_k$.

Case 9 $\gamma^{(2)}\varrho^{(1)} = \lambda_1...\lambda_k\beta^{(1)}$, and
$\gamma^{(2)}\sigma^{(1)} = \lambda_1...\lambda_h\beta^{(2)}$, $\gamma^{(2)} \gneqq \lambda_1...\lambda_k$, and $\gamma^{(2)} \gneqq \lambda_1...\lambda_h$.

Consider case 1.
Let $\lambda^{(1)} = \lambda_{k+1}...\lambda_n\lambda_1...\lambda_k$ and $\lambda^{(2)} = \lambda_{h+1}...\lambda_n\lambda_1...\lambda_h$. We can distinguish four cases.

Case 1.1 $\varrho^{(1)} \in {}_{\lambda_j \ldots \lambda_n \lambda_1 \ldots \lambda_k} l^{\lambda^{(1)}}_{\beta^{(1)}}$, and
$\sigma^{(1)} \in {}_{\lambda_j \ldots \lambda_n \lambda_1 \ldots \lambda_h} l^{\lambda^{(2)}}_{\beta^{(2)}}$, and $j > k+1$ and $j > h+1$.

Case 1.2 $\varrho^{(1)} \in {}_{\lambda_j \ldots \lambda_k} l^{\lambda^{(1)}}_{\beta^{(1)}}$, and
$\sigma^{(1)} \in {}_{\lambda_j \ldots \lambda_n \lambda_1 \ldots \lambda_h} l^{\lambda^{(2)}}_{\beta^{(2)}}$, and $j \leqslant k$ and $j > h+1$.

Case 1.3 $\varrho^{(1)} \in {}_{\lambda_j \ldots \lambda_n \lambda_1 \ldots \lambda_k} l^{\lambda^{(1)}}_{\beta^{(1)}}$, and
$\sigma^{(1)} \in {}_{\lambda_j \ldots \lambda_h} l^{\lambda^{(2)}}_{\beta^{(2)}}$, and $j > k+1$ and $j \leqslant h$.

Case 1.4 $\varrho^{(1)} \in {}_{\lambda_j \ldots \lambda_k} l^{\lambda^{(1)}}_{\beta^{(1)}}$, and
$\sigma^{(1)} \in {}_{\lambda_j \ldots \lambda_h} l^{\lambda^{(2)}}_{\beta^{(2)}}$, and $j \leqslant k$ and $j \leqslant h$.

Consider **case 1.1**.
Let m be the line ${}_{\lambda_j \ldots \lambda_n} l^{\lambda}_{e}$, then m is primary and related to l. Furthermore, the two lines $l_1 = {}_{\lambda_j \ldots \lambda_n \lambda_1 \ldots \lambda_k} l^{\lambda^{(1)}}_{\beta^{(1)}}$ and $l_2 = {}_{\lambda_j \ldots \lambda_n \lambda_1 \ldots \lambda_h} l^{\lambda^{(2)}}_{\beta^{(2)}}$ are associated with m. Together with the fact that $\varrho^{(1)} \in l_1 \cap P$ and $\sigma^{(1)} \in l_2 \cap P$ (thus, $l_1 \subseteq B^C_m$ and $l_2 \subseteq B^C_m$), this gives $\varrho^{(1)} \in P \cap B^C_m$ and $\sigma^{(1)} \in P \cap B^C_m$. Thus,

$$\eta_{B^C_m}(\varrho^{(1)}) = (s', r_1) \in \eta_{B^C_m}(P \cap B^C_m), \text{ and}$$
$$\eta_{B^C_m}(\sigma^{(1)}) = (t', r_2) \in \eta_{B^C_m}(P \cap B^C_m),$$

for some $r_1 \geqslant 0$, and $r_2 \geqslant 0$. And $\eta_{B^C_m}(P \cap B^C_m) = ST$ a strip template on the strip $S^0_{B^C_l}$, $ST \in ST_l$. Note that ${}_{\lambda_1 \ldots \lambda_k} l^{\lambda^{(1)}}_{\beta^{(1)}}$ is related to l_1 and ${}_{\lambda_1 \ldots \lambda_h} l^{\lambda^{(2)}}_{\beta^{(2)}}$ is related to l_2. Use lemma 4.8 to obtain that for all $v \geqslant 0$:

$$\eta_{B^c_l}(\lambda_1 \ldots \lambda_k (\lambda^{(1)})^{s'+v} \beta^{(1)}) = (s'+v, r_1) \in ST(v), \text{ and}$$
$$\eta_{B^c_l}(\lambda_1 \ldots \lambda_h (\lambda^{(2)})^{t'+v} \beta^{(2)}) = (t'+v, r_2) \in ST(v).$$

Recall that $\gamma^{(1)}\varrho^{(1)} = \lambda_1 \ldots \lambda_k (\lambda_{k+1} \ldots \lambda_n \lambda_1 \ldots \lambda_k)^s \beta^{(1)}$ and $\gamma^{(1)}\sigma^{(1)} = \lambda_1 \ldots \lambda_h (\lambda_{h+1} \ldots \lambda_n \lambda_1 \ldots \lambda_h)^t \, \beta^{(2)}$. Thus,

$$\eta_{B^c_l}(\gamma^{(1)}\varrho^{(1)}) \in ST(s - s'), \text{ and}$$
$$\eta_{B^c_l}(\gamma^{(1)}\sigma^{(1)}) \in ST(t - t').$$

Hence from the definition of validity of a skewing scheme on a strip follows that

$$s_{\gamma_1}(\eta_{B^c_l}(\gamma^{(1)}\varrho^{(1)})) \neq s_{\gamma_1}(\eta_{B^c_l}(\gamma^{(1)}\sigma^{(1)})).$$

Thus, from the construction follows that $s(\gamma_1\gamma^{(1)}\varrho^{(1)}) \neq s(\gamma_1\gamma^{(1)}\sigma^{(1)})$, hence

$s(\varrho) \neq s(\sigma)$. Contradiction.

Consider **case 1.2.**
Let m be the line ${}_{\lambda_j\ldots\lambda_k}l^{\lambda}_{e}$, and contradiction occurs analogously to case 1.1.

Case 1.3 can be handled analogously to case 1.2, because of symmetry reasons.

Consider **case 1.4.**
If $k \leqslant h$, then let m be the line ${}_{\lambda_j\ldots\lambda_k}l^{\lambda}_{e}$, otherwise let m be ${}_{\lambda_1\ldots\lambda_h}l^{\lambda}_{e}$. And again contradiction occurs analogously to case 1.1.

Consider **case 2.**
Then we have either $\varrho^{(1)} \in {}_{\lambda_j\ldots\lambda_n\lambda_1\ldots\lambda_k}l^{\lambda^{(1)}}_{\beta^{(1)}}$ and $\sigma^{(1)} \in {}_{\lambda_j\ldots\lambda_h}l^{\lambda^{(2)}}_{\beta^{(2)}}$, with $j > k+1$ and $j \leqslant h$, which is the same as case 1.3, or $\varrho^{(1)} \in {}_{\lambda_j\ldots\lambda_k}l^{\lambda^{(1)}}_{\beta^{(1)}}$ and $\sigma^{(1)} \in {}_{\lambda_j\ldots\lambda_h}l^{\lambda^{(2)}}_{\beta^{(2)}}$, with $j \leqslant k$ and $j \leqslant h$, which is the same as case 1.4.

Case 3 can be handled analogously to case 2, because of symmetry reasons.

Case 4 is the same as case 1.4.

Consider **case 5.**
$\varrho^{(1)} = \lambda_j\ldots\lambda_n(\lambda_1\ldots\lambda_n)^{s'}\lambda_1\ldots\lambda_k\beta^{(1)}$ and $\gamma^{(2)}\sigma^{(1)} = \lambda_1\ldots\lambda_h\beta^{(2)}$, with $\gamma^{(2)} \gneqq \lambda_1\ldots\lambda_h$. Let $\beta^{(2)} = \beta^{(2)}_1\ldots\beta^{(2)}_p$. Then there exists a r, $1 \leqslant r \leqslant p$, such that $\sigma^{(1)} = \beta^{(2)}_r\ldots\beta^{(2)}_p$. So $\lambda_1\ldots\lambda_h\beta^{(2)}_1\ldots\beta^{(2)}_{r-1} = \gamma^{(2)}$. Recall that $\gamma^{(3)}\gamma^{(2)} = \gamma^{(1)} = (\lambda_1\ldots\lambda_n)^{s''}\lambda_1\ldots\lambda_{j-1}$, for some $s'' \geqslant 0$, and $\gamma^{(3)} \in T$. Thus $\beta^{(2)}_1\ldots\beta^{(2)}_{r-1} = \lambda_{h+1}\ldots\lambda_{h+r-1}$, which is in contradiction with the definition of the tail of a primary line.

Case 6, case 7 and **case 8** can be handled analogously to case 5.

Consider **case 9.**
$\gamma^{(2)}\varrho^{(1)} = \lambda_1\ldots\lambda_k\beta^{(1)}$ and $\gamma^{(2)}\sigma^{(1)} = \lambda_1\ldots\lambda_h\beta^{(2)}$, for some $\gamma^{(1)} \gneqq \lambda_1\ldots\lambda_k$ and $\gamma^{(2)} \gneqq \lambda_1\ldots\lambda_h$. Then we can conclude that $h = k$, because otherwise $\beta^{(1)} = \lambda_{k+1}\ldots\lambda_{k+r-1}\beta^{(1)}_r\ldots\beta^{(1)}_{p_1}$, or $\beta^{(2)} = \lambda_{h+1}\ldots\lambda_{h+r-1}\beta^{(2)}_r\ldots\beta^{(2)}_{p_2}$, for some $r > 1$, and $\beta^{(1)}_1\ldots\beta^{(1)}_{p_1} = \beta^{(1)}$ and $\beta^{(2)}_1\ldots\beta^{(2)}_{p_2} = \beta^{(2)}$, both contradicting the definition of the tail of a primary line. Furthermore it follows that $s = t$. Let μ be such that $|\mu|$ is minimal and there exists a $q \geqslant 1$ with $\mu^q = \gamma^{(2)}$ ($\mu = \mu_1\ldots\mu_m$). Furthermore let $\varrho^{(1)} = \mu^v\mu_1\ldots\mu_i\varrho^{(2)}$ and $\sigma^{(1)} = \mu^w\mu_1\ldots\mu_j\sigma^{(2)}$,

with $v \geqslant 0$, $w \geqslant 0$, $1 \leqslant i \leqslant m$, $1 \leqslant j \leqslant m$, and $|\varrho^{(2)}|$ and $|\sigma^{(2)}|$ minimal. Then we have

$$\lambda_1 ... \lambda_k \beta^{(1)} = \mu^{q+v} \mu_1 ... \mu_i \varrho^{(2)}, \text{ and}$$
$$\lambda_1 ... \lambda_h \beta^{(2)} = \mu^{q+w} \mu_1 ... \mu_j \sigma^{(2)}.$$

Thus,

$$\lambda_1 ... \lambda_k \beta^{(1)} \in {}_{\mu_1 ... \mu_i} l_{\varrho^{(2)}}^{\mu_{i+1} ... \mu_m \mu_1 ... \mu_i} (= l_1), \text{ and}$$
$$\lambda_1 ... \lambda_h \beta^{(2)} \in {}_{\mu_1 ... \mu_j} l_{\sigma^{(2)}}^{\mu_{j+1} ... \mu_1 ... \mu_j} (= l_2).$$

Further $\varrho^{(1)} \in l_1$ and $\sigma^{(1)} \in l_2$. Consider the lines $m_1 = {}_{\lambda_1 ... \lambda_k} l_{\beta^{(1)}}^{\lambda_{k+1} ... \lambda_n \lambda_1 ... \lambda_k}$ and $m_2 = {}_{\lambda_1 ... \lambda_r} l_{\delta}^{\lambda_{r+1} ... \lambda_n \lambda_1 ... \lambda_r}$, with r is maximal such that $\lambda_1 ... \lambda_r \delta = \varrho^{(1)}$. Then $m_2 \subseteq B_l^{(0)}$, because m_2 is primary and associated with l, and $\varrho^{(1)} \in m_2 \cap P$. Further, head$(m_1)$tail$(m_2) \in l_1$ and head(m_2)tail$(m_2) \in l_1$. Together with the fact that $\varrho^{(1)} \in l_1$, this gives $l_1 \in TL_l^{(i)}$, for some $i \geqslant 1$. Applying lemma 4.7 gives $B_{l_1}^{(0)}(\lambda^v) \subseteq B_l^C$, for all $v \geqslant 0$. $l_2 \subseteq B_{l_1}^{(0)}$, thus $\varrho^{(1)} \in B_{l_1}^{(0)} \cap P$ and $\sigma^{(1)} \in B_{l_1}^{(0)} \cap P$. Let $B_{l_1}^{(0)} = \{l^{(1)}, l^{(2)}, ..., l^{(u)}\}$, and let $TT = \eta_1(B_{l_1}^{(0)} \cap P)$ and for each i, $1 \leqslant i \leqslant u$, $\pi_i\,(TT) = \eta_1(l^{(i)} \cap B_l^C)$. η_1 is defined by $\eta_1(\alpha) = j$ iff $\eta_{B_l^C}(\alpha) = (i, j)$. Then $TT \in TT_l$, and $\varrho^{(1)} \in TT(0,0)$ and $\sigma^{(1)} \in TT(0,0)$. Now we have $\eta_{B_l^C}(\gamma^{(1)}\varrho^{(1)}) = \eta_{B_l^C}(\lambda^s \lambda_1 ... \lambda_k \beta^{(1)}) = \eta_{B_l^C}(\lambda^s \gamma^{(2)} \varrho^{(1)}) = \eta_{B_l^C}(\lambda^s \mu^q \varrho^{(1)}) \in TT(s,q)$, and $\eta_{B_l^C}(\gamma^{(1)}\sigma^{(1)}) = \eta_{B_l^C}(\lambda^t \lambda_1 ... \lambda_h \beta^{(2)}) = \eta_{B_l^C}(\lambda^s \gamma^{(2)} \sigma^{(1)}) = \eta_{B_l^C}(\lambda^s \mu^q \sigma^{(1)}) \in TT(s,q)$. Hence from the definition of validity of a skewing scheme on a strip follows that

$$s_\gamma(\eta_{B_l^C}(\gamma^{(1)}\varrho^{(1)})) \neq s_\gamma(\eta_{B_l^C}(\gamma^{(1)}\sigma^{(1)})).$$

Thus, from the construction follows that $s(\gamma_1\gamma^{(1)}\varrho^{(1)}) \neq s(\gamma_1\gamma^{(1)}\sigma^{(1)})$, hence, $s(\varrho) \neq s(\sigma)$. Contradiction.

□

□

4.4 Some Applications and Simplifications of Theorem 4.6

The characterization of the minimal number of memory banks given in theorem 4.6 was rather complicated. In order to get a better understanding of this result we shall first reduce theorem 4.6, and in particular the definition of the bundle B_l^C, to a more useful form.

Definition 4.18 *Given a template P on a tree T_k and an arbitrary node $\lambda = \lambda_1...\lambda_n, \lambda \neq \varepsilon$.*
(i) For $j, 0 \leqslant j < n$, and $\alpha \in P$ define $\varphi_\lambda^j(\alpha)$ and $d_\lambda^j(\alpha)$ by: $\varphi_\lambda^j(\alpha) = \alpha^{(1)}$ and $d_\lambda^j(\alpha) = s$, where s is the maximal number such that $\lambda^s \in \text{Prefix}(\lambda_1...\lambda_j\alpha)$ and $\alpha^{(1)}$ is such that $\lambda^s\alpha^{(1)} = \lambda_1...\lambda_j\alpha$.
(ii) The λ-augmented template $(P)_\lambda$ is the set $\{\varphi_\lambda^j(\alpha) | \alpha \in P$ and $0 \leqslant j < n\}$. The collection of jth-degrees $D_P^j(\beta)$ of a node $\beta \in (P)_\lambda$ is the set $\{d_\lambda^j(\alpha) | \varphi_\lambda^j(\alpha) = \beta\}$.

With the help of definition 4.18 we can simplify the definition of $B_l^{(0)}$. For an arbitrary line m define odperi(m) by : odperi(m).head(prim(m)) = head(prim(m)).period(m).

Lemma 4.9 *Let l be a primary line and let C be a collection of templates on a tree T. Then*

$$B_l^{(0)} = \{\gamma |\ \textit{there exists a primary line } m, \textit{ which is associated with } l, \textit{ such that } \gamma \in m \textit{ and } \text{head}(m)\text{tail}(m) \in (P)_{\text{odperi}(l)}, \textit{ for some } P \in C\}.$$

Proof Let $\gamma \in m$, with m primary and associated with l. Then there exists a primary line m', related to m, such that $|m' \cap P| \geqslant 1$, for some $P \in C$. Let odperi(l) = $\lambda (= \lambda_1...\lambda_n)$. Then head($m$).tail($m$) = $\lambda_1...\lambda_i\beta$, for some i, $0 \leqslant i \leqslant n$, and $\beta \in T$. Because $m' \cap P \neq \emptyset$, there exists a node α such that $\alpha \in m' \cap P$. Then $\alpha = \lambda_j...\lambda_n\lambda_1...\lambda_i(\lambda_{i+1}...\lambda_n\lambda_1...\lambda_i)^s\beta$, for some j, $i+1 < j \leqslant n$, and $s \geqslant 0$. (Or, $\alpha = \lambda_j...\lambda_i(\lambda_{i+1}...\lambda_n\lambda_1...\lambda_i)^s\beta$ for some j, $1 \leqslant j \leqslant i$, and $s \geqslant 0$. But this case can be handled analogously.) Thus head(m).tail(m) = $\lambda_1...\lambda_i\beta = \varphi_\lambda^{j-1}(\alpha) \in (P)_\lambda$. So, $B_l^{(0)} \subseteq \{\gamma|$ there exists a primary line $m, ...\}$. By reversing the implications we get that $\{\gamma|$ there exists a primary line $m, ...\} \subseteq B_l^{(0)}$, which completes the proof. □

Corollary 4.1 *Let l be a primary line and let C be a collection of templates on the tree T. Then*

$$TL_l^{(1)} = \{m|\ \ |m \cap (\cup_{P \in C} P)_{\text{odperi}(l)}| \geqslant 2, \textit{ and } \text{head}(m_1)\text{tail}(m_1) \in (P)_{\text{odperi}(m_1)}, \textit{ with } m_1 = \text{prim}(m) \textit{ and } P \in C\}.$$

Proof Directly from lemma 4.9 and definition 4.13. □

By the following definition we reduce the bundle B_l^C as defined in definition 4.13 to the bundle $\overline{B}_l^C$ in such a way that the construction of each set $TL_l^{(i)}$ of transversal lines is not depending on all lines of $B_l^{(0)} \cup TL_l^{(1)} \cup ... \cup TL_l^{(i-1)}$, but only on the set $TL_l^{(i-1)}$ of transversal lines.

Definition 4.19 *Let l be a primary line, and let C be a collection of templates on a tree T.*

(*i*) $\overline{B}_l^{(0)} = \{\gamma |$ *there exists a primary line m which is associated with l, such that $\gamma \in m$ and* $\text{head}(m)\text{tail}(m) \in (P)_{\text{odperi}(l)}$, *for some $P \in C\}$.*

(*ii*) $\widetilde{\overline{TL}}_l^{(0)} = \{l\}$, *and for all $i \geqslant 1$*

$\overline{TL}_l^{(i)} = X_l^{(i)} \cup Y_l^{(i)}$, *where*

$X_l^{(i)} = \{m_1 |\ |m_1 \cap (\bigcup_{P \in C} P)_{\text{odperi}(m)}| \geqslant 2, m \in \widetilde{\overline{TL}}_l^{(i-1)}$, *and* $\text{head}(m')\text{tail}(m') \in (P)_{\text{odperi}(m')}$, *with* $m' = \text{prim}(m_1)$ *and $P \in C\}$,*

$Y_l^{(1)} = \emptyset$ *and for all $i \geqslant 2$,*

$Y_l^{(i)} = \{m_1 |\ m_1$ *is a primary line and there exists a node $\sigma \in P$, for some $P \in C$, such that $\sigma \in m_1$ and $\sigma^{(1)} \in m_1$, with $\sigma_1\sigma^{(1)} = \sigma$, for some σ_1 and $\sigma^{(1)} \neq \varepsilon\}$.*

$\widetilde{\overline{TL}}_l^{(i)}$ *is a maximal subset of $\overline{TL}_l^{(i)}$ such that for all $m_1 \in \widetilde{\overline{TL}}_l^{(i)}$ and $m_2 \in \widetilde{\overline{TL}}_l^{(i)}$, $m_1 \neq m_2 : m_1$ is not associated with m_2.*

(*iii*) *For each $i \geqslant 1$ and $m \in \widetilde{\overline{TL}}_l^{(i)}$,*

$\text{Pre}(m) = \{m_1 |\ |m \cap (\bigcup_{P \in C} P)_{\text{odperi}(m_1)}| \geqslant 2$, *for some $m \in X_l^{(i)}$, and $m_1 \in \widetilde{\overline{TL}}_l^{(i-1)}\}$.*

(*iv*) $\overline{TL}_l = \{m | m \in \widetilde{\overline{TL}}_l^{(1)}$, *or* $m = \{\text{base}(m_1).(\text{odperi}(m_1))^{s_1}.\text{base}(m_2).(\text{odperi}(m_2))^{s_2}...\text{base}(m_{i-1}).(\text{odperi}(m_{i-1}))^{s_{i-1}}.\varrho |\ \varrho \in m_i\}$ *for some $s_1 \geqslant 0$, $s_2 \geqslant 0$, ..., $s_{i-1} \geqslant 0$, $i \geqslant 2$, and* $m_1 \in \text{Pre}(m_2)$, $m_2 \in \text{Pre}(m_3)$, ..., $m_{i-1} \in \text{Pre}(m_i)$, $m_i \in \widetilde{\overline{TL}}_l^{(i)}\}$.

(*v*) $\overline{B}_l^C = \{(\text{odperi}(l))^s.\varrho | s \geqslant 0$ *and* $\varrho \in \overline{B}_{\text{prim}(m)}^{(0)}(\text{base}(m))$, *with $m \in \overline{TL}_l\}$.*

And $\overline{B}_l^C(\gamma)$ is defined by $\alpha \in \overline{B}_l^C$ iff $\gamma\alpha \in \overline{B}_l^C(\gamma)$.

Note : *If* base$(m) = \gamma\mu_j...\mu_n\mu^q$ *for some node* γ, $\mu\,(=\mu_1...\mu_n) =$ odperi(m), $1 \leqslant j \leqslant n$ *and* $q \geqslant 0$, *then we take* $\overline{B}^{(0)}_{\mu_j...\mu_n l^{\mu}_{s}}(\gamma)$ *instead of* $\overline{B}^{(0)}_{\mathrm{prim}(m)}(\mathrm{base}(m))$ *for defining* $\overline{B}^C_l$.

From lemma 4.7, lemma 4.9 and corollary 4.1 follows that the only difference between definition 4.19 and definition 4.13 consists of the different definitions of $\overline{TL}_l^{(i)}$ and $TL_l^{(i)}$. The relationship between $\overline{TL}_l^{(i)}$ and $TL_l^{(i)}$ is expressed by the following lemma.

Lemma 4.10

(i) $X_l^{(1)} = \overline{TL}_l^{(1)} = TL_l^{(1)}$.

(ii) For all $i \geqslant 2$:

$$X_l^{(i)} = \{m \mid m \in TL_l^{(i)} \textit{ and there exists a line } m' \in \overline{TL}_l^{(i-1)}, \textit{ such that } |\{\varrho \mid \mathrm{base}(m').\varrho \in m\} \cap (\textstyle\bigcup_{P\in C} P)_{\mathrm{odperi}(m')}| \geqslant 2\} \subseteq TL_l^{(i)}.$$

Proof Directly from the definitions. □

It is not always true that $Y_l^{(i)} \subseteq TL_l^{(i)}$. The additional lines contributed by $Y_l^{(i)}$ are the price to be paid for the reduction of $TL_l^{(i)}$ to $X_l^{(i)}$. See also case 1.4 in the proof of theorem 4.7. In spite of the fact that $\overline{TL}_l^{(i)}$ is not always a subset of $TL_l^{(i)}$, the next lemma shows that the reduction of $TL_l^{(i)}$ to $\overline{TL}_l^{(i)}$ is worthwhile.

Lemma 4.11 *For all* $i \geqslant 1$:

$$|\overline{TL}_l^{(i)}| \leqslant \prod_{j=1}^{i} \left(pd + \binom{p(|\lambda| + id)}{2} \right),$$

with $p = |\bigcup_{P\in C} P|$, $d = \max_{\alpha\in P\in C}$, *and* $\lambda =$ period(l).

Proof From definition 4.18 of the λ-augmented template follows that for all P and $\lambda \in T$: $|(P)_\lambda| \leqslant |\lambda|.p$. Further, from the definition of $\overline{B}^C_l$ follows that for all $i \geqslant 1$ and $m \in \widetilde{\overline{TL}}_l^{(i)}$: $|\mathrm{odperi}(m)| \leqslant d + \max_{m' \in \widetilde{\overline{TL}}_l^{(i-1)}} |\mathrm{odperi}(m')|$. Because $\widetilde{\overline{TL}}_l^{(0)} = \{l\}$, it follows that for all $i \leqslant 0$ and $m \in \widetilde{\overline{TL}}_l^{(i)}$: $|\mathrm{odperi}(m)| \leqslant |\mathrm{odperi}(l)| + i.d = |\lambda| + i.d$. Thus, for all $i \geqslant 1$: $|X_l^{(i)}| \leqslant \binom{p(|\lambda|+id)}{2} |\overline{TL}_l^{(i-1)}|$. Obviously $|Y_l^{(i)}| \leqslant p.d.|\overline{TL}_l^{(i-1)}|$, for all $i \geqslant 1$. Further $|\overline{TL}_l^{(0)}| = 1$. □

Note that from the definition of $TL_l^{(i)}$ follows that for all $i \geqslant 2$: $|TL_l^{(i)}|$ is infinite except for the trivial case that $B_l^{(0)} = B_l^{(1)} = \ldots = B_l^{C}$. For all $i \geqslant 2$ there even exists an infinite subset $T_l^{(i)}$ of $TL_l^{(i)}$, such that for all $m_1 \in T_l^{(i)}$ and $m_2 \in T_l^{(i)}$, $m_1 \neq m_2$, there does not exist a γ_1 and γ_2 such that $\{\gamma_1\varrho | \ \varrho \in \text{prim}(m_1)\} = \{\gamma_2\varrho | \ \varrho \in \text{prim}(m_2)\}$. Another valuable property of the reduced bundle $\overline{B}_l^{C}$ is the following.

Lemma 4.12 *For all* $i \geqslant 2$:

$$X_l^{(i)} = \{m | \text{ there exists a line } m' \in \overline{TL}_l^{(i-1)}, \text{ such that } m \in X^{(1)}_{\text{prim}(m')}\}.$$

Proof Directly from lemma 4.10 and definition 4.19. □

Define for $\overline{B}_l^{C}$, the standard decomposition $D_{\overline{B}_l^{C}}$, the corresponding cut strip $S^0_{\overline{B}_l^{C}}$, and the collection of templates $\overline{ST}_l$ and $\overline{TT}_l$, similar to $D_{B_l^C}$, $S^0_{B_l^C}$, ST_l and TT_l (definition 4.14, definition 4.15, definition 4.16 and definition 4.17). In spite of the fact that we have reduced the definition of the bundle B_l^C to $\overline{B}_l^{C}$ (lemma 4.12), the result of the previous section remains valid.

Theorem 4.7 *Let T be a k-ary tree and C a collection of templates on T. Then*

$$\mu_T(C) = \mu_{S^0_{\overline{B}_l^{C}}}(\overline{ST}_l \cup \overline{TT}_l),$$

with $l = {}_{e}l_{e}^{\lambda}$, λ *arbitrary.*

Proof Consider the proof of theorem 4.6 and substitute $\overline{B}_l^{C}$ for B_l^C, $S^0_{\overline{B}_l^{C}}$ for $S^0_{B_l^C}$, $\overline{ST}_l$ for ST_l, and $\overline{TT}_l$ for TT_l.

By lemma 4.10 we can conclude that we have to make only two adjustments to let this proof yield the desired result. The first adjustment consists of a revision of case 1 of the proof of claim 4.1.

Revised version of case 1 of claim 4.1.

Let i be the smallest integer such that there exists a line $\tilde{l}' \in \widetilde{\overline{TL}}_l^{(i)}$, with $l' = \{\vartheta.\alpha | \ \alpha \in \tilde{l}'\} \in \overline{TL}_l$ for some $\vartheta \in T$ and $\varrho \in \overline{B}^{(0)}_{\text{prim}(l')}(\gamma_1\lambda^s\text{base}(l'))$ for some $s \geqslant 0$. Thus, $\varrho = \gamma_1\lambda^s\text{base}(l')\varrho_1$ and $\varrho_1 \in \overline{B}^{(0)}_{\text{prim}(l')}$. Let m_1' be the line with $\varrho_1 \in m_1'$ and $m_1' \subseteq \overline{B}^{(0)}_{\text{prim}(l')}$, $m_1' = {}_{\lambda_1'\ldots\lambda_{k'}'}l^{\lambda_{k'+1}'\ldots\lambda_{n'}',\lambda_1'\ldots\lambda_{k'}'}_{\beta_1'\ldots\beta_{p'}'}$. Then we can distinguish four cases. Note that for all $s \geqslant 0$: $\{\gamma_1\lambda^s\text{base }(l')\alpha | \ \alpha \in m'\} \subseteq \overline{B}_l^{C}(\gamma_1)$.

Case 1.1 $\gamma = \gamma_1\lambda^s\text{base}(l')\lambda'_1...\lambda'_{k'}(\lambda'_{k'+1}...\lambda'_{n'}\lambda'_1...\lambda'_{k'})^{t'}\beta'_1...\beta'_{i'}$, $t' \geqslant 0$ and $i' \leqslant p'$.

Case 1.2 $\gamma = \gamma_1\lambda^s\text{base}(l')\lambda'_1...\lambda'_{k'}(\lambda'_{k'+1}...\lambda'_{n'}\lambda'_1...\lambda'_{k'})^{t}\lambda'_{k'+1}...\lambda'_{i'}$, $t' \geqslant 0$ and $i' > k'$, or,

$\gamma = \gamma_1\lambda^s\text{base}(l')\lambda'_1...\lambda'_{k'}(\lambda'_{k'+1}...\lambda'_{n'}\lambda'_1...\lambda'_{k'})^{t'}\lambda_{k'+1}...\lambda'_{n'}\lambda'_1...\lambda'_{i'}$, $t' \geqslant 0$ and $i' \leqslant k'$.

Case 1.3 $\gamma = \gamma_1\lambda^s\text{base}(l')\lambda'_1...\lambda'_{i'}$, $i' < k'$.

Case 1.4 $\gamma = \gamma_1\lambda^s\delta$, $\delta <\text{base}(l')$.

Consider **case 1.1**.
Then by exactly the same argument as in the old version of case 1 (substitute $\gamma_1\lambda^s\text{base}(l')$ for γ_1, m'_1 for m_1, and prim(l') for l, thus, $\lambda_1...\lambda_n = \lambda'_1\lambda'_{n'}, k = k'$, and $\beta_1...\beta_p = \beta'_1...\beta'_{p'}$) we get lines m'_2, l'_1 and l'_2. See figure 4.9, the lines l and m_1 are drawn starting from γ_1 and the lines l'_1, l'_2, m'_1 and m'_2 are drawn starting from $\gamma_1\lambda^s\text{base}(l')$. For these lines m'_2, l'_1, and l'_2 the same holds as for the lines m_2, l_1, and l_2 of the old version of case 1. Contradiction follows.

Consider **case 1.2**.
Substitute $\gamma_1\lambda^s\text{base}(l')$ for γ_1, m'_1 for m_1, and prim(l') for l in case 2 of the proof of claim 4.1. Then we get $\tau \in \overline{B}^{(0)}_{\text{prim}(l')}(\gamma_1\lambda^s\text{base}(l')) \subseteq \overline{B}^{C}_{l}(\gamma_1)$, a contradiction occurs.

Case 1.3 can be handled analogously to case 1.2.

Consider **case 1.4**.
Let $\varrho^{(1)}$ be the node with $\gamma\varrho^{(1)} = \varrho$. Then $\varrho^{(1)} \in P$ and

$$\varrho^{(1)} = \sigma^{(1)}\lambda'_1...\lambda'_{k'}(\lambda'_{k'+1}...\lambda'_{n'}\lambda'_1...\lambda'_{k'})^{t'}\beta'_1...\beta'_{p'},$$

with $\delta\delta^{(1)} = \text{base}(l')$. Write, for simplicity's sake, $\bar{\lambda}$ for $\lambda'_{k'+1}...\lambda'_{n'}\lambda'_1...\lambda'_{k'}$. Consider $l'_1 = {}_{\delta}l^{\delta^{(1)}}_{\lambda'_1...\lambda'_{k'}(\bar{\lambda})^{t'}\beta'_1...\beta'_{p'}}$, then $\{\varrho | \text{base}(l').\varrho \in l'_1\} = {}_{\epsilon}l^{\delta^{(1)}}_{\lambda'_1...\lambda'_{k'}(\bar{\lambda})^{t'}\beta'_1...\beta'_{p'}}$.
Thus,

$$\begin{aligned} \varrho^{(1)} &\in \{\varrho | \text{base}(l').\varrho \in l'_1\} \text{ and} \\ \lambda'_1...\lambda'_{k'}(\bar{\lambda})^{t'}\beta'_1...\beta'_{p'} &\in \{\varrho | \text{base}(l').\varrho \in l'_1\}. \end{aligned}$$

In addition we have that

$$tr(\lambda'_1...\lambda'_{k'}(\bar{\lambda})^{t'}\beta'_1...\beta'_{p'}) = \beta'_{p'}...\beta'_1(\lambda'_{k'}...\lambda'_1\lambda'_{n'}...\lambda'_{k'+1})^{t'}\lambda'_{k'}...\lambda'_1 \lneqq \tilde{\varrho}^{(1)}.$$

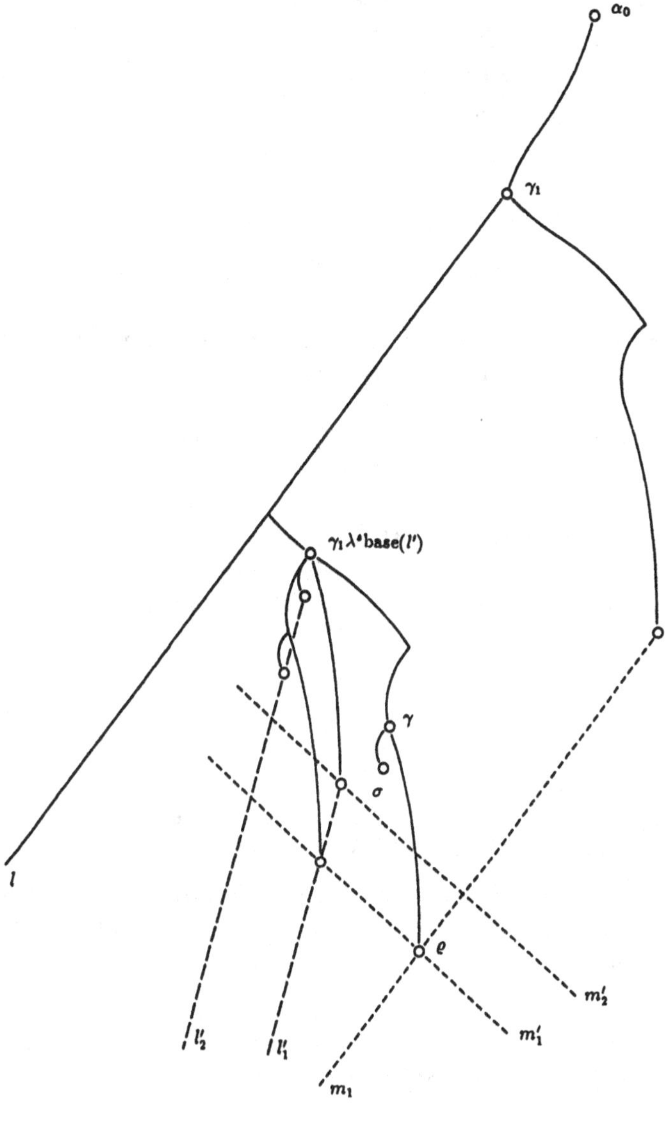

Figure 4.9: An illustration of the revised version of case 1.1.

Now, we have to distinguish two cases. If $\tilde{l}' \in X_l^{(i)}$, then $l_1' \in Y_l^{(i+1)} \subseteq \overline{TL}_l^{(i-1)}$. And, if $\tilde{l}' \in Y_l^{(i)}$, then there exists a line $l'' \in X_l^{(i-1)}$ such that $\{\varrho|$ base$(l'').\varrho \in l'\}$ is primary. Thus, base(l'') = base(l'). Hence $l_1' \in Y_l^{(i)} \subseteq \overline{TL}_l^{(i)}$. Consider σ and let $\sigma^{(1)}$ be such that $\gamma\sigma^{(1)} = \sigma$. Then $\sigma^{(1)} \in P$ and $\sigma^{(1)} \in l_2' \subseteq \overline{B}^{(0)}_{\text{prim}(l_1')}$ for some l_2'. Thus,

$$
\begin{aligned}
\sigma &= \gamma\sigma^{(1)} \\
&= \gamma_1\lambda^s\delta\sigma^{(1)} \\
&\in \{\gamma_1\lambda^s\text{base}(l_1')\varrho|\ \varrho \in \overline{B}^{(0)}_{\text{prim}(l_1')}\} \subseteq \overline{B}_l^{\mathcal{C}}(\gamma_1).
\end{aligned}
$$

Contradiction. See figure 4.10, the lines l and m_1 are drawn starting from γ_1 and the lines l_1', l_2' and m_1' are drawn starting from $\gamma_1\lambda^s$base(l').

The second adjustment consists of a revision of case 9 of the proof of claim 4.2, which can be handled in the same way as the first adjustment. □

From now on we shall focus our attention on the relationship between instances of templates on the tree and instances of the induced strip templates and transversal templates on the strip $S^0_{\overline{B}_l^{\mathcal{C}}}$. With respect to this the following lemma is helpful.

Lemma 4.13 *Let l be the line ${}_e l_e^{\lambda}$, with $\lambda = (\lambda_1...\lambda_n)$ arbitrary, and let $\mathcal{C}$ be a collection of templates on a tree T. For each $P \in \mathcal{C}$ and $\gamma \in T$:*
if $P(\gamma) \cap \overline{B}_l^{\mathcal{C}} \neq \emptyset$, then either,
$\gamma = \lambda^t\lambda_1...\lambda_i$, for some $t \geqslant 0$, $1 \leqslant i \leqslant n$, and there exists a strip template $ST \in \overline{ST}_l$ such that $\eta_{\overline{B}_l^{\mathcal{C}}}(P(\gamma)) = ST(x)$, for some $x \geqslant 0$, or,
$\gamma = \lambda^t\lambda_1...\lambda_i\beta_1...\beta_j$, for some $t \geqslant 0$, $1 \leqslant i < n$, $\beta_1...\beta_j \in T$, and there exists a transversal template $TT \in \overline{TT}_l$ such that $\eta_{\overline{B}_l^{\mathcal{C}}}(P(\gamma)) = TT(x, y)$, for some $x \geqslant 0$ and $y \geqslant 0$.

Proof Directly from the definitions, and from the proof of the revised version of claim 4.2, see the proof of theorem 4.7. □

Note that lemma 4.13 is valid for the old definition of the bundle, $B_l^{\mathcal{C}}$, also.

Theorem 4.8 *Let l be a primary line and let $\mathcal{C}$ be a collection of templates on a tree T. Let $m' \in \overline{TL}_l$, such that there does not exist a line m'', with*

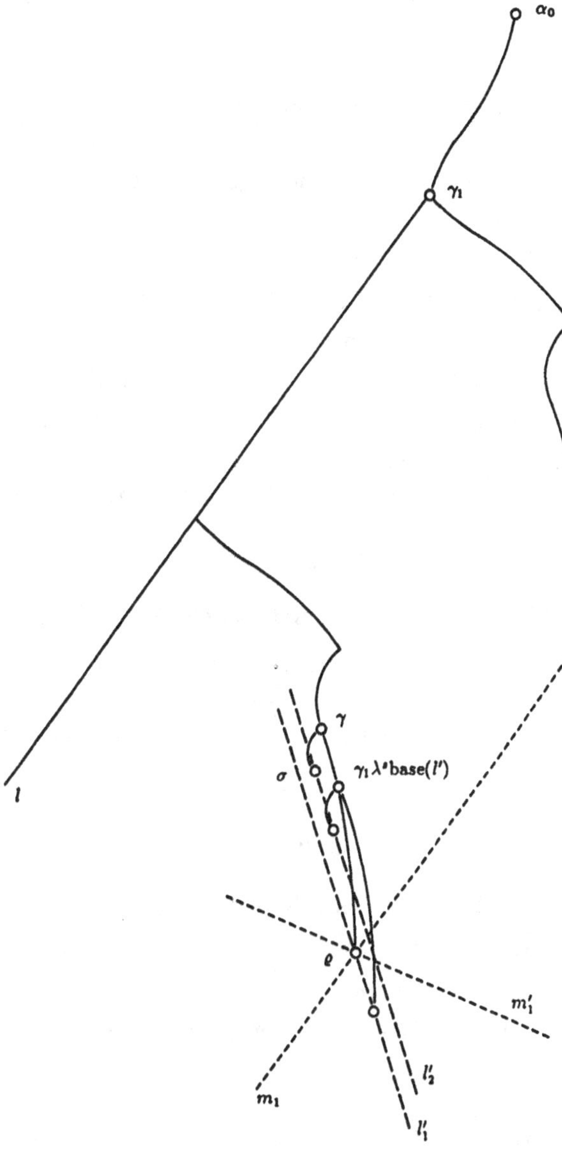

Figure 4.10: An illustration of case 1.4.

prim(m'') *associated with* prim(m'), *and* $m'' \in \widetilde{\overline{TL}}_l^{(1)}$. *Then for each line* $m \subseteq \overline{B}^{(0)}_{\text{prim}(m')}$ *and* $s \geqslant 0$:

$$|\{(\text{period}(l))^s.\text{base}(m').\varrho \mid \varrho \in m \text{ and there exists a } ST \in \overline{ST}_{\text{prim}(m')} \text{ and a } x \geqslant 0 \text{ such that } \eta_{\overline{B}_l^c}(\varrho) \in ST(x)\} \cap \overline{B}_l^{(0)}| \leqslant 1.$$

Proof For each $s \geqslant 0$, $|\{(\text{period}(l))^s.\text{base}(m').\varrho \mid \varrho \in m$ and there exists a $ST \in \overline{ST}_{\text{prim}(m')}\ldots\} \cap \overline{B}_l^{(0)}| = |\{\text{base}(m').\varrho \mid \varrho \in m$ and there exists a $ST \in \overline{ST}_{\text{prim}(m')}\ldots\} \cap B_l^{(0)}|$. By lemma 4.13 we can conclude that there exists a $t \geqslant 0$, $\overline{\beta} \in T$, and a $k, 1 \leqslant k \leqslant n$ ($\lambda = \lambda_1 \ldots \lambda_n$), such that for all $\varrho \in m$, for which there exist a $ST \in \overline{ST}_{\text{prim}(m')}$ and a $x \geqslant 0$ with $\eta_{\overline{B}_l^c}(\varrho) \in ST(x)$, holds that base$(m').\varrho = \lambda_1 \ldots \lambda_k (\lambda_{k+1} \ldots \lambda_n \lambda_1 \ldots \lambda_k)^t \overline{\beta}\beta_1$, for some $\beta_1 \in T$. Because of the definition of a transversal line t has to be equal to 0. Thus,

$$\text{base}(m').\varrho = \lambda_1 \ldots \lambda_k \overline{\beta}\beta_1.$$

Suppose that $|\{\text{base}(m').\varrho \mid \varrho \in m$ and there exists a $ST \in \overline{ST}_{\text{prim}(m')}\ldots\} \cap \overline{B}_l^{(0)}| \geqslant 2$. Then there exist nodes $\varrho_1 \in m$ and $\varrho_2 \in m$, $\varrho_1 \neq \varrho_2$ such that base$(m').\varrho_1 = \lambda_1 \ldots \lambda_k \overline{\beta}\beta^{(1)}$ and base $(m').\varrho_2 = \lambda_1 \ldots \lambda_k \overline{\beta}\beta^{(2)}$. Because $_{\lambda_1 \ldots \lambda_k} l^{\lambda_{k+1} \ldots \lambda_n \lambda_1 \ldots \lambda_k}_{\overline{\beta}\beta^{(1)}} \subseteq \overline{B}_l^{(0)}$ and $_{\lambda_1 \ldots \lambda_k} l^{\lambda_{k+1} \ldots \lambda_n \lambda_1 \ldots \lambda_k}_{\overline{\beta}\beta^{(2)}} \subseteq \overline{B}_l^{(0)}$, we have

$$\lambda_1 \ldots \lambda_k \overline{\beta}\beta^{(1)} \in (P_{j_1})_\lambda \text{ and}$$
$$\lambda_1 \ldots \lambda_k \overline{\beta}\beta^{(2)} \in (P_{j_2})_\lambda,$$

for some $P_{j_1} \in C$ and $P_{j_2} \in C$. Thus $|\{\text{ base}(m').\varrho \mid \varrho \in m\} \cap (\bigcup_{P \in C} P)_\lambda| \geqslant 2$. Further, $m \subseteq \overline{B}^{(0)}_{\text{prim}(m')}$, so head$(m)$tail$(m) \in (P_j)_{\text{odperi}(m')(=\text{odperi}(m))}$, for some $P_j \in C$. Hence, $\{\text{base }(m').\varrho \mid \varrho \in m\} \in \overline{TL}_l^{(1)}$. So, there exists a line m'' with prim(m'') associated with m, which is in turn associated with prim (m'), and $m'' \in \widetilde{\overline{TL}}_l^{(1)}$. Contradiction. □

Theorem 4.8 gives rise to the assumption that the influence of transversal templates, acting on $\eta_{\overline{B}_l^c}(\overline{B}^{(0)}_{\text{prim}(m)}((\text{period}(l))^s.\text{base}(m)))$, for $m \notin \widetilde{\overline{TL}}_l^{(1)}$, on the skewing scheme of $\eta_{\overline{B}_l^c}(\overline{B}_l^{(0)})$ could be neglected. This leads to the following conjecture.

Conjecture 4.3 *Let T be a k-ary tree T_k, and let $\mathcal{C} = \{P_1, P_2, ..., P_t\}$ be a collection of templates on T. Then*

$$\mu_T(\mathcal{C}) = \max_{l \in \mathcal{L}} \mu_{S^0_{\overline{B}_l^c}} (\overline{ST_l} \cup \{TT_{m,j} \mid 1 \leqslant j \leqslant t, \text{ and there exists a line } m' \in \widetilde{\overline{TL}}_l^{(1)} \text{ with prim}(m') \text{ related to prim}(m) \text{ and base}(m') = \text{base}(m)\}),$$

with $\mathcal{L} = \{\, l \mid l$ primary and $|l \cap P_j| \geqslant 2$, for some $P_j \in \mathcal{C}\}$.

Note that for each (primary) line l : $\mu_{S^0_{\overline{B}_l^c}} (\overline{ST_l} \cup \{TT_{m,j} \mid 1 \leqslant j \leqslant t$, and there exists a line $m' \in \widetilde{\overline{TL}}_l^{(1)}$ with ... $\}) = \mu_{S^0_{B_l^c}} (ST_l \cup \{TT_{m,j} \mid 1 \leqslant j \leqslant t$, and there exists a $m' \in \widetilde{TL}_l^{(1)}$ with ... $\})$.
The following lemma shows that it is not sufficient to maximize only over the $\mu_{S^0_{\overline{B}_l^c}} (\overline{ST_l})$'s.

Lemma 4.14 *There exists a collection of templates $\mathcal{C}$ such that*

$$\mu_T(\mathcal{C}) \neq \max_{l \in \mathcal{L}} \mu_{S^0_{\overline{B}_l^c}} (\overline{ST_l}),$$

with $\mathcal{L} = \{{}_e l_e^\lambda \mid \lambda$ arbitrary$\}$.

Proof Let T be a binary tree, and let $\mathcal{C} = \{P\}$, with $P = \{\varepsilon, e_1, e_1e_1, e_1e_1e_1, (e_1)^7, (e_1)^{11}, (e_1)^{15}, (e_1)^{19}, (e_1)^{20}(e_2)^{20}, e_2, e_2e_2, e_2e_2e_2, (e_2)^7, (e_2)^{11}, (e_2)^{15}, (e_2)^{19}\}$. In figure 4.11 P is depicted. Then $\mu_T(\mathcal{C}) = 21$, but $\max_{l \in \mathcal{L}} \mu_{S^0_{\overline{B}_l^c}} (\overline{ST_l}) = 20$. □

In addition to the previous results we can say that with the help of conjecture 4.1 and conjecture 4.2 of section 4.3 the calculation of $\mu_T(\mathcal{C})$ can even be simplified further.

4.5 Applications of Theorem 4.6 (Theorem 4.7) to Certain Collections of Templates

Despite the negative result of lemma 4.14, holding for arbitrary collections of templates, in this section (theorem 4.10) we are able to define templates for which it is sufficient to maximize only over the $\mu_{S^0_{\overline{B}_l^c}} (\overline{ST_l})$'s. This is done

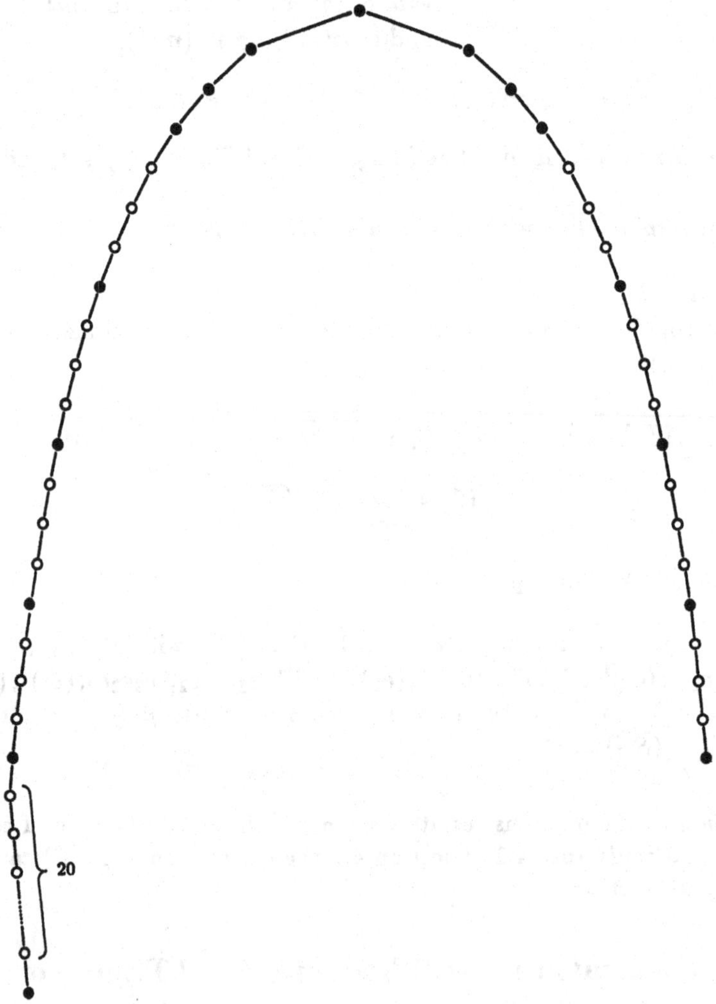

Figure 4.11: A template P such that for $\mathcal{C} = \{P\} : \mu_T(\mathcal{C}) \neq \max_{l \in \mathcal{C}} \mu_{S^0_{\overline{B}^c_l}}(\overline{ST_l})$.

in the following way.
Recall the definition of the collection of jth degrees $D^j_P(\beta)$ of a node $\beta \in (P)_\lambda$ (definition 4.18 (*ii*)).

Definition 4.20 *A collection C of templates on a tree T is called stable if the following two conditions are satisfied.*
(i) For all $\lambda\,(=\lambda_1...\lambda_n) \in T$, for all i, $0 \leqslant i < n$, and for all $\alpha \in \Gamma^\lambda_i$, and $\beta \in \Gamma^\lambda_i$ there exists a j, $0 \leqslant j < n$ and a template $P \in C$ such that $D^j_P(\alpha) \cap D^j_P(\beta) \neq \emptyset$, where $\Gamma^\lambda_i = \{\gamma |\ \gamma \in (\bigcup_{P\in C} P)_\lambda$ and the maximal i_1, such that there exists a node $\gamma^{(1)}$ with $\lambda_1...\lambda_{i_1}\gamma^{(1)} = \gamma$, is equal to $i\}$.
(ii) For all $P \in C$: if $\alpha\,(=\alpha_1...\alpha_n) \in P$, $\beta\,(=\beta_1...\beta_m) \in P$, $\alpha_1...\alpha_i = \beta_1...\beta_i$ and $\alpha_{i+1} \neq \beta_{i+1}$, for some i, $0 \leqslant i < n$ and $0 \leqslant i < m$, then $\alpha_{i+1}...\alpha_n \in P$ and $\beta_{i+1}...\beta_m \in P$.

The nodes λ in the first condition of definition 4.20 range over an infinite set of values. We can replace this condition by a condition in which the λ's range only over a finite set.

Lemma 4.15 *Given a collection C of templates on a tree T which satisfies condition (ii) of* definition 4.20. *Then C is stable iff*
(i′) for all $\lambda\,(=\lambda_1...\lambda_n)$, with $\lambda \leqslant \gamma$, for some $\gamma \in \bigcup_{P\in C} P$, for all i, $0 \leqslant i < n$, and for all $\alpha \in \Gamma^\lambda_i$ and $\beta \in \Gamma^\lambda_i$, there exists a j, $0 \leqslant j < n$ and a template $P \in C$ such that $D^j_P(\alpha) \cap D^j_P(\beta) \neq \emptyset$.

Proof $\Rightarrow$ Follows trivially.
$\Leftarrow$ Let C fulfill both (*ii*) and (*i′*). And let $\lambda\,(\lambda_1...\lambda_n)$ be arbitrary, $0 \leqslant i < n$, and $\alpha \in \Gamma^\lambda_i$ and $\beta \in \Gamma^\lambda_i$. Then $\alpha = \lambda_1...\lambda_i\alpha^{(1)}$ and $\beta = \lambda_1...\lambda_i\beta^{(1)}$, and there exists an j_1, $0 \leqslant j_1 < n$, j_2, $0 \leqslant j_2 < n$, $s_1 \geqslant 0$, $s_2 \geqslant 0$, a template $P_1 \in C$ and a template $P_2 \in C$, such that $\lambda_{j_1}...\lambda_n\lambda^{s_1}\lambda_1...\lambda_i\alpha^{(1)} \in P_1$ and $\lambda_{j_2}...\lambda_n\lambda^{s_2}\lambda_1...\lambda_i\beta^{(1)} \in P_2$. Let, without loss of generality, $j_1 \leqslant j_2$.

If $s_2 > 0$, then define μ by $\mu = \lambda_{j_2}...\lambda_n\lambda_1...\lambda_{j_2-1}$. Then $\lambda_{j_1}...\lambda_n\lambda^{s_1}\lambda_1...\lambda_i\alpha^{(1)} = \lambda_{j_1}...\lambda_{j_2-1}\mu^{s_1}\lambda_{j_2}...\lambda_n\lambda_1...\lambda_i\alpha^{(1)}$ and $\lambda_{j_2}...\lambda_n\lambda^{s_2}\lambda_1...\lambda_i\beta^{(1)} = \mu^{s_2}\lambda_{j_2}...\lambda_n\lambda_1...\lambda_i\beta^{(1)}$ and $i < j_2-1$. (If $i \geqslant j_2-1$, then we have $\lambda_{j_1}...\lambda_n\lambda^{s_1}\lambda_1...\lambda_i\alpha^{(1)} = \lambda_{j_1}...\lambda_{j_2}\mu^{s_1+1}\lambda_{j_2}...\lambda_i\alpha^{(1)}$ and $\lambda_{j_2}...\lambda_n\lambda^{s_2}\lambda_1...\lambda_i\beta^{(1)} = \mu^{s_2+1}\lambda_{j_2}...\lambda_i\beta^{(1)}$. But this case can be handled analogously.) Thus, $\mu_{n+j_1-j_2+1}...\mu_n\mu^{s_1}\mu_1...\mu_{n+i-j_2+1}\alpha^{(1)} \in P_1$ and $\mu^{s_2}\mu_1...\mu_{n+i-j_2+1}\beta^{(1)} \in P_2$. Hence $\mu_1...\mu_{n+i-j_2+1}\alpha^{(1)} \in \Gamma^\mu_{n+i-j_2+1}$ and $\mu_1...\mu_{n+i-j_2+1}\beta^{(1)} \in \Gamma^\mu_{n+i-j_2+1}$. Because $\mu \leqslant \gamma$, for some $\gamma\,(=\mu^{s_2}\mu_1...\mu_{n+i-j_2+1}) \in \bigcup_{P\in C} P$, there exists a j, $0 \leqslant j < n$ and a template $P \in C$ such that $D^j_P(\mu_1...\mu_{n+i-j_2+1}\alpha^{(1)}) \cap D^j_P(\mu_1...\mu_{n+i-j_2+1}\beta^{(1)}) \neq \emptyset$ (the collection of jth-degrees are taken with respect to μ). So, $\mu_j...\mu_n\mu^s\mu_1...$

$\mu_{n+i-j_2+1}\alpha^{(1)} \in P$ and $\mu_j...\mu_n\mu^s\mu_1...\mu_{n+i-j_2+1}\beta^{(1)} \in P$, for some $s \geqslant 0$. Thus, $\lambda_{j_2+j-1}...\lambda_n\lambda^{s+1}\lambda_1...\lambda_i\alpha^{(1)} \in P$, and $\lambda_{j_2+j-1}...\lambda_n\lambda^{s+1}\lambda_1...\lambda_i\beta^{(1)} \in P$ (and $j \leqslant n - j_2 + 1$), or $\lambda_{j_2+j-n-1}...\lambda_n\lambda^s\lambda_1...\lambda_i\alpha^{(1)} \in P$ and $\lambda_{j_2+j-n-1}... \lambda_n\lambda^s\lambda_1...\lambda_j\beta^{(1)} \in P$ (and $j > n-j_2+1$). So, either $s+1 \in D_P^{j_2+j-1}(\lambda_1...\lambda_i\alpha^{(1)})$ and $s + 1 \in D_P^{j_2+j-1}(\lambda_1...\lambda_i\beta^{(1)})$, or, $s \in D_P^{j_2+j-n-1}(\lambda_1...\lambda_i\alpha^{(1)})$ and $s \in D_P^{j_2+j-n-1}(\lambda_1...\lambda_i\beta^{(1)})$ (the degrees are taken with respect to λ).

If $s_2 = 0$ and $s_1 > 0$, then we can handle analogously to the aforesaid. If both $s_1 = 0$ and $s_2 = 0$, then take $\mu = \lambda_{j_1}...\lambda_n\lambda_1...\lambda_i$ and again we can handle analogously to the above. □

Examples

In all examples T is a binary tree.

1. Let P be the template $\{\varepsilon, e_1e_2, e_2, e_2e_1e_2, e_2e_1e_2e_1e_2\}$. Then $C = \{P\}$ is stable. Take, for example $\lambda = e_1e_2$, then $(P)_\lambda = \{\varepsilon, e_1, e_1e_1e_2, e_2, e_2e_1e_2, e_2e_1e_2e_1e_2\}$ and $D_P^0(\varepsilon) = \{0,1\}$, $D_P^1(\varepsilon) = \{1,2,3\}$, $D_P^1(e_1) = \{0\}$, $D_P^1(e_1e_1e_2) = \{0\}$, $D_P^0(e_2) = \{0\}$, $D_P^0(e_2e_1e_2) = \{0\}$, and $D_P^0(e_2e_1e_2e_1e_2) = \{0\}$. So condition ($i'$) is fulfilled for $\lambda = e_1e_2$. For all the other choices of λ see figure 4.12. Condition (ii) is trivially fulfilled.
2. $C = \{\tilde{P}\}$, with P from example 1, is also stable.
3. Let P be the template $\{\varepsilon, e_1, e_1e_2, e_1e_1e_2, e_2, e_2e_1\}$. Then $C = \{P\}$ is stable, whereas $C = \{\tilde{P}\}$ is not stable. Consider, for instance, $(\tilde{P})_{e_2} = \{\varepsilon, e_1, e_1e_1, e_1e_2\}$. Then $D_P^0(\varepsilon) = \{0,1\}$, $D_P^0(e_1) = \{0,1\}$, but $D_P^0(e_1e_1) = \{1\}$ and $D_P^0(e_1e_2) = \{0\}$.
4. For any $d \geqslant 0$, the collection C consisting of the subtree P of depth $d\,(P = \{\alpha \mid |\alpha| \leqslant d\})$ is stable. This is because, for all λ, $|\lambda| \leqslant d$, and for all i, $0 \leqslant i < n$, $\Gamma_\lambda^i \subseteq P(\lambda_1...\lambda_i)$. So, for all $\alpha \in \Gamma_\lambda^i$: $0 \in D_P^i(\alpha)$. Condition (ii) is fulfilled trivially.
5. For any $s_1 \geqslant 0$ and $s_2 \geqslant 0 : C = \{P_1, P_2\}$, with $P_1 = \{e_1^i \mid 0 \leqslant i \leqslant s_1\}$ and $P_2 = \{e_2^i \mid 0 \leqslant i \leqslant s_2\}$, is stable.

Theorem 4.9 *Let C be a stable collection of templates. Let l be an arbitrary primary line and let $m \in \overset{\approx}{\overline{TL}}{}_l^{(1)}$. Further, let $s_1 : \eta_{\overline{B}_l^c}(\overline{B}_l^{(0)}) \to \{0, 1, ..., M_1 - 1\}$ be an "incomplete" skewing scheme on $S^0_{\overline{B}_l^c}$, which is valid for $\overline{ST}_l$ and with M_1 minimal, and let $s_2 : \eta_{\overline{B}_l^c}(\overline{B}^{(0)}_{\mathrm{prim}(m)}((\mathrm{odperi}(l))^i\mathrm{base}(m))) \to \{0, 1, ..., M_2 - 1\}$, $i \geqslant 0$, be an "incomplete" skewing scheme on $S^0_{\overline{B}_l^c}$ which is valid for $\{TT_{m',j} \mid 1 \leqslant j \leqslant t$ and $\mathrm{prim}(m')$ related to $\mathrm{prim}(m)$ and $\mathrm{base}(m') =$*

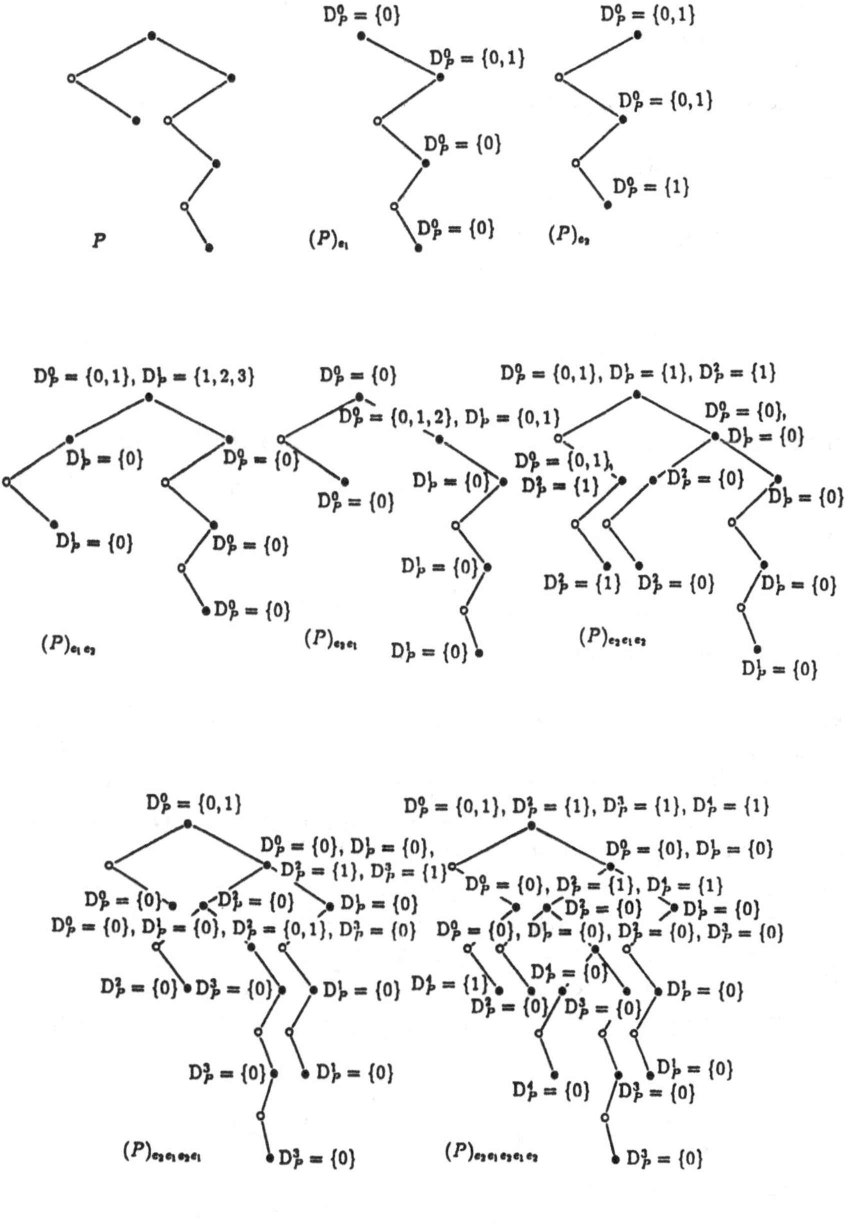

Figure 4.12: A template P for which $C = \{P\}$ is stable.

base(m)} *(see definition 4.17) and with* M_2 *minimal. Then there exists a permutation* $\eta : \{0,1,...,M_2-1\} \to \{0,1,...,M_2-1\}$ *such that the "incomplete" skewing scheme*

$$s : \eta_{\overline{B}_l^c}(\overline{B}_l^{(0)} \cup \overline{B}^{(0)}_{\text{prim}(m)}((\text{odperi}(l))^i(\text{base}(m)))) \to \{0,1,...,M-1\},$$

with $M = \max(M_1, M_2)$*, defined by*

$$\begin{cases} s(x,y) = s_1(x,y), & \text{if } (x,y) \in \eta_{\overline{B}_l^c}(\overline{B}_l^{(0)}), \\ s(x,y) = \eta(s_2(x,y)), & \text{otherwise}, \end{cases}$$

is valid for $ST_l \cup \{TT_{m',j} | \ 1 \leqslant j \leqslant |C|,$ prim(m') *related to* prim(m) *and* base(m') = base(m)}.

Proof Consider the set $C = \{\alpha | \alpha \in \overline{B}^{(0)}_{\text{prim}(m)}((\text{odperi}(l))^i\text{base}(m)) \cap \overline{B}_l^{(0)}$, and there exists a $\gamma \in T$ and a template $P \in C$ such that $P(\gamma) \not\subseteq \overline{B}_l^{(0)}$ and $\alpha \in P(\gamma)\}$. Thus, $C \subseteq \overline{B}_l^{(0)}$.

Claim 4.3 *For all* $\alpha \in C$ *and* $\beta \in C$, $\alpha \neq \beta$ *:*
(1) $s_1(\eta_{B_l^c}(\alpha)) \neq s_1(\eta_{B_l^c}(\beta))$*, and*
(2) $s_2(\eta_{B_l^c}(\alpha)) \neq s_2(\eta_{B_l^c}(\beta))$.

Proof Let $\alpha \in C$ and $\beta \in C$, $\alpha \neq \beta$. Then there exist nodes γ_1, γ_2, and templates $P_1 \in C$ and $P_2 \in C$, such that $\alpha \in P_1(\gamma_1)$, $\beta \in P_2(\gamma_2)$, $P_1(\gamma_1) \not\subseteq \overline{B}_l^{(0)}$ and $P_2(\gamma_2) \not\subseteq \overline{B}_l^{(0)}$. Thus, $\gamma_1 = \lambda^i\lambda_1...\lambda_j\delta^{(1)}$ and $\gamma_2 = \lambda^i\lambda_1...\lambda_j\delta^{(2)}$, for some $\delta^{(1)} \neq \varepsilon$, $\delta^{(2)} \neq \varepsilon$, $\lambda (= \lambda_1...\lambda_n) = \text{odperi}(l)$ and $j \leqslant n$. Then $\alpha = \lambda^i\lambda_1...\lambda_j\delta^{(1)}\varrho^{(1)}$ and $\beta = \lambda^i\lambda_1...\lambda_j\delta^{(2)}\varrho^{(2)}$, for some $\varrho^{(1)}$ and $\varrho^{(2)}$. $\alpha \in \overline{B}_l^{(0)}$ and $\beta \in \overline{B}_l^{(0)}$, so both $\lambda_1...\lambda_j\delta^{(1)}\varrho^{(1)} \in \Gamma_j^\lambda$ and $\lambda_1...\lambda_j\delta^{(2)}\varrho^{(2)} \in \Gamma_j^\lambda$. Because C is stable, there exists a j_1, $0 \leqslant j_1 < n$, and a template $P \in C$ such that $D_P^{j_1}(\lambda_1...\lambda_j\delta^{(1)}\varrho^{(1)}) \cap D_P^{j_1}(\lambda_1...\lambda_j\delta^{(2)}\varrho^{(2)}) \neq \emptyset$. Thus, there exists a $\sigma^{(1)} \in P$ and $\sigma^{(2)} \in P$ such that $\lambda_1...\lambda_{j_1}\sigma^{(1)} = \lambda^{i_1}\lambda_1...\lambda_j\delta^{(1)}\varrho^{(1)}$ and $\lambda_1...\lambda_{j_1}\sigma^{(2)} = \lambda^{i_1}\lambda_1...\lambda_j\delta^{(2)}\varrho^{(2)}$. From the validity of s_1 for ST_l now follows that for all $i' \geqslant 0$:

$$s_1(\eta_{\overline{B}_l^c}(\lambda^{i'}\lambda_1...\lambda_j\delta^{(1)}\varrho^{(1)})) \neq s_1(\eta_{\overline{B}_l^c}(\lambda^{i'}\lambda_1...\lambda_j\delta^{(2)}\varrho^{(2)})).$$

And condition (1) follows.

Further, $\alpha \in \overline{B}^{(0)}_{\text{prim}(m)}(\lambda^i\text{base}(m))$ and $\beta \in \overline{B}^{(0)}_{\text{prim}(m)}(\lambda^i\text{base}(m))$. Now we can distinguish two cases:

Case 1 base$(m) = \lambda_1 ... \lambda_{j_2}$, $j_2 \leqslant j$.
Case 2 base$(m) = \lambda_1 ... \lambda_j \zeta_1 ... \zeta_{j_2}$, $\zeta_1 ... \zeta_{j_2} \leqslant \delta^{(1)}\varrho^{(1)}$ and $\zeta_1 ... \zeta_{j_2} \leqslant \delta^{(2)}\varrho^{(2)}$.

Consider **case 1**.
Then $\lambda_{j_2+1} ... \lambda_j \delta^{(1)} \varrho^{(1)} \in \overline{B}^{(0)}_{\text{prim}(m)}$ and $\lambda_{j_2+1} ... \lambda_j \delta^{(2)} \varrho^{(2)} \in \overline{B}^{(0)}_{\text{prim}(m)}$. Let $\mu = \mu_1 ... \mu_k = \text{odperi}(m)$. Then we have two cases.

Case 1.1 $\lambda_{j_2+1} ... \lambda_j \delta^{(1)} \varrho^{(1)} = \mu^t \mu_1 ... \mu_v \tau^{(1)}$, and
$\lambda_{j_2+1} ... \lambda_j \delta^{(2)} \varrho^{(2)} = \mu^t \mu_1 ... \mu_v \tau^{(2)}$, $t \geqslant 0$, $0 \leqslant v < k$ and nodes $\tau^{(1)}$ and $\tau^{(2)}$.

Case 1.2 $\lambda_{j_2+1} ... \lambda_j \delta^{(1)} \varrho^{(1)} = \mu^{t_1} \mu_1 ... \mu_{v_1} \tau^{(1)}$, and
$\lambda_{j_2+1} ... \lambda_j \delta^{(2)} \varrho^{(2)} = \mu^{t_2} \mu_1 ... \mu_{v_2} \tau^{(2)}$, $t_1 \leqslant 0$, $t_2 \geqslant 0$, $0 \leqslant v_1 < k$, $0 \leqslant v_2 < k$ and nodes $\tau^{(1)}$, $\tau^{(2)}$ ($t_1 \neq t_2$ or $v_1 \neq v_2$).

Case 1.1 can be handled in the same way as the proof of condition (1) mentioned above.

Consider **case 1.2**.
Then $\lambda_1 ... \lambda_{j_1} \sigma^{(1)} = \lambda^{i_1} \lambda_1 ... \lambda_{j_2} \mu^{t_1} \mu_1 ... \mu_{v_1} \tau^{(1)}$, and $\lambda_1 ... \lambda_{j_1} \sigma^{(2)} = \lambda^{i_1} \lambda_1 ... \lambda_{j_2} \mu^{t_2} \mu_1 ... \mu_{v_2} \tau^{(2)}$. $\sigma^{(1)} \in P$ and $\sigma^{(2)} \in P$, and $t_1 \neq t_2$ or $v_1 \neq v_2$. Because of symmetry reasons we may assume that $\mu^{t_1} \mu_1 ... \mu_{v_1} \lneqq \mu^{t_2} \mu_1 ... \mu_{v_2}$. Then, because of the definition of the tail of a primary line, there exists a $t' \geqslant 0$ such that $\sigma^{(1)} = \mu_q ... \mu_k \mu^{t'} \mu_1 ... \mu_{v_1} \tau^{(1)}$ and $\sigma^{(2)} = \mu_q ... \mu_k \mu^{t'+t_2-t_1+1} \mu_1 ... \mu_{v_2} \tau^{(2)}$, for some q, $1 < q < k$. Then from condition (*ii*) of definition 4.20 follows that $\tau^{(1)} \in P$ and $\mu_{v_1+1} ... \mu_k \mu^{t_2-t_1-1} \mu_1 ... \mu_{v_2} \tau^{(2)} \in P$. Hence $\alpha \in P(\lambda^i \text{base}(m) \mu^{t_1} \mu_1 ... \mu_{v_1})$, and $\beta \in P(\lambda^i \text{base}(m) \mu^{t_1} \mu_1 ... \mu_{v_1})$. And the result follows.

Case 2 can be handled analogously to case 1. □

Let the permutation $\eta : \{0, 1, ..., M_2 - 1\} \to \{0, 1, ..., M_2 - 1\}$ be defined by

$$\begin{cases} \eta(x) = s_1(s_2^{-1}(x) \cap C) & \text{, if } s_2^{-1}(x) \cap C \neq \emptyset \\ \eta(x) = x & \text{, otherwise.} \end{cases}$$

Then from lemma 4.13 follows that the "incomplete" skewing scheme

$$s : \eta_{\overline{B}_l^c}(\overline{B}_l^{(0)} \cup \overline{B}^{(0)}_{\text{prim}(m)}((\text{odperi}(l))^i(\text{base}(m)))) \to \{0, 1, ..., M - 1\},$$

with $M = \max(M_1, M_2)$, defined by

$$\begin{cases} s(x, y) = s_1(x, y), & \text{if } (x, y) \in \eta_{\overline{B}_l^c}(\overline{B}_l^{(0)}), \\ s(x, y) = \eta(s_2(x, y)), & \text{otherwise ,} \end{cases}$$

is valid for $\overline{ST_l} \cup \{TT_{m',j} | 1 \leqslant j \leqslant |C|$, prim$(m')$ related to prim(m) and base(m') = base$(m)\}$. □

Thus, from theorem 4.9 we can conclude that for a stable collection of templates the assignment of $\overline{B}^{(0)}_{\text{prim}(l)}(\text{base}(l))$, l an arbitrary line, has no influence on the assignment of $\overline{B}^{(0)}_{\text{prim}(m)}$ (base(l)(odperi(prim(l)))^{i}base(m)), $m \in \widetilde{\overline{TL}}^{(1)}_{\text{prim}(l)}$ and $i \geqslant 0$, and visa versa. However, the notion of a stable collection of templates says nothing about the influence of the assignment of $\overline{B}^{(0)}_{\text{prim}(m_1)}$ ((odperi(l))^{i_1}base(m_1)) on the assignment of $\overline{B}^{(0)}_{\text{prim}(m_2)}$((odperi$(l)$)^{i_2}base$(m_2)$) for some primary line l, $i_1 \geqslant 0$, $i_2 \geqslant 0$, and $m_1 \in \overline{TL}_l$ and $m_2 \in \overline{TL}_l$ arbitrary. Thus, this notion is not strong enough to ensure that $\mu_T(C) = \max_{l \in \mathcal{L}} \mu_{S^0_{\overline{B}^C_l}}(\overline{ST_l})$, for some set $\mathcal{L}$ of primary lines. Therefore we need an additional constraint on a stable collection of templates. Recall the definition of connectedness of templates, see definition 4.6.

Definition 4.21 *A collection C of templates on a tree T is called semi-connected iff for each template $P \in C$: $\tilde{P}$ is connected.*

Lemma 4.16 *Let C be a collection of templates on a tree T.*
(i) If C is stable, then C is not necessarily semi-connected.
(ii) If C is semi-connected, then C is not necessarily stable.

Proof Example 1, p. 184 provides an example of a collection which is stable, but which is not semi-connected. Consider the collection C of templates on a binary tree which consists of the templates $P_1 = \{\varepsilon, e_1, e_2\}$ and $P_2 = \{\varepsilon, e_1, e_2e_1\}$. Then $(P_1 \cup P_2)_{e_1} = \{\varepsilon, e_2, e_2e_1\}$ and $D^0_{P_1}(e_2) = \{0\}$, $D^0_{P_2} = \emptyset$, $D^0_{P_1}(e_2e_1) = \emptyset$ and $D^0_{P_2} = \{0\}$. Thus condition (i) of definition 4.20 is not fulfilled and C is not stable. Further, C is obviously semi-connected. □

Example 5, p. 184 shows a collection C which is both stable and semi-connected.

Theorem 4.10 *Let C be a semi-connected and stable collection of templates on a tree T. Then*

$$\mu_T(C) = \max_{l \in \mathcal{L}} \mu_{S^0_{\overline{B}^C_l}}(\overline{ST_l}),$$

with $\mathcal{L} = \{ {}_{e}l^{\lambda}_{e} | \lambda \in T, \lambda \neq \varepsilon\}$.

Proof Let $l = {}_e l_e^\lambda$ be a primary line, with λ arbitrary, and let $\overline{TL}_l = \{\bar{l}_1, \bar{l}_2, ...\}$. Consider the set $\Lambda = \{l_0 (= l), l_1, l_2, ...\}$, with for all $i \geqslant 0$ there exists a $a_i \geqslant 1$ and $k_i \geqslant 0$ such that

$$l_i = \{(\text{odperi}(l))^{k_i} \varrho | \ \varrho \in \bar{l}_{a_i}\}$$

and for all $i \geqslant 0 : |\text{base}(l_i)| \leqslant |\text{base}(l_{i+1})|$. Now the following claim is valid.

Claim 4.4 *For all $i \geqslant 1$ there exists a $j_i < i$ such that for all $j < i$:*

$$\overline{B}^{(0)}_{\text{prim}(l_j)}(\text{base}(l_j)) \cap \overline{B}^{(0)}_{\text{prim}(l_i)}(\text{base}(l_i)) \subseteq \overline{B}^{(0)}_{\text{prim}(j_i)}(\text{base}(l_{j_i})).$$

Proof Let $i \geqslant 1$ be given.
Write for each $j \leqslant i : \gamma^{(j)} = \text{base}(l_j)$ and $\lambda^{(j)} (= \lambda_1^{(j)} ... \lambda_{n_j}^{(j)}) = \text{odperi}(\text{prim}(l_j))$.
Then let $j_i < i$ be such that

$$\gamma^{(j_i)}(\lambda^{(j_i)})^{t_{j_i}} \lambda_1^{(j_i)} ... \lambda_{p_{j_i}}^{(j_i)} \leqslant \gamma^{(i)}(\lambda^{(i)})^{t_i} \lambda_1^{(i)} ... \lambda_{p_i}^{(i)}$$

and $|\gamma^{(j_i)}(\lambda^{(j_i)})^{t_{j_i}} \lambda_1^{(j_i)} ... \lambda_{p_{j_i}}^{(j_i)}|$ is maximal, for some $t_{j_i} \geqslant 0$, $t_i \geqslant 0$, $0 \leqslant p_{j_i} < n_{j_i}$ and $0 \leqslant p_i < n_i$.
Suppose $\alpha \in \overline{B}^{(0)}_{\text{prim}(l_j)}(\gamma^{(j)}) \cap \overline{B}^{(0)}_{\text{prim}(l_i)}(\gamma^{(i)})$, for some $j < i$. Then

$$\alpha = \gamma^{(j)}(\lambda^{(j)})^{t_j} \lambda_1^{(j)} ... \lambda_{p_j}^{(j)} \beta^{(j)} = \gamma^{(i)}(\lambda^{(i)})^{t_i} \lambda_1^{(i)} ... \lambda_{p_i}^{(i)} \beta^{(i)}$$

for some $t_j \geqslant 0$, $t_i \geqslant 0$, $0 \leqslant p_j < n_j$, $0 \leqslant p_i < n_i$, and $\beta^{(j)} \in T$ and $\beta^{(i)} \in T$.
Further $\gamma^{(j)} \leqslant \gamma^{(i)}$. Thus, we can distinguish three cases.

Case 1 $\gamma^{(j)}(\lambda^{(j)})^{t_j} \lambda_1^{(j)} ... \lambda_{p_j}^{(j)} = \gamma_1^{(i)} ... \gamma_{q_1}^{(i)}$, and $\gamma_1^{(i)} ... \gamma_{q_i}^{(i)} \leqslant \gamma^{(i)}$.
Case 2 $\gamma^{(j)}(\lambda^{(j)})^{t_j} \lambda_1^{(j)} ... \lambda_{p_j}^{(j)} = \gamma^{(i)}(\lambda^{(i)})^{t'} \lambda_1^{(i)} ... \lambda_{q_i}^{(i)}$, and $0 \leqslant t' \leqslant t_i$ and $0 \leqslant q_1 < n_i$.
Case 3 $\gamma^{(j)}(\lambda^{(j)})^{t_j} \lambda_1^{(j)} ... \lambda_{p_j}^{(j)} = \gamma^{(i)}(\lambda^{(i)})^{t_i} \lambda_1^{(i)} ... \lambda_{p_i}^{(i)} \beta_1^{(i)} ... \beta_{q_1}^{(i)}$, and $\beta_1^{(i)} ... \beta_{q_1}^{(i)} \leqslant \beta^{(i)}$.

Consider **case 1**.
From the maximality of $|\gamma^{(j_i)}(\lambda^{(j_i)})^{t_{j_i}} \lambda_1^{(j_i)} ... \lambda_{p_{j_i}}^{(j_i)}|$ follows that $\gamma^{(j)}(\lambda^{(j)})^{t_j} \lambda_1^{(j)} ... \lambda_{p_j}^{(j)} \leqslant \gamma^{(j_i)}(\lambda^{(j_i)})^{t_{j_i}} \lambda_1^{(j_i)} ... \lambda_{p_{j_i}}^{(j_i)}$. Then we have two cases.

Case 1.1 $\gamma^{(j)}(\lambda^{(j)})^{t_j} \lambda_1^{(j)} ... \lambda_{p_j}^{(j)} = \gamma_1^{(j_i)} ... \gamma_r^{(j_i)}$, and $r < z$, $\gamma_1^{(j_i)} ... \gamma_z^{(j_i)} = \gamma^{(j_i)}$.
Case 1.2 $\gamma^{(j)}(\lambda^{(j)})^{t_j} \lambda_1^{(j)} ... \lambda_{p_j}^{(j)} = \gamma^{(j_i)}(\lambda^{(j_i)})^{t'} \lambda_1^{(j_i)} ... \lambda_r^{(j_i)}$, and $t_{j_i} \geqslant t' \geqslant 0$, $0 \leqslant r < n_{j_i}$.

Consider case 1.1
Then $\beta^{(i)} = \gamma_{r+1}^{(j_i)}...\gamma_z^{(j_i)}\bar{\beta}$, for some node $\bar{\beta}$. Because ${}_{\lambda_1^{(j)}...\lambda_{p_j}^{(j)}}l_{\beta^{(j)}}^{\lambda^{(j)}} \subseteq \overline{B}_{\text{prim}(l_j)}^{(0)}$ it is valid that $\lambda_1^{(j)}...\lambda_{p_j}^{(j)}\beta^{(j)} \in (\bigcup_{P\in C} P)_{\lambda^{(j)}}$. Thus, there exists a $k \geqslant 0$ and a template $P \in C$ such that $\lambda_1^{(j)}...\lambda_{p_j}^{(j)}(\lambda^{(j)})^k\beta^{(j)} \in P(\lambda_1^{(j)}...\lambda_w^{(j)})$, for some w, $0 \leqslant w < n_j$. Then from the connectedness of $\tilde{P}$ and the definition of the tail of a primary line follows that $\bar{\beta} \in P$. So, $\bar{\beta} \in \overline{B}_{\text{prim}(l_{j_i})}^{(0)}$. Thus

$$\begin{aligned}
\alpha &= \gamma^{(j)}(\lambda^{(j)})^{t_j}\lambda_1^{(j)}...\lambda_{p_j}^{(j)}\beta^{(j)} \\
&= \gamma_1^{(j_i)}...\gamma_r^{(j_i)}\gamma_{r+1}^{(j_i)}...\gamma_z^{(j_i)}\bar{\beta} \\
&= \gamma^{(j_i)}\bar{\beta} \\
&\in \overline{B}_{\text{prim}(l_{j_i})}^{(0)}(\text{base}(l_{j_i})).
\end{aligned}$$

In figure 4.13 (i) case 1.1 is depicted for $\gamma^{(j)} \leqslant \gamma^{(j_i)}$ and for $\gamma^{(j)} \geqslant \gamma^{(j_i)}$.

Consider case 1.2.
Then again we get that there exists a $k \geqslant 0$ and a template $P \in C$ such that for some w, $0 \leqslant w < n_j$, $\lambda_1^{(j)}...\lambda_{p_j}^{(j)}(\lambda^{(j)})^k\beta^{(j)} \in P(\lambda_1^{(j)}...\lambda_w^{(j)})$. Thus, $\beta^{(j)} \in P$ and, hence, $\lambda_1^{(j_i)}...\lambda_r^{(j_i)}\beta^{(j)} \in (\bigcup_{P\in C} P)_{\lambda^{(j_i)}}$. So ${}_{\lambda_1^{(j_i)}...\lambda_r^{(j_i)}}l_{\beta^{(j)}}^{\lambda^{(j_i)}} \subseteq \overline{B}_{\text{prim}(l_{j_i})}^{(0)}$, and

$$\begin{aligned}
\alpha &= \gamma^{(j)}(\lambda^{(j)})^{t_j}\lambda_1^{(j)}...\lambda_{p_j}^{(j)}\beta^{(j)} \\
&= \gamma^{(j_i)}(\lambda^{(j_i)})^{t'}\lambda_1^{(j_i)}...\lambda_r^{(j_i)}\beta^{(j)} \\
&\in \overline{B}_{\text{prim}(l_{j_i})}^{(0)}(\text{base}(l_{j_i})).
\end{aligned}$$

Case 2 can be handled analogously to case 1.

Consider **case 3.**
From the fact that $\gamma^{(j)} \leqslant \gamma^{(i)}$ follows that $\beta_1^{(i)}...\beta_{q_i}^{(i)} = \lambda_{p'}^{(j)}...\lambda_{n_j}^{(j)}(\lambda^{(j)})^{t'}\lambda_1^{(j)}...\lambda_{p_j}^{(j)}$, for some p', $1 < p' \leqslant n_j$ and $t' \geqslant 0$, and $\gamma^{(j)}(\lambda^{(j)})^{t_j-t'-1}\lambda_1^{(j)}...\lambda_{p'-1}^{(j)} = \gamma^{(i)}(\lambda^{(i)})^{t_i}\lambda_1^{(i)}...\lambda_{p_i}^{(i)}$. From the maximality of $|\gamma^{(j_i)}(\lambda^{(j_i)})^{t_{j_i}}\lambda_1^{(j_i)}...\lambda_{p_{j_i}}^{(j_i)}|$ follows that $\gamma^{(j)}(\lambda^{(j)})^{t_j-t'-1}\lambda_1^{(j)}...\lambda_{p'-1}^{(j)} \leqslant \gamma^{(j_i)}(\lambda^{(j_i)})^{t_{j_i}}\lambda_1^{(j_i)}...\lambda_{p_{j_i}}^{(j_i)}$. Because $\gamma^{(j_i)} \leqslant \gamma^{(i)}$ it follows that $\gamma^{(j)}(\lambda^{(j)})^{t_j-t'-1}\lambda_1^{(j)}...\lambda_{p'-1}^{(j)} = \gamma(\lambda^{(j_i)})^{t''}\lambda_1^{(j_i)}...\lambda_{p''}^{(j_i)}$, for some $t'' \geqslant 0$ and $0 \leqslant p'' < n_{j_i}$. ${}_{\lambda_1^{(i)}...\lambda_{p_i}^{(i)}}l_{\beta^{(i)}}^{\lambda^{(i)}} \subseteq \overline{B}_{\text{prim}(l_i)}^{(0)}$, thus $\lambda_1^{(i)}...\lambda_{p_i}^{(i)}\beta^{(i)} \in (\bigcup_{P\in C} P)_{\lambda^{(i)}}$. So, there exists a $k \geqslant 0$ and $P \in C$ such that $\lambda_1^{(i)}...\lambda_{p_i}^{(i)}(\lambda^{(i)})^k$

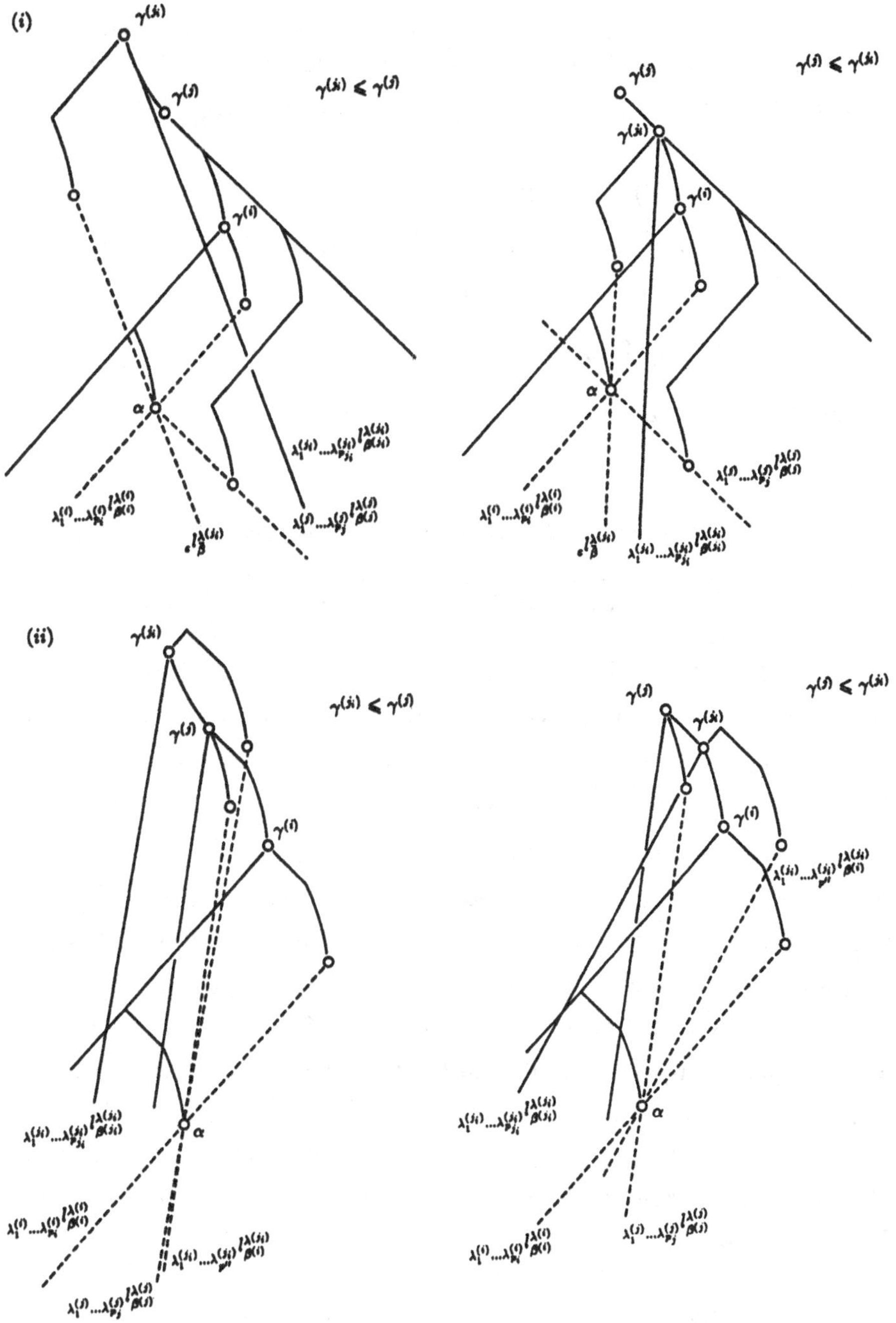

Figure 4.13: Case 1.1 and case 3.

$\beta^{(i)} \in P(\lambda_1^{(i)}...\lambda_w^{(i)})$, for some w, $0 \leqslant w < n_i$. From the connectedness of $\tilde{P}$ and the definition of the tail of a primary line follows that $\beta^{(i)} \in P$. So, $\lambda_1^{(j_i)}...\lambda_{p''}^{(j_i)}\beta^{(i)} \in (\bigcup_{P \in \mathcal{C}} P)_{\lambda^{(j_i)}}$. Thus, ${}_{\lambda_1^{(j_i)}...\lambda_{p''}^{(j_i)}} l_{\beta^{(i)}}^{(j_i)} \subseteq \overline{B}^{(0)}_{\mathrm{prim}(l_{j_i})}$ and

$$\begin{aligned}
\alpha &= \gamma^{(j)}(\lambda^{(j)})^{t_j}\lambda_1^{(j)}...\lambda_{p_j}^{(j)}\beta^{(j)} \\
&= \gamma^{(j)}(\lambda^{(j)})^{t_j-t'-1}\lambda_1^{(j)}...\lambda_{p'-1}^{(j)}\lambda_{p'}^{(j)}...\lambda_{n_j}^{(j)}(\lambda^{(i)})^{t'}\lambda_1^{(j)}...\lambda_{p'}^{(j)}\beta^{(j)} \\
&= \gamma^{(j_i)}(\lambda^{(j_i)})^{t''}\lambda_1^{(j_i)}...\lambda_{p''}^{(j_i)}\beta^{(i)} \\
&\in \overline{B}^{(0)}_{\mathrm{prim}(l_{j_i})}(\mathrm{base}(l_{j_i})).
\end{aligned}$$

See also figure 4.13 (*ii*).

□

The proof is obtained by constructing a skewing scheme $s : S^0_{\overline{B}_l^c} \to \{0, 1, ..., M-1\}$ which is valid for $\mathcal{ST}_l \cup \mathcal{TT}_l$ and with $M = \max_{l \in \mathcal{L}} M_l$, and $M_l = \mu_{S^0_{\overline{B}_l^c}}(\overline{\mathcal{ST}_l})$. (See theorem 4.7.) This is done by first assigning to each node $\alpha \in \eta_{\overline{B}_l^c}(\overline{B}_l^{(0)})$ a value $s(\alpha) \in \{0, 1, ..., M_{l_0} - 1\}$ according to the "incomplete" skewing scheme $s_0' : S^0_{\overline{B}_l^c} \to \{0, 1, ..., M_{l_0} - 1\}$ which is valid for $\overline{\mathcal{ST}}_{l_0}$. After that we successively extend for each $i = 1, 2, 3, ...$ the "incomplete" skewing scheme defined on $\eta_{\overline{B}_l^c}(\overline{B}_{l_0}^{(0)} \cup \overline{B}^{(0)}_{\mathrm{prim}(l_1)}(\mathrm{base}(l_1)) \cup ... \cup \overline{B}_{\mathrm{prim}(l_{i-1})}(\mathrm{base}(l_{i-1})))$ to an "incomplete" skewing scheme on $\eta_{\overline{B}_l^c}(\overline{B}_{l_0}^{(0)} \cup \overline{B}^{(0)}_{\mathrm{prim}(l_1)}(\mathrm{base}(l_1)) \cup ... \cup \overline{B}^{(0)}_{\mathrm{prim}(l_i)}(\mathrm{base}(l_i)))$, which is valid for $\{\mathcal{TT}_{m,j} | 1 \leqslant j \leqslant |\mathcal{C}|$ and $\mathrm{prim}(m)$ related to $\mathrm{prim}(\overline{l}_{a_i})$ and $\mathrm{base}(m) = \mathrm{base}(\overline{l}_{a_i})\} (= \mathcal{T}_{\overline{l}_{a_i}})$. This is achieved by assigning to each node $\alpha \in \eta_{\overline{B}_l^c}(\overline{B}^{(0)}_{\mathrm{prim}(l_i)}(\mathrm{base}(l_i)))$ which has not been assigned to yet a value $s_i(\alpha) \in \{0, 1, ..., M_{{}_{e}l_e^{\lambda^{(i)}}} - 1\}$, with $\lambda^{(i)} = \mathrm{odperi}(\mathrm{prim}(l_i))$, according to the "incomplete" skewing scheme s_i': $S^{(0)}_{\overline{B}^c_{\mathrm{prim}(l_i)}} \to \{0, 1, ..., M_{{}_{e}l_e^{\lambda^{(i)}}} - 1\}$, which is valid for $\overline{\mathcal{ST}}_{\mathrm{prim}(l_i)}$. With the help of theorem 4.9 and claim 4.4 we can prove that this actually can be done. Note that the skewing scheme constructed in this way is defined for the whole strip $S^0_{\overline{B}_l^c}$. Let for each $i \geqslant 1$

$$\bar{s}_i : \eta_{\overline{B}_l^c}(\overline{B}^{(0)}_{\mathrm{prim}(\overline{l}_i)}(\mathrm{base}(\overline{l}_i))) \to \{0, 1, ..., M_{{}_{e}l_e^{\bar{\lambda}^{(i)}}} - 1\},$$

$\bar{\lambda}^{(i)} = \text{odperi}(\text{prim}(\bar{l}_i))$, be the "incomplete" skewing scheme on $S^{(0)}_{\overline{B}_l^c}$ which is valid for $\mathcal{T}_{\bar{l}_i}$ and which corresponds to the "incomplete" skewing scheme $\bar{s}_i'$: $S^0_{\overline{B}_{\text{prim}(\bar{l}_i)}}{}^c \to \{0, 1, ..., M_{{}_e l_e^{\bar{\lambda}(i)}} - 1\}$, which is valid for $\overline{ST}_{\text{prim}(\bar{l}_i)}$. Then it follows that for each l_i, $i \geqslant 1$, the incomplete skewing scheme

$$s_i : \eta_{\overline{B}_l^c}(\overline{B}^{(0)}_{\text{prim}(l_i)}(\text{base}(l_i))) \to \{0, 1, ..., M_{{}_e l_e^{\bar{\lambda}(i)}} - 1\},$$

defined by

$$s_i(x, y) = \bar{s}_{a_i}(x - k_i, y) \text{ for all } (x, y),$$

is also valid for $\mathcal{T}_{\bar{l}_{a_i}}$.

Claim 4.5 *For each $i \geqslant 1$ there exists a permutation η: $\{0, 1, ..., M_{{}_e l_e^{\bar{\lambda}(a_i)}} - 1\}$ $\to \{0, 1, ..., M_{{}_e l_e^{\bar{\lambda}(a_i)}} - 1\}$ such that the "incomplete" skewing scheme*

$$s' : \eta_{\overline{B}_l^c}(\overline{B}^{(0)}_{\text{prim}(l_i)}(\text{base}(l_i))) \to \{0, 1, .., M' - 1\},$$

defined by

$$\begin{cases} s'(x, y) = s_{j_i}(x, y) & , \textit{if } (x, y) \in \eta_{\overline{B}_l^c}(\overline{B}^{(0)}_{\text{prim}(l_{j_i})}(\text{base}(l_{j_i}))) \\ s'(x, y) = \eta(s_i(x, y)) & , \textit{otherwise}, \end{cases}$$

and with $M' = \max(M_{{}_e l_e^{\bar{\lambda}(a_{j_i})}}, M_{{}_e l_e^{\bar{\lambda}(a_i)}})$ *and $j_i < i$ as in* claim 4.4, *is valid for* $\mathcal{T}_{\bar{l}_{a_i}}$.

Proof Let $i \geqslant 1$ be given. Write, for simplicity sake, $l^{(1)}$ for $\text{prim}(l_{j_i})$, $l^{(2)}$ for $\text{prim}(l_i)$, $\gamma^{(1)}$ for $\text{base}(l_{j_i})$, $\gamma^{(2)}$ for $\text{base}(l_i)$, $\lambda^{(1)}(= \lambda_1^{(1)}...\lambda_{n_1}^{(1)})$ for $\text{odperi}(l^{(1)})$, and $\lambda^{(2)}(= \lambda_1^{(2)}...\lambda_{n_2}^{(2)})$ for odperi $(l^{(2)})$.

If $\overline{B}^{(0)}_{l^{(1)}}(\gamma^{(1)}) \cap \overline{B}^{(0)}_{l^{(2)}}(\gamma^{(2)}) = \emptyset$, then take for η the identity and we are ready.

Suppose $\overline{B}^{(0)}_{l^{(1)}}(\gamma^{(1)}) \cap \overline{B}^{(0)}_{l^{(2)}}(\gamma^{(2)}) \neq \emptyset$. Then from theorem 4.9 and claim 4.4 follows that it suffices to show that $\tilde{l}^{(1)} \in \overline{TL}^{(1)}_{l^{(2)}}$, for some primary line $\tilde{l}^{(1)}$ associated with $l^{(1)}$, or $\tilde{l}^{(2)} \in \overline{TL}^{(1)}_{l^{(1)}}$, for some primary line $\tilde{l}^{(2)}$ associated with $l^{(2)}$. Note that theorem 4.9 remains valid if the roles of s_1 and s_2 are interchanged. Let $\varrho \in \overline{B}^{(0)}_{l^{(1)}}(\gamma^{(1)}) \cap \overline{B}^{(0)}_{l^{(2)}}(\gamma^{(2)})$ be such that $\varrho = \gamma^{(1)}(\lambda^{(1)})^{t_1}\lambda_1^{(1)}...\lambda_{p_1}^{(1)}\beta^{(1)} = \gamma^{(2)}\lambda_1^{(2)}...\lambda_{p_2}^{(2)}\beta^{(2)}$ and $|\gamma^{(2)}(\lambda^{(2)})^{t_2}\lambda_1^{(2)}...\lambda_{p_2}^{(2)}|$ is maximal, for some $t_1 \geqslant 0$, $t_2 \geqslant 0$, $0 \leqslant p_1 < n_1$, $0 \leqslant p_2 < n_2$ and $\beta^{(1)}$ and $\beta^{(2)}$ arbitrary. Then we can distinguish two cases.

Case 1 $\gamma^{(1)} = \gamma^{(2)}$.
Case 2 $\gamma^{(1)} < \gamma^{(2)}$.

Consider **case 1**.
Then $(\lambda^{(1)})^{t_1}\lambda_1^{(1)}...\lambda_{p_1}^{(1)}\beta^{(1)} = (\lambda^{(2)})^{t_2}\lambda_1^{(2)}...\lambda_{p_2}^{(2)}\beta^{(2)}$. Because of the definition of the tail of a primary line and the fact that $j_i < i$ it follows that either $t_1 = 0$ or $t_2 = 0$.
If $t_1 = 0$ and $t_2 \neq 0$, then $\lambda_1^{(1)}..\lambda_{p_1}^{(1)}\beta^{(1)} = (\lambda^{(2)})^{t_2}\lambda_1^{(2)}...\lambda_{p_2}^{(2)}\beta^{(2)}$. From the fact that ${}_{\lambda_1^{(1)}...\lambda_{p_1}^{(1)}}l_{\beta^{(1)}}^{\lambda^{(1)}} \subseteq \overline{B}_{l^{(1)}}^{(0)}$ follows that $(\lambda^{(2)})^{t_2}\lambda_1^{(2)}...\lambda_{p_2}^{(2)} \in (\bigcup_{P\in C} P)_{\lambda^{(1)}}$. From the connectedness of all $\tilde{P}$, $P \in C$, follows that $\lambda_1^{(2)}...\lambda_{p_2}^{(2)}\beta^{(2)}$ is also an element of $(\bigcup_{P\in C} P)_{\lambda^{(1)}}$. Thus, $|{}_{\lambda_1^{(2)}...\lambda_{p_2}^{(2)}}l_{\beta^{(2)}}^{\lambda^{(2)}} \cap (\bigcup_{P\in C} P)_{\lambda^{(1)}}| \geqslant 2$. Further $\lambda_1^{(2)}...\lambda_{p_2}^{(2)}\beta^{(2)} \in P$, for some $P \in C$ (${}_{\lambda_1^{(2)}...\lambda_{p_2}^{(2)}}l_{\beta^{(2)}}^{\lambda^{(2)}} \subseteq \overline{B}_{l^{(2)}}^{(0)}$). So, ${}_{\lambda_1^{(2)}...\lambda_{p_2}^{(2)}}l_{\beta^{(2)}}^{\lambda^{(2)}} \in \overline{TL}_{l^{(1)}}^{(1)}$.
If $t_2 = 0$ and $t_1 \neq 0$, then by the same argument we get ${}_{\lambda_1^{(1)}...\lambda_{p_1}^{(1)}}l_{\beta^{(1)}}^{\lambda^{(1)}} \in \overline{TL}_{l^{(2)}}^{(1)}$.
Let $t_1 = 0$ and $t_2 = 0$. Consider an arbitrary $\varrho'(\neq \varrho) \in C$. Then

$$\varrho' = \gamma^{(1)}(\lambda^{(1)})^{t_1'}\lambda_1^{(1)}...\lambda_{p_1'}^{(1)}\delta^{(1)} = \gamma^{(2)}(\lambda^{(2)})^{t_2'}\lambda_1^{(2)}...\lambda_{p_2'}^{(2)}\delta^{(2)}.$$

Again we have that either $t_1' = 0$ or $t_2' = 0$. If $t_1' \neq 0$ or $t_2' \neq 0$, then we can handle as above. So, we can assume that for all $\varrho' \in C : \varrho' = \gamma^{(1)}(\lambda^{(1)})^{t_1'}\lambda_1^{(1)}...\lambda_{p_1'}^{(1)}\delta^{(1)} = \gamma^{(2)}(\lambda^{(2)})^{t_2'}\lambda_1^{(2)}...\lambda_{p_2'}^{(2)}\delta^{(2)}$, for some $\delta^{(1)}$, $\delta^{(2)}$, $0 \leqslant p_1' < n_1$, $0 \leqslant p_2' < n_2$ and both $t_1' = 0$ and $t_1' = 0$. Let p be maximal such that $\lambda_1^{(1)}..\lambda_p^{(1)} = \lambda_1^{(2)}...\lambda_p^{(2)}$. Thus for all $\varrho' \in C$ holds that $\varrho' = \gamma^{(1)}\lambda_1^{(1)}...\lambda_p^{(1)}\lambda_{p+1}^{(1)}...\lambda_{p_1'}^{(1)}\delta^{(1)} = \gamma^{(1)}\lambda_1^{(1)}...\lambda_p^{(1)}\delta^{(2)}$, or $\varrho' = \gamma^{(1)}\lambda_1^{(1)}...\lambda_p^{(1)}\delta^{(1)} = \gamma^{(1)}\lambda_1^{(1)}...\lambda_p^{(1)}\lambda_{p+1}^{(2)}...\lambda_{p_2'}^{(2)}\delta^{(2)}$, or $\varrho' = \gamma^{(1)}\lambda_1^{(1)}...\lambda_{p'}^{(1)}\delta^{(1)} = \gamma^{(1)}\lambda_1^{(1)}...\lambda_{p'}^{(1)}\delta^{(2)}$, for some $p' < p$. So, we have for all $p' \leqslant p$ and $P \in C$: $P(\gamma^{(1)}\lambda_1^{(1)}...\lambda_{p'}^{(1)}) \subseteq \overline{B}_{l^{(1)}}^{(0)}(\gamma^{(1)})$. Further, for all $p' > p$ and for all $P \in C$: if $\alpha \in P(\gamma^{(2)}\lambda_1^{(2)}...\lambda_{p'}^{(2)})$ then $\alpha = \gamma^{(1)}\lambda_1^{(1)}...\lambda_p^{(1)}\delta$, with $\delta \neq \varepsilon$. Then from the assumption that C is stable follows that for all $\alpha \in \bigcup_{p'>p,P\in C} P(\gamma^{(2)}\lambda_1^{(2)}...\lambda_{p'}^{(2)}) \cap C$ and for all $\beta \in \bigcup_{p'>p,P\in C} P(\gamma^{(2)}\lambda_1^{(2)}...\lambda_{p'}^{(2)}) \cap C$:

$$s_{j_i}(\eta_{\overline{B}_l^c}(\alpha)) \neq s_{j_i}(\eta_{\overline{B}_l^c}(\beta)) \text{ and}$$
$$s_i(\eta_{\overline{B}_l^c}(\alpha)) \neq s_1(\eta_{\overline{B}_l^c}(\beta)).$$

And the existence of a permutation η, which fits the constraints, follows.

Consider **case 2.**
Then $(\lambda^{(1)})^{t_1}\lambda_1^{(1)}...\lambda_{p_1}^{(1)}\beta^{(1)} = \bar{\gamma}(\lambda^{(2)})^{t_2}\lambda_1^{(2)}...\lambda_{p_2}^{(2)}\beta^{(2)}$ and $\gamma^{(1)}\bar{\gamma} = \gamma^{(2)}$. We can distinguish two cases.

Case 2.1 $\bar{\gamma} = (\lambda^{(1)})^t\lambda_1^{(1)}...\lambda_q^{(1)}$, and $t < t_1$ or $t = t_1$, $q < p_1$.
Case 2.2 $\bar{\gamma} = (\lambda^{(1)})^t\lambda_1^{(1)}...\lambda_{p_1}^{(1)}\beta_1^{(1)}...\beta_q^{(1)}$, and $\beta_1^{(1)}...\beta_z^{(1)} = \beta^{(1)}$, $1 \leqslant 1 < z$.

Consider **case 2.1.**
Then $\lambda_{q+1}^{(1)}...\lambda_{n_1}^{(1)}(\lambda^{(1)})^{t_1-t}\lambda_1^{(1)}...\lambda_{p_1}^{(1)}\beta^{(1)} = (\lambda^{(2)})^{t_2}\lambda_1^{(2)}...\lambda_{p_2}^{(2)}\beta^{(2)}$. And we can handle analogously to case 1, except that we have to substitute $\lambda_{q+1}^{(1)}...\lambda_{n_1}^{(1)}\lambda_1^{(1)}...\lambda_q^{(1)}$ for $\lambda^{(1)}$, and $\lambda_{q+1}^{(1)}....\lambda_{p_1}^{(1)}$ for $\lambda_1^{(1)}...\lambda_{p_1}^{(1)}$ if $q \leqslant p_1$ and $\lambda_{q+1}^{(1)}...\lambda_{n_1}^{(1)}\lambda_1^{(1)}...\lambda_{p_1}^{(1)}$ for $\lambda_1^{(1)}...\lambda_{p_1}^{(1)}$ if $q > p_1$.

Consider **case 2.2.**
Then $\beta_{q+1}^{(1)}...\beta_z^{(1)} = (\lambda^{(2)})^{t_2}\lambda_1^{(2)}...\lambda_{p_2}^{(2)}\beta^{(2)}$. Because ${}_{\lambda_1...\lambda_{p_1}}l_{\beta^{(1)}}^{\lambda^{(1)}} \subseteq \overline{B}_{l^{(1)}}^{(0)}$, $\lambda_1^{(1)}...\lambda_{p_1}^{(1)}\beta^{(1)} \in (\bigcup_{P\in C} P)_{\lambda^{(1)}}$. Further, from the connectedness of each $\tilde{P}$, with $P \in C$ follows that $\beta_{q+1}^{(1)}...\beta_z^{(1)} \in P$, for some $P \in C$.

Let $\lambda^{(3)}(= \lambda_1^{(3)}..\lambda_{n_3}^{(3)})$ be such that $(\lambda^{(3)})^t = \lambda_1^{(1)}...\lambda_{p_1}^{(1)}\beta_1^{(1)}...\beta_q^{(1)}$ for some $t \geqslant 1$ and $|\lambda^{(3)}|$ is minimal. Consider the line $l^{(3)} = {}_e l^{\lambda^{(3)}}_{(\lambda^{(2)})^{t_2}\lambda_1^{(2)}...\lambda_{p_2}^{(2)}\beta^{(2)}}$. Then

$$\begin{aligned} \lambda_1^{(1)}...\lambda_{p_1}^{(1)}\beta^{(1)} &= (\lambda^{(3)})^t(\lambda^{(2)})^t\lambda_1^{(2)}...\lambda_{p_2}^{(2)}\beta^{(2)} \in l^{(3)} \text{ and} \\ \beta_{q+1}^{(1)}...\beta_z^{(1)} &= (\lambda^{(2)})^{t_2}\lambda_1^{(2)}...\lambda_{p_2}^{(2)}\beta^{(2)} \in l^{(3)}. \end{aligned}$$

Together with the fact that $\beta_{q+1}^{(1)}...\beta_z^{(1)} \in P$, for some $P \in C$, this gives $l^{(3)} \in \overline{TL}_{l^{(1)}}^{(1)}$. Thus there exists a line $l_{i'} \in \Lambda$ such that $l_{i'} = \{\gamma^{(1)}(\lambda^{(1)})^{t_1}\alpha | \alpha \in l^{(3)}\}$. Further, base$(l_{i'}) = \gamma^{(1)}(\lambda^{(1)})^{t_1}$ ($l^{(3)}$ is primary). Let $\gamma^{(3)} =$ base $(l_{i'})$. Then, because $|\gamma^{(3)}| \lneqq |\gamma^{(2)}|$, $i' < i$. Thus from the definition of j_i follows that $\overline{B}_{l^{(3)}}^{(0)}(\gamma^{(3)}) \cap \overline{B}_{l^{(2)}}^{(0)}(\gamma^{(2)}) \subseteq \overline{B}_{l^{(1)}}^{(0)}(\gamma^{(1)}) \cap \overline{B}_{l^{(2)}}^{(0)}(\gamma^{(2)})$.

Consider an arbitrary $\varrho' \in \overline{B}_{l^{(1)}}^{(0)}(\gamma^{(1)}) \cap \overline{B}_{l^{(2)}}^{(0)}(\gamma^{(2)})$. Then $\varrho' = \gamma^{(1)}(\lambda^{(1)})^{t_1'}\lambda_1^{(1)}...\lambda_{p_1'}^{(1)}\delta^{(1)} = \gamma^{(2)}(\lambda^{(2)})^{t_2'}\lambda_1^{(2)}...\lambda_{p_2'}^{(2)}\delta^{(2)}$, for some $\delta^{(1)}$, $\delta^{(2)}$, $t_1' \geqslant 0$, $t_2' \geqslant 0$, $0 \leqslant p_1' < n_1$ and $0 \leqslant p_2' < n_2$. From the maximality of $|\gamma^{(2)}(\lambda^{(2)})^{t_2}\lambda_1^{(2)}...\lambda_{p_2}^{(2)}|$ follows that $t_2' \leqslant t_2$ or $p_2' \leqslant p_2$. Because ${}_{\lambda_1^{(2)}...\lambda_{p_2'}^{(2)}}l_{\delta^{(2)}}^{\lambda^{(2)}} \subseteq \overline{B}_{l^{(2)}}^{(0)}$,

$$\lambda_1^{(2)}...\lambda_{p_2'}^{(2)}\beta^{(2)} \in (\bigcup_{P\in C} P)_{\lambda^{(2)}}.$$

And because C is semi-connected we have that $\delta^{(2)} \in P$, for some $P \in C$. $t_2' \leqslant t_2$ or $p_2' \leqslant p_2$, so, $\lambda_1^{(1)}...\lambda_{p_1}^{(1)}\beta_1^{(1)}...\beta_q^{(1)}(\lambda^{(2)})^{t_2'}\lambda_1^{(2)}...\lambda_{p_2'}^{(2)}\delta^{(2)} \in (\bigcup_{P\in C} P)_{\lambda^{(3)}}$, if $t = 1$. (If $t > 1$ then we can handle similarly.) Thus, $\lambda_1^{(1)}...\lambda_{p_1}^{(1)}\beta_1^{(1)}...\beta_q^{(1)}(\lambda^{(2)})^{t_2'}\lambda_1^{(2)}..\lambda_{p_2'}^{(2)}\delta^{(2)} \in \overline{B}_{l(3)}^{(0)}$. So,

$$\begin{aligned}
\varrho' &= \gamma^{(2)}(\lambda^{(2)})^{t_2'}\lambda_1^{(2)}...\lambda_{p_2'}^{(2)}\delta^{(2)} \\
&= \gamma^{(1)}\overline{\gamma}(\lambda^{(2)})^{t_2'}\lambda_1^{(2)}...\lambda_{p_2'}^{(2)}\delta^{(2)} \\
&= \gamma^{(1)}(\lambda^{(1)})^{t_1}\lambda_1^{(1)}...\lambda_{p_1}^{(1)}\beta_1^{(1)}...\beta_q^{(1)}(\lambda^{(2)})^{t_2'}\lambda_1^{(2)}...\lambda_{p_2'}^{(2)}\delta^{(2)} \\
&\in \overline{B}_{l(3)}^{(0)}.
\end{aligned}$$

Concluding we have that $\overline{B}_{\mathrm{prim}(l_i)}^{(0)}(\mathrm{base}(l_{i'})) \cap \overline{B}_{\mathrm{prim}(l_i)}^{(0)}(\mathrm{base}(l_i)) = \overline{B}_{\mathrm{prim}(l_{j_i})}^{(0)}(\mathrm{base}(l_{j_i})) \cap \overline{B}_{\mathrm{prim}(l_i)}^{(0)}(\mathrm{base}(l_i))$, and $\mathrm{base}(l_i) = \mathrm{base}(l_{i'}) = \mathrm{base}(l_{i'})\lambda_1^{(3)}...\lambda_{q'}^{(3)}$, for some $q' < n_3$. So the roles of l_{j_i} and $l_{i'}$ can be exchanged.

Let $\bar{\varrho} \in \overline{B}_{l(3)}^{(0)}(\gamma^{(3)}) \cap \overline{B}_{l(2)}^{(0)}(\gamma^{(2)})$. Then $\varrho = \gamma^{(3)}(\lambda^{(3)})^{t_3}\lambda_1^{(3)}...\lambda_{p_3}^{(3)}\beta^{(3)} = \gamma^{(2)}(\lambda^{(2)})^{\bar{t}_2}\lambda_1^{(2)}...\lambda_{\bar{p}_2}^{(2)}\bar{\beta}^{(2)}$, for some $\beta^{(3)}$, $\bar{\beta}^{(2)}$, $t_3 \geqslant 0$, $\bar{t}_2 \geqslant 0$, $0 \leqslant p_3 < n_3$ and $0 \leqslant \bar{p}_2 < n_2$. And $\gamma^{(2)} = \gamma^{(3)}\lambda_1^{(3)}...\lambda_{q'}^{(3)}$ which is the same as case 2.1.

□

□

With the help of the fact that for strip skewing every arbitrary collection C of strip and transversal templates $\mu_{S^0}(C)$ is "the minimum number M such that for all $K \geqslant 0$ there exists a skewing scheme $s: S^0 \to \{0, 1, ..., M-1\}$ such that for all $ST \in C$, $TT \in C$, $0 \leqslant x \leqslant K$, $y \geqslant 0$, and $i \in \{0, 1, ..., M-1\}$: $|ST(x) \cap s^{-1}(i)| \leqslant 1$ and $|TT(x, y) \cap s^{-1}(i)| \leqslant 1$", we can prove the following nice consequence of theorem 4.10. See also lemma 4.4.

Theorem 4.11 *Let C be a semi-connected and stable collection of templates on a tree T. Then there exists an infinite path $p: \alpha_0$ (the root), $\alpha_1, \alpha_2, ...$ with for all $i \geqslant 0: \alpha_i \in T$ and $\alpha_i \prec \alpha_{i+1}$ such that*

> *$\mu_T(C)$ = the minimal number M such that there exist a skewing scheme $s: T \to \{0, 1, ..., M-1\}$ with for all $j \geqslant 0$, $P \in C$, and $i \in \{0, 1, ..., M-1\}: |P(\alpha_j) \cap s^{-1}(i)| \leqslant 1$.*

Proof Let $\lambda_0\lambda_1, \lambda_2, ...$ be an enumeration of all nodes in T. Consider the set $\Gamma = \{\alpha | \exists i$ such that $\alpha \leqslant \lambda_0\lambda_1...\lambda_i\}$. Then $\Gamma = \{\alpha_0, \alpha_1, \alpha_2, ...\}$ with for all $i \geqslant 0 : \alpha_i \leqslant \alpha_{i+1}$. Define the path p by $p : \alpha_0, \alpha_1, \alpha_2, ...$ Then from theorem 4.10 and the fact mentioned above the result follows. □

4.6 Some Specific Results

In the remainder of this section we shall study the case that C consists of only one template. Recall the relationship between transversal templates on the set $\eta_{\overline{B}_l^c}(\overline{B}^{(0)}_{\text{prim}(m)}$ (base(m))) for some $m \in \overline{TL}_l$ and the strip templates on the set $\eta_{\overline{B}_l^c}(\overline{B}_l^{(0)})$ (cf. theorem 4.8).

Theorem 4.12 *Let l be a primary line and let $C = \{P\}$ be a collection of templates on a tree T, consisting of only one template. Then for all $ST_1 \in \overline{ST}_l$ and $ST_2 \in \overline{ST}_l$ there exists a bijective mapping ψ: $ST_1 \to ST_2$, such that for all (x_1, y_1) and (x_2, y_2), with $\psi(x_1, y_1) = (x_2, y_2)$:*

if $x_1 \geqslant 1$ then $y_2 > y_1$ and $x_2 = 0$,
if $x_2 \geqslant 1$ then $y_1 > y_2$ and $x_1 = 0$, and
if $x_1 = 0$ and $x_2 = 0$ then $y_1 \neq y_2$.

Proof Let $ST_1 \in \overline{ST}_l$ and $ST_2 \in \overline{ST}_l$, and let $\lambda\ (= \lambda_1...\lambda_n) = \text{odperi}(l)$. For each i, $1 \leqslant i \leqslant n$, write $\bar{\lambda}^{(i)}$ for $\lambda_{i+1}...\lambda_n\lambda_1...\lambda_i$. Then $\overline{B}_l^{(0)} = {}_{\alpha^{(i_1)}}l^{\bar{\lambda}^{(i_1)}}_{\beta^{(1)}} \cup {}_{\alpha^{(i_2)}}l^{\bar{\lambda}^{(i_2)}}_{\beta^{(2)}} \cup ... \cup {}_{\alpha^{(i_p)}}l^{\bar{\lambda}^{(i_p)}}_{\beta^{(p)}}$ with for all j, $1 \leqslant j \leqslant p$, $\alpha^{(i_j)} = \lambda_1...\lambda_{i_j}$ and $\beta^{(1)} \prec \beta^{(2)} \prec ... \prec \beta^{(p)}$. Because $ST_1 \in \overline{ST}_l$ and $ST_2 \in \overline{ST}_l$ there exists a k_1 and k_2, $k_1 \neq k_2$, such that

$$ST_1 = \eta_{\overline{B}^c_{\lambda_{k_1}...\lambda_n}l^{\lambda}_{\beta}}(P) \text{ and } ST_2 = \eta_{\overline{B}^c_{\lambda_{k_2}...\lambda_n}l^{\lambda}_{\beta}}(P),$$

for $\beta = \text{tail}(l)$. Let ψ_1 denote $\eta_{B^c_{\lambda_{k_1}...\lambda_n}l^{\lambda}_{\beta}}$ and ψ_2 for $\eta_{B^c_{\lambda_{k_2}...\lambda_n}l^{\lambda}_{\beta}}$. Define the map $\psi : ST_1 \to ST_2$ by $\psi(x, y) = \psi_2(\psi_1^{-1}(x, y))$. Let $\psi(x_1, y_1) = (x_2, y_2)$ for some (x_1, y_1) and (x_2, y_2). Then $\psi_1^{-1}(x_1, y_1) = \psi_2^{-1}(x_2, y_2)$. Thus, there exists a $\varrho \in P$ such that $(x_1, y_1) = \psi_1(\varrho)$ and $(x_2, y_2) = \psi_2(\varrho)$. Then $\varrho = \lambda_{k_1}...\lambda_{i_{y_1}}(\bar{\lambda}^{(i_{y_1})})^{x_1}\beta^{(y_1)}$ and $k_1 \leqslant i_{y_1}$, or $\varrho = \lambda_{k_1}...\lambda_n\lambda_1...\lambda_{i_{y_1}}(\bar{\lambda}^{(i_{y_1})})^{x_1}\beta^{(y_1)}$ and $k_1 > i_{y_1}$. And $\varrho = \lambda_{k_2}...\lambda_{i_{y_2}}(\bar{\lambda}^{(i_{y_2})})^{x_2}\beta^{(y_2)}$ and $k_2 \leqslant i_{y_2}$, or $\lambda_{k_2}...\lambda_n\lambda_1...\lambda_{i_{y_2}}(\bar{\lambda}^{(i_{y_2})})^{x_2}\beta^{(y_2)}$ and $k_2 > i_{y_2}$.

Consider the case that $\varrho = \lambda_{k_1}...\lambda_{i_{y_1}}(\bar{\lambda}^{(i_{y_1})})^{x_1}\beta^{(y_1)} = \lambda_{k_2}...\lambda_{i_{y_2}}(\bar{\lambda}^{(i_{y_2})})^{x_2}\beta^{(y_2)}$ and $k_1 \leqslant i_{y_1}$ and $k_2 \leqslant i_{y_2}$. The other three cases can be handled similarly.

Let $x_1 \geqslant 1$. Suppose $x_2 \geqslant 1$, then from the definition of the tail of a primary line follows that $\beta^{(y_1)} = \beta^{(y_2)}$, $x_1 = x_2$ and $k_1 = k_2$. Contradicting the fact that $k_1 \neq k_2$. Thus, $x_2 = 0$. So, $\lambda_{k_1}...\lambda_{i_{y_1}}(\lambda_{i_{y_1}+1}...\lambda_n\lambda_1...\lambda_{i_{y_1}})^{x_1}\beta^{(y_1)} = \lambda_{k_2}...\lambda_{i_{y_2}}\beta^{(y_2)}$. Then $|\beta^{(y_2)}| = i_{y_1} - k_1 + 1 + x_1 n - i_{y_2} + k_2 - 1 + |\beta^{(y_1)}| \geqslant |\beta^{(y_1)}| + x_1 n - (n-1) \gneqq |\beta^{(y_1)}|$. Thus, $y_1 < y_2$.
If $x_2 \geqslant 1$ then by an analogous argument we get $x_1 = 0$ and $y_2 > y_1$. If $x_1 = 0$ and $x_2 = 0$ then $\lambda_{k_1}...\lambda_{i_{y_1}}\beta^{(y_1)} = \lambda_{k_2}...\lambda_{i_{y_2}}\beta^{(y_2)}$. Suppose $y_1 = y_2$. Then $\beta^{(y_1)} = \beta^{(y_2)}$ and $k_1 = k_2$. Contradicting the fact that $k_1 \neq k_2$. Thus, $y_1 \neq y_2$. □

Corollary 4.2 *Let l be a primary line and let $C = \{P\}$. Then for each $y_0 \geqslant 0$,*

$$\sum_{ST \in \overline{ST_l}} |\{(x, y_0) | (x, y_0) \in ST\}| \leqslant |P|.$$

Proof Let $\overline{ST_l} = \{ST_1, ST_2, ..., ST_n\}$. Then from the previous theorem follows that there exists bijective maps $\psi_2' : ST_1 \rightarrow ST_2$, $\psi_3' : ST_1 \rightarrow ST_3$, ..., $\psi_n' : ST_1 \rightarrow ST_n$, such that for each $i \geqslant 2 : \psi_i' = \psi_i \circ \psi_1^{-1}$, $\psi_i : P \rightarrow ST_i$, and such that for all $i \geqslant 2$, $j \geqslant 2$, $i \neq j$, $(x_i, y_0) \in ST_i$ and $(x_j, y_0) \in ST_j$: $\psi_i^{-1}(x_i, y_0) \neq \psi_j^{-1}(x_j, y_0)$. The result now follows. □

Define for each $ST \in \overline{ST_l}$ its depth d_{ST} by

$$d_{ST} = |\{y | \exists x \text{ such that } (x, y) \in ST\}|.$$

Corollary 4.3 *Let l be a primary line and let $C = \{P\}$. Then for each pair $ST_1 \in \overline{ST_l}$ and $ST_2 \in \overline{ST_l}$: $d_{ST_1} + d_{ST_2} \geqslant |P| + 1$.*

Proof Let $\psi : ST_1 \rightarrow ST_2$ be the mapping which fits the constraints of theorem 4.12. Let X denote the set $\{(x, y) | x = 0 \text{ and } \psi(x, y) = (0, y') \text{ for some } y' \neq y\}$. Then $|\{(x, y) | x > 0 \text{ and } (x, y) \in ST_1\}| = |\{(x, y) | x = 0 \text{ and } (x, y) \in ST_2\}| - |X|$. Thus

$$\begin{aligned}
&|\{(x, y) | x = 0 \text{ and } (x, y) \in ST_1\}| + |\{(x, y) | x = 0 \text{ and } (x, y) \in ST_2\}| \\
&\quad = |\{(x, y) | x > 0 \text{ and } (x, y) \in ST_2\}| + |\{(x, y) | x = 0, (x, y) \in ST_2\}| + |X| \\
&\quad = |P| + |X|.
\end{aligned}$$

Because for both $i = 1$ and $i = 2 : d_{ST_i} \geqslant |\{(x, y) | x = 0 \text{ and } (x, y) \in ST_i\}|$ we have that $d_{ST_1} + d_{ST_2} \geqslant |P| + |X|$.

If $X \neq \emptyset$ then we are ready. Let $X = \emptyset$. Note that $\psi^{-1} : ST_2 \to ST_1$ fits also the constraints of theorem 4.12. Let $(x_0, y_0) \in ST_1 \cup ST_2$ such that y_0 is minimal. Assume that $(x_0, y_0) \in ST_1$ (the case that $(x_0, y_0) \in ST_2$ can be handled similar). If $x_0 = 0$ then from the fact that ψ fits the constraint of theorem 4.12 and $X = \emptyset$ follows that there exists a $(x, y)(= \psi(x_0, y_0)) \in ST_2$ such that $x \geqslant 1$ and $y < y_0$. If $x_0 \neq 0$ then there exists a (x, y) (with $\psi^{-1}(x, y) = (x_0, y_0)) \in ST_2$ such that $x = 0$ and $y < y_0$. And both cases lead to contradiction. □

The previous observations inspire us to the following interesting theorem. Define for each primary line $l = {}_\alpha l_\beta^\lambda$, with $|l \cap P| \geqslant 2$, $\eta_l(l \cap P) = \{s | \alpha\lambda^s\beta \in P\}$ and the corresponding collection of templates $C_l = \{\eta_m(m \cap P) | \, m$ a primary line related to $l\}$ on a 1-dimensional array. Note that for each $y_0 \geqslant 0$ there exists a primary line m such that $\{\{x | (x, y_0) \in ST\} | \, ST \in \overline{ST_l}\} = C_m$.

Theorem 4.13 *Let* $C = \{P\}$. *Then*

$$\mu_T(C) = \sum_{l \in \mathcal{L}} \mu_Z(C_l) + |\{\varrho | \varrho \in P \text{ and there does not exist a } l \in \mathcal{L} \text{ with } \varrho \in \mathcal{L}\}|,$$

with $\mathcal{L} = \{l | \, l$ *primary and* $|l \cap P| \geqslant 2\}$.

Proof Let $\mathcal{L} = \{l_0, l_1, ..., l_{p-1}\}$, for some $p \geqslant 0$, and let for all i, $0 \leqslant i \leqslant p-1$, $s_i : Z \to \{M_i, M_i + 1..., M_i - 1 + \mu_Z(C_{l_i})\}$, with $M_0 = 0$ and $M_i = \sum_{j<i} \mu_Z(C_{l_j})$, be a skewing scheme which is valid for C_{l_i}. Note that for all $\varrho \in P$ and $\sigma \in P$ there exists a primary line l with $\varrho \in l$ and $\sigma \in l$ iff $\tilde{\varrho} \leqslant \tilde{\sigma}$ or $\tilde{\sigma} \leqslant \tilde{\varrho}$. Define for each $l \in \mathcal{L}$ the transposed line $\tilde{l}$ by: $\varrho \in l$ iff $\tilde{\varrho} \in \tilde{l}$. $\tilde{l}$ is not necessarily primary. Let $T = \{\alpha_0, \alpha_1, \alpha_2, ...\}$, with $\alpha_0 \prec \alpha_1 \prec \alpha_2 ....$ Let M denote the number $\sum_{l \in \mathcal{L}} \mu_Z(C_l) + |\{\varrho | \varrho \in P$ and there does not exist a $l \in \mathcal{L}$ such that $\varrho \in \mathcal{L}\}|$. The skewing scheme $\tilde{s} : T \to \{0, 1, ..., M-1\}$ is defined by the following three stages. Let $\Gamma = \{\varrho | \, \exists l \in \mathcal{L} : \varrho \in \tilde{l}\} \cap \tilde{P}$.

Stage 1 Assign successively for each l_i, $i = 0, 1, ..., p-1$, to each node $\alpha\lambda^t\beta$ the integer value $\tilde{s}(\alpha\lambda^t\beta) = s_i(t)$, with $t \geqslant 0$ and $\tilde{l}_i = {}_\alpha l_\beta^\lambda$. Thereupon assign to each node $\alpha \in \tilde{P}$ which has not been assigned to yet a distinct integer value $\tilde{s}(\alpha) \geqslant \sum_{l \in \mathcal{L}} \mu_Z(C_l)$ (and $\tilde{s}(\alpha) \leqslant M-1$).
Stage 2 Assign to each node $\alpha \in T$, which has not been assigned to yet and for which there exists a $\varrho \in \Gamma$ such that $\varrho \leqslant \alpha$, the value $\tilde{s}(\alpha) = \tilde{s}(\bar{\varrho})$, with $\bar{\varrho} \in \Gamma, \bar{\varrho} \leqslant \alpha$ and $|\bar{\varrho}|$ is maximal.
Stage 3 Assign to each node $\alpha \in T$, which has not been assigned to in stage 1 or 2, an arbitrary integer value $\tilde{s}(\alpha) \in \{0, 1, ..., M-1\}$.

Define the skewing scheme $s : T \to \{0, 1, ..., M-1\}$ by $s(\alpha) = \tilde{s}(\tilde{\alpha})$ for all $\alpha \in T$.

Suppose s is not valid for P. Then there exists a node $\gamma \in T$ and nodes $\varrho \subset P$ and $\sigma \in P$, $\varrho \neq \sigma$, such that $s(\gamma\varrho) = s(\gamma\sigma)$.
Consider $\tilde{\varrho}\tilde{\gamma}$ and $\tilde{\sigma}\tilde{\gamma}$. Then from the definition of $\tilde{s}$ it is clear that both $\tilde{s}(\tilde{\varrho}\tilde{\gamma})$ and $\tilde{s}(\tilde{\sigma}\tilde{\gamma})$ are assigned in stage 1 or 2. Let $\bar{\varrho} \in \Gamma$ and $\bar{\sigma} \in \Gamma$ be such that $\bar{\varrho} \leqslant \tilde{\varrho}\tilde{\gamma}$, $\bar{\sigma} \leqslant \tilde{\sigma}\tilde{\gamma}$, and $|\bar{\varrho}|$ is maximal and $|\bar{\sigma}|$ is maximal.

If $\bar{\varrho} \notin \{\varrho | \exists l \in \mathcal{L} : \varrho \in \tilde{l}\}$ or $\bar{\sigma} \notin \{\varrho | \exists l \in \mathcal{L} : \varrho \in \tilde{l}\}$ then from the definition of $\tilde{s}$ directly follows that $\tilde{s}(\tilde{\varrho}\tilde{\gamma}) = \tilde{s}(\bar{\varrho}) \neq \tilde{s}(\bar{\sigma}) = \tilde{s}(\tilde{\sigma}\tilde{\gamma})$. Thus, $s(\gamma\varrho) \neq s(\gamma\sigma)$. Contradiction.
Let $l_{i_1} \in \mathcal{L}$ and $l_{i_2} \in \mathcal{L}$, such that $\bar{\varrho} \in \tilde{l}_{i_1}$ and $\bar{\sigma} \in \tilde{l}_{i_2}$. If $i_1 \neq i_2$ then, again, directly follows that $\tilde{s}(\bar{\varrho}) \neq \tilde{s}(\bar{\sigma})$ and $s(\gamma\varrho) \neq s(\gamma\sigma)$. This leaves us with the case that $i_1 = i_2$. Note that for all i, $0 \leqslant i \leqslant p-1$: tail$(\tilde{l}_i) = \varepsilon$. Thus, $\tilde{l}_{i_1} = {}_{\alpha}l^{\lambda}_{\epsilon}$, and $\bar{\varrho} = \alpha\lambda^{t_1}$, $t_1 \geqslant 0$, and $\bar{\sigma} = \alpha\lambda^{t_2}$, $t_2 \geqslant 0$. Further, $\bar{\varrho} \geqslant \tilde{\varrho}$ and $\bar{\sigma} \geqslant \tilde{\sigma}$. So, $\tilde{\varrho}\tilde{\gamma} = \alpha\lambda^{t_1}\gamma^{(1)}$, $\tilde{\sigma}\tilde{\gamma} = \alpha\lambda^{t_2}\gamma^{(2)}$, and $\tilde{\varrho} \leqslant \alpha\lambda^{t_1}$ and $\tilde{\sigma} \leqslant \alpha\lambda^{t_2}$. Thus, $\tilde{\gamma} = \lambda_j...\lambda_n\lambda^t\bar{\gamma}$, for some j, $1 < j \leqslant n+1$, $t \geqslant 0$, $\lambda_1...\lambda_n = \lambda$ and $\bar{\gamma} = \gamma^{(1)} = \gamma^{(2)}$. Further, $t \leqslant \min(t_1, t_2)$, if $j = n+1$, and $t \leqslant \min(t_1, t_2) - 1$, otherwise. Then $\tilde{\varrho} = \alpha\lambda^{t_1-t-1}\lambda_1...\lambda_{j-1}$ and $\tilde{\sigma} = \alpha\lambda^{t_2-t-1}\lambda_1...\lambda_{j-1}$. So there exists a template $A \in C_{l_{i_1}}$ such that $t_1 - t - 1 \in A$ and $t_2 - t - 1 \in A$, or, $t_1 - t \in A$ and $t_2 - t \in A$. Thus, $s_{i_1}(t_1) \neq s_{i_1}(t_2)$, and $\tilde{s}(\tilde{\varrho}\tilde{\gamma}) \neq \tilde{s}(\tilde{\sigma}\tilde{\gamma})$. Contradiction. □

Corollary 4.4 *Let $C = \{P\}$ be a collection of templates on a tree T. If there exists a primary line l such that $l \cap P = P$, then*

$$\mu_T(C) = \mu_{\mathbf{Z}}(\eta_l(l \cap P)).$$

Proof Directly from theorem 4.13. □

Corollary 4.5 *Let $C = \{P\}$ be a collection of templates on a tree T. If for all $\varrho \in \tilde{P}$ there exists at most one $\varrho' \in \tilde{P}$, $\varrho' \neq \varrho$, such that $\varrho' \leqslant \varrho$ or $\varrho \leqslant \varrho'$, then*

$$\mu_T(C) = |P|.$$

Proof Let P be a template such that for all $\varrho \in \tilde{P}$ there exists at most one $\varrho' \in \tilde{P}$ with $\varrho' \neq \varrho$ and $\varrho' \leqslant \varrho$ or $\varrho \leqslant \varrho'$. Then for each node $\varrho \in P$ there exists at most one primary line l such that $\varrho \in l$ and $|l \cap P| \geqslant 2$. Further, for each primary line $l : |l \cap P| \leqslant 2$. So for each primary line l, with $|l \cap P| \geqslant 2$, holds that $\mu_{\mathbf{Z}}(C_l) = 2$. Apply theorem 4.13. □

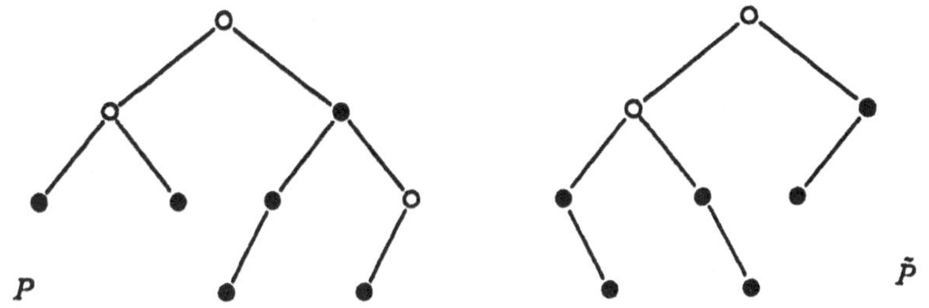

Figure 4.14: An example of a template for which corollary 4.5 yields an optimal result.

Whereas corollary 4.4 is quite obvious, corollary 4.5 has some nice applications. An example is shown below.

Example
Let T be a binary tree. Let $\mathcal{C} = \{P\}$, with $P = \{e_1e_1, e_1e_2, e_2, e_2e_1, e_2e_1e_1, e_2e_2e_1\}$. In figure 4.14 P and $\tilde{P}$ are shown. Then $\mathcal{C}$ fulfills the constraints of corollary 4.5. Thus, $\mu_T(\mathcal{C}) = |P| = 6$.

Chapter 5

Compactly Representable Skewing Schemes for Trees

As pointed out in chapter 3, arbitrary skewing schemes are not always of much practical interest. In this chapter we only study compactly representable skewing schemes for trees, i.e., skewing schemes for trees which allow for a short representation and which are quickly computable. The compactly representable skewing schemes for d-dimensional arrays were obtained by requiring that whenever two elements x and y of a d-dimensional array are mapped into the same memory bank then every two points which are in the same relative position to each other as x and y are mapped into the same memory bank also. This appeared to be a natural way of defining compactly representable skewing schemes. So, we will apply the same idea to skewing schemes for trees. By this approach we obtain various kinds of compactly representable skewing schemes for trees: regular, semi-regular, linear and simple skewing schemes. As in chapter 4 we will assume that trees are infinite, complete, k-ary, and have a fixed orientation.

The first part of this chapter uses a representation of trees based on the path-labeling as introduced in chapter 4. Nodes of a tree T represented by the path-labeling are denoted by a string (word) over the alphabet $A = \{e_1, e_2, ..., e_k\}$. Where the relationship between this representation of trees and the theory of codes was only briefly mentioned in chapter 4, in the first part of this chapter we will fully exploit this close connection. The mathematical background for this part of the chapter is available from standard texts on the theory of codes [BP85].

The second part of this chapter is based on another representation of trees: the level-labeling. A node of a tree T is represented by the pair (i, n) where i denotes the level of T in which the node resides and n the position of the node in level i. By this representation we are able to define compactly representable skewing schemes that are based upon the concept of linearity, see section 3.1.

This chapter is organized as follows. In section 5.1 we introduce some basic notions of the theory of codes. In section 5.2 we define the semi-regular skewing schemes for trees which are derived from the regular (periodic) skewing schemes for d-dimensional arrays. Whereas the regular skewing schemes for d-dimensional arrays were quite feasible, in this section we show that there exists only a limited number of semi-regular skewing schemes that can be finitely represented. Further, in section 5.3, we show that the actual representation costs for a semi-regular skewing scheme that is valid for a collection of templates are too high. In section 5.4 we strengthen the notion of semi-regularity and obtain a suitable notion of regular skewing schemes for trees. In section 5.5 we show that in several applications the regular skewing schemes are optimal in the sense that they use a minimum number of memory banks. In section 5.6 we introduce linear (and simple) skewing schemes for trees which are based on the level-labeling representation of trees. Linear (and simple) skewing schemes have the advantage over regular skewing schemes that the time to evaluate them is reduced to a minimum.

5.1 Preliminaries

In this section we introduce some basic notions of the theory of codes, restricting ourselves only to those notions which will fit our purposes. For a more thorough introduction to this topic see [BP85]. Let A be an alphabet, $A = \{e_1, e_2, ..., e_k\}$. Let A^* denote the set of all words over the alphabet A. On A^* we can define an associative operation, the concatenation of two sequences

$$(\alpha_1\alpha_2...\alpha_n)(\beta_1\beta_2...\beta_m) = (\alpha_1\alpha_2...\alpha_n\beta_1\beta_2...\beta_m).$$

The empty sequence is denoted by ε (, or, 1). Because ε acts as a neutral element for the concatenation, A^* is a monoid. A^* is called the *free monoid* on A.

For each word $w \in A^*$ we define its *length* $|w|$ as the number of symbols in w. The *reverse* of a word $w \in A^*$, $w = \alpha_1\alpha_2...\alpha_n$, $\alpha_i \in A$ is $\tilde{w} = \alpha_n...\alpha_2\alpha_1$. A *factorization* of a word $w \in A^*$ is a sequence $u_1, u_2, ..., u_n$ of n words $(n \geqslant 0)$

in A^* such that $w = u_1 u_2 ... u_n$.

For a subset X of A^* we denote by X^* the submonoid generated by X,

$$X^* = \{x_1 x_2 ... x_n | \, n \geqslant 0, \, x_i \in X\}.$$

Similarly, we denote by X^+ the subsemigroup generated by X,

$$X^+ = \{x_1 x_2 ... x_n | \, n \geqslant 1, \, x_i \in X\}.$$

Definition 5.1 *A subset X of the free monoid A^* is a code over A if for all $x \in X^+$ there exists a unique factorization in words in X.*

A word $w \in A^*$ is called a left factor of a word $x \in A^*$ if there exists a word $u \in A^*$ such that $x = wu$. The relationship "is a left factor of" is a partial order on A^* called the prefix ordering. We write $w \leqslant x$ when w is a left factor of x, and $w < x$ if $w \leqslant x$ and $w \neq x$, see also chapter 4. In a symmetric way we can define the relation "is a right factor of".

A subset (code) $X \subseteq A^*$ is *prefix* if no element of X is a proper left factor of another element of X. A subset X of A^* is *suffix* of no element of X is a proper right factor of another element of X. A subset of A^* which is both prefix and suffix is called *biprefix.*

Proposition 5.1 [BP85] *Any prefix (suffix, biprefix) set of words $X \neq \{\varepsilon\}$ is a code.*

Definition 5.2 *Let M be a monoid and N be a submonoid of M. Then N is right unitary (in M) if for all $u, v \in M$:*

$$u, uv \in N \Rightarrow v \in N.$$

N is left unitary if for all $u, v \in M$:

$$u, vu \in N \Rightarrow v \in N.$$

N is called bi-unitary if it is both left and right unitary.

Proposition 5.2 [BP85] *A submonoid M of A^* is right unitary (resp. left unitary, bi-unitary) if and only if its (unique) minimal set of generators is a prefix (suffix, biprefix) code.*

A code X is *maximal* if X is not properly contained in any other code. A subset Q of a monoid M is called *dense* in M if for all $m \in M$, there exist elements u and v of M such that $umv \in Q$. A code $X \subseteq M$ is called *complete* in M if X^* is dense in M.

Theorem 5.1 [BP85] *A code X is complete if and only if X is dense or X is maximal.*

5.2 Semi-Regular Skewing Schemes

We first recall the path-labeling of a tree as introduced in chapter 4, cf. definition 4.1. Let T be a k-ary tree with root α_0. Let the edges emanating from a node of T to its sons be labeled $e_1, ..., e_k$ from left to right.

Definition 5.3 *The mapping* lab : $T \to A^*$, *with* $A = \{e_1, e_2, ..., e_k\}$ *is defined as follows :*
(i) $\text{lab}(\alpha_0) = \varepsilon$,
(ii) for all $\alpha \neq \alpha_0$, $\text{lab}(\alpha) = \lambda_1\lambda_2...\lambda_n$, *with for all* i, $1 \leqslant i \leqslant n : \lambda_i \in A$ *and* $\lambda_1\lambda_2...\lambda_n$ *is the sequence of labels on the unique path from* α_0 *to* α.

So, from now on, we identify the nodes of T with words over the alphabet $A = \{e_1, e_2, ..., e_k\}$ and T with A^*. In terms of the theory of codes, T is the literal representation of A^*.

Recall also the definition of a template P on T, a skewing scheme s for T, and the number $\mu_T(\{P_1, P_2, ..., P_t\})$ denoting the minimum number M such that there exists a skewing scheme $s : T \to \{0, 1..., M-1\}$ that is valid for $\{P_1, P_2, ..., P_t\}$, cf. definition 4.2 and definition 4.3.

The semi-regular skewing schemes are obtained by a direct translation from the notion of regularity (periodicity), see section 3.2, to trees.

Definition 5.4
(i) A skewing scheme $s : T \to \{0, 1, ..., M-1\}$ *is called semi-regular if the following condition holds : if for some* α, $\alpha\gamma \in T : s(\alpha\gamma) = s(\alpha)$, *then for all* $\delta \in T : s(\delta\gamma) = s(\delta)$.
(ii) Let s *be semi-regular, then* $L_s = \{\gamma|$ *there exists a* $\alpha \in T$ *such that* $s(\alpha) = s(\alpha\gamma)\}$.

Proposition 5.3 *For all semi-regular skewing schemes* s, L_s *is a dense bi-unitary submonoid of* T.

Proof That L_s is a bi-unitary submonoid follows directly from definition 5.4. Suppose L_s is not dense. Then there exists a $\gamma \in T$ such that for all $\beta \in T : \gamma\beta \notin L_s$. That means that $s(\alpha) \neq s(\alpha\gamma\beta)$ for all $\alpha \in T$ and $\beta \in T$. Consider the numbers $s(\alpha), s(\alpha\gamma), s(\alpha\gamma^2), ...$ Then for all $i \geqslant 0$, $j \geqslant 0, i \neq j : s(\alpha\gamma^i) \neq s(\alpha\gamma^j)$, contradicting the fact that M is finite. □

Lemma 5.1 *Let* s *be a semi-regular skewing scheme. Then the minimal set of generators of* L_s *is a maximal biprefix code* B_s.

Proof From proposition 5.2 and proposition 5.3 follows that the minimal set of generators of L_s is a biprefix code B_s. Thus, the set B_s is not dense. Theorem 5.1 together with proposition 5.3 yields that B_s is a maximal code. □

B_s is also called the base of L_s. Further, from the theory of codes follows that B_s is uniquely determined.

Because L_s is a bi-unitary submonoid of T we can define an equivalence relation $\equiv_{L_s}$ on T by: $\alpha \equiv_{L_s} \beta$ iff $\exists\gamma$ such that $\alpha \in \gamma L_s$ and $\beta \in \gamma L_s$. If $\alpha \equiv_{L_s} \beta$ then α and β are said to be equivalent modulo L_s.

Proposition 5.4 *Let $s\colon T \to \{0, 1, ..., M-1\}$ be a semi-regular skewing scheme. Then*

$$M \leqslant |T/L_s|.$$

Proof Directly from definition 5.4. □

Definition 5.5 *Let L_s be a dense bi-unitary submonoid of T and let $B_s = \{\omega_1, \omega_2, ..., \omega_n\}$ be its basis. The fundamental domain F_s of L_s is the set*

$$\{\alpha|\ \textit{for all } i \leqslant n : \tilde{\alpha} \notin T_{\tilde{\omega}_i}\},$$

where T_ω denotes the complete subtree of T with root ω.

In other words, F_s is the set of all proper right factors of nodes $\in B_s$. In figure 5.1 some examples of bases and their fundamental domains are shown. The next lemma shows that the fundamental domain F_s actually is an embedding of T/L_s.

Lemma 5.2 *F_s is isomorphic to T/L_s.*

Proof Follows from the observation that $\alpha \in F_s$ if and only if there do not exist a α' ($\neq \alpha$) and $i_1, i_2, ..., i_k \leqslant n$ such that $\alpha = \alpha'\omega_{i_1}\omega_{i_2}...\omega_{i_k}$. □

Lemma 5.3 *There is no infinite sequence $\alpha_1, \alpha_2, ...$ with for all $i \geqslant 1 : \alpha_i \in F_s$ and $\alpha_i < \alpha_{i+1}$.*

Proof The proof relies on the following fact from the theory of codes:

Fact 5.1 [BP85] *Any maximal biprefix code B_s has a finite degree d.*

Here the degree d is the maximum number N such that there exists a node α with N left factors $\in F_s$. The result follows directly. □

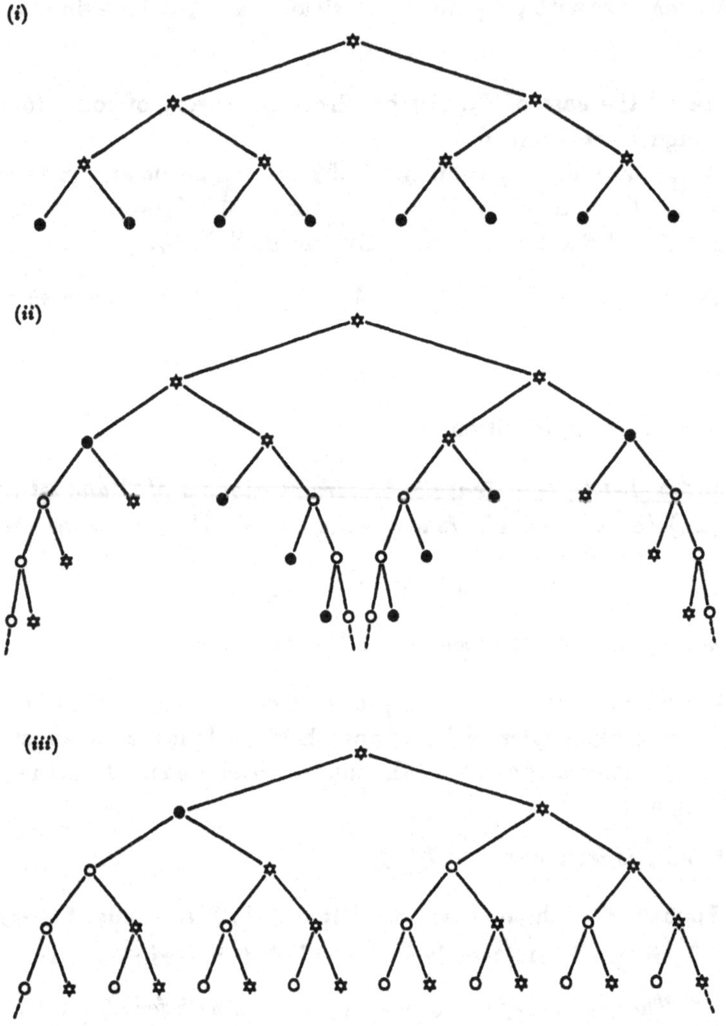

● : the elements of the bases of L_s.

✡ : the elements of F_s, the fundamental domain of L_s.

Figure 5.1: Some bases together with their fundamental domains.

The next theorem gives another characterization of semi-regular skewing schemes.

Theorem 5.2 *$s: T \rightarrow \{0, 1, ..., M-1\}$ is a semi-regular skewing scheme if and only if there exists a bi-unitary submonoid L_s with fundamental domain F_s, and a map $\eta_s : F_s \rightarrow \{0, 1, ... M-1\}$ with for all $\alpha, \beta \in F_s$, $\alpha < \beta$, $\eta_s(\alpha) \neq \eta_s(\beta)$, such that for all $\alpha \in T$: $s(\alpha) = \eta_s(\delta_s(\alpha))$. ($\delta_s(\alpha)$ is the unique $\delta \in F_s$ with $\delta \equiv_{L_s} \alpha$).*

Proof $\Rightarrow$ Follows directly.
$\Leftarrow$ Let $s(\alpha) = s(\alpha\gamma)$, for some $\alpha \in T$ and $\gamma \in T$. Suppose $\gamma \notin L_s$. Then $\delta_s(\alpha) \neq \delta_s(\alpha\gamma)$. Because $\delta_s(\alpha) \leqslant \alpha$ and $\delta_s(\alpha\gamma) \leqslant \alpha\gamma$, we have that $\delta_s(\alpha) < \delta_s(\alpha\gamma)$ or $\delta_s(\alpha\gamma) < \delta_s(\alpha)$. So, $\eta_s(\delta_s(\alpha)) \neq \eta_s(\delta_s(\alpha\gamma))$. Contradiction. Thus $\gamma \in L_s$ and, hence, for all $\delta \in T$: $s(\delta) = s(\delta\gamma)$. □

Corollary 5.1 *Let $s: T \rightarrow \{0, 1, ..., M-1\}$ be a semi-regular skewing scheme, and let F_s be the fundamental domain of L_s. Then*

$$\max_{\alpha \in F_s} |\{\beta | \beta \leqslant \alpha\}| \leqslant M \leqslant |F_s|.$$

Note, that by theorem 5.2 a semi-regular skewing scheme s is fully determined by L_s, F_s and η_s. Also L_s is fully determined by its base B_s. So, the representation cost of a semi-regular skewing scheme s is fixed by the cardinality of B_s and F_s. The constraint that a semi-regular skewing scheme s should be compactly representable directly induces that $|B_s|$ and $|F_s|$ should at least be finite. We also have the following two results.

Lemma 5.4 *Let s be a semi-regular skewing scheme which uses M memory banks and with $|B_s|$ finite. Then M is finite iff $|F_s|$ is finite.*

Proof If $|F_s|$ is finite then from corollary 5.1 follows that M is finite. Let $|F_s|$ be infinite. Because $|B_s|$ is finite there exist nodes α_0 (the root of T), $\alpha_1, \alpha_2, ...$ such that for all $i \geqslant 0 : |\alpha_i| = |\alpha_{i+1}| - 1$ and $\alpha_i \in F_s$. Thus $\max_{\alpha \in F_s} |\{\beta | \beta \leqslant \alpha\}|$ is infinite. Hence, from corollary 5.1 follows that M is infinite. □

Note that by the definition of a skewing scheme M is always finite.

Lemma 5.5 *If $|F_s|$ is finite, then $|B_s|$ is finite.*

Proof Follows from the fact that for all semi-regular skewing scheme s, B_s is a biprefix code (cf. lemma 5.1). □

For a 2-ary tree T this result can even be strengthened to: if $|F_s|$ is finite, then $|B_s| = |F_s| + 1 = |\{\beta | \exists \alpha \in B_s: \beta < \alpha\}| + 1$. Because of the results so far, we will assume that for a semi-regular skewing scheme s, $|B_s|$ and $|F_s|$ are finite, unless explicitly stated otherwise.

Theorem 5.3 *For every semi-regular skewing scheme s, B_s is a finite maximal biprefix code.*

Proof Directly from lemma 5.1. □

Finite maximal biprefix codes have quite remarkable properties and have received special attention in the literature [Sch61,Ces79]. We state some properties. For more details, see [BP85].

Recall that the degree d of a finite maximal biprefix code X equals the maximum number m such that there exists a word x with m left factors $\in S$, where S is the set of all proper right factors of words $\in X$, see also fact 5.1.

Proposition 5.5 [Ces79] *Let $X \subseteq A^*$, $X \neq \{\varepsilon\}$, be a finite maximal biprefix code of degree d. Then for each symbol $\alpha \in A : \alpha^d \in X$.*

Proposition 5.6 [BP85] *Let $X \subseteq A^*$, be a finite maximal biprefix code of degree d, and A be a k-symbol alphabet. Then $|X| \geqslant k^d$.*

Theorem 5.4 [Sch61] *Let A be a k-symbol alphabet and let $d \geqslant 1$. There are only a finite number ($\beta_k(d)$) of finite maximal biprefix codes over A with degree d.*

It is obvious that $\beta_1(d) = 1$ for all $d \geqslant 1$. Also it is clear that $\beta_k(1) = 1$ and $\beta_k(2) = 1$ for all k. But in general the determination of $B_k(d)$ appears to be very tedious. For instance $\beta_2(3) = 3$, $\beta_2(4) = 73$, $\beta_2(5) = 5056783$. $\beta_2(5)$ was computed with the help of a computer program written by M.Leonard in 1984.

In figure 5.2 all finite maximal biprefix codes over the alphabet $\{e_1, e_2\}$ of degree 3 are depicted.

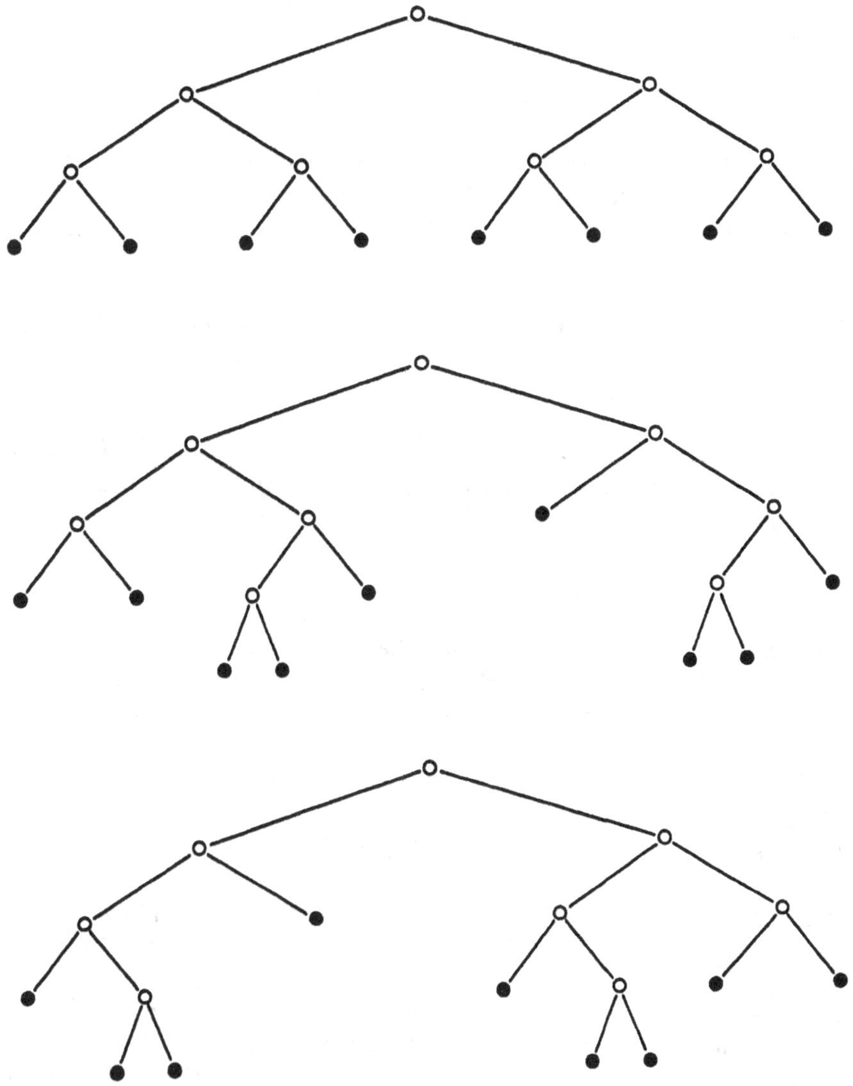

Figure 5.2: All finite maximal biprefix codes over the alphabet $\{e_1, e_2\}$ of degree 3.

5.3 The Insufficiency of Semi-Regular Skewing Schemes

In this section we give conditions for a semi-regular skewing scheme to be valid for one or more templates. As we shall see they are similar to the conditions of validity of periodic skewing schemes for d-dimensional arrays (cf. section 3.2.1). Further, we will show that the representation costs for a semi-regular skewing scheme are too high if it has to be valid for a collection of templates.

Definition 5.6 *For any finite subset (template) P of T and for any semi-regular skewing scheme s, define the reduced subset P_s by $P_s = \{\alpha_s | \alpha_s \in F_s$ and $\exists \alpha \in P$ with $\alpha_s \equiv_{L_s} \alpha\}$.*

Theorem 5.5 *Let s be a semi-regular skewing scheme and $C = \{P_1, P_2, ..., P_t\}$ be a collection of templates. Then s is valid for C iff (i) for all $P_i \in C$, $\delta \in T | (\delta.P_i)_s| = |P_i|$, and (ii) for all ϱ, $\sigma \in F_s$ with $s(\varrho) = s(\sigma)$, there does not exist a node δ and a template $P_i \in C$ such that $\varrho \in \delta.(P_i)_s$ and $\sigma \in \delta.(P_i)_s$.*

Proof Let s be not valid for C. Then there exist nodes α, β and γ and a template $P_i \in C$ such that $\alpha \in \gamma P_i$, $\beta \in \gamma P_i$ and $s(\alpha) = s(\beta)$ (Recall that an instance $P_i(\alpha)$ of a template P_i is the set αP_i.) Let $\alpha = \gamma\alpha'$ and $\beta = \gamma\beta'$. Then we have two possible cases.
Case 1 $\exists \varrho \in F_s$ $\alpha \in \varrho L_s$ and $\beta \in \varrho L_s$. Then again we can consider two cases.

If $\gamma \leqslant \varrho$, then from $\alpha \equiv_{L_s} \varrho$ and $\beta \equiv_{L_s} \varrho$ follows that $\alpha' \equiv_{L_s} \beta'$. Hence $|P_s| < |P|$ ($\alpha' \in P$ and $\beta' \in P$).

If $\gamma > \varrho$, then let δ be such that $\delta \in \varrho L_s$, $\varrho \leqslant \delta \leqslant \gamma$ and $|\delta|$ is maximal. Let δ' be such that $\delta\delta' = \gamma$. Then $\delta' \in F_s$. Further, $\delta'\alpha' \equiv_{L_s} \delta'\beta'$. So, $|(\delta'.P_i)_s| < |P|$.
Case 2 $\exists \varrho, \sigma \in F_s(\varrho \neq \sigma) : \alpha \in \varrho L_s$ and $\beta \in \sigma L_s$. Because $s(\alpha) = s(\beta)$, it follows that neither $\varrho \leqslant \sigma$ nor $\varrho \geqslant \sigma$. Thus, $\gamma \leqslant \varrho$ and $\gamma \leqslant \sigma$. Let $\varrho = \gamma\varrho'$ and $\sigma = \gamma\sigma'$. Then $\alpha' \equiv_{L_s} \varrho'$ and $\beta' \equiv_{L_s} \sigma'$. From the definition of P_s follows that $\varrho' \in (P_i)_s$ and $\sigma' \in (P_i)_s$. Thus, $\varrho \in \gamma.(P_i)_s$ and $\sigma \in \gamma.(P_i)_s$.

Note that the converse of all implications stays valid. □

Examples
In both examples T is a binary tree. Further, in example 2 we have a semi-regular skewing scheme with both $|B_s|$ and $|F_s|$ infinite.

1. Let $C = \{$ "all paths of length p"$\}$, for some $p \geqslant 1$. So if $P \in C$, then $P = \{\alpha_1, \alpha_2, ..., \alpha_p\}$, with $\forall i : |\alpha_i| \leqslant p$ and $\alpha_i < \alpha_{i+1}$. Let $s : T \to \{0, 1, ..., p\}$ be the semi-regular skewing scheme, given by $B_s = \{\alpha | \, |\alpha| = p + 1\}$ and the following assignment of F_s:

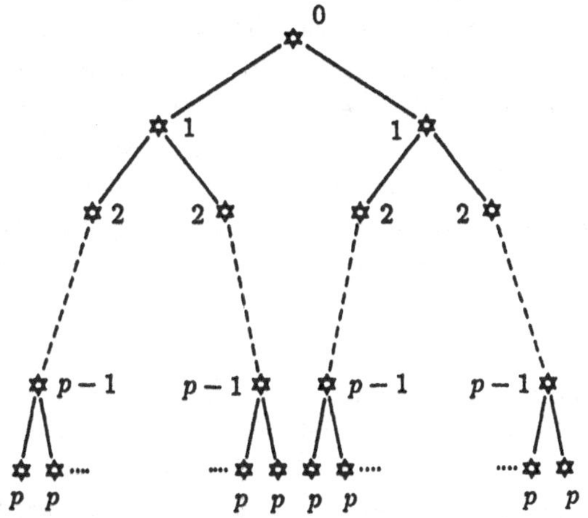

Then s is valid for C.

2. The semi-regular skewing scheme $s : T \to \{0, 1, 2\}$, given by the base of figure 5.1(ii) and the following assignment of F_s, is valid for {} .

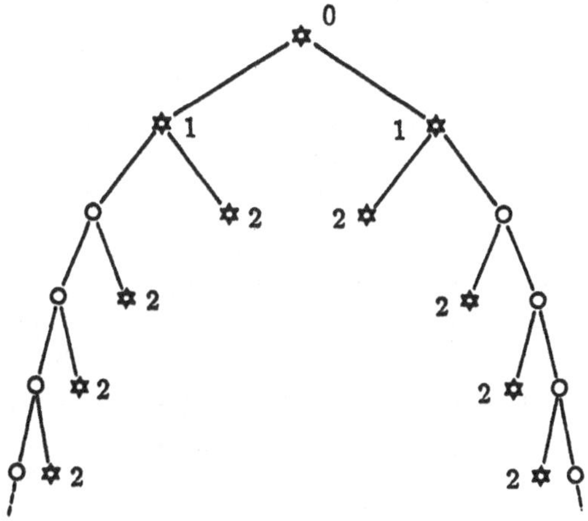

In the following theorem we show that example 2 is characteristic for a large class of templates.

Theorem 5.6 *Let P be a template on a k-ary tree, such that $\exists \alpha, \beta \in P$ $\exists \gamma \in T$ with $|\alpha| = |\beta| = |\gamma| + 1$ and $\gamma \leqslant \alpha$ and $\gamma \leqslant \beta$. Then there does not* *exist a semi-regular skewing scheme $s: T \rightarrow \{0, 1, ..., M-1\}$ with $|B_s|$ and $|F_s|$ finite, that is valid for P.*

Proof We claim that for all semi-regular skewing schemes s, with $|B_s|$ and $|F_s|$ finite, there exists a $\gamma \in T$ such that for all $\alpha \in \{e_1, e_2, ..., e_k\} : \gamma\alpha \in B_s$.

Suppose not. Then from the fact that $|B_s|$ is finite it follows that there exists an infinite path α_0 (= the root of T), $\alpha_1, \alpha_2, ...$ such that for all $i \geqslant 0 : \alpha_i \notin B_s$. Let $j \geqslant 0$ be such that $|\alpha_j| > \max_{\gamma \in B_s} |\gamma|$. Then from the fact that B_s is finite biprefix code, cf. lemma 5.1, it follows that $B_s \cup \{\alpha_j \tilde{\alpha}_j\}$ is a finite biprefix code, proposition 5.1. This is in contradiction with the maximality of B_s, implied by theorem 5.3. Use theorem 5.5 to complete the proof. □

From theorem 5.6 we can conclude that the templates P for which there exists a valid semi-regular skewing scheme should have the property that for all $\alpha \in P$ there exists at most one $\beta \in P$, with $|\beta| = |\alpha| + 1$ and $\alpha < \beta$. The most notable templates that have this property are the "paths" of finite length on a tree T, i.e., the templates $\{\alpha_0, \alpha_1, ..., \alpha_p\}$ such that for all i, $0 \leqslant i < p : |\alpha_i| = |\alpha_{i+1}| - 1$, and $\alpha_i \leqslant \alpha_{i+1}$.

However, even for these templates we can show that the representation costs of a valid semi-regular skewing scheme are too high.

Theorem 5.7 *Let $P = \{\alpha_0, \alpha_1, ..., \alpha_p\}$ be a (path) template on a k-ary tree T, such that there exists a $e_j \in \{e_1, e_2, ..., e_k\}$ with for all i, $0 \leqslant i < p$: $\alpha_{i+1} = \alpha_i e_j$. Then for all semi-regular skewing schemes s valid for P : $|B_s| \geqslant k^{p+1}$.*

Proof Let s be a semi-regular skewing scheme valid for P. If $|B_s|$ is infinite then we are done. Let $|B_s|$ be finite. From theorem 5.3 we know that B_s is a finite maximal biprefix code of some degree $d \geqslant 0$. By proposition 5.5 we have that $e_j^d \in B_s$. Then from the validity of s and theorem 5.5 follows that $d = p + 1$. So, by proposition 5.6, $|B_s| \geqslant k^d = k^{p+1}$. □

Concluding we can say that the notion of semi-regularity in the given form is too weak to guarantee the existence of compactly representable skewing schemes valid for a collection of templates. In the next section we shall adjust the notion of semi-regularity and obtain compactly representable skewing schemes that are feasible for several applications.

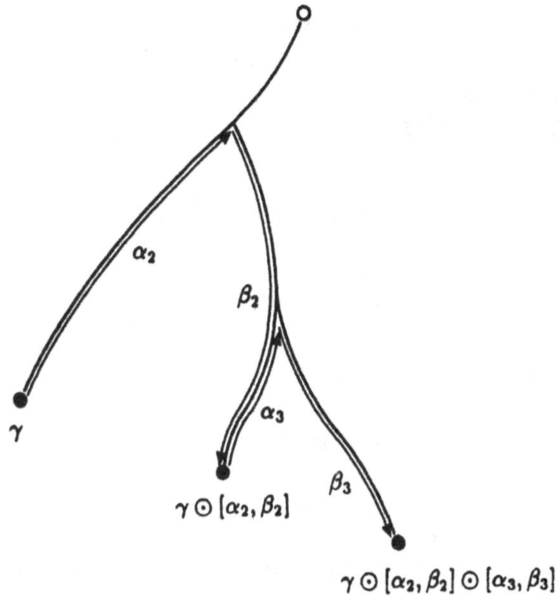

Figure 5.3: The operation $\odot$.

5.4 Regular Skewing Schemes

In this section we will strengthen the notion of semi-regularity in such a way that the structure of these skewing schemes remains the same, but the representation costs, i.e., the cardinality of the base B_s and of the fundamental domain L_s, are reduced. This will be achieved by defining an associative operation $\odot$, different from the concatenation of two words. This operation $\odot$ is defined on pairs of nodes $[\alpha_1, \beta_1]$ and $[\alpha_2, \beta_2]$ of which α_2 is a right factor of β_1, by $[\alpha_1, \beta_1] \odot [\alpha_2, \beta_2] = [\alpha_1, \bar{\beta}_1\beta_2]$ where $\bar{\beta}_1$ is defined such that $\bar{\beta}_1\alpha_2 = \beta_1$. Further, the operation $\odot$ can act on a node γ and a pair of nodes $[\alpha_2, \beta_2]$, with α_2 is a right factor of γ, by defining $\gamma \odot [\alpha_2, \beta_2] = \bar{\gamma}\beta_2$ with $\bar{\gamma}\alpha_2 = \gamma$. The effect of $\gamma \odot [\alpha_2, \beta_2] \odot [\alpha_3, \beta_3]$ is illustrated in figure 5.3. So, instead of moving downwards in the tree T only as with the simple concatenation of words, the operation $\odot$ enables us to move more arbitrarily. Based on this operation we can define for each $\gamma \in T$ a subset $\gamma \odot \mathsf{L}$ of T which in fact is the union of a number of δL 's, where L is a bi-unitary submonoid of T. For all $\gamma \in T$ the subsets $\gamma \odot \mathsf{L}$ are generated from the same finite set of generators B. We denote this implicit generative mechanism by L, and call B the hyperbase of L. Because the operation $\odot$ is more tedious than the concatenation of two words, we have to be careful in stating the conditions to ensure the minimality of B.

Definition 5.7
(i) A hyperbase B *is a set* $\{[\alpha_1,\beta_1],[\alpha_2,\beta_2],...,[\alpha_n,\beta_n]\}$ *such that*

(1) *for all* i, $1 \leqslant i \leqslant n : |\alpha_i| \leqslant |\beta_i|$,
(2) *for all* i, $1 \leqslant i \leqslant n : \alpha_i$ *is less than* β_i *in lexicographic order, and the only left factor of* α_i *that is a left factor of* β_i *is* ε,
(3) *for all* i, j, $1 \leqslant i \leqslant n$, $1 \leqslant j \leqslant n$, $i \neq j : \beta_i$ *is not a right factor of* β_j, *and if* $\alpha_i \neq \varepsilon$ *and* $\alpha_j \neq \varepsilon$, *then* $\alpha_i \neq \alpha_j$,
(4) *for all* $[\alpha_{i_1},\beta_{i_1}],[\alpha_{i_2},\beta_{i_2}],[\alpha_{j_1},\beta_{j_1}],[\alpha_{j_2},\beta_{j_2}]$, $(j_1 \neq j_2)$: *if*
α_{i_1} *is a right factor of* β_{j_1} *and*
α_{i_2} *is a right factor of* β_{j_2} *and*
$\alpha_{j_1} = \varepsilon$ *and* $\alpha_{j_2} = \varepsilon$, *then*
$\bar{\beta}_{j_1}$ *is not a left factor of* β_{j_2}, *with* $\bar{\beta}_{j_1}\alpha_{i_1} = \beta_{j_1}$ *and* $\bar{\beta}_{j_2}\alpha_{i_2} = \beta_{j_2}$.

(ii) For each $\gamma \in T$ *and hyperbase* B *define*

$$\gamma \odot \mathsf{L} = \{\gamma \odot [\alpha_{i_1},\beta_{i_1}] \odot [\alpha_{i_2},\beta_{i_2}] \odot ... \odot [\alpha_{i_t},\beta_{i_t}] \mid \text{for all } j, 1 \leqslant j \leqslant t : [\alpha_{i_j},\beta_{i_j}] \in \mathsf{B},\ \alpha_{i_1} \text{ is a left factor of } \gamma, \text{ and for all } j,\ 1 \leqslant j \leqslant t-1 : \alpha_{i_{j+1}} \text{ is a left factor of } \beta_{i_j}\}.$$

Condition $(i)(1)$ ensures the fast computability of a regular skewing scheme, see theorem 5.10. Condition $(i)(2)$ guarantees a unique description of the base elements. Conditions $(i)(3)$ and $(i)(4)$ are needed to prove the minimality of B as will appear from the next results.

Define for each $\gamma \in T$ the set

$$\Gamma_\gamma = \{\gamma \odot [\alpha_{i_1},\beta_{i_1}] \odot [\alpha_{i_2},\beta_{i_2}] \odot ... \odot [\alpha_{i_t},\beta_{i_t}] \mid \text{for all } j, 1 \leqslant j \leqslant t : [\alpha_{i_j},\beta_{i_j}] \in \mathsf{B} \text{ and } \alpha_{i_j} \neq \varepsilon,\ \alpha_{i_1} \text{ is a right factor of } \gamma, \text{ and for all } j,\ 1 \leqslant j \leqslant t-1 : \alpha_{i_{j+1}} \text{ is a right factor of } \beta_{i_j}\}.$$

Proposition 5.7 *Let* $\gamma \in T$, *and* L *be generated by a hyperbase* B. *Then*

$$\gamma \odot \mathsf{L} = \bigcup_{\delta \in \Gamma_\gamma} \delta.(\varepsilon \odot \mathsf{L}).$$

Proof Directly from definition 5.7. □

In the same way we can define the set L_ε by

$$\mathsf{L}_\varepsilon = \{\varepsilon \odot [\alpha_{i_1}, \beta_{i_1}] \odot [\alpha_{i_2}, \beta_{i_2}] \odot ... \odot [\alpha_{i_t}, \beta_{i_t}] | \\ \alpha_{i_1} = \varepsilon \text{ and for all } j, 2 \leqslant j \leqslant t : \alpha_{i_j} \neq \varepsilon, \\ \text{for all } j, 1 \leqslant j \leqslant t : [\alpha_{i_j}, \beta_{i_j}] \in \mathsf{B}, \text{ and} \\ \text{for all } j, 1 \leqslant j \leqslant t-1 : \alpha_{i_{j+1}} \text{ is a right factor of } \beta_{i_j}\}.$$

Then it is obvious that L_ε is a proper subset of $\varepsilon \odot \mathsf{L}$, except for the case that $\mathsf{L}_\varepsilon = \{\varepsilon\}$ and $\varepsilon \odot \mathsf{L} = \{\varepsilon\}$. And we have $\varepsilon \odot \mathsf{L} = \{\gamma_1\gamma_2...\gamma_t |$ for all i, $1 \leqslant i \leqslant t$: $\gamma_i \in \mathsf{L}_\varepsilon\}$, so L_ε generates $\varepsilon \odot \mathsf{L}$.

Proposition 5.8 *L_ε is a biprefix code, except for the degenerated case that $\mathsf{L}_\varepsilon = \{\varepsilon\}$.*

Proof From the definition of L_ε follows that each element of L_ε is of the form $\bar{\beta}_{i_1}\bar{\beta}_{i_2}...\bar{\beta}_{i_{t-1}}\beta_{i_t}$, with for all j, $1 \leqslant j \leqslant t-1$: $\bar{\beta}_{i_j}\alpha_{i_{j+1}} = \beta_{i_j}$. Let γ $(= \bar{\beta}_{i_1}\bar{\beta}_{i_2}...\bar{\beta}_{i_{t-1}}\beta_{i_t}) \in \mathsf{L}_\varepsilon$ and $\gamma_2(= \bar{\beta}_{j_1}\bar{\beta}_{j_2}...\bar{\beta}_{j_{s-1}}\beta_{j_s}) \in \mathsf{L}_\varepsilon$. If γ_1 is a right factor of γ_2, then from the condition that for all i and j, β_i is not a right factor of β_j, follows that $i_t = j_s$. So, $\alpha_{i_t} = \alpha_{j_s}$. Thus by the same argument $i_{t-1} = j_{s-1}$, and so on. Hence $\gamma_1 = \gamma_2$. If γ_1 is a left factor of γ_2 then from condition $(i)(4)$ follows that $i_1 = j_1$. Further from the condition that for all i, the only left factor of α_i that is a left factor of β_i is ε, follows that $\bar{\beta}_{i_1} = \bar{\beta}_{j_1}$. So $\alpha_{i_2} = \alpha_{j_2}$. From the definition of L_ε follows that $\alpha_{i_2} \neq \varepsilon$ and $\alpha_{j_2} \neq \varepsilon$, hence $i_2 = j_2$. Thus $\bar{\beta}_{i_2} = \bar{\beta}_{j_2}$. By repeating this argument we obtain that $\bar{\beta}_{i_3} = \bar{\beta}_{j_3}, ..., \bar{\beta}_{i_{t-1}} = \bar{\beta}_{j_{s-1}}$, and $\beta_{i_t} = \beta_{j_s}$. From proposition 5.1 now follows that L_ε is a biprefix code. □

Note that the set $\{\beta | [\alpha, \beta] \in \mathsf{B}\}$ is a suffix code for all hyperbases B.

Proposition 5.9 *$\varepsilon \odot \mathsf{L}$ is a bi-unitary submonoid of T and L_ε is its minimal set of generators.*

Proof Directly from proposition 5.8 and proposition 5.2. □

Again we can define an equivalence relation $\equiv_\mathsf{L}$ by: $\alpha \equiv_\mathsf{L} \beta$ iff there exists a γ such that $\alpha \in \gamma \odot \mathsf{L}$ and $\beta \in \gamma \odot \mathsf{L}$. If $\alpha \equiv_\mathsf{L} \beta$, then α and β are said to be equivalent modulo L. As for the equivalence relation $\equiv_L$, T/L is isomorphic to the fundamental domain F of L which is defined next.

Definition 5.8 *Let* L *be generated by the hyperbase* $\mathsf{B} = \{[\alpha_1, \beta_1], [\alpha_2, \beta_2], ..., [\alpha_n, \beta_n]\}$. *Then the fundamental domain* F *of* L *is defined by*

$$\mathsf{F} = \{\alpha| \text{ for all } i,\ 1 \leqslant i \leqslant n : \tilde{\alpha} \in T_{\tilde{\beta}_i}\}.$$

Lemma 5.6 *Let* L *be generated by a hyperbase* B. *Let* F *be the fundamental domain of* L *and let* F *be the fundamental domain of the bi-unitary submonoid* $\varepsilon \odot \mathsf{L}$ (cf. definition 5.5). *Then* $\mathsf{F} \subseteq F$ *and for all* $\gamma \in F : |\Gamma_\gamma \cap \mathsf{F}| = 1$.

Proof Directly from the definitions. □

We are now ready to define the regular skewing schemes.

Definition 5.9 *A skewing scheme* $s\colon T \to \{0, 1, ..., M-1\}$ *is called regular iff there exists a* L_s, *generated by a hyperbase* B_s, *with a finite fundamental domain* F_s *such that for all* i, $0 \leqslant i \leqslant M-1$, *there exists a* $\gamma \in \mathsf{F}_s$ *such that* $s^{-1}(i) = \gamma \odot \mathsf{L}_s$.

So, under a regular skewing scheme s all nodes of F_s are assigned different values, whereas in the semi-regular skewing schemes it is only required that nodes $\alpha, \beta \in F_s$ are assigned different values if $\alpha \leqslant \beta$, or $\beta \leqslant \alpha$, cf. the characterization of semi-regular skewing schemes given by theorem 5.2. Notice also lemma 5.6. This is the reason why for regular skewing schemes a stronger version of proposition 5.4 holds.

Lemma 5.7 *Let* $s\colon T \to \{0, 1, ..., M-1\}$ *be a regular skewing scheme. Then*

$$M = |T/\mathsf{L}_s|.$$

Proof Directly from definition 5.9. □

Lemma 5.8 *For all regular skewing schemes* s, $\varepsilon \odot \mathsf{L}$ *is a dense bi-unitary submonoid of* T *and* L_ε *is a maximal biprefix code (where* $\mathsf{L} = \mathsf{L}_s$*).*

Proof Similar to the proof of proposition 5.3 and lemma 5.1. □

Theorem 5.8 *Let* $s\colon T \to \{0, 1, ..., M-1\}$ *be a regular skewing scheme. Then* s *is semi-regular and* $L_s = \varepsilon \odot \mathsf{L}_s$.

Proof Directly from proposition 5.7, lemma 5.8, lemma 5.6 and definition 5.9. □

The next theorem gives another characterization of the regular skewing schemes which resembles the characterization of the semi-regular skewing schemes given in definition 5.4(i). As a consequence of this result we also have that not every semi-regular skewing scheme is regular. So, the regular skewing schemes form a proper subset of the semi-regular skewing schemes.

Theorem 5.9 *A skewing scheme* $s : T \to \{0, 1, ..., M-1\}$ *is regular iff the following condition holds : if* $s(\gamma\alpha) = s(\gamma\beta)$, *for some* $\alpha \in T$, $\beta \in T$ *and* $\gamma \in T$ *then for all* $\delta \in T : s(\delta\alpha) = (\delta\beta)$.

Proof $\Rightarrow$ Follows directly from definition 5.9.
$\Leftarrow$ From the definition of a semi-regular skewing scheme, cf. definition 5.4, follows that s is semi-regular. Thus the set $L = \{\alpha |\ s(\alpha) = s(\alpha_0)\}(= L_s)$, α_0 = the root of T, is a dense bi-unitary submonoid of T with a maximal biprefix code $B(= B_s)$. We will first prove that there exists a finite hyperbase B such that $\varepsilon \odot \mathsf{L} = L$, with L generated by B.

Let $B = \{\omega_1, \omega_2, ...\}$, such that for al $i \geqslant 1$: $|\omega_i| \leqslant |\omega_{i+1}|$ and if $|\omega_i| = |\omega_{i+1}|$, then ω_i is less than ω_{i+1} in lexicographic order. The construction of B is given by the following algorithm .

Algorithm "**hyperbase-construction**":
$\mathsf{B} := \emptyset$;
$A := B$; $\bar{A} := \emptyset$;
repeat
  let $\omega_i \in A$ with i is minimal ;
  if for all $\omega \in \bar{A}$ the only common left factor of ω_i and ω equals ε
  then $\mathsf{B} := \mathsf{B} \cup \{[\varepsilon, \omega_i]\}$
  else begin
    let $\omega_{k_i} \in \bar{A}$, such that the (maximal) left factor
    of ω_i and ω_{k_i} equals $\sigma_i(\neq \varepsilon)$, and k_i is maximal,
    let $\sigma_i\omega_i' = \omega_i$ and $\sigma_i\omega_{k_i}' = \omega_{k_i}$;
    $\mathsf{B} := \mathsf{B} \cup \{[\omega_{k_i}', \omega_i']\}$
    end ;
  let ϱ_i be the maximal right factor of ω_i such that
  there exists a $\omega \in \bar{A}$ with ϱ_i is a right factor of ω, and
  let $\omega_i''\varrho_i = \omega_i$;
  $A := A - \{\gamma |\ \gamma \in A \text{ and } \gamma \geqslant \omega_i''\}$;
  $\bar{A} := \bar{A} \cup \{\omega_i\}$
until $A = \emptyset$

The effect of **hyperbase-construction** on the maximal biprefix code $B' = \{e_2e_1, e_2e_2, e_1e_1e_1, e_1e_1e_2, e_1e_2e_1e_1, e_1e_2e_1e_2, e_1e_2e_2e_1e_1, e_1e_2e_2e_1e_2, ...\}$ is illustrated in figure 5.4. Conditions $(i)(1)$, $(i)(2)$, $(i)(3)$ and $(i)(4)$ of definition 5.7 follow from the constraint that, if $s(\gamma\alpha) = (\gamma\beta)$, then for all $\delta \in T : s(\delta\alpha) = s(\delta\beta)$ (*).

So, in order to prove that B is a (finite) hyperbase we only have to show that **hyperbase-construction** ends after a finite number of steps. This will be done by proving that for all β with $[\alpha, \beta] \in \mathsf{B}$ there exist no β_1 and β_2 with $\tilde{\beta}_1 < \tilde{\beta}$, $\tilde{\beta}_2 < \tilde{\beta}$, $\beta_1 \neq \beta_2$ and $s(\beta_1) = s(\beta_2)$. Suppose there exist a $[\alpha, \beta]$, β_1 and β_2 which fit these constraints. Assume, without loss of generality that $\beta_2 < \beta_1$. Then from the condition that $\tilde{\beta}1 < \tilde{\beta}$ follows that there exists a γ such that $\gamma\beta_1 = \beta$. From the condition that $[\alpha, \beta] \in \mathsf{B}$ follows that there exists a δ such that $\delta\beta \in B$. Because B is a biprefix code and condition (*) follows that $\delta\gamma\beta_2 \in B$. Then by the construction of B given by the algorithm, there exists a node β' such that $[\alpha', \beta'] \in \mathsf{B}$ for some α' and $\tilde{\beta}' \leqslant \tilde{\beta}_1 < \tilde{\beta}$, contradicting condition $(i)(2)$. So, we can conclude that for all β, with $[\alpha, \beta] \in \mathsf{B}$ for some α, all β' with $\tilde{\beta}' < \tilde{\beta}$ are assigned to different values by s (**).

Suppose **hyperbase-construction** takes an infinite number of steps. Then there is an infinite number of β's such that $[\alpha, \beta] \in \mathsf{B}$. Because all these β's form a suffix code, cf. condition $(i)(2)$, it follows that all $s(\beta)$'s with $[\alpha, \beta] \in \mathsf{B}$ for some α are different. So for each number $n \geqslant 0$ there exists a β with $|\beta| = n$ and $[\alpha, \beta] \in \mathsf{B}$ for some α. By ($$) this implies that there are $n-1$ nodes which are assigned to different values by s, contradicting the finiteness of M.

The proof is completed by showing that for all $i \in \{0, 1, ..., M-1\}$ there exists a $\delta \in \mathsf{F}$ (the fundamental domain of L generated by B) such that $s^{-1}(i) = \delta \odot \mathsf{L}$. Let $i \in \{0, 1, ..., M-1\}$. Let γ_0 be such that $s(\gamma_0) = i$ and there exists no γ such that $s(\gamma) = i$ and $\gamma \prec \gamma_0$ ($\gamma \prec \gamma_0$ iff $|\gamma| \leqslant |\gamma_0|$ and if $|\gamma| = |\gamma_0|$ then γ is less than γ_0 in lexicographic order, cf. chapter 4). Then $s^{-1}(i) = \{\gamma | \, s(\gamma) = s(\gamma_0)\}$. Take $\delta = \gamma_0$. The inclusion $s^{-1}(i) \supseteq \delta \odot \mathsf{L}$ follows from the construction of B given by the algorithm . Let $\gamma \in s^{-1}(i)$, then $s(\gamma) = s(\gamma_0)$, and, hence, $\gamma_0 \prec \gamma$. Define $[\alpha_1, \beta_1]$ by $\gamma = \gamma_1\beta_1$ for some γ_1, $s(\gamma_1\alpha_1) = s(\gamma_0)$ and $|\beta_1|$ is minimal. Define $[\alpha_2, \beta_2]$ in an analogous way but substitute $\gamma_1\alpha_1$ for γ. By iterating this definition we obtain a sequence $[\alpha_1, \beta_1], [\alpha_2, \beta_2], ..., [\alpha_t, \beta_t]$. From the minimality of each β_i follows that each $[\alpha_i, \beta_i] \in \mathsf{B}$. By condition $(i)(1)$ this sequence necessarily is finite and $\gamma_t\alpha_t = \gamma_0$. This implies that $\gamma \in \gamma_0 \odot \mathsf{L} = \delta \odot \mathsf{L}$. Thus $s^{-1} \subseteq \delta \odot \mathsf{L}$. □

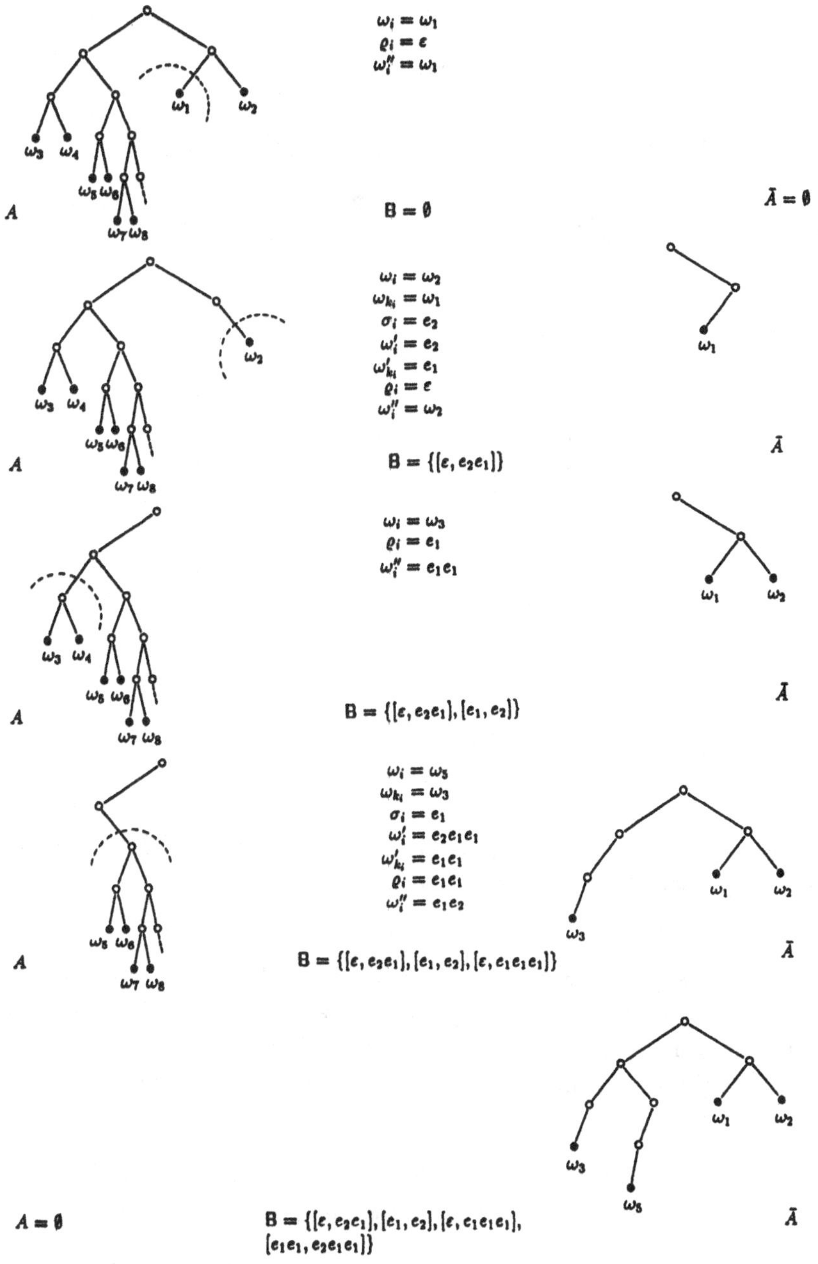

Figure 5.4: The effect of algorithm **hyperbase-construction**.

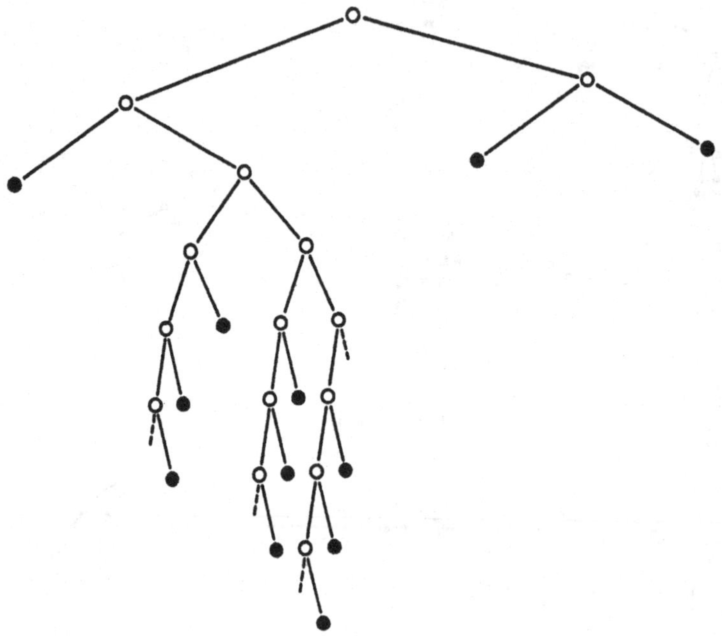

Figure 5.5: A dense bi-unitary submonoid for which there exists no finite hyperbase.

It is not always true that for every dense bi-unitary submonoid L there exists a (finite) hyperbase B with L generated by B and $\varepsilon \odot \mathsf{L} = L$.

Example
Let T be a binary tree and let B be defined by $B = \{e_1e_1, e_2e_1, e_2e_2\} \cup \{e_1(e_2)^m(e_1)^n e_2 | m \geqslant 1 \text{ and } n \geqslant 1\}$. See figure 5.5. Then B is a maximal biprefix code. Thus, L generated by B is a dense bi-unitary submonoid of T. However, because $e_1e_2 \notin L$, there is no finite hyperbase B such that $\varepsilon \odot \mathsf{L} = L$ with L generated by B.

As a final result in this section we show that each regular skewing scheme can indeed be represented at a low cost and computed efficiently.

Theorem 5.10 *Let s be a regular skewing scheme and let B_s be the hyperbase of L_s. Further, let $|\mathsf{B}_s| = b$ and $max_{[\alpha,\beta]\in \mathsf{B}_s}|\beta| = d$. Then s can be* *represented in space* $O(bd)$, *such that for all* $\alpha \in T$: $s(\alpha)$ *can be computed in time* $O(bd|\alpha|)$.

Proof Consider the subtree $\tilde{T}$ of T which is defined by $\tilde{T} = \{\gamma | \exists [\alpha, \beta] \in \mathsf{B}_s : \gamma \leqslant \tilde{\beta}\}$. Call the nodes γ of $\tilde{T}$ for which there exists a $[\alpha, \beta] \in \mathsf{B}_s$ with $\gamma = \tilde{\beta}$, the leaves of $\tilde{T}$. Assign to each leaf γ of $\tilde{T}$, the node $B(\gamma) = \alpha$, with $[\alpha, \beta] \in \mathsf{B}_s$ and $\gamma = \tilde{\beta}$. Assign to each node $\gamma \in \tilde{T}$ that is not a leaf the number $f(\gamma) = s(\tilde{\gamma})$. Then the following algorithm computes $s(\alpha)$, for arbitrary α.

```
Algorithm "s-evaluation":
γ : = the root of T̃;
ζ : = α̃;
repeat
    if γ is a leaf of T̃
    then begin
        ζ := B(γ).ζ ;
        γ : = the root of T̃
        end
    else begin
        define e_j, ζ' such that ζ = e_j ζ';
        ζ := ζ';
        γ := γ e_j
        end
until ζ = ε;
result: = f(γ)
```

s-evaluation is correct and takes $O(bd|\alpha|)$ time. Furthermore the representation costs are

$$\begin{aligned} &\approx \text{"the size of } \tilde{T}\text{"} + \text{"the value's } f(\gamma)\text{"} + \text{"the value's } B(\gamma)\text{"} \\ &\approx |\tilde{T}| + |\mathsf{F}_s| + |\mathsf{B}_s|.d \\ &\approx 2.|\mathsf{B}_s| + |\mathsf{B}_s| + |\mathsf{B}_s|.d \\ &= (d+3).b = O(bd). \end{aligned}$$

□

5.5 The Validity of Regular Skewing Schemes

We can make use of theorem 5.5 to derive the conditions for a regular skewing scheme to be valid for a given collection of templates.

Theorem 5.11 *Given a regular skewing scheme $s\colon T \to \{0, 1, ..., M-1\}$ and a collection of templates $C = \{P_1, P_2, ..., P_t\}$. Then s is valid for C iff (i) for all $P_i \in C$ and $\gamma \in \mathsf{F}_s : |\{\delta \mid \delta \equiv_{\mathsf{L}_s} \gamma\alpha,\ \alpha \in P_i, \text{ and } \delta \in \mathsf{F}_s\}| = |P_i|$ and (ii) for all $[\alpha, \beta] \in \mathsf{B}_s$: if there does not exist a $[\alpha', \beta'] \in \mathsf{B}_s$ with $\alpha \in$ Suffix(β') then there does not exist a γ such that both $\gamma\alpha \in P_i$ and $\gamma\beta \in P_i$, for some P_i.*

Proof Follows directly from theorem 5.5 together with theorem 5.8 and lemma 5.6. □

We first give some examples.

Examples
In all examples T is a binary tree.
1. Consider the regular skewing scheme $s : T \to \{0, 1, 2\}$ given by L_s generated by the hyperbase $\mathsf{B}_s = \{[\varepsilon, e_1e_1], [\varepsilon, e_2e_2], [e_1, e_2e_1], [e_2, e_1e_2]\}$. In addition let $s(\varepsilon) = 0$, $s(e_1) = 1$, and $s(e_2) = 2$ ($\mathsf{F}_s = \{\varepsilon, e_1, e_2\}$). Then $\varepsilon \odot \mathsf{L}_s$ is equal to the set L of example 2, p. 212 and s is valid for the template $\{\varepsilon, e_1, e_2\}$. Figure 5.6 shows the elements α of T with $s(\alpha) = 0$. So, we can conclude that s is valid for the same template as the semi-regular skewing scheme of example 2 p. 212. But in contrast to the latter one $|\mathsf{B}_s|$ and $|\mathsf{F}_s|$ are finite.
2. Consider the regular skewing scheme $s : T \to \{0, 1, 2, 3, 4\}$, defined by L_s generated by the hyperbase $\mathsf{B}_s = \{[\varepsilon, e_2e_1e_1], [\varepsilon, e_1e_1e_1], [e_2, e_1e_1e_2], [e_1, e_2e_1e_2], [e_1e_2, e_2e_2], [e_1e_1, e_2e_1]\}$. In addition let $s(\varepsilon) = 0$, $s(e_1) = 1$, $s(e_1e_1) = 2$, $s(e_2) = 3$, $s(e_2e_1) = 4$ ($\mathsf{F}_s = \{\varepsilon, e_1, e_1e_1, e_2, e_2e_1\}$). $\varepsilon \odot \mathsf{L}_s$ and F_s are depicted in figure 5.7. As can be seen from figure 5.7 s is valid for both

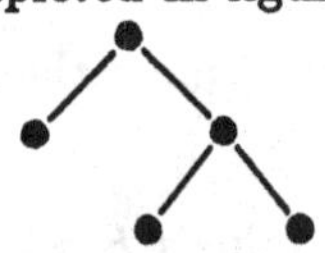

and

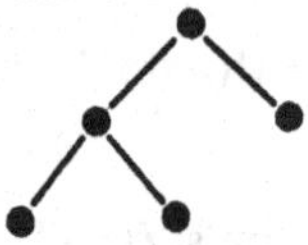

Later on we shall generalize this result.

We will now show that for two important classes of templates there always exists a valid regular skewing scheme which out of all possible skewing schemes uses a minimum number of memory banks.

Theorem 5.12 *Let T be a binary tree. Let P be the template $\{\alpha \mid |\alpha| \leqslant d\}$, for some $d \geqslant 0$. (Thus, P is the complete subtree of depth d.) Then there exists a regular skewing scheme $s\colon T \to \{0, 1, ..., 2^{d+1}-2\}$ that is valid for P, and where $|\mathsf{F}_s| = |\mathsf{B}_s| - 1 = 2^{d+1} - 1$. Moreover, we have that $2^{d+1} - 1 = \mu_T(P)$.*

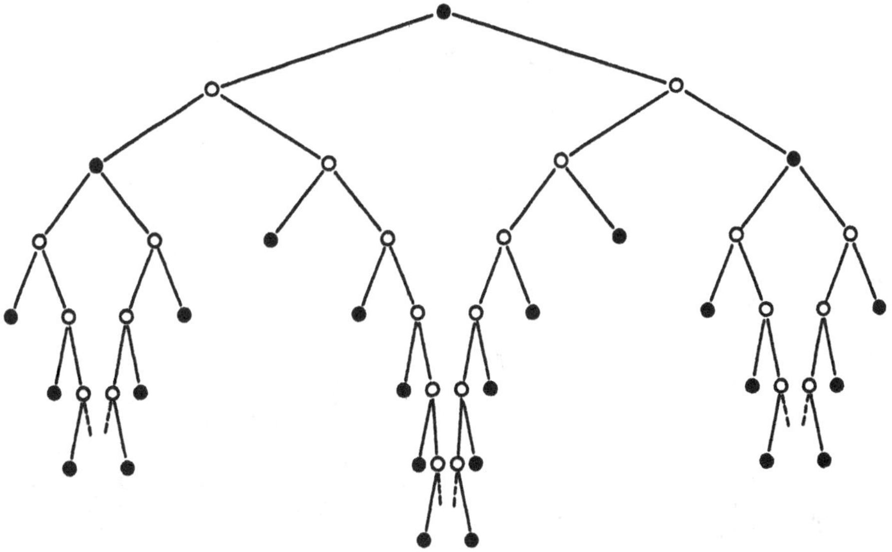

Figure 5.6: The elements $\alpha \in T$ with $s(\alpha) = 0$.

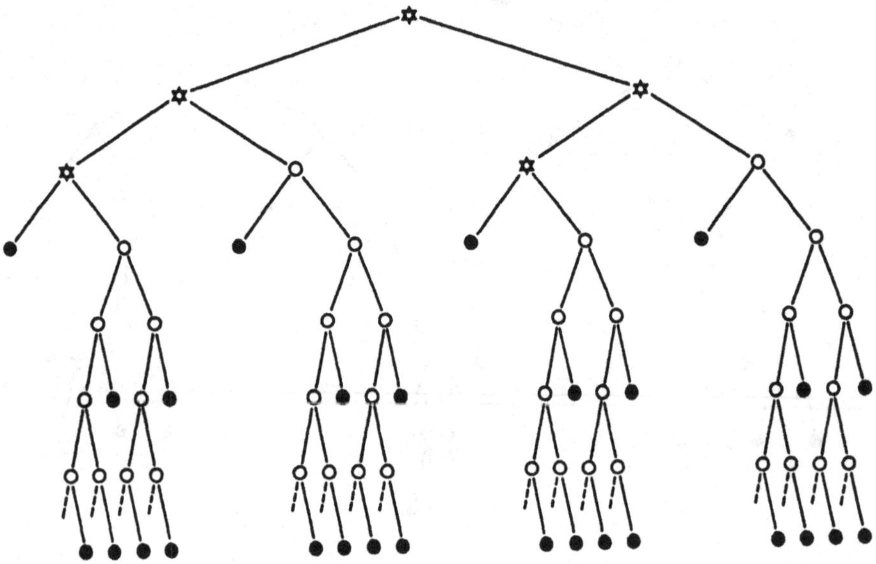

Figure 5.7: $\varepsilon \odot \mathsf{L}_s$ and F_s.

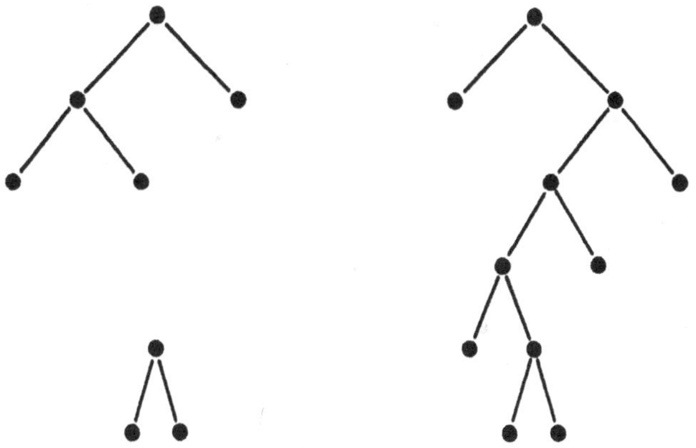

Figure 5.8: Some double-paths.

Proof Let $\{e_1\alpha||\alpha| < d\} = \{\alpha^1_1, \alpha^1_2, ..., \alpha^1_{2^d-1}\}$, $\{e_2\alpha||\alpha| < d\} = \{\alpha^2_1, \alpha^2_2, ..., \alpha^2_{2^d-1}\}$, $\{e_1.\beta||\beta| = d$ and $\beta \neq e_1e_1...e_1\} = \{\beta^1_1, \beta^1_2, ..., \beta^1_{2^d-1}\}$, and $\{e_2.\beta||\beta| = d$ and $\beta \neq e_2e_2...e_2\} = \{\beta^2_1, \beta^2_2, ..., \beta^2_{2^d-1}\}$. Let L be generated by the hyperbase $\mathsf{B} = \{[\varepsilon, \underbrace{e_1e_1...e_1}_{d+1}], [\varepsilon, \underbrace{e_2e_2...e_2}_{d+1}], [\alpha^1_1, \beta^2_1], ..., [\alpha^1_{2^d-1}, \beta^2_{2^d-1}], [\alpha^2_1, \beta^1_1], ..., [\alpha^2_{2^d-1}, \beta^1_{2^d-1}]\}$. Then s with $\mathsf{L}_s = L$ satisfies the condition of the theorem. □

Example 1 shows the regular skewing scheme valid for $P = \{\alpha| \, |\alpha| \leqslant 1\}$.

Definition 5.10 *Let T be a binary tree. A template P is called a double-path of length d iff there exists a path α_0 (= the root), $\alpha_1, \alpha_2, ..., \alpha_{d-1}$ of length $d-1$, such that $P = \{\beta| \, \exists\alpha_i \, (0 \leqslant i \leqslant d-1) : \beta = \alpha_ie_1$ or $\beta = \alpha_ie_2\}$.*

In figure 5.8 some examples of double-paths are shown.

Theorem 5.13 *Given a binary tree T and C the collection of all double-paths of length d, for some $d \geqslant 1$. Then there exists a regular skewing scheme s: $T \rightarrow \{0, 1, ..., 2d\}$ that is valid for C, where $|\mathsf{F}_s| = |\mathsf{B}_s| - 1 = 2d+1$. Moreover, we have that $2d+1 = \mu_T(C)$.*

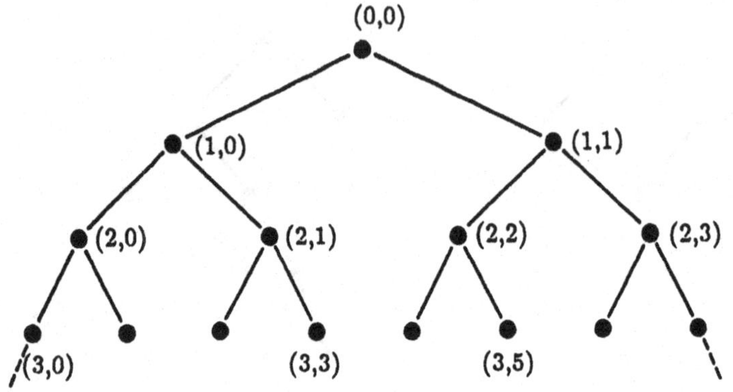

Figure 5.9: The level-labeling.

Proof Consider L generated by the hyperbase

$$\begin{aligned} \mathsf{B} \;=\; & \{[\varepsilon, \underbrace{e_1e_1...e_1}_{d+1}], [\varepsilon, e_2\underbrace{e_1e_1...e_1}_{d}], [e_1, e_2\underbrace{e_1e_1...e_1}_{d-1}e_2], [e_2, \underbrace{e_1e_1...e_1}_{d}e_2]\} \cup \\ & \{[e_1e_1\alpha, e_2e_1\alpha] \mid \alpha = e_1e_1...e_1 \text{ and } 0 \leqslant |\alpha| \leqslant d-2\} \cup \\ & \{[e_1\alpha e_2, e_2\alpha e_2] \mid \alpha = e_1e_1...e_1 \text{ and } 0 \leqslant |\alpha| \leqslant d-2\}. \end{aligned}$$

Then s with $\mathsf{L}_s = \mathsf{L}$ satisfies the condition of the theorem. □

The case of double-paths of length 2 can be found in example 2. Theorem 5.12 and 5.13 can be generalized in a natural way for k-ary trees with $k > 2$.

5.6 Linear Skewing Schemes for Trees

Another approach to obtain compactly representable skewing schemes is to use the level-labeling instead of the path-labeling.

Definition 5.11 *Given a (k-ary) tree T with root α_0. The level-labeling* lab_l *of T is the mapping* $\text{lab}_l : T \to \{(i,n) \mid i \in \mathsf{Z}^+\}$ *defined by*
(i) $\text{lab}_l(\alpha_0) = (0,0)$,
(ii) $\text{lab}_l(\alpha) = (i,n)$ *iff α has level i and α is the nth node from left to right in level i.*

In figure 5.9 lab_l is illustrated for a binary tree. The relationship between $\text{lab}(\alpha)$ and $\text{lab}_l(\alpha)$ is expressed by the following lemma.

Lemma 5.9 *If* $\text{lab}(\alpha) = e_{i_1} e_{i_2} \ldots e_{i_r}$, *then*

$$\text{lab}_l(\alpha) = (r, (i_1 - 1)k^{r-1} + (i_2 - 1)k^{r-2} + \ldots + (i_{r-1} - 1)k + i_r - 1).$$

The conversion from lab_l to lab easily follows from lemma 5.9 as well. Throughout this section we will identify a node α with $\text{lab}_l(\alpha)$, which uniquely defines it.

Using the level-labeling the nodes of a tree T can be seen as elements of a 2-dimensional array. The linear skewing schemes for trees are obtained by a translation of the notion of linearity for 2-dimensional arrays, cf. section 3.1.

Definition 5.12 *A skewing scheme* $s : T \to \{0, 1, ..., M-1\}$ *is called linear iff there exists a* $m \geqslant 1$ *and linear skewing schemes* $s_i : \mathbb{Z} \to \{c_i, c_i + 1, ..., c_i + M_i - 1\}, 0 \leqslant i \leqslant m - 1$, *with for all* $i : s_i = c_i + (a_i x + b_i) \bmod M_i$, $\gcd(a_i, M_i) = 1$, *and* $c_i + M_i \leqslant M$, *such that for all* $(n, j) \in T : s(n, j) = s_{n \bmod m}(j)$.

Call m the period of s. It is easily seen that linear skewing schemes on trees are compactly representable and can be computed fast.

Theorem 5.14 *Given a linear skewing scheme* $s: T \to \{0, 1, ..., M-1\}$ *with period* m. *Then* s *can be represented in* $O(m)$ *space, and can be computed in* $O(c)$ *time.*

The next theorem shows that the linear skewing schemes are quite different from the regular schemes as introduced in the previous section.

Theorem 5.15
(*i*) *There exist linear skewing schemes, which are not regular.*
(*ii*) *There exist regular skewing schemes, which are not linear.*

Proof Let T be a binary tree.

(*i*) Take, for instance, for arbitrary $a, b, M > 1$, and $\gcd(a, M) = 1$, the linear skewing scheme s defined by $s(n, j) = (aj + b) \bmod M$. Suppose s is regular, then from $s(n, 0) = s(n + 1, 0)$ follows that $s(n, 2) = s(n + 1, 2) = s(n, 1)$. From the linearity of s follows that $s(n, i) = s(n, j)$, for all i, j. This contradicts the fact that $M > 1$.

(*ii*) Take, for instance, the skewing scheme s with L_s generated by $\mathsf{B}_s = \{[\varepsilon, e_1], [\varepsilon, e_2 e_2], [e_2 e_1, e_1 e_2]\}$. In addition let $s(\varepsilon) = 0$ and $s(e_2) = 1$ ($\mathsf{F}_s = \{\varepsilon, e_2\}$). In figure 5.10 the first 4 levels of T and the values of s are shown. It is clear that there does not exist any a, b, c, d such that s: $x \to c + (ax + b) \bmod d$, and $s(0) = 0$, $s(1) = 1$, $s(2) = 1$, $s(3) = 0$.

More examples of regular skewing schemes which are not linear were constructed in theorem 5.13. □

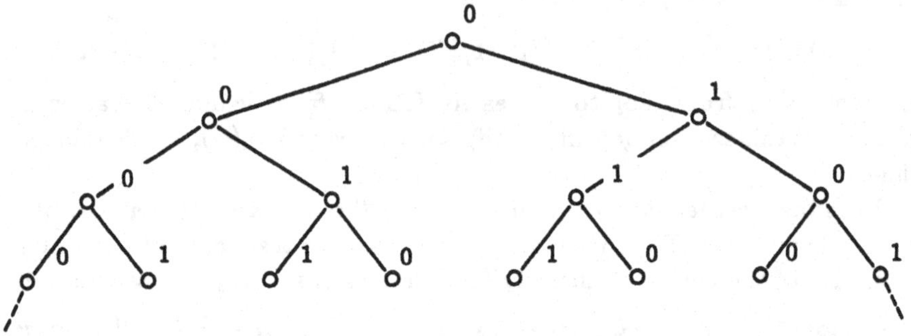

Figure 5.10: A regular skewing scheme which is not linear.

A relatively small subset of the linear skewing schemes can be used to derive the following upperbound on the number of memory banks needed for skewing an arbitrary collection of templates conflict-free. An arbitrary template P can be seen as consisting of "slices" $P^0, P^1, ..., P^q$ such that for each $i : P^i \subseteq \mathbf{Z}$ and $P = \bigcup_{0 \leqslant i \leqslant q} \{(i, x) | x \in P^i\}$.

Theorem 5.16 *Given an arbitrary collection of templates* $C = \{P_1, P_2, ..., P_t\}$. *Let for each* $j : P_j = \bigcup_{0 \leqslant i \leqslant q_j} \{(i, x) | \; x \in P_j^i\}$ *and let* $q = \max q_i$. *Furthermore let* $s' : \mathbf{Z} \rightarrow \{0, 1, ..., M-1\}$ *be a linear skewing scheme,* $s'(x) = (ax+b) \bmod M$ *with* M *minimal and for all* $1 \leqslant j \leqslant t$, $0 \leqslant i \leqslant q_j$, $0 \leqslant k \leqslant \lfloor 2^{q_j - i - 1} \rfloor$:

$$|\{s'(x) | \; x - k2^i \in P_j^i\}| = |P_j^i|.$$

Then there exists a linear skewing scheme s *which uses* $(q+1)M$ *memory banks and which is valid for* C.

Proof Take for $s_0, s_1, ..., s_q$ the following (linear) skewing schemes:

$s_0 : \mathbf{Z} \rightarrow \{0, 1, ..., M-1\}$, and $s_0(x) = (ax+b) \bmod M$,
$s_1 : \mathbf{Z} \rightarrow \{M, M+1, ..., 2M-1\}$, and $s_1(x) = M + (ax+b) \bmod M$,
$s_2 : \mathbf{Z} \rightarrow \{2M, 2M+1, ..., 3M-1\}$, and $s_1(x) = 2M + (ax+b) \bmod M$,
$\vdots$
$s_q : \mathbf{Z} \rightarrow \{qM, qM+1, ..., (q+1)M-1\}$, and $s_q(x) = qM + (ax+b) \bmod M$.

Let s be the skewing scheme from T into $\{0, 1, ..., (q+1)M-1\}$ defined by $s(n, j) = s_{n \bmod (q+1)}(j)$. Then s is valid for C, and s uses $(q+1)M$ memory banks. □

Corollary 5.2 *Given a binary tree T and the collection of templates $C = \{P | P$ is a double path of length $d\}$, for some $d \geqslant 1$* (cf. theorem 5.13). *Then there exists a linear skewing scheme s, with period $d+2$, which uses $2(d+2)$ memory banks and which is valid for C.*

Proof Consider s': $Z \to \{0,1\}$ with $s'(x) = x \bmod 2$. Then s' fits the constraints of the previous theorem and the result follows. □

Notice that the minimum number of memory banks needed by a regular skewing scheme in order to be valid for a collection of double-paths was equal to $2d+1$, cf. theorem 5.13.

Theorem 5.17 *Given a binary tree T and the template $P = \{\alpha | |\alpha| \leqslant d\}$ for some $d \geqslant 0$. Then there exists a linear skewing scheme s^d, with period $d+1$, which uses $2^{d+1} - 1$ memory banks, and which is valid for P.*

Proof Let the (linear) skewing schemes $s_0, s_1, \ldots, s_d$ be defined by

$$\begin{aligned}
s_0(x) &= (2^{d+1}x + 2^d)\mathrm{mod}2^{d+1} - 1,\\
s_1(x) &= (2^d x + 2^{d-1})\mathrm{mod}2^{d+1} - 1,\\
&\vdots\\
s_{d-1}(x) &= (4x + 2) \quad \mathrm{mod}2^{d+1} - 1, \text{ and}\\
s_d(x) &= (2x + 1) \quad \mathrm{mod}2^{d+1} - 1.
\end{aligned}$$

Define the linear skewing scheme s^d: $T \to \{0, 1, \ldots, 2^{d+1} - 2\}$ by $s^d(n,j) = s_{n \mathrm{mod}(d+1)}(j)$.

For each $(n,j) \in T$ we have that $P(n,j) = \{(n,j), (n+1, 2j), (n+1, 2j+1), (n+2, 4j), (n+2, 4j+1), (n+2, 4j+2), (N+2, 4j+3), \ldots, (n+d, 2^d j), (n+d, 2^d j+1), \ldots, (n+d, 2^d j + 2^d - 1)\}$.

Suppose s^d is not valid for P. Then there exist n, j, n_1, n_2, j_1, j_2, with $0 \leqslant n$, $0 \leqslant n_{1,2} \leqslant d$, $0 \leqslant j \leqslant 2^n - 1$, $0 \leqslant j_1 \leqslant 2^{n_1} - 1$, and $0 \leqslant j_2 \leqslant 2^{n_2} - 1$, such that

$$s^d(n + n_1, 2^{n_1} j + j_1) = s^d(n + n_2, 2^{n_2} j + j_2)$$

and $j_1 \neq j_2$ or $n_1 \neq n_2$. Let for simplicity $n_1 \geqslant n_2$. (The case that $n_2 \geqslant n_1$ can be handled analogously.) Let $a = (n+n_1) \bmod d$ and $b = (n+n_2) \bmod d$. Then we have

$$2^{d-a+1}(2^{n_1} j + j_1) + 2^{d-a} \equiv_{2^{d+1}-1} 2^{d-b+1}(2^{n_2} j + j_2) + 2^{d-b},$$

where $\equiv_{2^{d+1}-1}$ denotes: equivalent modulo $2^{d+1} - 1$. Because $n_1 \geqslant n_2$, we can distinguish two cases.

Case 1 $a - b = n_1 - n_2$. Then $2^{a-b}(2^{d-a+1}(2^{n_1}j + j_1) + 2^{d-a}) \equiv_{2^{d+1}-1} 2^{a-d}(2^{d-b+1}(2^{n_2}j + j_2) + 2^{d-b})$. Thus

$$\begin{aligned} 2^{n_1+1}j + 2j_1 + 1 &\equiv_{2^{d+1}-1} 2^{n_1-n_2}(2^{n_2+1}j + 2j_2 + 1) \\ \Rightarrow 2^{n_1+1}j + 2j_1 + 1 &\equiv_{2^{d+1}-1} 2^{n_1+1}j + 2^{n_1-n_2+1}j_2 + 2^{n_1-n_2} \\ \Rightarrow 2j_1 + 1 &\equiv_{2^{d+1}-1} 2^{n_1-n_2}(2j_2 + 1). \end{aligned}$$

Then there exists a $k \in \mathbf{Z}$ such that $2^{n_1-n_2}(2j_2 + 1) = 2j_1 + 1 + k.2^{d+1} - k$.

Suppose $n_1 = n_2$, then $2j_2 + 1 = 2j_1 + 1 + k2^{d+1} - k$. Thus $2(j_2 - j_1) = k2^{d+1} - k$. So k is even, and there exists a $l \in \mathbf{Z}$, such that $j_2 - j_1 = l2^{d+1} - l$. Because $0 \leqslant j_1 \leqslant 2^{n_1} - 1$ and $0 \leqslant j_2 \leqslant 2^{n_2} - 1$, we get $-2^{n_1} + 1 \leqslant l2^{d+1} - l \leqslant 2^{n_2} - 1$. Thus $-2^d + 1 \leqslant l2^{d+1} - l \leqslant 2^d - 1$. Hence $l = 0$ and $j_1 = j_2$. Contradiction.

Let $n_1 > n_2$. Then $2j_1 + 1 - k = 2^{n_1-n_2}(2j_2 + 1 - k2^{d-n_1+n_2+1})$. Thus k has to be odd and there exists a $l \in \mathbf{Z}$ such that $k = 2l - 1$. Furthermore there exists a $q \in \mathbf{Z}$ such that $2q - 1 = 2j_2 + 1 - (2l - 1)2^{d-n_1+n_2+1}$ and $(2q - 1)2^{n_1-n_2} = 2j_1 + 1 - (2l - 1)$. Thus $j_1 = (2q - 1)2^{n_1-n_2-1} + l - 1$ and $j_2 = (2l - 1)2^{d-n_1+n_2} + q - 1$. Furthermore we have that $0 \leqslant j_1 \leqslant 2^{n_1} - 1$ and $0 \leqslant j_2 \leqslant 2^{n_2} - 1$. So

$$1 - (2q - 1)2^{n_1-n_2-1} \leqslant l \leqslant 2^{n_1} - (2q - 1)2^{n_1-n_2-1}, \text{ and} \quad (5.1)$$

$$1 - (2l - 1)2^{d+n_2-n_1} \leqslant q \leqslant 2^{n_2} - (2l - 1)2^{d-n_2-n_1}. \quad (5.2)$$

Substitute equation 5.2 in equation 5.1, and we get $1 - 2^{n_1} + (2l - 1)2^d + 2^{n_1-n_2-1} \leqslant l \leqslant 2^{n_1} - 2^{n_1-n_2-1} + (2l - 1)2^d$. Thus $-2^d + 1 - 2^{n_1} + 2^{n_1-n_2-1} \leqslant l(1 - 2^{d+1}) \leqslant 2^{n_1} - 2^{n_1-n_2-1} - 2^d$. Hence $(0 \leqslant n_2 < n_1 \leqslant d)$ $1 - 2^{d+1} < l(1 - 2^{d+1}) < 0$. Contradiction.

Case 2 $a - b = n_1 - n_2 - d$. Then $2^{d-a}(2^{n_1+1}j + 2j_1 + 1) \equiv_{2^{d+1}-1} 2^{d-b}(2^{n_1+1}j + 2j_2 + 1)$. Thus $2^d(2^{n_1+1}j + 2j_1 + 1) \equiv_{2^{d+1}-1} 2^{n_1-n_2}(2^{n_1+1}j + 2j_2 + 1)$. So, there exists a $k \in \mathbf{Z}$, such that $2^{d+1}(2^{n_1}j + j_1) + k.2^{d+1} + 2^d - k = 2^{n_1-n_2}(2^{n_2+1}j + 2j_2 + 1)$. Thus there exists a $k' \in \mathbf{Z}$ such that $2^{d+1}.k' + 2^d - k' + 2^{n_1}j + j_1 = 2^{n_1-n_2}(2^{n_2}j + 2j_2 + 1)$. So, $2^{n_1}j + 2j_1 + 2^{d+1}.k' - k' + 2^d = 2^{n_1-n_2}(2^{n_2}j + 2j_2 + 1)$, and a contradiction is obtained analogously to case 1. □

Concerning theorem 5.17 we can make the following two observations.

Observation 5.1 *Each linear skewing scheme $s^d: T \to \{0, 1, ..., 2^{d+1} - 2\}$ as constructed in the proof of* theorem 5.17 *is a regular skewing scheme. In fact the linear skewing schemes s^d are a subset of the regular skewing schemes as constructed in* theorem 5.12.

To illustrate this consider s^3, and let B_s be the hyperbase $\{[\varepsilon, e_1e_1e_1e_1]$, $[\varepsilon, e_2e_2e_2e_2]$, $[e_1, e_2e_1e_2e_2]$, $[e_2, e_1e_2e_1e_1]$, $[e_1e_1, e_2e_1e_1e_2]$, $[e_2e_2, e_1e_2e_2e_1]$, $[e_1e_2, e_2e_2e_1e_2]$, $[e_2e_1, e_1e_1e_2e_1]$, $[e_1e_1e_1, e_2e_1e_1e_1]$, $[e_2e_2e_2, e_1e_2e_2e_2]$, $[e_1e_1e_2, e_2e_1e_2e_1]$, $[e_2e_2e_1, e_1e_2e_1e_2]$, $[e_1e_2e_1, e_2e_2e_1e_1]$, $[e_2e_1e_2, e_1e_1e_2e_2]$, $[e_1e_2e_2, e_2e_2e_2e_1]$, $[e_2e_1e_1, e_1e_1e_1e_2]\}$. Take for the assignment of F_s: $\varepsilon \mapsto 8$, $e_1 \mapsto 4$, $e_2 \mapsto 12$, $e_1e_1 \mapsto 2$, $e_1e_2 \mapsto 6$, $e_2e_1 \mapsto 10$, $e_2e_2 \mapsto 14$, $e_1e_1e_1 \mapsto 1$, $e_1e_1e_2 \mapsto 3$, $e_1e_2e_1 \mapsto 5$, $e_1e_2e_2 \mapsto 7$, $e_2e_1e_1 \mapsto 9$, $e_2e_1e_2 \mapsto 11$, $e_2e_2e_1 \mapsto 13$, $e_2e_2e_2 \mapsto 0$. Then the regular skewing scheme s with L_s generated by the hyperbase B_s is equal to s^3.

The second observation is based upon the notion of the perfect shuffle [Sto71]. The perfect shuffle is a useful mapping for applications in the field of parallel computations. The perfect shuffle σ_d of order d is the mapping σ_d: $\{0,1,...,2^d-1\} \rightarrow \{0,1,...,2^d-1\}$, with $\sigma_d([x_1x_2...x_d]) = [x_dx_1...x_{d-1}]$. ($[x_1...x_d]$ denotes the binary representation of a number x). In figure 5.11 σ_4 is depicted.

Observation 5.2 *For all d, (n,j) : $s^d(n,j) = \sigma^n_{d+1}((j+2^d) \bmod 2^{d+1}-1)$.*

This observation has some nice consequences for the problem of scrambling and unscrambling vectors, as described in [Swa74]. Here we content ourselves by mentioning that when an architecture is provided with a perfect shuffle network (see e.g. [Sto71,Sto80]) then access to a consecutive set of nodes of one level of the tree T which is stored by the map s^d, can be achieved by only a shift and a number of iterations through the perfect shuffle network.

Thus, concluding we can say that for the case of templates which are double-paths or subtrees the linear skewing schemes perform almost as well as the regular schemes. Besides the representation costs are less than the representation costs of regular schemes. That this is not always the case shows the following example.

Example
Given a binary tree T, and let $d \geqslant 2$. Define the collection of templates $C = \{\{\underbrace{e_1e_1...e_1}_{d}, e_2\alpha\} \mid |\alpha| = d-1\}$. Then $\mu_T(C) = 2$. Let the hyperbase B_s be the set

$$\{[\varepsilon, \underbrace{e_1e_1...e_1}_{d}], [\varepsilon, e_2e_2\underbrace{e_1e_1...e_1}_{d-1}], [\underbrace{e_2e_2...e_2}_{d}, e_1e_2\underbrace{e_1e_1...e_1}_{d-1}],$$
$$[e_1, e_2], [e_1, e_2e_1], ..., [e_1, e_2\underbrace{e_1e_1...e_1}_{d-2}]\}.$$

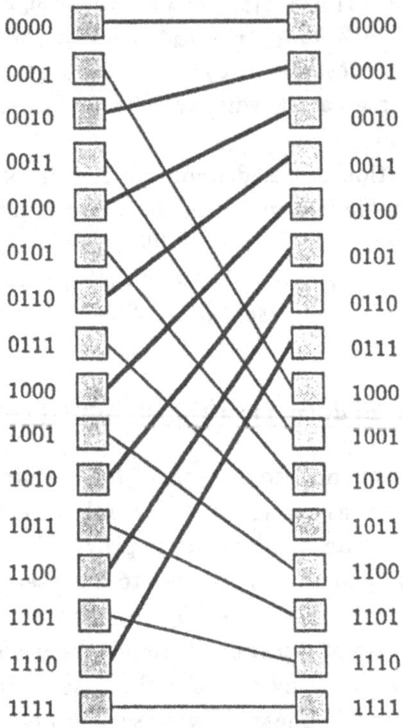

Figure 5.11: The perfect shuffle σ_4.

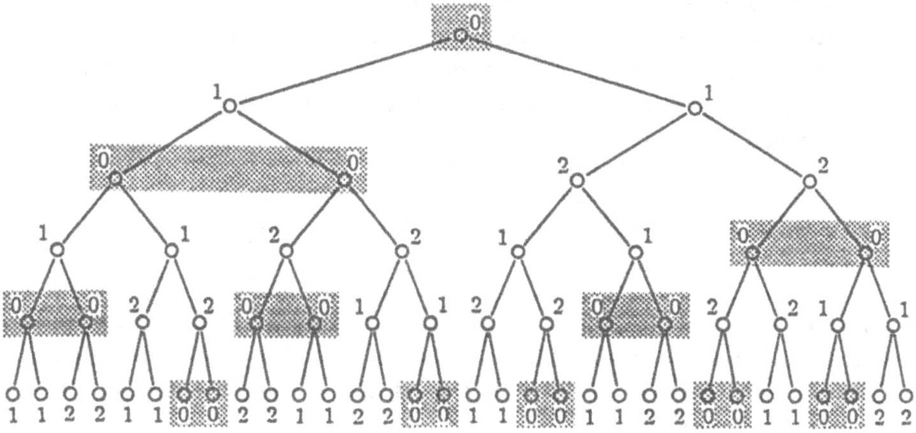

Figure 5.12: An application of a regular skewing scheme for which there exists no suitable linear skewing scheme.

Choose an arbitrary assignment of F_s, and let s be the regular skewing scheme with L_s generated by the hyperbase B_s. Then s is a skewing scheme from T to $\{0, 1, ..., d\}$, and s is valid for C. An example of s for the case that $d = 2$ is given in figure 5.12. Thus, there exists a regular skewing scheme which is valid for C, and which uses $d + 1$ memory banks. However a linear skewing scheme which is valid for C needs at least 2^d memory banks.

The previous example gives rise to another kind of compactly representable skewing schemes.

Definition 5.13 ***A skewing scheme s: $T \to \{0, 1, ..., M-1\}$ is called simple iff there exist $\alpha_1, \alpha_2, ..., \alpha_p \in T$, and a map $\eta : \{\alpha_1 \alpha_2, ..., \alpha_p\} \to \{0, 1, ..., M-1\}$, $p \geqslant M$, such that for all $\gamma \in T$: if there exists a $\gamma' \in T$, with $\gamma' \alpha_i = \gamma$, for some α_i, $1 \leqslant i \leqslant p$, and there does not exist a $\gamma'' < \gamma'$, such that $\gamma = \gamma'' \alpha_j$, for some α_j, $1 \leqslant j \leqslant p$, then $s(\gamma) = \eta(\alpha_i)$.***

p is called the size of s, and $\alpha_1, \alpha_2, ..., \alpha_p$ are the generating nodes of s.

For the collection C of templates mentioned in the previous example, there exists a simple skewing scheme which is valid for C and which uses only 2 memory banks! Namely, let for a given d : $\alpha_1 = e_1 e_1 ... e_1$, $|\alpha_1| = d$, $\alpha_2 = e_1$, and $\alpha_3 = e_2$, and let $\eta : \{\alpha_1, \alpha_2, \alpha_3\} \to \{0, 1\}$ be defined by

$\eta(\alpha_1) = 0$, $\eta(\alpha_2) = 1$, $\eta(\alpha_3) = 1$. Then the simple skewing scheme with generating nodes α_1, α_2 and α_3 is valid for C.

Although these simple skewing schemes are far more feasible than the regular and linear skewing schemes for the collection of templates given in the previous example, in general they work out very badly. This is shown by the following theorem.

Theorem 5.18 *Given a template P such that there exist $\lambda, \beta \in T$, $s \geqslant 0$, $t > 0$ with $\lambda^s\beta \in P$ and $\lambda^{s+t}\beta \in P$. Then there does not exist a simple skewing scheme that is valid for P.*

Proof From definition 5.13 follows that for every simple skewing scheme s, there exists a $k \geqslant 0$, such that $s(\lambda^k\beta) = s(\lambda^{k+1}\beta) = s(\lambda^{k+2}\beta) = ...$ But from the fact that $\lambda^s\beta$, $\lambda^{s+t}\beta \in P$ follows that whenever s is valid for P, then $s(\lambda^k\beta) \neq s(\lambda^{k+t}\beta)$. □

Note that almost all templates fulfill the constraint of theorem 5.18.

Bibliography

[Bar68] G.H. Barnes et al. The ILLIAC IV computer. *IEEE Trans. Comput.*, C-17:746–757, 1968.

[Bat80] K.E. Batcher. Design of a Massively Parallel Processor. *IEEE Trans. Comput.*, C-29:836–840, 1980.

[Ber72] G.D. Bergland. A parallel implementation of the FFT algorithm. *IEEE Trans. Comput.*, C-21:366–370, 1972.

[BK71] P. Budnik and D.J. Kuck. The organization and use of parallel memories. *IEEE Trans. Comput.*, C-20:1566–1569, 1971.

[BP85] J. Berstel and D. Perrin. *Theory of Codes.* Volume 117 of *Pure and Applied Mathematics*, Academic Press, New York, 1985.

[Ces79] Y. Césari. Propriétés combinatoires des codes biprefixes. In D. Perrin, editor, *Théorie des Codes*, pages 20–46, LITP, Paris, 1979.

[CLR82] B. Chor, C.E. Leiserson, and R.L. Rivest. An application of number theory to the organisation of raster-graphics memory. In *Conf. Rec. 23rd Annual IEEE Symp. Foundations of Computer Science*, pages 92–99, Chicago, 1982.

[Cor] Control Data Corporation. Introducing the Control Data CYBER-205: the supercomputer for the 80's. CDC, St. Paul, Minnesota.

[Cox61] H.S.M. Coxeter. *Introduction to Geometry.* J. Wiley & Sons, New York, 1961.

[Eul82] L. Euler. Recherches sur une nouvelle espèce des quarrés magiques. *Verh. Zeeuwsch Gen. Wetensch. Vlissingen*, 9:85–239, 1782.

[Fen72] T. Feng. Some characteristics of associative parallel processing. In *1972 Sagamore Comp. Conf. Parall. Proc.*, pages 5–16, 1972.

[FJL85] J.M. Frailong, W. Jalby, and J. Lenfant. Xor-schemes: a flexible data organization in parallel memories. In D. Degroot, editor, *Int. Conf on Parallel Proc.*, pages 276–283, IEEE Computer Society Press, Washington, 1985.

[Fla82] P.M. Flanders. A unified approach to a class of data movements on an array processor. *IEEE Trans. Comput.*, C-31:809–819, 1982.

[Fly72] M.J. Flynn. Some computer organisations and their effectiveness. *IEEE Trans. Comput.*, C-21:948–960, 1972.

[Gar77] M. Gardner. Mathematical games. *Scientific American*, :July, 112–117, August, 112–115, December, 116–119, 1975, January, 110 -121, 1977.

[GE70] J.K. Goldhaber and G. Ehrlich. *Algebra*. The MacMillan Comp., Toronto, 1970.

[Gen84] W. Gentzsch. Benchmark results on physical flow problems. In J.S. Kowalik, editor, *High Speed Computation, Nato ASI Series, Series F*, pages 221–229, Springer Verlag, Berlin, 1984.

[Ger74] E. Gergely. A simple method for constructing doubly diagonalised Latin squares. *J. Combin. Theory*, Ser. A(16):266–272, 1974.

[GJ78] M.R. Garey and D.S. Johnson. *Computers and Intractability*. W.H. Freeman and Company, San Francisco, 1978.

[Gob79] F. Göbel. Geometrical packing and covering problems. In A. Schrijver, editor, *Packing and Covering in Combinatorics*, pages 179–199, Mathematisch Centrum, Amsterdam, 1979. MC Tract 106.

[Gol66] S.W. Golomb. Tiling with polyominoes. *J.Combin. Theory*, 1:280–296, 1966.

[Gol70] S.W. Golomb. Tiling with sets of polyominoes. *J.Combin. Theory*, 9:60–71, 1970.

[Han66] M. Hanan. On Steiner's problem with rectilinear distance. *SIAM J. Appl. Math.*, 14:255–265, 1966.

[Han77] W. Händler. The impact of classification schemes on computer architecture. In *Int. Conf. on Parallel Proc.*, pages 7–15, 1977.

[HB85] K. Hwang and F.A. Briggs. *Computer Architecture and Parallel Processing.* McGraw-Hill Book Comp., New-York, 1985.

[HC64] D. Hilbert and S. Cohn-Vossen. *Anschauliche Geometrie.* Dover Publ., New York, 1964.

[Hed77] A. Hedayat. A complete solution to the existence and non-existence of Knut Vik designs and orthogonal Knut Vik designs. *J. Combin. Th.*, 22(Series A):331–337, 1977.

[HF75] A. Hedayat and W.T. Federer. On the non-existence of Knut Vik designs for all even orders. *Ann. Stat.*, 3:445–447, 1975.

[HHS76] W. Händler, F. Hofmann, and H.J. Schneider. A general purpose array with a broad spectrum of applications. In W. Händler, editor, *Computer Architecture, Workshop of the GI 1975, Informatik-Fachberichte 4*, pages 311–335, Springer Verlag, Berlin, 1976.

[Hil73] A.J.W. Hilton. On double diagonal and cross Latin squares. *J. London Math. Soc.*, II(6):679–689, 1973.

[HJ81] R.W. Hockney and C.R. Jesshope. *Parallel Computers.* Hilger, Bristol, 1981.

[HS81] K. Hwang and S.P. Su. Vector computer architecture and processing techniques. In M.C. Yovits, editor, *Adv. in Computers, vol. 20*, pages 115–197, Acad. Press., New York, 1981.

[HW79] G.H. Hardy and E.M. Wright. *An Introduction to the Theory of Numbers.* Clarendon Press, Oxford, 5th edition, 1979. (First edition 1938).

[Hwa76] F.K. Hwang. On Steiner minimal trees with rectilinear distance. *SIAM J. Appl. Math.*, 30:104–114, 1976.

[JFJ84] W. Jalby, J.M. Frailong, and J.Lenfant. *Diamond Schemes: an Organization of Parallel Memories for Efficient Array Processing.* Technical Report 342, INRIA, Centre de Rocquencourt, 1984.

[Kar72] R.M. Karp. Reducibility among combinatorial problems. In R.E. Miller and J.W. Thatcher, editors, *Complexity of Computer Computations*, pages 85–103, Plenum Press, New York, 1972.

[KOMW67] M. Knowles, B. Okawa, Y. Muroaka, and R. Wilhelmson. *Matrix Operations on ILLIAC IV.* Report 222, Dept. of Computer Science, University of Illinois, Urbana, Illinois, 1967.

[KS82] D.J. Kuck and R.A. Stokes. The Burroughs Scientific Processor (BSP). *IEEE Trans. Comput.*, C-31:363–376, 1982.

[Kuc68] D.J. Kuck. ILLIAC IV software and application programming. *IEEE Trans. Comput.*, C-17:758–770, 1968.

[Kur56] A.G. Kurosh. *The Theory of Groups.* Volume 1, Chelsea Publ. Comp., New York, 1956. Translated from the Russian and edited by K.A. Hirsch.

[Law75] D.H. Lawrie. Access and alignment of data in an array processor. *IEEE Trans. Comput.*, C-24:1145–1155, 1975.

[Lek69] C.G. Lekkerkerker. *Geometry of Numbers.* Wolters-Noordhoff (North-Holland), Amsterdam, 1969.

[Lev34] P. Levi. Sur une généralisation du théorème de Rolle. *C.R. Acad. Sci.*, 198:424–425, 1934.

[LMM85] O. Lubeck, J. Moore, and R. Mendez. A benchmark comparison of three supercomputers: Fujitsu VP-200,Hitachi S810/20 and CRAY X-MP/2. *IEEE Computer Magazin*, :10–23, December 1985.

[LV82] D.H. Lawrie and C.R. Vora. The prime memory system for array access. *IEEE Trans. Comput.*, C-31:435–442, 1982.

[Mel61] Z.A. Melzak. On the problem of Steiner. *Canadian Mathematical Bulletin*, 4:143–148, 1961.

[MV84] K. Mehlhorn and U. Vishkin. Randomized and deterministic simulations of PRAMs by parallel machines with restricted granularity of parallel memories. *Acta Informatica*, 21:339–374, 1984.

[New72] M. Newman. *Integral Matrices.* Volume 45 of *Pure Applied Mathematics Series*, Academic Press, New York, 1972.

[Pea77] M.C. Pease. The indirect binary n-cube microprocessor array. *IEEE Trans. Comput.*, C-26:458–473, 1977.

[Pol18] G. Pólya. Über die "Doppelt-Periodischen" Lösungen des n-Damenproblemes. In W. Ahrens, editor, *Mathematische Unterhaltungen und Spiele*, pages 364–374, Teubner, Leipzig, 1918.

[Pot85] J.L. Potter, editor. *The Massively Parallel Processor. Scientific Computation Series*, MIT Press, Cambridge(US), 1985.

[Rus78] R.M. Russell. The CRAY-1 computer system. *Comm. of ACM*, 17:63–72, 1978.

[Sam86] A.H. Sameh et al. Parallel algorithms on the CEDAR system. In W. Händler et al., editor, *CONPAR 86, Lecture Notes in Comp. Science 237*, pages 25–39, Springer Verlag, Berlin, 1986.

[Sch61] M.P. Schützenberger. On a special class of recurrent events. *Ann. Math. Statist.*, 32:1201–1213, 1961.

[Sha75] H.D. Shapiro. Storage schemes in parallel memories. In *1975 Sagamore Comp. Conf. Parall. Proc.*, pages 159–166, 1975.

[Sha78a] H.D. Shapiro. Generalized latin squares on the torus. *Discr. Math.*, 24:63–77, 1978.

[Sha78b] H.D. Shapiro. Theoretical limitations on the efficient use of parallel memories. *IEEE Trans. Comput.*, C-27:421–428, 1978.

[Shi86] M. Shigeharu. Hierarchical Array Processor system (HAP). In W. Händler et al., editor, *CONPAR 86, Lecture Notes in Comp. Science 237*, pages 311–318, Springer Verlag, Berlin, 1986.

[Sho28] K. Shoda. Über die Automorphismen einer endlichen Abelschen Gruppe. *Math. Ann.*, 100:674–686, 1928.

[Sie81] H.J. Siegel et al. PASM: a partitionable SIMD/MIMD system for image processing and pattern recognition. *IEEE Trans. Comp.*, C-30:934–947, 1981.

[Ste72] S.K. Stein. A symmetric star body that tiles but not as a lattice. *Proc. Amer. Math. Soc.*, 36:543–548, 1972.

[Sto71] H.S. Stone. Parallel processing with the perfect shuffle. *IEEE Trans. Comput.*, C-20:153–161, 1971.

[Sto77] R.A. Stokes. Burroughs Scientific Processor. In D.J. Kuck et al., editor, *High Speed Computer and Algorithm Organization*, pages 85–89, Academic Press, New York, 1977.

[Sto80] H.S. Stone. Parallel Computers. In H.S. Stone, editor, *Introduction to Computer Architecture*, pages 363–425, SRA Inc., Chicago, 1980.

[Swa74] R.C. Swanson. Interconnections for parallel memories to unscramble *p*-ordered vectors. *IEEE Trans. Comput.*, C-23:1105–1115, 1974.

[Tap] J. Tappe. Algebraische Hilfsmittel zur Organisation paralleler Speicher. Informatik-Kolloquium über Parallelverarbeitung, Lessach, 1984.

[TR86] K.D. Thalhofer and K.D. Reinartz. A classification of algorithms which are well suited for implementations on the DAP as a basis for further research on parallel programming. In W. Händler et al., editor, *CONPAR 86, Lecture Notes in Comp. Science 237*, pages 376–384, Springer Verlag, Berlin, 1986.

[Tro86] U. Trottenberg. SUPRENUM - an MIMD multiprocessor system for multi-level scientific computing. In W. Händler et al., editor, *CONPAR 86, Lecture Notes in Comp. Science 237*, pages 48–52, Springer Verlag, Berlin, 1986.

[TvLW84] J. Tappe, J. van Leeuwen, and H.A.G. Wijshoff. *Parallel Memories, Periodic Skewing Schemes and the Theory of Finite Abelian Groups.* Technical Report RUU-CS-84-7, Dept. of Computer Science, University of Utrecht, Utrecht, 1984. To appear in the IEEE Trans. Comp.

[TvLW86] G. Tel, J. van Leeuwen, and H.A.G. Wijshoff. *The one-dimensional skewing problem.* Techn. Rep. RUU-CS-86-8, Dept. of Computer Science, University of Utrecht, Utrecht, 1986.

[TW85] G. Tel and H.A.G. Wijshoff. *Hierarchical parallel memory-systems, and multi-periodic skewing schemes.* Techn. Rep. RUU-CS-85-24, Dept. of Computer Science, University of Utrecht, Utrecht, 1985.

[Vik24] K. Vik. Bedømmelse av feilen på forsøksfelter med og uten malestokk. *Meldinger fra Norges Landbrukshøgskole*, 4:129–181, 1924.

[vLW83] J. van Leeuwen and H.A.G. Wijshoff. *Data Mappings in Large Parallel Computers.* Technical RUU-CS-83-11, Dept. Computer Science, University of Utrecht, Utrecht, 1983. Also appeared in I. Kupka (ed.), GI-13 Jahrestagung, Informatik Fb 73, Springer Verlag, 8-20, 1983.

[vVM78] D.C. van Voorhis and T.H. Morrin. Memory systems for image processing. *IEEE Trans. Comput.*, C-27:113–125, 1978.

[Wan65] H. Wang. Games, logic and computers. *Scientific American*, 213:98–106, 1965.

[Wey40] H. Weyl. *Algebraic Theory of Numbers*. Volume 1 of *Annals of Mathematics Studies*, Princeton University Press, Princeton, New Jersey, 1940.

[WvL83a] H.A.G. Wijshoff and J. van Leeuwen. *A Linearity Condition for Periodic Skewing Schemes*. Techn. Rep. RUU-CS-83-10, Dept. of Computer Science, University of Utrecht, Utrecht, 1983.

[WvL83b] H.A.G. Wijshoff and J. van Leeuwen. Periodic storage schemes with a minimum number of memory banks. In M. Nagl and J. Perl, editors, *International Workshop on Graphtheoretical Concepts in Computer Science*, pages 381–393, Trauner Verlag, Linz, 1983.

[WvL84] H.A.G. Wijshoff and J. van Leeuwen. Periodic versus arbitrary tessellations of the plane using polyominos of a single type. *Inf. Control*, 62:1–25, 1984.

[WvL85] H.A.G. Wijshoff and J. van Leeuwen. The structure of periodic storage schemes for parallel memories. *IEEE Trans. Comput.*, C-34:501–505, 1985.

[WvL87] H.A.G. Wijshoff and J. van Leeuwen. On linear skewing schemes and *d*-ordered vectors. *IEEE Trans. Comp.*, C-36:233–239, 1987.

Index